Exploring Gender Relations

A Canadian Perspective

Marlene Mackie

Butterworths
Toronto

Exploring Gender Relations: A Canadian Perspective
© 1983—Butterworth & Co. (Canada) Ltd.

Printed and bound in Canada

4 5   AP   88 87

Canadian Cataloguing in Publication Data

Mackie, Marlene.
   Exploring gender relations: a Canadian perspective

Bibliography: p.
Includes index.
ISBN 0–409–84780–1

1. Sex role.   2. Sex differences (Psychology).
3. Socialization.   I. Title.

HQ1075.M32   305.3   C82-094764-4

The Butterworth Group of Companies

Canada:
Butterworth & Co. (Canada) Ltd., Toronto and Vancouver

United Kingdom:
Butterworth & Co. (Publishers) Ltd., London

Australia:
Butterworths Pty. Ltd., Sydney

New Zealand:
Butterworths of New Zealand Ltd., Wellington

South Africa:
Butterworth & Co. (South Africa) Ltd., Durban

United States:
Butterworth (Publishers) Inc., Boston
Butterworth (Legal Publishers) Inc., Seattle
Mason Publishing Company, St. Paul

Contents

Tables

About the Author

Marlene Mackie obtained her Ph.D. at the University of Alberta and later joined the University of Calgary, where she has been since 1969. She is currently associate professor of sociology and teaches gender relations, social psychology, and collective behavior. She has done research in the area of gender relations for the past ten years and also serves on the executive committee of the Canadian Sociology and Anthropology Association.

To my parents, Marjorie and Albert Martin

Acknowledgments

A number of people contributed to this book. It would not have been written without the encouragement of Walter Lindenbach, Merlin Brinkerhoff, and Karen Mackie. I would like to thank Myra Phipps and Stella Herring for help with the typing, and Fran Kimmel for help with the Glossary. The comments of reviewer, Professor Sharon Abu-Laban, and editor, Kathleen Hamilton, led to a greatly improved manuscript.

This book drew upon an earlier study of the interrelationship of work and family. Principal investigators in this research were Merlin B. Brinkerhoff, James S. Frideres, Eugen Lupri, Donald L. Mills, and myself, from the University of Calgary. Funds for the research were provided by the University of Calgary Research Policy and Grants Committee.

1 Introduction and Overview

THE SUBJECT of this book is gender in contemporary Canadian society. The focus is upon one central question: What does it mean to be female or to be male? Although the wording used to formulate this question will vary as we move from chapter to chapter and consider it from many different perspectives, the fundamental issue throughout will be the implications of femininity and masculinity for the individual and for society.

Gender and Sex

Before we can proceed further, it is necessary to define briefly the word *gender*, and to distinguish it from the closely related word *sex*. (This terminological distinction is not as straightforward as it first appears. We will return to it later on.) Like all definitions, this one is a matter of conventional usage. For present purposes, *sex* can be viewed as the physiological differences between males and females and *gender* as the sociocultural elaborations of these differences. Sex is the biological dichotomy between females and males. It is determined at conception and is, for the most part, unalterable. Gender, on the other hand, is what is socially recognized as femininity and masculinity (Gould and Kern-Daniels, 1977:83-84). The cultural norms and values of a particular society at a particular time identify certain ways of behaving, feeling and thinking as appropriate for females and other ways of behaving, feeling and thinking as appropriate for males. Although the expectations based upon anatomy differ among cultures and historical periods, and the precise definitions of masculinity and femininity current in our own society are being subjected to critical scrutiny, the gender distinction appears to be a cultural universal.

Determining whether it is sex or gender that is responsible for a given female-male difference is one of the tasks of this book. This "nature-

1

nurture" question is often complicated because masculinity is almost invariably associated with male sex organs and femininity with female sex organs. Nevertheless, we will argue that gender, not sex, is the fundamental "fact of life." In Lambert's (1971:2) words, "beliefs about the roles of the sexes are threads running through the fabric of society, having multiple effects upon human institutions and themselves nourished and sustained by these institutions." Sex (the biological fact) matters to the individual and to society. However, gender (the cultural embellishment on anatomy) matters even more.

The Importance of Gender

Our argument for the importance of gender rests upon two major points that will be further developed throughout the book. First, in Canadian society, as in all human societies, the sexes are differentiated. The sex difference is both noted and emphasized. This fact is of course the essence of the meaning of *gender*. The following paragraphs outline some of the more central male-female differences and set aside, for the time being, male-female similarities. Second, the sexes are ranked and society places more value on males than females. As a category, males have more prestige and power than females. After the discussion of male-female differentiation, we will turn to male-female evaluation.

The impact of gender upon the individual begins at the moment of birth and continues until the moment of death. The parents of a newborn infant ask, "Is it a boy or a girl?" Though at this stage the infant is little more than a bundle of tissue with potentiality, members of society immediately begin to react to it in terms of its gender. Usually, it will be wrapped in a pink or blue blanket and given a name that signals its sex.

Parents' perceptions of their infants after birth continue to be sextyped. Aberle and Naegele (1952) reported that fathers expected their daughters to be pretty, fragile, sweet and delicate, and their sons to be athletic and aggressive. Rubin et al. (1974) interviewed thirty pairs of parents at a Boston hospital within twenty-four hours of the birth of their first child. Fifteen of the couples had daughters and fifteen had sons. Infant girls were described by the parents as "softer," "finer-featured," "littler" and "prettier," and boys as "bigger," "stronger," "firmer" and "more alert." Although males are generally slightly longer and heavier at birth (Barfield, 1976), the hospital records showed that these particular male and female infants did not differ in birth length, weight or health. From birth onward, parents continually react to their child as a girl or as a boy.

The experiences of people born with genital anomalies emphasize how thoroughly children learn the lessons of gender during their early years. "Attempts to reassign gender, to take a child previously treated as a boy, for example, and begin to treat it as a girl, are usually unsuccessful after the age of three or four" (Yussen and Santrock, 1978:397).

Throughout life, gender permeates every social relationship and every sphere of human activity. There are girls' games and boys' games, girls' clothes and boys' clothes. Although girls find school more congenial than do boys, they soon learn that attracting a suitable mate takes priority over serious occupational commitment. Boys too expect to marry but work is their major life goal. Even when the same occupation is chosen, the male (a physician, for example) has different experiences than his female counterpart. And on it goes. Being a wife, mother, divorcée, widow or elderly woman is not the same as being a husband, father, divorcé, widower or elderly man.

Humorist Nora Ephron (1975:1) expresses the importance of gender to children:

> In grammar school, in the fifth and sixth grades, we were all tyrannized by a rigid set of rules that supposedly determined whether we were boys or girls. The episode in *Huckleberry Finn* where Huck is disguised as a girl and gives himself away by the way he threads a needle and catches a ball —that kind of thing. We learned that the way you sat, crossed your legs, held a cigarette, and looked at your nails—the way you did these things instinctively was absolutely proof of your sex. Now obviously most children did not take this literally, but I did. I thought that just one slip, just one incorrect cross of my legs or flick of an imaginary cigarette ash would turn me from whatever I was into the other thing; that would be all it took, really.

We argued above that gender is an axis of individual and social experience because the sexes are differentiated. If the sexes were equally valued, if society in general shared Maurice Chevalier's sentiment of "Vive la différence!" the women's liberation movement would never have come into existence. However, masculinity is evaluated more highly than femininity. Since the ramifications of this inequality are a continuing theme of this book, only a few observations will be offered here. The point requires emphasis because many people wrongly believe that equality of the sexes has already been achieved, that utopia has arrived.

In 1967 the Royal Commission on the Status of Women was set up to inquire into the situation of Canadian women and to "recommend what steps might be taken by the Federal Government to ensure for women equal opportunities with men in all aspects of Canadian society" (*Report of the Royal Commission on the Status of Women in Canada*, 1970:vii). Three years later, the Commission tabled its report, which contained 167 recommendations in the areas of the economy, education, the family, taxation, poverty, public life, immigration and citizenship, and criminal law.

Among these recommendations was the suggestion that a Canadian Advisory Council on the Status of Women be established to act as a watchdog on women's issues. A few years ago, the Advisory Council assessed the progress that had been made over the decade in implementing the 122 Royal Commission recommendations falling within the jurisdiction of the federal government (Canadian Advisory Council on the Status of Women, 1979). According to its analysis, 43 recommendations have been implemented, 53 have been partially implemented, 24 have not been implemented and 2 are no longer applicable. It is clear that the task of implementation "is far from finished." In addition:

> Many new and pressing issues concern women today that were not at all evident in 1970. The whole question of employment for women, . . . the worsening situation of economic security for women which makes wage gaps and lack of pensions even more important than before, are of paramount importance today. The need for equality of treatment on such issues as unemployment insurance, maternity benefits, the health needs of women, the problems of increasing violence against women, support systems for parents, the elimination of sex stereotyping which colors and influences the way society, and even women themselves, see women, the worsening child care situation—even though more and more mothers are working—all of these and many more issues . . . will have to be addressed and tackled in the 1980's. [Canadian Advisory Council on the Status of Women, 1979:5]

Perhaps it is easier to understand intuitively the extent of female-male inequality if we look at it from a less abstract vantage point. Remember the newborn infant that we brought into being a few pages ago? When the parents asked the doctors what sex the baby was, in all likelihood they were hoping for a particular answer. If the baby was their first child or intended to be their only child, the parents tended to prefer a boy, according to research (e.g., Markle, 1974). Which sex would you yourself prefer to be? If we can assume that twenty-year-old study results are still valid, the chances are that if you are female, you wish you were male and if you are male, you are quite satisfied to remain male. Why do people condone and even admire the masculine behavior of a twelve-year-old girl and abhor the feminine behavior of a twelve-year-old boy? (Even the labels for these children, "tomboy" and "sissy," communicate societal sentiment.) Why do female fashions often mimic male fashions, while the reverse rarely occurs (Chafetz, 1974:75)? The answer to these questions and many more like them is both simple and not so simple: society values males more highly than females.

Our objective up to this point has been to establish the crucial nature of gender. Before we move on to other matters, some additional remarks are needed in order to ensure that the impression we have created is a balanced one. First, it should be emphasized that the norms associated with gender and the differential evaluation of the sexes are no longer taken for granted. That these societal arrangements are being questioned is demonstrated by such everyday occurrences as the confusion about who precedes whom through doorways, and by the semantics of "chairperson," "Ms." and "girls." Second, we must keep in mind that gender presents problems for males as well as females. Being expected to achieve at work, to conceal emotions, to be strong and aggressive constricts the human potential of males. Since the traditional expectations of masculinity and femininity are closely interrelated, *both* sets are currently being subjected to critical scrutiny. However, the fact that it is the males who enjoy the superior power and prestige explains why gender problems are usually seen as exclusively female problems.

DEFINITION OF THE FIELD

Since this book claims to be about gender relations, some specification of the term's meaning is required. All definitions are arbitrary conventions but textbook authors and readers feel more comfortable when definitions are made explicit.

The Sociology of Gender Relations

The term *gender relations* applies to the study of the causes and consequences of the cultural identification of emotional, attitudinal, intellectual and behavioral traits as either masculine or feminine. These causes and consequences are examined from the point of view of individuals, groups and society as a whole.

Although for the time being enough has already been said about the term *gender*, other aspects of this very inclusive definition need further comment. The use of the word *relations* to label this area of study takes advantage of its multiple connotations. For one thing, it signals our interest in interaction. In order to understand the ramifications for the individual and society of the traits associated with anatomical sex differences, we must attend to social relationships. We shall be interested, then, in same-sex and cross-sex interaction, parent-child interaction, employer-employee interaction, husband-wife interaction, etc. Second, the term *relations* connotes dynamics and process. Cultural definitions of masculinity and femininity are not laid down once and for all. Culture is an abstraction, not a god who inscribes norms on tablets of stone. These definitions are worked out over time, and can change. They gain reality and legitimacy only through their operation in day-to-day social transactions. Finally, *relations* here means interdependence among individuals, groups and societal institutions. The lives of individual Canadians have been shaped by gender-related experiences in the family, school and workplace. Some of the norms of these institutions reflect and also maintain the gender norms current in Canadian society. However, individuals and groups (especially the latter) can challenge norms. A parent wonders why only girls are allowed to take home economics classes, and boys woodworking classes. A group of nurses' aides objects to doing the same work as hospital orderlies for less pay. Sometimes the norms change.

In the above definition, traits are described as "feminine" or "masculine." This dichotomization is at the heart of the meaning of gender. There are girls and boys, women and men, women's behavior and men's behavior. Females are sentimental and weepy, while males are tough and don't cry. Females are followers, while males are leaders. Females are intuitive thinkers, while males are rational thinkers. At least, they are seen to be that way in our society. However, the societal emphasis on difference should not encourage us to lose sight of the similarities shared by the sexes, or of the overlap between male-female characteristics and behavior (Tresemer, 1975). In some cases, folk knowledge is accurate, and males and females are truly quite different. (Males have penises and females have vaginas.) Sometimes the sexes are the same. (Canadian men and women have almost identical attitudes toward the issue of multiculturalism [Berry, Kalin and Taylor, 1977:242].) In yet others, masculine and feminine traits overlap. (Males *in general* are more aggressive than females *in general* but females are not utterly lacking in aggressiveness, and *some* females are more aggressive than *some* males.) To sum up, the cultural or folk meaning of *gender* polarizes the sexes and views them as quite different. For social scientists, the commonsensical definition of the situation constitutes the subject matter to be studied. However, we must keep in mind that male-female traits fall along a continuum (Tresemer, 1975), from very different through increasing degrees of overlap to exactly the same. Where to place a particular trait on this continuum is an empirical question that research must answer.

Related Definitions

The delimitation of the boundaries of a given academic field of inquiry, as well as the choice of the label for this intellectual territory, are matters of pragmatism and trial and error. Scholars come to believe that an area deserves intensive study. Because the new area needs a name, labels and definitions evolve over time. The next section will treat the very short history of the social-scientific examination of men's and women's experiences and problems. Here, we want to contrast the label, "gender relations," with related labels, "women's studies," "men's studies" and "sex roles," which the student is likely to encounter in his/her reading.

Although the precise content of women's studies textbooks and courses varies from book to book and university to university, the title indicates comprehensive inquiry into *women's* experiences. "Women's studies" is a generic term that refers to the analysis of women in a variety of fields within the humanities and social sciences. The focus is on women rather than men and women, and the approach is interdisciplinary (Nemiroff, 1978). Proponents of women's studies believe that partitioning women's experiences into the Psychology of Women, the Sociology of Women, the Biology of Women, the Literature by Women and so on leads to the fragmentation of knowledge. They therefore argue for a synthesis of approaches that transcends university disciplines and departments. Although they are right that no one discipline can completely account for human experiences, depth of study within individual disciplines is also necessary. The field of "gender relations," then, is narrower in scope than the more inclusive "women's studies." It is a perspective that draws upon other disciplines, but which is primarily sociological in orientation.

As the title suggests, "men's studies" concentrate on issues of concern to men (Powers, 1978). They too adopt an interdisciplinary approach. The field emerged very recently as a reaction to women's studies. In Canada, courses are rare and, at this time, textbooks nonexistent. The field of gender relations differs from men's studies and women's studies by its attempt to encompass the situation and experiences of women *and* men, both individually and in relation to one another.

Finally, the nomenclature commonly applied to the scholarly study of the sexes includes the unsatisfactory label, "sex roles." Since objections have been raised to both concepts contained in this title, it has fallen into disuse. "Gender" has replaced "sex" because, for the most part, social scientists are interested in the cultural, rather than the biological, meaning of femaleness and maleness. Although the differences of opinion are somewhat greater here, some sociologists argue with good reason that the word "role" is inappropriate. Behaving as a girl or a boy, a woman or a man is not so much a social role as a pervasive gender identity that affects all, or almost all, the social roles played (Lopata, 1976:172-73). Canadian men and women are constantly reminded of their gender identity in all their roles. They are expected to behave somewhat differently even in allegedly identical roles. For example, *university student* is a supposedly identical role for both, but the expectations and behavior of male and female students are *not* really equivalent. For this reason, the more inclusive term "relations" has replaced "role" in current definitions.

ORIENTATION OF THE BOOK

Because the subject matter of gender relations covers a large area, a book on this topic must of necessity be written from certain selected perspectives. Some of the choices made here reflect the author's academic training and experience in teaching gender relations courses. Others stem from personal conviction. The five guiding themes set out below are the outcome of this decision making.

Emphasis on Both Sexes

This book focuses upon both females and males. Although there is a massive and ever-growing literature that attempts to understand women's experience, comparatively little thought has been devoted to men's experience. This statement refers to the analysis of masculinity as gender, not to generic man. To say this another way, the consideration of the implications of cultural beliefs about maleness, by social scientists, is a very recent phenomenon. However, the bulk of the social science literature has been written by men on topics of interest to men. Furthermore, these descriptions of the male experience have often been presented as descriptions of the *human* experience. These observations will be discussed more fully later in this chapter.

Here, we take the position that it is futile to attempt to study one sex in isolation from the other. Masculinity and femininity derive their meaning from the relation of one to the other. The tendency for them to be culturally defined as complementary opposites is only one example of what is meant. Moreover, the roles most influenced by gender (for example, husband and wife) are reciprocal roles. The changes currently taking place in female roles inevitably affect male roles. Indeed, the growing literature on men is "clearly a response to the cultural ferment generated by feminism" (Harrison, 1978:324). We will attempt to achieve a balance of emphasis on female and male experiences. Sometimes, however, the relative scarcity of research on the latter will hinder the attainment of this objective.

A Sociological and Social-Psychological Perspective

As mentioned earlier, men's and women's studies encompass extremely broad areas. The expertise of all the humanities and social sciences would be required in order to tell the complete story, and that story will never really be finished. In the meantime, any one book must be restricted in scope. Although the perspective of this book is to a certain extent interdisciplinary, and draws upon material from psychology, anthropology, history and literature, among others, its primary vantage points are sociology and social psychology.

Aside from the fact that sociology and social psychology represent the author's areas of competence, the two disciplines, supplemented by the ones mentioned above, offer an effective approach to gender relations. Sociology is the study of social relationships and social institutions. Therefore, sociology can inform us about gender-related interaction (e.g., socialization and courtship) and social structure (e.g., the labor market and social stratification systems). Social psychology, a subdiscipline on the border line between sociology and psychology, examines social influences upon the *individual*. Hence, this approach is uniquely suited to understanding the impact of gender upon individual persons. The anthropologist Malinowski (1922:25), although he was writing sixty years ago (and his language was sexist by today's standards), set out goals for the study of preliterate people, which we could well apply to our study of contemporary Canadians: "to grasp the native's point of view, his relation to life, to realize *his* vision of *his* world [emphasis in original]."

A Canadian Focus

This book concentrates on gender relations in Canadian society. Although social science research done elsewhere is included, a major objective is to provide an integrated discussion of the Canadian literature. Specifying what is meant by "Canadian research" can become complicated. Eichler's (1977a) definition has been adopted here. She says, "I shall simply define as Canadian any research that is informed by the Canadian experience, irrespective of the birth, residence, or citizenship status of a researcher" (Eichler, 1977a:410). Related objectives are to discover gaps in our knowledge of the Canadian situation and to consider relevant differences that may exist between Canada and other societies and within Canada itself.

Nationalistic sentiment is *not* the reason for this book's Canadian emphasis. Rather, Canadian scholars and students require an understanding of the meaning of gender in their own society. Though a great deal of the international research and theory probably does apply to our country, the equivalence of Canadian experiences with those elsewhere cannot be assumed. For one thing, the patterns of male-female relations and the institutions shaping and shaped by them have developed over time, and our history is not the history of other societies.

Canadian society is a heterogeneous society. It is differentiated by regionalism, ethnicity, religion, social class, age and urban-rural residence. Though much more research needs to be done, dimensions such as these are intricately interrelated with gender. We can hypothesize that gender will have both shared and unique meanings for a young, working-class woman in the Newfoundland outport of Tickle Cove and an elderly, upper-middle-class woman in Vancouver, British Columbia. The detailed patterns of differentiation in Canadian society do not mirror those found elsewhere.

Some aspects of gender are universal and some are unique to particular societies. Therefore, research into the particularities of the Canadian situation is required, and research (and theorizing) done in this country will be emphasized. However, because of the universal aspects of gender and the relative scarcity of Canadian work, ideas from elsewhere will be included in this book after they have passed critical scrutiny.

Selective Integration

A fourth objective of this book is to integrate the existing knowledge about gender relations in a selective fashion. This integrative function requires us to consolidate in one volume the somewhat scattered work of Canadian scholars and to place it within the context of the general sociology and social psychology of gender relations. Where relevant, the author's own research will be described. Labelling the book's orientation as "selective" emphasizes the fact that no claim is made to be totally comprehensive. Because so much material exists, no one volume can possibly deal with all of it. The criteria for selectivity are the other themes listed in this section, as well as the author's own notions of what is important.

Scholarship versus Propaganda

The book's final feature is its adoption of a scholarly stance as opposed to an ideological feminist stance. Women's studies came into being as a result of the women's liberation movement, and the majority of the academics involved were (and still are) women. Consequently, many have a dual motivation for their work: to explain *and* to improve women's situation. This combination of intellectual curiosity and value commitment is not confined to gender relations specialists, of course. And, although this combination can produce undesirable consequences (which will be discussed shortly), completely impartial or value-free scholarship is neither possible nor desirable. A gender relations specialist with absolutely no interest in making the world a better place is almost impossible to imagine. We all have values and passions that are bound to infuse our work.

Nevertheless, the coalescence of personal and social movement sympathies with scholarship poses potential dangers to the study of gender relations (Mackie, 1977a). There is a temptation to mistake our ideological preferences and pronouncements for social "reality," to confuse facts with values. For example, in the Preface to her book on the psychology of women, Judith Bardwick (1972:xi) wrote that "rhetoric, passion, and extremism characterize most of what has been recently published." In general, social science's protection against the retention of faulty generalizations lies in the self-corrective mechanisms of science as a *social* enterprise. Mistakes are discovered by the "accumulation of different perspectives on the subject matter" (Berger and Luckmann, 1966:10). However, the field of gender relations is especially vulnerable to the intrusion of bias precisely because specialists share the same ideological position. Therefore, the corrective function of multiple ideological positions is less likely to be in operation.

How can this dilemma be resolved? Although the study of gender relations has achieved some maturity over the past decade, there are still no pat answers. As far as this book is concerned, an attempt will be made to avoid equating personal sentiments with social scientific pronouncements. The use of nonemotive language should help restrain the urge to present propaganda under the guise of scholarship. In addition, the book will try to distinguish between statements that are hypotheses or conjectures and those that are empirically grounded generalizations. Where no answers yet exist, it will admit inadequacies of evidence rather than suggest closure. The focus on men as well as women should aid us in achieving these lofty goals. However, as we have seen, the safeguards against bias are social. Therefore, it is simply beyond the power of the individual author or researcher to guarantee the impartiality of his/her work. Readers of this book will have to judge how well it achieves this, as well as its other objectives.

SOCIAL SCIENCE AND GENDER RELATIONS

A discipline, or a subfield within a discipline, makes more sense to newcomers if they have some appreciation of its history. Although a detailed history is of interest only to specialists, some general background knowledge places the neophyte in a better position to understand what practitioners are attempting to accomplish, why certain topics are emphasized, and the reasons for shortcomings and gaps in the evidence. This evidence is especially pertinent for the area of gender relations. Because it is so new, its contemporary developments are, to a considerable extent, outgrowths of its beginning stages.

Gender relations, as a field of study, came into being in 1969, the year that North American sociologists discovered the existence of women. At the 1969 meeting of the American Sociological Association, a women's caucus met to protest discrimination against female sociologists in the profession, discrimination against women in society at large, and the sexist bias in the study of sociology (Bernard, 1973:775). Similar concerns were expressed by women in the other social sciences in both Canada and the United States, though the Canadian reaction came somewhat later.

In 1971 the Canadian Sociology and Anthropology Association passed a resolution opposing discrimination on the grounds of sex, age or marital status and encouraging the recruitment of women. In the same year, Robson and Lapointe published a comparison of Canadian academic men's and women's salaries and fringe benefits for the Royal Commission on the Status of Women. This report, as well as a series of studies of women's status in particular Canadian universities, was analyzed in Hitchman (1974). The first issue of the *Canadian Newsletter of Research on Women* was published in May 1972 under the editorship of Margrit Eichler and Marylee Stephenson. The newsletter, now titled *Resources for Feminist Research*, communicates information on feminist research and the teaching of gender relations courses. The first two Canadian academic books on women (Andersen, 1972; Stephenson, 1973) also appeared in the early 1970s. The formation of an association of women in sociology and anthropology was announced in 1974.

In retrospect, it seems odd that the realization of the importance of gender did not originate in social science research. After all, sociologists are the professional students of society and one might expect that their studies would have alerted them to the fact that the world contains women as well as men. Be that as it may, the actions of academic women were stimulated by the women's liberation movement. The decade of the 1960s was marked by protest against the system and demands for just treatment from Indians, blacks, the poor, university students and, eventually, women. Indeed, female sociologists in North America did not speak out until *after* Commissions on the Status of Women had been established by the Canadian and American governments.

A second reason explaining why the male-female distinction became an issue in sociology was the increasing number of female sociologists. Canadian sociology as a whole was growing. Only two doctorates in sociology were awarded in 1960-61; by 1971-72, thirty-one had been awarded (Hiller, 1979:130). In 1973, there were 648 professional sociologists resident in Canada (Canadian Sociology and Anthropology Association *Bulletin*, October 1974:14). Although the proportion of females (16.4%) was low, in absolute numbers they, along with female graduate students, were becoming a visible, self-conscious minority within the profession.

The genesis of gender relations was not complete until the definition of the area included men as well as women. Women, as the protesting, disadvantaged sex, tended naturally to confine their attention to their own situation. However, the reciprocal relationship between the sexes made it impossible to discuss one sex in isolation from the other. In addition, men were reacting to the feminist movement. Though some of their early books, such as Vance Packard's *The Sexual Wilderness* (1968), predicted dire consequences unless the sexual revolution was curtailed (Harrison, 1978:328), their gradual realization that men too have been trapped by traditional role definitions resulted in critical analysis of men's roles (e.g., Farrell, 1974). This new literature on men does not yet include a specifically Canadian book, although a few books such as this one and Ambert (1976) discuss the experiences of both sexes.

The Female Sociologists' Complaints

Their eyes having been opened by the women's liberation movement, the women in sociology looked critically at their own lives and at their discipline and put forth three complaints. First, they protested their own status, both in the profession and in the university. Second, they were troubled about the devalued status of women in general. Finally, they charged the field of sociology with sexual bias. These issues are interconnected, and some attention will be given to the relevance of all three to the contemporary state of the field. However, our main concern here is the third accusation. Specifically, we need to explain what is meant by "sexual bias" in the discipline. This complaint can be summed up by saying that the sociology that had previously been accepted as the science of society was really the male science of male society (Bernard, 1973:781).

The charge that sociology is androcentric, and hence incomplete and distorted, rests upon these general arguments:

1. With a few exceptions (Hacker, 1951; Komarovsky, 1946), the social behavior of females has been ignored in the past by sociologists. There appear to be two reasons for the exclusion of women. Sociologists, who were primarily male, seem to have believed that what women did was trivial and unworthy of serious study (Daniels, 1975:346). As well as making this point, the following quotation illustrates the relationship between women's lowly status in the discipline and the sexually biased content of the field. "If, in spite of the insecurity of our positions, the interminable packing and unpacking as we went from one temporary job to another, we managed to do research and publish, we were told that the work we did was competent but uninteresting. Who really gives a damn about reading studies, particularly feminist studies about women, their dilemmas, their problems, their attempts at solution" (Bart, 1971b:735).

2. A second reason was the tendency of male sociologists to focus their attention on social institutions and settings in which males predominate, such as the occupational, political and legal systems. Where women were noticed at all, it was their connection to men that counted. Consequently, matters of interest to women were neglected. For example, urban sociology overlooked the behavior of mothers and

children in parks, women at beauty parlors, widows in coffee shops (Lofland, 1975). Labelling the suburb as the "bedroom community" because the *men* leave during the day conveyed the message that what women and children did was not important (Richardson, 1981). In addition, there was a tendency to assume that the results of studies of male behavior applied to women as well, e.g., that people responded to leaders generally as they responded to male leadership. On other occasions it was assumed that what was true of men could be reversed for a description of women (Fuller, 1978:147). For example, the traits of ambitiousness, aggressiveness and competitiveness are often associated with masculinity and disassociated from femininity.

3. The critics of pre-1970s sociology argued that the exclusion of women's social behavior as legitimate subject matter and the inferior position of women sociologists carried the further implication of the exclusion of the feminine intellectual perspective. This sociology-of-knowledge argument contends that different locations in the social structure produce different ways of thinking, or different intellectual orientations toward social reality. Karl Marx (1904:11) put it this way: "It is not the consciousness of men that determines their existence, but, on the contrary, their social existence determines their consciousness." A contemporary researcher (Jacobson, 1979:103) speaks specifically of women's experience: "Women play different roles, hold different positions, carry out different tasks, have different upbringings and different expectations. We do not experience the world in the same way nor do we understand it from the same perspective as do men." Men and women live in social worlds that are separate at some points and overlapping at others. It is hypothesized that separate experiences result in unique mental content. The public world of men compared to the domestic world of women is one critical difference. The "status world" of women and the "cash-nexus" world of men is another (Bernard, 1973:782). (In a status world, bonds are based on love or duty. In a cash-nexus world, monetary exchange is the primary bond.) However, even when the two sexes share the same social role or social milieu, their perspectives are not identical. As we have argued before, being a female university student is not the same thing as being a male university student. Within the same marriage, being a wife is not the same as being a hus-

band (Bernard, 1971). Therefore, *how* one thinks and *what* one thinks are influenced by gender. The invisibility of women in sociology means the exclusion of both female views of reality.

From the sociology-of-knowledge vantage point, the unequal numbers and power of female sociologists have had profound consequences for the discipline. According to Smith (1974:7), "how sociology is thought—its methods, conceptual schemes and theories—has been based on and built up within, the male social universe. . . ." The issue here is that the models of social reality are the models of the males who hold the power in the profession (Smith, 1975). Until recently, women sociologists were trained by males and functioned in a male-dominated system where only masculine thought-patterns held legitimacy. Although misogynous plotting was not responsible for all this, the result was an androcentric sociology.

According to feminist sociologists, the omission of women's social behavior and intellectual perspective had unfortunate effects on pre-1970s sociology, and remedial action was necessary. Although the debate has focused on women, it soon became evident that many dimensions of male experience were also missing. Indeed, sociologists had failed almost entirely to appreciate the role of gender in human social affairs. This foreshortened viewpoint influenced the topics studied, the theories of social behavior, research techniques and the teaching of sociology. Each of these problems will be discussed in turn.

Topics of Study

As noted above, sociology concentrated on topics of interest to male sociologists, such as work, economics, politics and education, and relegated women to the sociology of the family. Because work has long been a central area of sociology, it provides a good illustration of what the discipline looked like before and after the "discovery of women." Until recently, books often bore titles such as *Man and His Work* (Ritzer, 1972) and concentrated on masculine occupations and work problems. For example, analyses of bureaucracies overlooked the role of female clerks and secretaries in these enterprises. If women's work was mentioned at all, it tended to be confined to a special section. (A major book coyly labelled this section "A Job of Her Own.") Until 1978 (Blishen and Carroll), the most widely used index for measuring socioeconomic status in Canada (Blishen, 1967; Blishen and McRoberts, 1976), completely omitted female occupations. An award-winning study of the American occupational structure (Blau and Duncan, 1967) excluded the two-fifths of the labor force constituted by women, and discussed women only as contributors to their husbands' careers (Bernard, 1973:782). Little was known about teachers, nurses, waitresses, typists or beauticians. Housework, an activity engaged in by nearly all adult women, was not even regarded as real work.

Since the early 1970s, the topics of study have been expanded considerably to take into account both women's interests and the role of gender. Some of this remedial work was done by extending traditional areas such as social stratification, work, criminology and politics to include women as well as men. In Canada, concern with women at work comes before all other subjects. Professional women in general, and academic women in particular, have received disproportionate attention (Eichler, 1975a:474). In addition, many new topics of special import to women have emerged, such as the sociology of emotions, voluntary childlessness, violence in the family, the menopause and rape. A recognition has grown that though sociology in the past was male sociology, it emphasized formal-official, as opposed to *informal* male behavior (Millman and Kanter, 1975:x). Newly defined topics such as male inexpressiveness and fatherhood are attempts to fill this lacuna.

In general, the women's liberation movement alerted sociologists to the role played by gender in social affairs. As a result, the sociology of gender relations was provoked into being. The area differs from other, more specialized subfields of sociology in that it attempts to analyze previously ignored social behavior across *all* sociology. The type of article published by sociology journals is an excellent gauge of the state of the discipline. The 1964-69 issues of the *Canadian Review of Sociology and Anthropology* (the official journal of the Canadian Sociology and Anthropology Association) contained no articles at all on gender relations. The 1979 and 1980 issues together contained four articles on the subject (7% of the total). Progress is being made but made slowly. However, in recent years several journals devoted exclusively to gender relations have been established. These include *Atlantis, Canadian Women's Studies*, the *International Journal of Women's Studies* and *Resources for Feminist Research* in Canada, and *Signs* and *Psychology of Women Quarterly* in the United States. At the moment, the tabloid *Changing Men* published by the Men's Resource Center in Portland, Oregon is the closest thing available to a journal on men's studies.

Theory

Taking a sociology-of-knowledge stance, some feminist scholars argue that sociology's failure to incorporate women's intellectual perspectives has resulted in the hegemony of male theories of social behavior. Though this criticism is related to topic choice (discussed above), what concerns us here are the deficiencies in the abstract frameworks of ideas. These theories or theoretical orientations[1] are designed to guide research, to integrate diverse empirical observations and to explain social behavior. As usual, the discussion, like the Roman god Janus, looks forward and backward at the same time: the critique of past sociology is accompanied by a program for future improvement.

There are two major reasons for finding previous theoretical formulations objectionable. Since they are rooted in male perception and experience and omit the feminine perspective, it is hypothesized that these partial views of reality have limited explanatory power. For example, existing theories tend to emphasize the male interest in rational, formal dimensions of social behavior, and to omit irrational, emotional and informal dimensions. Because the behavior of people "out there" involves both dimensions, existing one-sided theories are deficient. To take another example, theories of deviance based exclusively on male deviance are bound to be misleading (Harris, 1977). Note that this argument rests on the twin sociology-of-knowledge assumptions that reality is socially constructed and that males and females, being differentially located in the social structure, inhabit different worlds and employ different concepts to think about their worlds. According to the sociology-of-knowledge perspective, reality is not something "out there," independent of our experience of it. Rather, reality must be defined and interpreted, and this definition and interpretation are social activities (Berger and Luckmann, 1966:21-23). Differences in male and female social experiences lead to differences in their interpretations of the world. Take color as an example. Various shades of purple are not *intrinsically* magenta, mauve or burgundy. The color labels, indeed the perceptual distinctions themselves, are social inventions. Moreover, color distinctions pertain more to the female world than to the male world. Consequently, we can hypothesize that females are more likely to notice colors and to give them their proper social names. So it is with the social reality as theoretically interpreted by female and male sociologists.

Second, some theory is criticized on the grounds that "scholarly" arguments are used to justify a sexist status quo. To illustrate, the theory of functionalism as put forward by Parsons (1955a,b) is accused of presenting a *"Kinder, Küche, Kirche"* view of women's place, as though efficient societal operation demanded that women stay home and play their traditional, or expressive, role. Indeed, sociology's founding fathers have been called "sexists to a man" (Schwendinger and Schwendinger, 1971).

Suggestions for remedying the sexism in sociological theorizing range from the obvious to the near utopian. Challenging a stereotypical depiction of women (or men) wherever it occurs represents an obvious step. The injection of an appreciation of gender into some theories that attempt to explain limited aspects of social reality has stimulated creativity and improved theorizing in a number of areas (e.g., social stratification

[Acker, 1973; Nielsen, 1979] and emotionality [Hochschild, 1975]). Eichler's (1977) warning to Canadian sociologists against the willy-nilly adoption of ideas that are both androcentric *and* American has served to provoke skepticism in defense.

A much more controversial position is taken by people such as Bernard (1973), Harrison (1978), Smith (1974) and Rubin (1976), who expect the recognition of gender to affect theory *radically*, in the literal sense of producing alterations that go to the very roots of the discipline of sociology. They talk about "paradigm crises" and the "shattering of old paradigms."[2] More specifically, Smith (1975:357, 367) argues that since "It is men who produce for women . . . the means to think and image," academic women "are confronted virtually with the problem of reinventing the world of knowledge, of thought, of symbols and images." Others (e.g., Epstein, 1974a) do not believe that there are essentially different male and female perspectives or that existing theoretical frameworks possess any intrinsic limitations for the analysis of women's experiences. The sociology-of-knowledge hypothesis is empirically testable and the "paradigm crisis" notion will receive the test of time.

At the time of writing, the theoretical progress made seems to have been restricted, for the most part, to *internal* development of women's studies. In the author's opinion, the fundamental corpus of sociological theory remains untouched. Sociology is generally still guided by high-order assumptions that are male creations. A new epistemology has not emerged; old thought-forms are simply applied to both sexes. Speaking for psychology, Parlee (1979:129) observes that "nowhere is it possible to find evidence suggesting that the scientific importance of a feminist perspective is recognized by those in the mainstream."

Methodology

Sociology's indifference toward women in the past has affected methodology (the logic and techniques of carrying out research) as well as the related areas of topic choice and theory. Because such matters as definition of problems for study, concept development and research grounded in theory are related to all three areas, there is no need to repeat here what has already been said. Similarly, we have already mentioned the tendency in the past to generalize the results from exclusively male samples to people in general (or to assume, again without evidence, that feminine behavior is the reverse of masculine behavior). The risk involved in mixing scholarly research with activist sympathies has received comment above. Finally, evidence is mounting that the sex of the researcher often influences the quality of the research when fieldwork is involved. For example, mature women are effective door-to-door interviewers. Male anthropologists learn almost nothing about the women's sphere in preindustrial cultures because their interest is interpreted as sexual (Wax, 1979). Only one important issue remains for discussion here, namely, the "machismo" and "communal" approaches to research (Bernard, 1973).

The "machismo factor" is the label for the overall research style allegedly preferred by male sociologists. This style contrasts sharply with female "communal" preferences. The machismo element involves quantitative, usually survey, research. "Hard" statistical data are controlled and manipulated. "The scientist using this approach creates his own controlled reality. He can manipulate it. He is master. He has power. He can add or subtract or combine variables. He can play with a simulated reality like an Olympian god. He can remain at a distance, safely invisible behind his shield, uninvolved. The communal approach is much humbler. It disavows control, for control spoils the results" (Bernard, 1973:785).

Machismo research stresses the similarities between sociology and the natural sciences.

Feminist researchers, on the other hand, consider the type of research described above as inappropriate for the study of women's behavior. They prefer qualitative methods, such as informal interviews, case studies and participant observation, which allow them to "take the role of the other," to see the world through the eyes of the people being studied. Understanding the experiences of women, treated as subjects, not objects to be manipulated, takes priority over translating "data" into "statistics." The language of variables really does not apply and a positivistic view of sociology (that is, one that stresses its similarities with the physical sciences) is not embraced. Whether sociology is or is not a science is not a very interesting question to these women researchers. A sense of history and of cooperation with practitioners in other disciplines are considered to be more important. Finally, the researcher's own experiences and biography play a prominent role in the research process. For one thing, feminist researchers view their own biographies as legitimate material for analysis. One criterion for the plausibility of ideas is their accordance with the researcher's own experiences (Parlee, 1979:130). Many feminist researchers have experienced the enhancement of self-esteem that comes from viewing the deficiencies of social institutions, rather than character defects, as responsible for "private troubles" (Mills, 1959).[3] Therefore, the scientist-subject, "I-them" dichotomy holds little appeal. The desire for personal growth and for improvement in the general situation of women supplements simple intellectual curiosity as motivation for research (Vaughter, 1976:146). Although these ideas have developed because traditional methods were judged unsuitable for the study of women's unique experiences, the goal is to develop approaches "suitable to the study of persons" (Vaughter, 1976), in order to grasp the subtle nuances of human behavior.

The "communal" orientation is the way that feminists *say* they prefer to do research. What is the relationship between words and deeds? Do female social scientists live up to their ideals? Although (to the author's knowledge) no systematic study of research styles has been done, we might hypothesize that the work of female social scientists published in the mainstream sociology journals would tend to be in the "machismo" style, and, in the nonacademic publication outlets, more "communal." The reasoning here is that the more conventional, more prestigious, "hard" techniques would be needed in order to get past the editorial gatekeepers of mainstream journals. In addition, female researchers might be motivated to use conventional techniques in order to improve the reputation of women's studies.[4]

An analogous situation occurred fifty years ago in the discipline of sociology. In a personal communication to Irwin Deutscher (1966:240), Richard La Piere explains that "well into the 1930s the status of sociology and hence of sociologists was abominable, both within and outside the academic community." He describes the personal "hurt of its lowly status." The adoption of methods that suggested sociology's affinity to the physical sciences was, according to La Piere, one attempt to enhance the discipline's status.

Teaching

In addition to carrying out research, most Canadian sociologists teach in postsecondary educational institutions. Understandably enough, the discipline's insensitivity to gender and its neglect of women in research has also affected the content of its curriculum. Until the women's movement removed blinders, no one really noticed that students were being taught the sociology of male society.

The premovement situation is easily summarized. Though sex was treated as a standard demographic variable, that usage had little to do with gender. Students might learn that the sex ratio is higher in Dawson City than in Ottawa. Or that females are more knowledgeable than males about heart disease (Mackie, 1973b). Sociology-of-the-family courses did consider women worth discussing. In general sociology and in social psychology, women turned up once in a while as rather pathetic creatures with low self-esteem, who conformed more than men to pressure, whose attitudes were easily swayed, who concealed their intelligence in order to snare a husband, who feared success and were susceptible to hysterical contagion. (An example of hysterical contagion: the fainting of more than 100 female employees on a Texas assembly line was attributed to Elvis Presley's sudden death. Though plant employers had feared toxic gas, the outbreak was blamed on the mass anxiety of overweight, middle-aged women who thought of themselves as liable to sudden death. The question of why the male employees didn't faint too can be left to the reader to ponder.)

In textbook presentations of that era, women tended to be stereotyped or absent altogether. Gray (1977) describes a statistics text published in 1971, which begins with a story about the author at his office window observing the "splendid displays of beautiful young birds," and delighting in the fact that "with the advent of the miniskirt, they're becoming even more splendid and more beautiful." The concept of *correlation* is illustrated in the text by speculation on the relationship between skirt heights and the rate of traffic accidents. The old days were "when men were men and girls wore flour sack underwear." An easy statistical test is one that "even little old ladies wearing straw hats decorated with flowers can be taught to do."

Sometimes the types of pictures chosen by authors and editors to illustrate books are a subtle revelation of social attitudes. Schneider and Hacker (1973:13) report that the pictures contained in twelve of the best-selling sociology introductory texts tended to support the hypothesis of women's relative invisibility. More particularly, content analysis showed that, taking all the books together, 42% of the pictures showed only men. The range over the twelve texts was from 25% to 63%. Comparable figures for pictures showing only women was an overall average of 8%, with a range of zero to 22%.

Sociology's discovery of women has affected the undergraduate textbooks and curriculum. In Canada, an important role was played by the *Canadian Newsletter of Research on Women*, which provided for the exchange of ideas about women's courses. In addition to the development of specialized women's (and to a lesser extent, men's) studies courses, many traditional sociology courses have modified their approaches in order to incorporate some gender relations content. Although the remedial work required in this neglected area warrants specialized courses for some time yet, the material should eventually be integrated into the more traditional courses. Otherwise, prolonged isolation of gender relations from mainstream sociology could result in unhealthy sectarianism. Over the long run, such ghettoization of thought would be detrimental to both gender relations and mainstream sociology.

In summary, the women's liberation movement raised women sociologists' consciousness regarding the state of their own discipline. What had been accepted until then as the sociology of human behavior was consequently accused of being the sociology of male behavior. Research had been conducted primarily by males (and females who had been socialized to accept the masculine ruling ideas), on topics of interest to males, using male techniques. The sheer awareness that a problem existed represented an important breakthrough. As we have seen, remedial action is being taken to make up for deficiencies and distortions of thought. However, it is well to remember just how recent all these events are. There is a long way to go. Men's studies have really just begun.

One optimistic note is the fact that both women *and* men currently share an awareness of the problems discussed above. Indeed, the term *feminist* applies to people of both sexes who believe in the equality of the sexes. One of the most visible male feminists, the actor Alan Alda, explains: "I come from a long line of women."

OVERVIEW OF CHAPTERS

The content of this book is divided into eight chapters. The intent of the present chapter is to provide the reader with a general introduction to the field of gender relations. Chapter Two poses the key question: What similarities and differences characterize females and males? The following five chapters attempt to answer this question. Chapter Three considers the extent to which biology is responsible for gender. Chapter Four adopts the social psychological perspective and inquires into gender socialization. This chapter focuses on various socialization theories. Chapters Five and Six discuss primary group (family, peer group) and secondary and symbolic (schools, mass media, language) sources of socialization, respectively. Chapter Seven explores social structural explanations of gender. The concept of sexual stratification is a central component of that chapter. Finally, Chapter Eight looks to the future and assesses the changes that are occurring in gender relations, as well as problem areas that still remain. The female and male liberation movements figure prominently here.

This book is intended to be an integrated, comprehensive text, appropriate for gender relations courses in sociology and psychology, as well as social problems and Canadian society courses. Although prior exposure to an introductory level sociology course would be helpful, it is not necessary. The Glossary at the end of the book explains the meaning of specialized concepts.

2 Female/Male Similarities and Differences

O NCE upon a time thoroughly masculine man met thoroughly feminine woman at a cocktail party. Man is big, hairy and deep-voiced. Woman is dainty and soft of skin and voice. Both smell nice. His scent is called Brut, her scent is called Caresse. They talk about themselves. Especially the male. He is an engineer. She teaches the second grade. He plays squash. She does needlepoint. Though both enjoy music, he thinks poetry is for sissies. They order drinks from the waiter, he Scotch on the rocks, she a concoction of Amaretto, Grand Marnier and whipping cream. They may go out to dinner, get married and live happily ever after (for a year or two)—if he overcomes his fear of rejection in asking for a date. Meanwhile, she waits.

SEX DIFFERENTIATION

The caricatured couple described above serves to illustrate the pervasiveness of sex differentiation in twentieth-century Canadian society and indeed in every other society and historical period. Sex differentiation is the essence of the meaning of gender, and it is the subject of the present chapter. (Chapter One gave only a brief introduction to it.) At birth (or even earlier, during gestation) everyone is placed in one of two categories: female or male. This categorization is completely dichotomous. That is, one is either 100% male or 100% female. (Nonetheless, it is estimated that nearly .5% of the population, or one person in 200, is hermaphroditic or biologically intersexual [Tresemer, 1975:314].) Males and females are assigned different roles, rights and privileges, and are subject to different rules of conduct. In addition, men and women are assumed to possess distinctive abilities and temperaments that justify the perpetuation of the societal role structure (Spence and Helmreich, 1978:4). In other words, the categorization based upon anatomy (sex) is in turn linked

23

to cultural and psychological definitions of femininity and masculinity (gender). Alleged differences in psychological makeup are used to explain and to justify the roles to which each sex is assigned (Spence and Helmreich, 1978:ix).

MISLEADING FEMALE-MALE COMPARISONS

The "battle of the sexes" and the "mating game" stretch back into the mists of prehistory (Tavris and Offir, 1977). Both of these related endeavors involve the question of how men and women differ and how they are alike. Therefore, the question has provided intriguing subject matter for folk thought and scientific thought alike. Because so much emotion and mystery surround male-female relations, it is not surprising that many of the assumptions made about sex differences have been biased (Tresemer, 1975). As a result of the political ferment aroused by the women's movement, the whole issue has become a topic for intense debate.

Three misleading notions have proved to be particularly significant. First, there has been a tendency for scientists and nonscientists alike to emphasize the differences between males and females and to treat their similarities as inconsequential. On the biological level, we are fascinated with differences in anatomy. However, according to Oakley (1972:18), "Far from falling into two discrete groups, male and female have the same body ground plan, and even the anatomical difference is more apparent than real. Neither the phallus nor the womb are organs of one sex only: the female phallus (the clitoris) is the biological equivalent of the male organ, and men possess a vestigial womb."

An example from psychology involves aggressiveness. According to commonsensical views, males are aggressive while females are passive. However, research shows that differences between the sexes can be represented by overlapping *normal curves*. The trait appears to be distributed normally within each category, but the group *means* differ. (The Glossary contains definitions of these terms.) That is, males and females alike vary within their category, between being highly aggressive and very unaggressive. However, the average for males as a group is somewhat higher. Nevertheless, a substantial number of females will be equally or more aggressive than a substantial number of males. Moreover, differences within a category are greater than differences *between* categories (Chafetz, 1974:34).

Finally, social science journals are reluctant to fill valuable space with negative findings or findings of "no difference." This reluctance has served to highlight sex differences and to minimize sex similarities. Take this hypothetical case. (Deutscher [1973:201-203] exaggerates less to make the same point.) Suppose that over time twenty experiments were carried out comparing female-male housekeeping abilities. Suppose further that seventeen showed no sex difference in cooking, dusting and garbage-toting, while three showed female superiority. Only a few of the seventeen "no difference" studies would likely be published because journal editors would find them uninteresting and/or unconvincing. In comparison, probably all three studies that did show a difference would get published. Consequently, science would have proved female superiority in housekeeping!

A famous, true example of sex differences being exaggerated in social science research is the sad tale of "poor Anne." Until 1968, almost all the research on the need for achievement involved males. Therefore, Matina Horner (1969) set out to study the reactions of women to achievement-oriented situations. One aspect of her study required female undergraduates to tell a story in response to this cue: *After first-term finals, Anne finds herself at the top of her medical-school class.* The resulting stories were scored for the "motive to avoid success."

The most frequent response reflected strong fears of social rejection. For example, "Anne starts proclaiming her surprise and joy. Her fellow classmates are so disgusted with her behavior that they jump on her in a body and beat her. She is maimed for life." More specifically, these female students showed anxiety about Anne becoming lonely and unmarriageable: "Anne is an acne-faced bookworm. She runs to the bulletin board and finds she's at the top. As usual she smarts off. A chorus of groans is the rest of the class's reply. She studies twelve hours a day, and lives at home to save money. 'Well it certainly paid off. All the Friday and Saturday nights without dates, fun—I'll be the best woman doctor alive.' And yet a twinge of sadness comes through—she wonders what she really has. . . ."

These female undergraduates also expressed worry about definitions of womanhood: "[Anne] is worried about herself and wonders if perhaps she isn't normal . . . [she] decides not to continue with her medical work but to take courses that have a deeper personal meaning for her." A third group of stories denied the possibility of a woman achieving such success: "Anne is a *code name* for a nonexistent person created by a group of med. students. They take turns writing exams for Anne. . . ." "Anne is really happy she's on top, though *Tom is higher than she*—though that's as it should be. . . . Anne doesn't mind Tom winning." "Anne is talking to her counselor. Counselor says she will make a fine *nurse*."

Horner reported that college women responded more frequently with such negative imagery to the Anne cue than did college men to a fictitious John who found himself at the top of his medical class. Her finding of a sex difference, which apparently fit social scientists' expectations, was widely accepted as valid. However, dozens of replication studies, summarized in Tresemer (1974), have found that males responded with negative, "fear of success" stories about as often as females. Two early Canadian studies (Kimball, 1973; Luce, 1973) were among those that found no female-male differences.

A second mistaken notion is the bipolarity assumption, or the assumption of dichotomy (Tresemer, 1975:314). This assumption is closely related to the one we have just discussed. To begin with, males and females are considered to be diametrically opposite beings. Little girls are made of "sugar and spice and everything nice," and little boys of "snakes and snails and puppy dogs' tails" (Clarke, 1978:223-24). Men and women are seen as *either* this *or* that, not both. The characteristics in question are viewed as complete opposites. For example, women are regarded as passive and men as aggressive. Passivity and aggressiveness are conceptualized as logical opposites. The possibility of both sexes having the capacity to be both aggressive and tender is ruled out. In this type of thinking, "femininity is equated with lack of masculinity and masculinity with lack of femininity" (Spence and Helmreich, 1978:17). Femininity and masculinity are, from this vantage point, clusters of entirely separate and opposite characteristics.

The final point to be made here is that the basic inequality of the sexes represents *bias* in the most literal sense of the word. Because males are the powerful sex in our society, male attitudes toward women are of much greater consequence than female attitudes toward men. Indeed, the English language has no word for *man-hating* that parallels *misogyny*, the hatred of women (Tavris and Offir, 1977:2).

Obviously, male sentiments concerning women cover a spectrum of emotions. The "pedestal-gutter syndrome" is one label for these apparently opposite attitudes.

> Woman has been esteemed, worshipped, and protected as often as she has been loathed, ignored, and reviled. . . . Woman is goddess and devil, virgin and whore, sweet madonna and malevolent mom. She can bring a man up to salvation or drag him down with her to hell. On the face of it, the pedestal-gutter syndrome appears to reflect views that are diametrically opposed: woman is good, woman is bad. But in fact these views represent a single attitude: Woman is different. After all, whether you are looking up to women or stooping down to them, you don't have to look them in the eye. [Tavris and Offir, 1977:3]

The following studies illustrate prejudice toward women.

Labovitz (1974) asked 335 University of Calgary students to evaluate a brief written description of a sociological study. The same description was attributed to four different, fictitious authors in order to determine the extent to which sex and ethnicity influence student reactions. The alleged authors were: Edward Blake (English-Canadian male), Edith Blake (English-Canadian female), Joseph Walking Bear (Canadian Indian) and Marcel Fournier (French-Canadian). The description was judged to be of lower quality when it was attributed to a woman than when it was attributed to a man. (However, the non-Anglo-Saxon names elicited more critical evaluations than did the female name.)

Our second example is an unpublished study of humor conducted by Zimbardo and Meadow (1974) and described in Tavris and Offir (1977:21-22). These authors analyzed one thousand jokes that appeared in the *Reader's Digest* during the 1940s, 1950s and 1960s. Jokes were classified as antifemale if they portrayed women in a derogatory fashion, depended on the target being female rather than male, or contained a punch line that characterized women negatively. Parallel criteria were used to identify antimale jokes. Zimbardo and Meadow found six times as many antifemale as antimale jokes. Typically, women were depicted as stupid or foolish. Antifemale humor was especially prevalent just after World War II, when such jokes made up nearly one-third of the total. (Why might this have been so?) However, even in the late 1960s, the ratio of antifemale to antimale jokes had not changed, though the total had dropped to 12% of the grand total.

SEX DIFFERENCE RESEARCH AND SOCIAL SCIENTISTS' BIAS

Some readers may have been surprised that the previous section attributed mistaken thinking about male-female comparisons to social scientists as well as to laypersons. Until quite recently, research on sex differences was often a value-laden activity, used as "battle weapons against women" (Bernard, 1976:13). In the past, the scientists' motive to seek knowledge was sometimes subverted by illegitimate attempts to document male superiority and to rationalize unequal social arrangements. For this reason, gender relations specialists have been as intrigued by the sociology-of-knowledge aspects of this research as by its substantive findings. However, it is important to note that because contemporary psychologists are alert to the possibility of bias, the following remarks pertain more to the past than to the present. Nevertheless, the fact that more women are entering the field opens the possibility of prejudice in reverse (Parlee, 1978:62). Therefore, sex differences constitute an area of research where a historical perspective is essential.

In 1910 Helen Woolley (quoted in Shields, 1975:739) expressed these sentiments: "There is perhaps no field aspiring to be scientific where flagrant personal bias, logic martyred in the cause of supporting a prejudice, unfounded assertions, and even sentimental rot and drivel, have run riot to such an extent as here." The main problem was the attempt to "prove" that (a) any male-female differences demonstrated male superiority, and (b) the differences involved were innate, biological differences.

The brain controversy, which raged between 1900 and 1930, is a famous historical case of this misuse of science (Parlee, 1978). At first the debate revolved around the question, "Which sex has the larger brain?" Because it was assumed that both brain size and intelligence increased with movement up the phylogenetic scale, it seemed obvious that the sex with the smaller brain was the inferior sex. (Apparently, the fact that elephants have larger brains than humans did not occur to these scholars.) The brain size of cadavers was measured, and male brains were reported to be the larger. However, contemporary critics believe that the finding of male superiority was affected by the fact that the male researchers knew the sex of the corpse before they did their measuring. In other words, this information influenced their judgment.

The second phase of the brain controversy emerged when scientists discovered that various psychological abilities were localized in various parts of the brain. At first, the frontal lobes were viewed as the seat of the intellect. Not surprisingly, "research" showed that men had larger frontal lobes, relative to the parietal lobes, than did women. Later on, the parietal lobes came to be regarded as the source of higher intellectual functions. Scientific opinion reversed itself; studies began to report that men had relatively larger parietal lobes than women. Today scholars agree that neither overall brain size, nor proportions of brain parts, differ by sex.

Although the brain controversy seems somewhat silly in the 1980s, a relatively recent article by psychologist Olga Favreau (1977) argues that this type of thinking still occurs. "The previously reported greater tactile sensitivity of females which is already apparent at birth may contribute to their greater manual dexterity and early in life direct them toward activities which require manual skills such as sewing, knitting, embroidery, dental laboratory work and microscopic research in biology and biochemistry" (Garai and Scheinfeld, 1968:205). Favreau objects to the inferential leaps that Garai and Scheinfeld make in order to justify the existing social structure. She also wonders why the professions of dentistry and surgery, which might also benefit from women's manual dexterity, are omitted.

Understandably enough, feminists have reacted strongly against research that claimed to demonstrate women's inferiority and justify their low status (Bernard, 1976:13-14). This feminist reaction has involved several strategies. One strategy has been the denial of sex differences—the argument that no relevant differences exist between men and women to justify differences in social roles and experiences. A second type of feminist response accepts sex differences. After all, they ask, why should women want to be just like men? Sometimes a note of pride in the distinctiveness of feminine traits and achievements creeps in. Whatever the strategy, the idea that such sex differences are intrinsic determinants of social roles is challenged. Frequently the argument is mounted by showing that sex differences vary from culture to culture, as well as from one historical period to another. A third strategy is often linked with the second, namely, an insistence that any role-relevant sex differences that do exist are the result of socialization, not biology. After all, biology is immutable but child-rearing practices can be altered. Many female psychologists feel that the energy devoted to sex-difference research could be better expended on other issues of interest to women (Parlee, 1978). In other words, they are objecting to the traditionalism of a subdiscipline that examines women only *in relation to* men.

Although all of the above defensive arguments help women to feel better about themselves, their *scientific* utility is of course measured by the adequacy of the empirical evidence. Replacing male biases with female biases does not benefit the disciplines of psychology or sociology. Fortunately, *The Psychology of Sex Differences* (1974), a book written by feminists Maccoby and Jacklin, has had a salutary influence within the field. Their thorough evaluation of the sex-difference literature has encouraged a balanced use of research data and a recognition of the ease with which value judgments and politics can intrude.

The remainder of this chapter will consider the following questions: What is the content of the images of males and females? To what degree is the self-imagery of men and women affected by stereotypes? And finally, according to the research evidence, what actual differences exist between men and women?

Subsequent chapters will inquire into the problem of how sex differences come about. Of vital concern here is the relationship between sex and gender. To put it another way, do innate sex differences account for the observed social differences between females and males? The inequality and powerlessness of women at the societal level is of particular interest.

IMAGES OF FEMALES AND MALES

Analyzing the imagery of men and women that is subscribed to in our society offers some insight into male-female similarities and differences. Here we will examine the sex comparisons made by ordinary people rather than those made by social scientists.

Myths of Women

Beliefs about the essential nature of women abound in the religion and literature of every culture (Williams, 1978). This universal mythology[1] appears to serve several functions. The creation of such images of women provides men with the conviction that they understand this otherwise mysterious phenomenon. "Such belief systems and preconceptions are ways of knowing that predate scientific explanations and continue, even, to exist alongside them" (Williams, 1978:222). In addition to their explanatory power, myths provide men with the hope that they can *control* the somewhat frightening phenomena. The procreative and sexual powers of women have both awed and threatened men.

The following images of women appear to be universal (Williams, 1978). They are neither exhaustive nor mutually exclusive.

1. *Woman as mother nature.* Because woman gives birth, she is close to the earth. Like nature, she is powerful and capricious. According to the Canadian author, Margaret Atwood (1972:200), the "nature-as-woman" metaphor permeates Canadian literature, and the type of woman portrayed is an "old, cold, forbidding and possibly vicious one." Because of the impact of Canada's landscape upon our history and mentality, most of the strong and vividly portrayed female characters in Canadian literature are old women.[2]
2. *Woman as enchantress-seductress.* Motivated by evil intent, she uses her beauty and deadly magic to effect man's downfall.
3. *Woman as saint.* As the embodiment of all virtues, the conservator of goodness in society, woman is man's superior.
4. *Woman as inferior, insignificant nonperson.* At best, she is a necessary evil. She is useful as a sex object and childbearer, but is of no importance in the essential affairs of men.[3]
5. *Woman as mystery.* Because she is a qualitatively different order of being, the laws and rules by which behavior are normally understood do not explain her.

If, as the literature suggests, males have formulated a mythology of women to provide some semblance of prediction and control, have women produced a parallel male mythology? Surely it is reasonable to expect that women, the less powerful sex, experience a need at least equal to men's to reduce the opposite sex symbolically to manageable proportions.

Since literature is one of the main sources of sex imagery, Atwood's (1972) analysis of themes in Canadian literature would seem to be a likely source of information on male imagery. She discusses the mythical ancestral figures of explorers, settlers and immigrants, failed heroes and martyrs, paralyzed artists, moralistic grandfathers. Yet nowhere is there found a depiction of maleness per se, much less a portrayal of masculinity as a projection of female desires, fears or weaknesses.

Simone de Beauvoir (1952:132-33) explains why women have created no complementary mythology of males in religion or literature.

Women do not set themselves up as subject and hence have erected no virile myth in which their projects are reflected; they have no religion or poetry of their own: they still dream through the dreams of men. Gods made by males are the gods they worship. . . . Representation of the world, like the world itself, is the work of men; they describe it from their own points of view, which they confuse with absolute truth.

Perhaps the myth of woman will some day be extinguished; the more women assert themselves as human beings, the more the marvelous quality of the other will die out in them.

SEX STEREOTYPES

The topic of sex stereotypes is one of the most intensively researched in the area of gender relations. We will begin our discussion with a definition of the frequently misunderstood concept, *stereotype.* "*A stereotype refers to those folk beliefs about the attributes characterizing a social category on which there is substantial agreement*" (Mackie, 1973a).

The term refers to nonscientists' consensual beliefs about the traits that appropriately describe categories of people, such as old people, lower-class people and university students. Stereotypes are *not* false by definition. Beyond the truism that all generalizations fail to reflect the minutiae of "reality," the degree of accuracy is an empirical question. Stereotypes are not "good" or "bad" or "desirable" or "undesirable." They simply are. The categorization involved appears to be a necessary aspect of human cognition. Our limited sensory apparatus cannot encode afresh each time, in detail, the multiplicity of stimuli rushing at us. Therefore, we place relevant stimuli into those categories designated as important from previous personal-cultural experience, and ignore the rest.

A brief description of a very simple study carried out by the author (Mackie, 1971) will show exactly what is meant by the abstract concept *sex stereotype.* (In this case, the stereotype measured was a stereotype of women.) In addition, the study demonstrates the willingness of people to stereotype others. The sample of three hundred Edmonton (Alberta) adults was asked to supply adjectives that described "women in general." Only 2% of the sample was unable to comply with these instructions. The technique used here is called *open-ended* because the respondents volunteered adjectives that they felt were appropriate. (In contrast, the *adjectival checklist* technique provides respondents with descriptions preselected by the researcher. The respondents then choose the adjectives from these lists.) For the purpose of this study, *consensus* was operationally defined as mention of a trait by 10% or more of the sample.

The results shown in Table 2.1 illustrate what many analysts see to be the major axis of Western societies' definitions of masculinity and femininity. Theorists such as Bakan (1966) have defined the essence of femininity in a *communal* orientation, or a concern for the relations between self and others (and contrasted it with the masculine *agentic* or in-

TABLE 2.1
Open-Ended Description of "Women in General"
N = 300

Trait	%N
Concerned with family responsibilities	37.7
Warm, nurturant	29.0
Extroverted/talkative	27.9
Emotional	25.6
Fashion conscious	24.2
Ambitious	17.2
Attractive/sexy	16.2
Dominating	13.5
Cold/manipulative	13.1
Competent at work	11.8
Submissive	9.8

SOURCE: Mackie (1971)

strumental orientation). In other words, the traditional gender role norms expect men to be *instrumental* specialists who seek occupational goals, and women to be *expressive* specialists who seek familial goals. Men are expected to work outside the home, marry and support their families, while women are expected to marry, carry the major responsibility for child rearing, and rely on men for financial support and social status. For women, attracting a suitable mate takes priority over serious occupational commitment. These gender-distinctive activities are accompanied by appropriate attitudes and skills, namely, nurturance and dependence in females and aggressiveness and competitiveness in males.

As Table 2.1 shows, women are seen to be socioemotional specialists and their identity is perceived to revolve about their relationship with men. They are either guardians of an established family or slaves of the fashion world in order to attract men. The results so far agree with American studies to be discussed below. However, the Canadian sample also ascribed some so-called masculine traits to women, e.g., ambitious, dominating. Although we should not make too much of one study, it would be worthwhile to replicate it for both sexes to see if differences do in fact exist between Canadian and American sex stereotypes.

The most thorough investigation of sex stereotypes was an American study carried out by Broverman et al. (1972). These researchers showed that the images of women and men are traditional in content and shared by groups who differ in sex, age, religion, marital status and education. Moreover, the similarity of their findings with more recent results (Ward and Balswick, 1978) suggests that despite the resurgence of the women's movement, sex stereotypes are remarkably stable over time.

Broverman et al. asked their American respondents to indicate the extent to which 122 phrases on an adjectival checklist characterized an adult man or an adult woman. The checklist gave bipolar traits such as "not at all aggressive–very aggressive." If 75% or more of the sample agreed that "very aggressive" was more descriptive of an average man than an average woman, that item was defined as stereotypic. Their findings are given in Table 2.2.

TABLE 2.2
Sex-Role Stereotypes

| *Competency Cluster: Masculine Pole is More Desirable* | |
Masculine	Feminine
Very aggressive	Not at all aggressive
Very independent	Not at all independent
Not at all emotional	Very emotional
Almost always hides emotions	Does not hide emotions at all
Very objective	Very subjective
Not at all easily influenced	Very easily influenced
Very dominant	Very submissive
*Likes math and science very much	Dislikes math and science very much
Not at all excitable in a minor crisis	Very excitable in a minor crisis
Very active	Very passive
Very competitive	Not at all competitive
*Very logical	Very illogical
*Very worldly	Very home-oriented
*Very skilled in business	Not at all skilled in business
*Very direct	Very sneaky
Knows the way of the world	Does not know the way of the world
*Feelings not easily hurt	Feelings easily hurt
*Very adventurous	Not at all adventurous
Can make decisions easily	Has difficulty making decisions
Never cries	Cries very easily
Almost always acts as a leader	Almost never acts as a leader
Very self-confident	Not at all self-confident
Not at all uncomfortable about being aggressive	Very uncomfortable about being aggressive
Very ambitious	Not at all ambitious
Easily able to separate feelings from ideas	Unable to separate feelings from ideas
Not at all dependent	Very dependent
Never conceited about appearance	Very conceited about appearance
Thinks men are always superior to women	Thinks women are always superior to men
Talks freely about sex with men	Does not talk freely about sex with men

SOURCE: Broverman et al. (1972)

* Trait mentioned by appropriate sex in Twenty Statement Test self-imagery (Mackie,

1980b). One-tailed, chi square, <.05 level (a statistically significant association exists between the attitudinal item and the demographic variable).

Warmth-Expressiveness Cluster: Feminine Pole is More Desirable	
Feminine	Masculine
Doesn't use harsh language at all	Uses very harsh language
Very talkative	Not at all talkative
Very tactful	Very blunt
Very gentle	Very rough
Very aware of feelings of others	Not at all aware of feelings of others
Very religious	Not at all religious
Very interested in own appearance	Not at all interested in own appearance
Very neat in habits	Very sloppy in habits
Very quiet	Very loud
Very strong need for security	Very little need for security
*Enjoys art and literature	Does not enjoy art and literature at all
Easily expresses tender feelings	Does not express tender feelings at all easily

Three points are worth noting from the Broverman et al. study.

1. These researchers found that sex-role stereotypes fall into a feminine warmth-expressiveness cluster and a masculine competency cluster. (This result parallels the communal-agentic distinction mentioned above.) The competency cluster includes traits such as being independent, active, competitive and ambitious. A relative absence of these traits characterizes women. That is, relative to men, women are seen to be dependent, passive, noncompetitive, etc. The warmth-expressiveness cluster, on the other hand, consists of attributes such as gentle, quiet and sensitive to the feelings of others. Relative to women, men are perceived as lacking these traits.

2. In addition, Broverman et al. found that masculine traits were valued more highly than feminine traits. Respondents of both sexes found masculinity to be more socially desirable than femininity.

3. In a related study, Broverman and colleagues (1970) administered a questionnaire to seventy-nine mental-health clinicians (clinical psychologists, psychiatrists, psychiatric social workers) of both sexes. The questionnaire asked these people to define a healthy person, a healthy man, and a

healthy woman. Male and female clinicians alike responded in terms of sex stereotypes. A mentally healthy man was seen as aggressive, independent, competitive, etc. A mentally healthy woman was seen as submissive, unaggressive, dependent, suggestible and so on. Moreover, a mentally healthy adult of unspecified sex was described in the same terms as a healthy man. These findings have unsettling implications for female identity, mental health and counselling. For one thing, *what men are* appears to set the standards of mental health, and furthermore, a healthy woman is an unhealthy adult.

Impact of Sex Stereotypes upon Self-Imagery

Although more research is needed in order to explore possible Canadian-American differences, a substantial literature does document the sheer *existence* of sex stereotypes. (In addition to the studies already cited, see Ashmore and Del Boca, 1979; Clifton, McGrath and Wick, 1976; Fernberger, 1948; Lunneborg, 1970; McKee and Sherriffs, 1959; Neufeld, Langmeyer and Seeman, 1974; Sherriffs and Jarrett, 1953; Sherriffs and McKee, 1957.) Sex stereotyping in both Canadian and American mass media (a topic to be discussed in Chapter Six) has been particularly well studied. The more interesting problem now concerns the *consequences* that stem from these societal expectations for "appropriate" masculine and feminine attitudes, temperament and behavior. How much do sex stereotypes matter in people's everyday lives?

In very general terms, sex stereotypes can be assumed to affect individuals in two ways. First, other people who subscribe to the stereotype may use it to guide their perception and treatment of an individual. For example, parents who believe that boys are stoical and aggressive may chastise their son for tears and encourage fistfights. (Gender socialization is discussed in Chapter Four.) Second, an individual's self-image and behavior may reflect stereotype content. The female employee, believing that women are too emotional to assume positions of authority, may rule herself out of the competition. A study by the author (Mackie, 1980b) focused on one aspect of the latter type, namely, the relationship between sex stereotypes and self-imagery. To quote Broverman et al. (1972:61), "the sex-role definitions are implicitly and uncritically accepted to the extent that they are incorporated into the self-concepts of both men and women."

This research, which was part of a larger study of family and work,[4] involved a systematic, random sample of 797 adult Calgarians. Their self-imagery was measured by means of the Twenty Statements Test (TST) (Kuhn and McPartland, 1954), which asks respondents to write twenty different answers to the question, "Who am I?" It was predicted that men would describe themselves significantly more frequently than women in terms of the Broverman et al. (1972) masculine competency cluster traits, and that women would describe themselves significantly more frequently than men in terms of the Broverman et al. feminine warmth-expressiveness cluster traits. Asterisks have been placed on Table 2.2 to indicate the characteristics for which this prediction proved accurate.

The impact of the masculine stereotype upon male self-imagery was considerably less than predicted.[5] Of the thirty competency cluster traits shown on Table 2.2, four received no mention at all ("not uncomfortable about being aggressive," "thinks men are superior to women," "never cries," "talks freely about sex with men"). Only three ("independent," "ambitious," "direct") were mentioned by 10% or more of the male respondents. When male-female frequencies were compared, significant differences emerged for eight traits (see Table 2.2). More men than women viewed themselves as "acting as leaders," "adventurous," "worldly," "skilled in business," "logical," "liking mathematics and science," "not having their feelings easily hurt" and "direct." In general, males perceive themselves as actors in the public sphere beyond the home. Although their self-observation as logical thinkers fits this pattern, it is interesting that significantly more women described themselves as intelligent (a trait excluded from the Broverman et al. stereotype).

The relationship between female self-imagery and the warmth-expressiveness traits was also weaker than expected. Two traits ("doesn't use harsh language," "easily expresses tender feelings") received no mention at all. Only three ("religious," "aware of others' feelings," "enjoys art and literature") exceeded the 10% level. Only one male-female difference was statistically significant ("enjoys art and literature"). Because common sense suggests that interests do distinguish between the sexes, the TST self-imagery was analyzed for additional interests beyond the scope of the Broverman et al. traits. Males described themselves as more interested than females in mechanics, automobiles and sports. On the other hand, animals played a more important role in the self-imagery of females.

Femininity has been equated with a communal orientation (a concern for the relationship between self and others). However, male and female sample members did not differ in their self-descriptions of the manner in which they relate to people, such as being aware of others' feelings, tactful or gentle. Moreover, analysis of self-imagery beyond the Broverman et al. stereotypes showed no differences in liking people, helping others, giving advice or being unselfish, though females do view themselves more often as "listeners." Nevertheless, some support for female communal orientation is provided by the fact that relationships *per se* comprised a significantly greater proportion of female, than male, self-imagery. That is, women described themselves in terms of relationships such as wife, daughter, friend or neighbor more often than did men.

To summarize, this study addressed the question, "To what extent do thoughts about the self reflect traditional sex stereotypes?" Although the results did provide limited support for the impact on self-imagery of the broad sex distinctions implied by the label "agentic-communal," the relationship was weaker than predicted. If we assume that the self-concept mediates between society's sex-role norms and the individual's sex-typed behavior, the implication of these conclusions is that sex stereotypes, as such, channel and constrict the human potentiality of both sexes much less than was expected. However, caution must be exercised. Replicating studies are needed, particularly studies that use other ways of measuring self-imagery, before we can develop a high level of confidence in this study's conclusion that the self-concept is only minimally affected by sex stereotypes. Whenever sociologists use interviews or questionnaires as their research technique, what they learn about "reality" is partially a function of the questions chosen to measure it.

The foregoing section has considered people's beliefs about the nature of women and men. As we have seen, this imagery current in our culture considers the sexes to be quite different and views male-associated traits as the preferable ones. Although the evidence suggests that sex stereotypes do not greatly constrain *adult* self-perception, they do embody society's expectations for appropriate sex-typed behavior. For this reason, stereotypes are important to students of gender relations.

Has the challenge to traditional definitions of femininity and masculinity, associated with the women's and men's liberation movements, resulted in discernible changes in the stereotypes? Some provocative results have been reported. For example, when O'Leary and Depner (1975) asked male college students to describe their ideal woman, they portrayed a superwoman. Their ideal was more competent, more successful, more adventurous than women's ideal *man*. In contrast, however, other investigators report that stereotypes have not drastically altered. Therefore, observers (Deaux, 1976:21) suspect that the superwoman image results more from the research subjects' attempts to please the investigator, to avoid being labelled "chauvinist pigs," than from any real change in their convictions.

We turn now from the question, "What do people think men and women are like?" to the question, "What differences actually distinguish females and males?" To reiterate, such differences, whether real or alleged, do matter because they provide the foundation for the sociocultural conception of gender.

ACTUAL FEMALE/MALE DIFFERENCES

This section will consider sex differences under three categories: physiological differences, sex differences in abilities and sex differences in personality. Here, the differences will be simply listed. The possible origins of such differences will be explored in later chapters. Because of space limitations and the fact that the author is neither a biologist nor a differential psychologist, only the briefest summary of the enormously complicated research literature is offered here.

Physiological Differences

The biological concept of sex (female or male) really has four highly inter-related aspects (Frieze et al., 1978:83-84):

1. *Genetic sex* (XX or XY chromosomes). Normal human beings have twenty-three pairs of *chromosomes*. One of these pairs determines the genetic sex of the individual. In males, this pair is made up of an X and a Y chromosome, while in females it is composed of two X chromosomes. A person's sex is determined at the moment of conception, when the egg, carrying an X chromosome, is united with the sperm, which carries *either* an X or a Y chromosome. The fertilized eggs with two X chromosomes are females; those with an X and a Y chromosome are males. Normally, XX embryos develop ovaries containing potential eggs, a female reproductive tract and external genitals consisting of a clitoris and two pairs of skin folds. Embryos with the XY genetic constitution will eventually acquire testes with potential sperm, a male reproductive tract and glands, and external genitals composed of a penis and scrotal sac. Four to five months are required for these sex differences to develop. Until the seventh week after conception, the only distinguishing characteristic is genetic, that is, chromosomal (Barfield, 1976:62-63).

2. *Hormonal sex* (relative levels of estrogen and testosterone). Hormones are chemical substances that the endocrine glands secrete into the bloodstream. The chief male sex hormone is *testosterone*, which is one of a group of hormones called *androgens*. Females also secrete testosterone in very small amounts (Chafetz, 1974:24). Until about the seventh week after conception, the fetus retains the potential to develop into either a male or a female. After this point, embryos with an XY genetic constitution develop testes, and the testes begin to secrete androgens. The androgens cause the male genital development to proceed. The XX embryo does not produce androgens *or* the female sex hormones. In this absence of hormonal stimulation, female genital development takes place (Barfield, 1976:63). *Estrogen* and *pro-*

gesterone (which are also present in males in very small amounts) are the primary female sex hormones. As children of both sexes approach puberty, the sex hormone production increases significantly and influences the development of sex glands and organs, and the elaboration of secondary sex characteristics. The release of female hormones is related to the menstrual cycle.

3. *Gonadal sex* (ovaries or testes). An embryo's genetic sex determines whether its *gonadal cells* become ovaries or testes. The exact means by which this occurs is not yet fully understood. If the embryo carries an X and a Y chromosome, testes are formed approximately seven weeks after conception. These testes then begin to produce male hormones. On the other hand, if the embryo carries two X chromosomes, the gonadal tissue remains undifferentiated until approximately twelve weeks after conception. Two ovaries form from this tissue somewhat later during the gestation period (Frieze et al., 1978:84).

4. *Genital sex* (penis or clitoris/vagina). As noted above, secretion of the male sex hormones by the embryonic testes results in development of the penis and scrotum. In the XX embryo, it is the absence of hormonal stimulation that produces female development.

As we have seen, the four components of femaleness and maleness are closely interrelated. The genetic sex normally determines the hormonal sex, which in turn determines the gonadal and genital sex. That is, an XY embryo develops into a fetus with testes, which secrete male hormones, which in turn trigger the development of male genitals. An XX embryo, on the other hand, develops without hormone production into a fetus having female genitals. However, inconsistencies occasionally occur, which provide researchers with the opportunity to explore the relative contributions of the various physiological factors to sex and gender. For example, a genetic female (XX chromosomes) may, as a result of hormone irregularities, be born with masculine-appearing genitals (Frieze et al., 1978:83).

Obviously, men and women differ in their reproductive functions. "Only women menstruate, gestate, and lactate. Only men produce semen" (Armstrong and Armstrong, 1978:97). In addition, a number of secondary sex characteristics are apparent, which become more pronounced with puberty (Barfield, 1976:65-70). On the average, males are taller and heavier, and a greater percentage of their total body weight is made up of muscle while a smaller proportion is made up of fat. Females have lighter skeletons, different shoulder and pelvis proportions, different pelvic bone shapes and different socket shapes at the hip and shoulder. These differences contribute to such feminine characteristics as less strength (particularly in the upper body), less endurance in heavy labor, more difficulty in overarm throwing and better ability to float.

Males are more susceptible than females to physical disorders, diseases and death. During the first year of life, one-third more males die. The male death rate continues to be higher in every age group. As Ashley Montagu informed us in *The Natural Superiority of Women* (1952), the fact that males have only one of the important X chromosomes makes them more vulnerable to some sixty genetically transmitted disorders, such as hemophilia and color blindness. Males are more prone to speech defects, reading disabilities, deafness and mental defectiveness (Barfield, 1976:68).

Both biological predisposition and social factors seem to be responsible for the higher male incidence of heart disease, strokes, stomach ulcers and so on, and for the variations in the physical symptoms of psychological stress. Because of their social roles, males, in the past at least, have had more physically active and stressful occupations. However, it does appear that males are biologically the more vulnerable sex. More males than females die very young, long before male-female activities become differentiated. Therefore, the reasons for death-rate differences seems to be biological. Moreover, an interesting study (Madigan, 1957), quoted in Barfield (1976:69), of men and women living in religious cloisters and having very similar diets, housing, work and living conditions showed that females still survived better at every age, although both sexes had above-average life expectancies. Though the females were just as prone to infectious diseases, they fared better with the degenerative diseases.

All this having been said, it is necessary to restore some sort of balance to this comparison of male-female physiology. Although the discussion so far has focused on sex differences, males and females also share many physiological characteristics. In the words of Armstrong and Armstrong (1978:97-98):

> The sexes differ in terms of chromosomes, hormone production, and reproductive functions. . . . In addition, because men on the average tend to have more muscle mass than women, they are often physically stronger than women, although there are many individual exceptions. These differences between the sexes cannot be ignored. However, the investigations of the basic physiological differences between the sexes indicate that no simple duality exists, that the opposite sexes are not so opposite.

For social scientists, the more interesting (and controversial) questions concern the possible links between physiological sex differences on the one hand, and psychological characteristics and sociocultural gender arrangements on the other. Because of the inevitability of biological causation, scholars sympathetic to women's situation would prefer that differences between the sexes result from learning, not biology. Marcel Kinsbourne, a neurologist at the Hospital for Sick Children in Toronto (quoted in Goleman, 1978:48), put it this way: "The real danger in this line of research is that the findings could be misinterpreted and used as a scientific justification for sexism, just as ambiguous genetic findings were often cited to provide a scientific basis for racism."

Sex Differences in Intellectual Ability

Whenever the situation of women is debated in mixed-sex groups, the discussion invariably turns to the relative absence of eminent women in history, art, literature and science. On the international scene, Joan of Arc, Marie Curie, the Brontë sisters, Margaret Thatcher and Margaret Mead exhaust most people's mental lists of "great women." Coming up with Canadian names is an even more challenging parlor game. Laura Secord? Nellie McClung? Margaret Atwood? Barbara Frum? Occasionally, someone has the temerity to put forth the sexual analogy: soft body, soft mind (Ellmann, 1968:74). Sex stereotypes, too, suggest that women lack the intellectual ability to excel. Is this so? What does research have to say on this matter?

In this section, the following characteristics are discussed: IQ, verbal ability, mathematical ability, spatial skills and cognitive style, and creativity. Once again a caveat must be entered: the differences to be considered are average, not absolute, differences. When we say that in terms of ability *X*, males are better than females, we do *not* mean that all males are superior to all females. The various abilities overlap and are matters of degree.

1. *IQ.* According to Maccoby and Jacklin's (1974:65) systematic review of the literature, through most of the age ranges studied, males and females do not differ in tests of general intellectual abilities. One reason for their conclusion is that most IQ tests are designed to minimize sex differences. That is, specific tasks and abilities at which females succeed are balanced by tasks and abilities at which males succeed. The aptitudes that are reviewed below are components of intelligence.

2. *Verbal Ability.* For psychologists, verbal ability includes the simple measures of articulation, spelling, punctuation, sentence complexity, vocabulary size and fluency, and more sophisticated measures of reading comprehension, creative

writing and use of language in logical reasoning (Tavris and Offir, 1977:35). Recent studies have cast doubt on earlier research that concluded that in the first few years of life, girls talk earlier and more than boys. Although boys are more likely than girls to stutter and to have reading difficulties, preadolescent linguistic competence is otherwise equivalent. However, from the age of ten or eleven through high school, female superiority increases, with girls doing better in both "lower" and "higher" measures of verbal performance.

3. *Mathematical Ability*. Girls and boys are similar in their early acquisition of quantitative concepts and mastery of arithmetic. However, beginning at puberty, boys' mathematical skills increase faster than girls'. According to Maccoby and Jacklin's (1974:352) review of the literature, the males' greater rate of improvement does not appear to be entirely a function of the number of mathematics courses taken. It is in the areas of reasoning and problem solving that males excel.

4. *Spatial Skills*. The predominance of men over women in science and mathematics is often attributed to male superiority in tasks involving spatial skills. Such skills refer to the ability to visually manipulate, locate or make judgments about the spatial relationships of items located in two- or three-dimensional space. Tests of spatial skills include, for example, embedded figures (locating smaller figures in a larger design), adjusting a bar or rod to a horizontal or vertical position against a tilted background, and body orientation tests. Males do indeed consistently excel in visual-spatial skills. Once again there is a development trend, with young children showing no difference, and a male advantage emerging at the beginning of adolescence and continuing into adulthood (Freize et al., 1978:62-63).

5. *Creativity*. Interest in possible sex differences in the ability to produce unique ideas arises in part from the observation that men are more heavily represented than women among creative artists, writers and scientists. Psychologists test creativity by measures such as the Alternative Uses Test, which asks people to list as many uses as they can for common objects, such as a brick. An obvious answer to this is, "You use a brick to build a house." Creative people list unique and almost endless solutions. (One creative soul, quoted by Tavris and Offir [1977:37], suggested using a brick as a "bug-hider." "You leave it on the ground for a

few days, then pick it up and see all the bugs that have been hiding.") Another test involves showing subjects a picture and requesting them to list all the questions they would need to have answered in order to understand the events in the picture. Such creativity tests tend to have two components, a verbal fluency component and a component involving productivity of unusual ideas. Therefore, they tend to reflect the documented female superiority in verbal skills. When the "ideational variety" component is analyzed, research shows that females are at least as capable as males of producing a variety of unusual ideas (Maccoby and Jacklin, 1974:111-14).

In summary, research shows no sex differences in general intelligence or in creativity. However, females excel in verbal abilities and males excel in mathematical and spatial skills. We must point out that for both sexes, intellect is only *one* factor contributing to eminence. Drive and opportunity are also required. Subsequent chapters will consider the sources and implications of sex differences in intellectual functioning.

Personality Traits

Charting the similarities and differences between the sexes becomes increasingly complicated as we move from physiological characteristics to intellectual capacities and, finally, to personality traits. The conceptualization and measurement of the aspects of personality to be considered here (emotionality, nurturance, sociability, dependence, aggression) present researchers with a series of problems. Although we cannot pursue them here, because of space limitations, the interested reader might consult Maccoby and Jacklin (1974). (Although more recent journal articles consider this trait or that, Maccoby and Jacklin (1974) is still the best source for an integrated overview.)

1. *Emotionality*. Stereotypes portray women as the emotional sex. They are viewed as sensitive, moody, anxious and prone to tears and hurt feelings. (Note, however, that the type of emotionality involved here is not the acting-out, aggressive type that is associated with males.) Attempts to test the accuracy of this particular stereotype trait have focused on only one aspect of emotionality, namely, anxiety and fearfulness. The evidence is confusing. Observational studies of sex differences in young children show no consistent results. However, paper-and-pencil measures of anxiety and fearfulness seem to support the expectation that females are more emotional than males. But social desir-

ability (the tendency to respond in culturally desirable ways) enters the picture; the results may mean that females are simply more willing to report fears and anxieties. Most authorities conclude that whether or not females are more emotional than males remains to be determined (Frieze et al., 1978:57-58).

2. *Nurturance*. The stereotypical expectation that women will be warm and helpful toward children, animals and men is illustrated by a statement made by the famous child expert, Bruno Bettelheim (quoted in Tavris and Offir, 1977:51): "We must start with the realization that, as much as women want to be good scientists or engineers, they want first and foremost to be womanly companions of men and to be mothers." From their review of the evidence, Maccoby and Jacklin (1974:354) conclude that it is impossible to say whether women are more disposed to behave maternally than men are to behave paternally. For example, the fact that girls more frequently play with dolls has been taken as spontaneous nurturance. However, dolls are presented to girls, not boys, and much doll play is not nurturant. Dolls are hugged and tucked into bed but they are also "scolded, spanked, subjected to surgical operations, and . . . even scalped" (Maccoby and Jacklin, 1974:220).

Two studies described by Maccoby and Jacklin (1974:221) suggest that males are not given sufficient credit for their potential nurturance. One aspect of a study by Bem (1975) provided the opportunity to observe college students' reactions toward a kitten. One part of the study instructed them to play with the kitten. During another part, kitten play was one of several activities from which subjects could choose. Bem reported no significant difference between male and female students in interest in the kitten, amount of contact with it or enjoyment of playing with it. In another study, Parke and O'Leary (1974) measured amounts of nurturant interaction (looking, touching, rocking, holding, smiling) displayed by fathers and mothers of newborn infants. In comparison with mothers, both middle-class and working-class fathers engaged in as much or more nurturant behavior. In short, neither sex appears to be inherently more nurturant. Oddly enough, research on the related trait of sociability has led to similar conclusions (Tavris and Offir, 1977:46).

3. *Dependency*. The results of research on sex differences in dependency behavior (clinging to others and help-seeking)

are also equivocal (Frieze et al., 1978:55). For example, findings with young children have been very inconsistent. Of forty-eight observational studies of children's touching and proximity to parents, and of resistance to separation from a parent, eight found girls more dependent, seven found boys more dependent and the rest found no sex differences. Although some studies done in the past have suggested that women may become more dependent as they grow older, current research fails to show consistent sex differences.

4. *Aggression*. A variety of different types of studies of aggression consistently show the stereotype to be true: males are more aggressive than females. This sex difference emerges as early as social play begins (at two years of age) and is found cross-culturally. Males engage in more physical aggression, more verbal aggression and more aggressive fantasies. Although the aggressiveness of both sexes declines with age, males remain more aggressive at least throughout the university years (Maccoby and Jacklin, 1974:352).

CONCLUSIONS

There has been a strong tendency in both folk and scientific thought to emphasize female-male differences and to overlook the similarities between the sexes. Nevertheless, Maccoby and Jacklin's (1974) evaluation of the relevant psychological research resulted in their conclusion that only four sex differences are well established: girls have greater verbal ability than boys; boys excel in visual-spatial ability; boys excel in mathematical ability; males are more aggressive. Although these four characteristics are included in the content of traditional sex-role stereotypes, the latter also contain a large number of apparently fictitious female-male psychological differences. In addition, stereotypes refer to social as well as psychological differences.

The recent furor over mathematical ability demonstrates that the *source* of sex differences remains a sensitive issue. From their study of the performance of junior high school students on the Scholastic Aptitude Test, Benbow and Stanley (1980) concluded that males have inherently superior mathematical ability. The annual meeting of the American Mathematical Society was held a month after the study appeared in the prestigious journal, *Science*. At a news conference, a half dozen mathematicians of both sexes called the finding "ridiculous" and "disturbing" and said that it would be "virtually impossible to undo the damage" of the publicity surrounding the report. Professor Stanley observed, "People are so eager not to believe that there is a difference in mathematical reasoning ability between boys and girls that all kinds of people are taking potshots" (*Time*, 22 March 1982). In the next chapter, we turn to a general consideration of the etiology of female-male distinctions.

3 Biological Explanations of Sex Differences

ALTHOUGH the distinctions between females and males have been exaggerated in both scientific and folk thought, and feminist social scientists have recently sought to correct such wrongheaded notions, sex differences cannot simply be dismissed as traditional nonsense. Not even the most impassioned supporter of women's rights would wish to argue that men and women are identical creatures. For one thing, research evidence contradicts such an absurd stance. Males and females differ in terms of chromosomes, hormones, primary and secondary sex characteristics, and reproductive functions. Their anatomical differences are enhanced by fashions in clothing and hairstyles. As we saw in Chapter Two, there are some sex differences in personality traits and intellectual abilities. Last, and probably most important (at least to sociologists), is the fact that certain assigned roles (e.g. soldier, nurse) embody disparate and distinctly "masculine" versus "feminine" norms. Other social roles, which are similar in title and formal outline for either sex, are often played with "masculine" or "feminine" style, depending on the sex of the occupant (e.g., professor, store clerk).

A second reason for which feminists are inclined to proclaim, rather than to deny, sex differences springs from a sentiment of pride amalgamated with hardheaded, social-movement pragmatism (Mackie, 1973a). Remember that this most recent women's liberation movement emerged as an offshoot of the ethnic rights movements in the late 1960s and early 1970s. Black Americans, for instance, were telling the world that their characteristics were not optical illusions, that "black is beautiful" and that they had "soul." The Red Power movement exhorted Indians to regard their traditional culture with pride, not shame. Moreover, the desire to preserve and enhance "feminine identity" was accompanied by the desire to bring about social change. In many cases, a first step in seeking "justice" was to encourage outsiders to recognize women's distinctive "character" and "needs."

From the feminist perspective, the difficulties associated with the topic of sex differences emerge from two related sources: confusion of *difference* with *inequality*, and insistence on genetic rather than environmental causation. The first objection is straightforward. As we have repeatedly remarked, males enjoy more power and prestige than females. The specific issue here is the cultural devaluation of feminine traits and the glorification of masculine traits. According to Vaughter (1976:128), "the theme that the masculinity of men is more highly valued than the femininity of women is one of the most consistent themes to be found in current research data." The second objection is more complicated. Up to this point, we have concentrated on enumerating sex differences rather than explaining them. The key questions (and the subject matter of this chapter) are as follows: To what extent does gender have a biological basis? What are the relative contributions of genetic factors and of learning to female-male differences? Feminists tend to prefer explanations that emphasize socialization and differential learning, not biology.

Why should women's rights advocates (and male liberationists too, for that matter) be biased against explanations of sex differences that are rooted in physiology, and welcome socialization explanations? (The biologically based reproductive functions would, of course, be acknowledged.) The major reason is that assumptions and "theories" about people's biologically innate nature have been used by conservative thinkers to rationalize and to justify inequality (Petryszak, 1980:132). "Undesirable" Jewish characteristics provided the Nazis with a rationalization for their "final solution." The allegedly lower intellectual potential of blacks was used to justify school segregation in the southern United States. If "anatomy is destiny," then the traditional subordination of females to males is right and proper, and the contemplation of alternatives to the gender status quo makes absolutely no sense. On the other hand, behavior patterns that are learned are arbitrary and hence replaceable with other behavior patterns. However, those that are "wired in" at birth, "God-given or instinct-driven" (Tavris and Offir, 1977:94), remain immutable. To give a concrete example, it would be pointless for Canadian women to organize for the purpose of seeking more power in the political parties and then in the House of Commons, if male leadership and female powerlessness were biologically preordained. Under hypothetical circumstances such as these, femininity would constitute a genetic defect!

This debate concerning the constitutional versus the environmental determination of sex differences is, of course, one version of the antiquated nature-nurture controversy, which Bardwick (1972:1) aptly describes as a "phoenix of a cliché that continually experiences vigorous rebirth." Most scientists have abandoned the simplistic dichotomy of nature *versus* nurture. Traits are not *either* innate *or* learned, but rather, the product of an *interplay* between biological predispositions and social learning (van den Berghe, 1975:31). Sophisticated models of sex differences are *interactive*, in that they emphasize the interaction between *environmental* factors, such as cultural norms, education and parental attitudes, and *inheritable* factors, such as anatomical and neuroendocrinological differences, rather than stating the differences in terms of a learned-versus-innate dichotomy. For example, a researcher employing this interactive approach might examine whether the nervous system of the developing child, by virture of being male or female, facilitates the learning of certain sex-linked behaviors (Archer, 1976:241, 253).

Weitz (1977:6) expresses the notion of interplay in another way. She says, "Although many would minimize the contribution of biology in our complex technological society, it does not make sense to suppose that roles would have evolved that are entirely out of sorts with biological predisposition, nor that they could endure for so long without any sort of biological base whatsoever."

Today, then, there is agreement that human behavior, including sex differences, is influenced by both biological and social shaping. The debate now centers on the relative importance of each factor and the mechanisms of interaction between the two (Frieze et al., 1978:72).

As the mathematical ability controversy has illustrated, the topic remains one of the most precarious areas within the field of gender relations. Professor Weyant (1979:372-73) summarizes the problems involved:

> The sheer mass and variability of the literature makes it difficult to summarize briefly what the empirical findings on gender-related differences really are. . . . Given the variability of the data and the gender-related preconceptions which we all carry about with us, it is not surprising that there is also a good deal of variability in interpretation and causal attribution. The most obvious dimension of variability in interpretation would have "totally innate" at one end and "totally environmental" at the other. The extremes are rarely used, except by social propagandists. Most of the variability in interpretation is a matter of emphasis. . . . The social propagandists, of course, have usually decided what the facts and their causes are prior to examining the data. Indeed, in many cases *despite* the data [emphasis in original].

Increasingly, gender specialists are coming to realize that the biological as well as the socialization evidence needs to be carefully evaluated. While sympathy can be shown for the political concerns of activist feminists, it is important to distinguish between conclusions drawn from scientific research, and ideology promulgated by a movement. In the long run, being open-minded may serve activist interests, if we can assume that "real progress in sex-role change depends on an accurate understanding of the factors underlying current sex-role behaviors" (Frieze et al., 1978:72).

The present chapter examines the biological basis of gender. (The relative contribution of socialization will be discussed in Chapter Four.) A variety of approaches will be taken in this present chapter, partly because the question of the impact of biology upon sex differences has fascinated practitioners in many academic disciplines. In addition, the inherent difficulties involved in establishing the relative importance of biology and of learning have stimulated many solutions to the problem. We will inquire into this question from the following perspectives: animal research; the anthropological approach; sociobiology; the psychoanalytic argument; sex differences in infants; hormone and gene research; psychosexual abnormalities.

SEXUAL DIMORPHISM AMONG THE LOWER ANIMALS

Harlow's Remarkable Monkeys

Two decades ago, Harry Harlow and his associates carried out a series of experiments on the effects of isolation on rhesus monkeys. The most famous of these studies (Harlow, 1959) involved comparing the importance of the act of nursing with the importance of bodily contact, in engendering the infant monkey's attachment to its mother. Two surrogate "mother" monkeys were constructed. Both were wire cylinders surmounted by wooden heads. One was bare. The wire of the other was cushioned by a terry-cloth sheath. Each "mother" had the nipple of a feeding bottle protruding from its "breast." Eight newborn monkeys were separated from their natural mothers a few hours after birth and placed in individual cages. They were given access to both types of surrogate "mothers." Four monkeys were fed from the wire "mother" and four from the cloth "mother." All the infants developed a strong attachment to the cloth "mother" and little or none to the wire "mother," regardless of which one provided the milk.

Harlow's demonstration of the importance of bodily contact in developing the infant-mother affectional bond is known to every properly educated social science student. A few years later (1962, 1965) Harlow published his observations on sex differences in monkeys. Those observations have achieved notoriety (rather than fame) among gender relations specialists. We will consider Harlow's conclusions at some length in order to illustrate both the rationale for and the shortcomings of animal studies, as an approach to the question, "Are human sex differences biologically determined or socially learned?"

In subsequent articles, Professor Harlow described the behavior of the monkeys who had had surrogate "mothers," when they were placed in special playrooms. The play behavior was found to be sexually dimorphic. That is, males and females displayed rather different types of behavior. When the monkeys were brought together after two months of isolation, the males, in comparison with the females, were more aggressive, engaged in more rough-and-tumble play, and initiated more games.

Harlow (1965:242, quoted in Tavris and Offir, 1977:95, 97) concluded that sexual dimorphism in the rhesus monkey must be innate:

> It is illogical to interpret these sex differences as learned, culturally ordered patterns of behavior because there is no opportunity for acquiring a cultural heritage, let alone a sexually differentiated one, from an inanimate cloth surrogate. When I first saw these data, I was very excited, and told my wife that I believed that we had demonstrated biologically determined sex differences in infants' behavior. She was not impressed and said, "Child psychologists have known that for at least thirty years, and mothers have known it for centuries."

Finally, Harlow (1962) believed that conclusions drawn from his animal research applied to human beings as well.

> I am convinced that these data have almost total generality to man. Several months ago I was present at a school picnic attended by twenty-five second-graders and their parents. While the parents sat and the girls stood around or skipped about hand in hand, thirteen boys tackled and wrestled, chased and retreated. No little girl chased any little boy, but some little boys chased some little girls. . . .
>
> These secondary sex-behavior differences probably exist throughout the primate order and, moreover, they are innately determined biological differences regardless of any cultural overlap.
>
> However, let us not belittle the female, for they also serve who only stand and wait.

The Logic of Animal Research

The task confronting scientists is to develop explanations for human sex differences and the related matter of male-female inequality. There are several alternate strategies for tackling this problem. Each of the available methods offers some advantages and involves some unavoidable difficulties. Such is the case with animal studies. Harlow's work with the neglected little rhesus monkeys provides us with a concrete example of these advantages and disadvantages.

The point to be emphasized is that this type of animal research is motivated by interest in human beings, not in the so-called lower animals themselves. Indeed, the research can be described as "argument by analogy" (Tavris and Offir, 1977:94). Selected features of selected animals are taken as analogs for human features, and comparisons are drawn. Very often, the creature chosen is one of the primate species. To scientists like Harlow, it seems logical to look to monkeys and apes for answers, because in the primate heritage of our species, "we can find patterns which form similarities and continuities with human behavior, and we can find sharp contrasts which will highlight specializations peculiar to human beings" (Lancaster, 1976:23).

Animals are used to inquire into human sex differences for these reasons:

1. *Ethical/practical restrictions.* The type and extent of experimental research that can be done with human beings is obviously much more restricted than that done with animals (Armstrong and Armstrong, 1978:94). Harlow's study of the effects of social deprivation is a case in point. Although social scientists have long suspected that an infant's biological potential cannot be actualized without close emotional attachment to at least one adult, no one would dream of deliberately separating a human child from its parents at birth. However, ethical considerations did not rule out this strategy with monkeys. (Cases of human social deprivation that were *not* arranged by researchers have nevertheless been studied. See, for example, Davis [1940, 1947].) The rationale for Harlow's linkage between monkey isolation and monkey sexual dimorphism is given below.

2. *Alleged ease of distinguishing between socially learned and biologically determined behavior.* Another major reason for studying our "evolutionary cousins," the monkeys and apes, relates to the "argument by analogy" mentioned earlier. The assumption is that because these primates are like human beings, but do not undergo the intensive learning that we do, an examination of their behavior can tell us about our own biological inheritance (Tavris and Offir, 1977:94). As we have seen, Professor Harlow was convinced that any sexual dimorphism observed in his monkeys after two months of isolation was innate. Regardless of whether or not we agree with Harlow's conclusion (and we are not obliged to), research in recent years has increased scientists' respect for the influence of learning, group traditions and ecological patterns on primate behavior (Lancaster, 1976:24).

3. *Primate behavior foreshadows human evolutionary development.* Interest in sex differences among monkeys and apes is partially explained by the hints that their behavior provide about the evolutionary record of human

beings (Lancaster, 1976:45). Feminists of various academic backgrounds have been preoccupied with a quest for the origins of sex/gender patterns. They ask, "Were things always as they are today?" "When did 'it' start?" (Rosaldo, 1980:391). Primate behavior provides some scholars with useful conjectures concerning the roots of primordial gender. The anthropological and evolutionary, biosocial approaches will be considered in subsequent sections. Here we simply want to point out the connection with animal studies; evaluation of these approaches will be deferred until later.

4. *Avoidance of researcher bias.* As we noted in Chapter Two, social scientists investigating the subject of sex differences are far from immune to the emotionalism surrounding this topic. Until the accumulating evidence began to indicate otherwise, many believed that the use of animal rather than human subjects offered some protection against the intrusion of scientists' value preferences upon their conclusions (in addition to the safeguards generally inherent in the logic of scientific research).

It was hoped that animal studies would avoid the unwitting communication of the experimenter's expectations to the research subjects, and the consequent confounding reactions of the subjects (Armstrong and Armstrong, 1978:93). Unfortunately, the "Rosenthal effect" (as the above has come to be called) can influence studies with animal as well as human subjects (Middlebrook, 1974:32-33). In a study done by Rosenthal and Fode (1963), a group of university students, who were enrolled in an experimental psychology course, believed that they were to do an experiment on the rates at which rats of different abilities learned a maze. Half of the students were told that they were to work with "maze-bright" rats, which had been bred to learn mazes easily. Half were told that they had been assigned "maze-dull" rats, which would likely show little evidence of learning. Actually, the rats (which did not differ in ability) had been randomly assigned to the students. Nevertheless, the rats performed as the students expected. Rats identified as "maze-bright" performed significantly better than those identified as "maze-dull." Apparently, without knowing it, the student experimenters had treated their rats differently, and their expectations had produced the expected results.

Critics such as Rosenberg (1976:112) suspect that Harlow's research on monkeys was affected by observer expectations concerning the results. In our culture, where a premium is placed on aggressive behavior and on being male, observers may have *expected* more rough-and-tumble behavior from the male monkeys.

Other examples of researcher bias, more directly related to sexual dimorphism, clearly indicate that animal studies are not exempt from the intrusion of values. Lancaster (1976:24) points out that early field studies overemphasized the behavior of adult male primates. Although these males were large and behaved conspicuously, they constituted only 10% to 20% of the total membership of a primate society. However, the social relations of this small minority of adult males were seen as being the social organization of the entire group.

A researcher has considerable discretion in deciding which animal species provides a suitable analog for *homo sapiens*. The decision is important because the choice of species may affect the investigators' conclusions. According to Rosenberg's (1976:111) reading of the evidence, "every imaginable mode of relationship between the sexes exists in different species, from the female lion who does most of the hunting and killing . . . to the male marmoset who does most of the child care . . . to the gibbon, very close to humans in the evolutionary sense, among whom there is little if any personality differentiation between the sexes, and males and females are barely distinguishable in their behavior and physical appearance."

Weisstein (1971:79) went one step further when she accused social scientists of citing only those primates that "exhibit exactly the kind of behavior that the proponents of the biological basis of human female behavior wish were true for humans." This perhaps explains the popularity of rhesus monkeys (Harlow's choice), which exhibit some of the most aggressive behavior found in primates. (Harlow's use of rhesus monkeys has also been criticized (Rosenberg, 1976:113) on the grounds that this species is distant from humans in the evolutionary scheme.)

Some Conclusions about Animal Studies

What can be learned about human sex differences from primate studies? First of all, expert Jane Lancaster (1976:54) concludes that such studies provide "very little real evidence for major unlearned differences in the psychology of male and female primates." In the past, many generalizations were made about primate sex differences in aggressiveness, dominance, maternal behavior and so on. However, recent research has made it clear that while there may be major sex differences in certain behavior patterns in one primate species (e.g., male aggressiveness in rhesus monkeys), these differences may not be apparent in another primate species (e.g., the peaceful gibbon). Lancaster (1976:55) says that "the overriding conclusion of more than a decade of primate studies is that each primate species has its own adaptive pattern in terms of the relationship between the sexes.

A second lesson that deserves particular emphasis here concerns the matter of extrapolation from animals to human beings. By now it should be obvious that Harlow's enthusiasm was misguided; extreme caution must be exercised in making such generalizations. For one thing, interspecies comparisons are risky. For example, early exposure to the sex hormone testosterone appears to be related to aggressiveness in adult mice and rats. Prenatally androgenized female rhesus monkeys (that is, genetically female monkeys that received a shot of the male hormone, testosterone, before birth) exhibit a high incidence of aggressive play. However, the implications of such findings for masculine-feminine differentiation in humans are unclear. Generalizing from rodents to humans, or from monkeys to humans, is difficult. In addition, as the evolutionary ladder is ascended, the effect of hormones on behavior becomes less dramatic, and the role of learning more important (Frieze et al., 1978:85-86). Furthermore, as noted above, extrapolation of findings from one primate species to another is often illegitimate. A most extreme position is taken here by Weisstein (1971), who argues that the misuse of animal studies constitutes a flagrant case of observer bias. She rules out all extrapolation because "there are no grounds to assume that anything primates do is necessary, natural, or desirable in humans, *for the simple reason that humans are not non-humans* [emphasis added]" (Weisstein, 1971:77).

Two additional caveats against animal-to-human generalizations should be entered. Often the same label is used for the characteristic in animal behavior and the characteristic in human behavior that investigators wish to compare. Nevertheless, the behaviors may not be at all comparable. Take, for instance, the label "aggression." The animal findings refer to aspects of aggression such as threat displays, the latency of initial attack and the outcome of fights, whereas the human studies of aggression refer to quite different aspects, such as verbal aggression, teachers' ratings of assertiveness, etc. (Archer, 1976:249-50).

A related consideration is that even when the behavior of two species really is similar, the reasons for that behavior are not necessarily the same. A fascinating illustration of this point is provided by Tavris and Offir (1977:98). The psychologist Maurice Temerlin and his wife, Jane, reared a chimpanzee named Lucy. Until Lucy reached sexual maturity, she treated Maurice affectionately and bestowed many wet, exuberant kisses on him. When Lucy began to menstruate, however, the relationship with her "human father" changed. She refused to kiss and hug him and repulsed affection from him. Periods of estrus characteristically mark sexual receptivity, and Lucy offered blatant sexual invitations to men other than Temerlin. Says Temerlin (1975:62), "With any man but me . . . she would jump into his arms, cover his mouth with hers, and thrust her genitals against his body. This behavior disconcerted Fuller Brush men, Bible salesmen, and census takers who happened to knock on our door." Because Lucy's behavior was so closely related to her hormone-controlled menstrual cycle, Temerlin concluded that chimpanzees may have a biologically based incest taboo. Every human society also has an incest taboo. However, the moral of this anecdote is that Lucy's story *does not tell us whether or not the human incest taboo is biologically based.* Unlike chimpanzees, humans have the ability to create and to communicate norms in order to control their behavior. Therefore, the pressures in human society to control sex within the family may very well be social rather than biological. In short, humans and animals may demonstrate "identical" behavior. However, the sources of that behavior need not be the same.

Do criticisms and cautions such as these mean that animal studies are worthless to students of human sex differences? Not at all. This type of research can open new avenues of thought about human behavior. For instance, because of the overemphasis on the behavior of adult males, dominance appeared to be the major axis of social organization in primate groups. Recently, another major theme has been discovered: the mother-infant bond, which over time develops into a *matrifocal* subunit. Some anthropologists (Lancaster, 1976) believe that the role of the mother-infant bond in human societies has not yet been fully appreciated.[1] Research into sexual dimorphism in animals, then, is best viewed as a source of hypotheses, rather than definitive answers, concerning sex differences in *homo sapiens*.

THE ANTHROPOLOGICAL APPROACH

Anthropologists have provided yet another perspective on the question: To what extent do men's and women's psychological characteristics and societal roles have their source in physiology? Feminists as well as their antagonists have found in anthropology inspiration for their particular point of view. Rosaldo (1980:392) gives eloquent expression to the significance of her discipline for scholars of feminist persuasion:

Feminists (and I include myself) have with good reason probed the anthropological record for evidence which appears to tell us whether 'human nature' is the sexist and constraining thing that many of us were taught. Anthropology is, for most of us, a monument to human possibilities and constraints, a hall of mirrors wherein what Anthony Wallace called the 'anecdotal exception' seems to challenge every would-be law; while at the same time, lurking in the oddest shapes and forms, we find a still familiar picture of ourselves, a promise that, by meditating on New Guinea menstrual huts, West African female traders, ritualists, or queens, we can begin to grasp just what—in universal terms—we 'really' are.

The Logic of Cultural Universals

With regard to this issue, the presence or absence of *cultural universals* in the anthropological record is taken to be evidence for or against a biological explanation of gender relations. If a certain type of behavior is found in many cultures, despite other sorts of variation in cultural patterns, that behavior is assumed to be biologically determined, or at least linked in some way to physiology. If, however, cultural comparisons show inconsistency, if social arrangements are sometimes this way and sometimes that, this cross-cultural inconsistency is interpreted as evidence for *social* causation. Unfortunately, the method is complicated by the fact that the concept of *cultural universal* has not been consensually defined. Does it apply to all known cultures, or are there allowable exceptions? Obviously, the logic is open to the intrusion of values at this point.

We will illustrate the thinking involved in the anthropological approach by describing three instances of its application. Margaret Mead's analysis of three primitive New Guinean societies presents a classic argument for cultural conditioning of sex differences. In our second example, Steven Goldberg's theory of male dominance, the opposite position is taken; biological determination of gender patterns is claimed. The third case, Rosaldo's concept of domestic and public orientations, represents the theoretical position of a number of feminist anthropologists; this position allows for the interaction of biological and social causation.

Sex and Temperament in Three Primitive Societies

In 1931 Margaret Mead set out on a two-year expedition to New Guinea in order to discover to what degree temperamental differences between the sexes were innate and to what extent they were culturally determined. In North American society, females are responsible for the domestic sphere and males for the economic sphere beyond the home. Contrasting psychological qualities are associated with this role division: females are passive, noncompetitive and submissive, while males are active, aggressive and dominant. (These qualities are central to sex stereotypes, at least, if not to actual behavior.) Fifty years ago, such sex differences certainly seemed quite "natural." Mead tested the universality of temperamental sex differences among three tribes located within a 100-mile area on the island of New Guinea: the gentle, mountain-dwelling Arapesh, the fierce, cannibalistic Mundugumor and the head-hunters of Tchambuli.

Arapesh men and women alike displayed an unaggressive, maternal personality that would seem feminine in our society. The mild-mannered Arapesh "see all life as an adventure in growing things, growing children, growing pigs, growing yams and taros and coconuts and sago, faithfully, carefully, observing all of the rules that make things grow" (Mead, 1935:24). An Arapesh boy "grew" his wife. The girl was betrothed when she was seven or eight to a boy about six years older. Although the marriage was not consummated until both reached sexual maturity, the Arapesh male's greatest claim on his wife was that he had contributed the food that became the flesh and bone of her body. Later, both parents participated in childbirth. Conception was believed to require repeated sexual union in order to feed and shape the child in the mother's womb. Both parents lay down to bear the child and observed the birth taboos and rituals (the *couvade*). Mead (1935:42) said that "if one comments upon a middle-aged man as good-looking, the people answer: 'Good-looking, Y–e–s? But you should have seen him before he bore all those children.' " Aggressiveness was eschewed by both sexes. For example, the ideal Arapesh male never provoked a fight, and rape was unknown. Males considered leadership to be an onerous duty.

Mead found that the Mundugumor tribe offered a striking contrast to the Arapesh. Whereas the Arapesh standardized the personality of both men and women in a mold that, out of traditional bias, we would describe as womanly and maternal, the Mundugumor went to the opposite extreme. Again, ignoring sex as the basis for establishing sex differences, they standardized the behavior of both men and women as actively (almost pathologically) masculine (p. 131). Both sexes were expected to be violent, aggressive, jealous, competitive and active.

The structure of the Mundugumor family system appeared to be the source of these insecure, aggressive personalities. Here, the social organization was based on a "theory" of natural hostility among members of the same sex. Because father and daughters formed one rival group (called a "rope") and mother and sons another, neither parent welcomed pregnancy. The resulting offspring could abet the forces of the opposing group. The infant, regardless of sex, was not cherished by its mother. For example, weaning consisted of slapping the child. Hostility existed among siblings. All this unpleasantness was intensified by the fact that polygyny (a man having more than one wife at a time) was the ideal. Although wives brought wealth, additional marriages fuelled hostility and jealousy.

Sex often took the form of a rough-and-tumble athletic tryst in the bushes. The delights of these bush encounters could be enhanced by copulating in other people's gardens, an act that would spoil their yam crops. The fact that this society was rich was the reason that it managed to exist at all, with so little of its structure based on genuine cooperation.

Among the lake-dwelling Tchambuli, Mead found that the gender roles and the accompanying temperament reversed Western notions of normalcy. The woman was the "dominant, impersonal, managing partner, the man the less responsible and the emotionally dependent person" (p. 205). The Tchambuli derived their greatest satisfaction from art. Economic affairs were relegated to the women, while the men devoted themselves to art and ceremony. Although the system was patrilineal (descent was traced through the male line), it was the women who exercised the real power. The latter worked together in amiable groups and enjoyed the theatricals the men put on, "whereas the lives of the men are one mass of petty bickering, misunderstanding, reconciliation, avowals, disclaimers, and protestations accompanied by gifts, the lives of the women are singularly unclouded with personalities or with quarrelling" (p. 192).

The women were described as "solid, preoccupied, powerful, with shaven unadorned heads" (p. 192) and the men as having "delicately arranged curls," "handsome pubic coverings of flying-fox skin highly ornamented with shells," "mincing steps and self-conscious mien" (p. 186). The women were more "urgently sexed" than the men. And from early childhood, males continued to be emotionally dependent on the women.

From her observations of the three tribes, Mead (p. 206) arrived at the following conclusion. "The material suggests that we may say that many, if not all, of the personality traits which we have called masculine or feminine are as lightly linked to sex as are the clothing, the manners, and the forms of head dress that a society at a given period assigns to either sex. . . . [The] evidence is overwhelmingly in favour of the strength of social conditioning."

The Inevitability of Patriarchy

Steven Goldberg's "theory" of gender relations (*The Inevitability of Patriarchy*, 1973) is built upon the argument that male dominance is a cultural universal. Other anthropologists inform us that this observation is accurate: in all known cultures, males are dominant over women of equal status and age (Frieze et al., 1978:80-82). However, the meaning here of *male dominance* is quite subtle. In behavioral terms, male dominance does not assume a universal content or a universal shape. Women often have *some* power, influence and autonomy. However, everywhere men have *some* authority over women. Men occupy the high-status positions, exercise political power and tend to be dominant at the interpersonal level. Moreover, no matter what specific activities men and women engage in, society values the roles played by men more than those played by women. These generalizations apply even to Margaret Mead's tribes. Tchambuli society regarded masculine artistic and ritualistic knowledge as superior to the feminine economic knowledge. The Arapesh wife was the "daughter" of her husband (Rosaldo, 1974:19-20).

According to Goldberg (1973), simple biology provides the explanation for the universality of male dominance. Here is his rather simplistic line of reasoning. Male bodies contain more of the sex hormone, testosterone, than do female bodies. Aggressive behavior is linked to testosterone. Because of hormonal differences, males are, on the average, more aggressive than females. Therefore, patriarchy is inevitable since the male competitive edge over women allows men always to occupy the high-status, public positions. Again, because of hormone differences, women are better suited for motherhood and homemaking. Goldberg feels that it violates nature for women to seek public leadership. Instead, he suggests that motherhood should be more highly valued. Faced with this "biological reality," societies choose to socialize the sexes so that they do not compete with one another. Females are protected from inevitable failure by being socialized into roles that males either cannot play (childbearing) or do not wish to play (low-status positions) (Frieze et al., 1978:71).

Needless to say, Goldberg's ideas have been more enthusiastically challenged than Mead's. (An alternate explanation of male dominance will be offered shortly.) First of all, research with humans has not demonstrated a clear link between testosterone levels and aggressiveness or competitiveness. Although male hormones and aggressiveness are related in animals, as we have seen, generalizing from animals to human beings is a risky business. Also, as Chapter Two emphasized, the sex difference in aggressiveness means that the *average* male is more aggressive than the *average* female. It does not mean that *all* males are more aggressive than *all* females. These average differences cannot explain the pervasiveness of role and status differentiation in our culture (Frieze et al., 1978:81). Furthermore, in order to explain cross-cultural differences in male aggressiveness in terms of biology, differences in testosterone levels would have to be demonstrated. In other words, we would have to establish that Mundugumor men had more testosterone surging through their systems than the Arapesh men.

Domestic and Public Orientations

In 1974 sixteen women anthropologists published their analysis of women's place in human societies in a volume edited by Rosaldo and Lamphere, entitled *Woman, Culture and Society*. Rosaldo provided the theoretical overview for the book. Although she has modified her position somewhat in a recent paper (Rosaldo, 1980), the perspective taken in the book involves (1) scrutiny of the anthropological record for variability and universality in male-female interactional patterns and (2) an explanation of these patterns that emphasizes the operation of social causation upon the biological foundation.

According to Rosaldo (1974:18), the variability that Mead discovered in male-female temperaments in New Guinea attaches to almost every conceivable kind of behavior. "[There] are societies in which women trade or garden, and those in which men do; societies where women are queens and those in which they must always defer to a man; in parts of New Guinea, men are (like Victorian women) at once prudish and flirtatious, fearful of sex yet preoccupied with love magic and cosmetics that will lead the maidens—who take the initiative in courtship —to be interested in them." Nevertheless, there are definite limitations to the variability of male-female patterns, and it is these limitations that interest Rosaldo.

Two cultural universals are emphasized, the *universal asymmetry in cultural evaluations of the sexes* and *male authority*. The first universal refers to the fact that all cultures value males more than females. If a particular area of activity is defined as exclusively or predominantly male, it is seen as important. Mead (1935:302) recognized that "the prestige values always attach to the activities of men." The second universal, that of male authority, is seen as a corollary of the first. Although women may have a good deal of informal influence, everywhere men have some authority over women. Everywhere, males have a culturally legitimated right to subordinate females.[2] For example, even the Iroquois, whose society was the closest approximation that ever existed to the hypothetical form called a *matriarchate*, were not ruled by women. Iroquois women might install and depose their rulers, but the chiefs were men (Rosaldo, 1974:20).

How are these universals to be explained? Rosaldo (1974, 1980) and her colleagues claim that an opposition between women's "domestic" orientation and men's "public" orientation is at the root of female subordination and the differential evaluation of the sexes. Women's sphere of activity is built around reproductive, affective and familial bonds. Though female economic activities are varied, they are relatively less public than those of men. Males, by necessity, fill the more public roles (hunting, politics, military activities, religion, etc.) The fact that women give birth to and nurse children provides the simplest distinction in adult division of labor. Therefore, the biological fact of women's reproductive role has operated in a universal, though nonnecessary, way to shape the pattern of male dominance. However, this *natural* fact must be understood in *social* terms. It is the encrustation of cultural meanings upon the biological facts, not biology itself, which is at issue. Men's public activities give them privileged access to resources and symbols that enhance their power and provide disproportionate rewards. Men build up rituals of authority that define them as superior. Correspondingly, women gain power by entering the men's public world or by getting male participation in domestic life.

It is not difficult to empathize with the rage of some feminists at women's entrapment by social elaborations on female reproductive capacities. The radical feminist, Shulamith Firestone (1971), appeals to science to eliminate the biological differences between males and females, either by developing *in vitro* (test-tube) reproduction, or by having males suffer equally the burdens of pregnancy and child rearing. In Firestone's (p. 206) terms, the ultimate revolution requires "the freeing of women from the tyranny of their reproductive biology by every means available, and the diffusion of the childbearing and childrearing role to the society as a whole, men as well as women."

In summary, contemporary feminist anthropologists argue first that, throughout history, biological considerations have been an essential element in women's situation and, second, that these biological facts must be interpreted in a social context. The constraints of pregnancy and child care, and perhaps the superiority of male strength, limit women's access to prestigious male pursuits. That is, every social system uses facts of biological sex to organize and explain male-female roles and opportunities (Rosaldo, 1980:395). Another implication is the association of women with "nature" and of men with "culture." Because the latter participate in the socially elaborated institutions, theirs is the world of "culture." Women, on the other hand, are more closely defined through their biological and sexual functions.

> Their status is derived from their stage in a life cycle, from their biological functions, and, in particular, from their sexual or biological ties to particular men. What is more, women are more involved than men in the 'grubby' and dangerous stuff of social existence, giving birth and mourning death, feeding, cooking, disposing of feces, and the like. . . . And women, as wives, mothers, witches, midwives, nuns, or whores, are defined almost exclusively in terms of their sexual functions. [Rosaldo, 1974:30-31]

Nevertheless, biology alone cannot explain gender relations; biological facts must be understood in social terms. The division of labor and the evaluation of males and females involve beliefs and patterns of expectations. These are sociocultural, not biological matters. Women come to be seen as inferior to men when women's activities and bodily processes are culturally defined as less important or as polluting (Lamphere, 1977:613). In short, the " 'brute' biological facts have everywhere been shaped by social logics" (Rosaldo, 1980:399). This interpretation of biology is considerably more sophisticated than that of Goldberg.

THE POINT OF VIEW OF SOCIOBIOLOGY

A biologically deterministic interpretation of sex differences has been advanced by the new discipline of sociobiology. This perspective first became well known with the publication of *Sociobiology: The New Synthesis*, by Wilson (1975). Other volumes (Barash, 1977b; Dawkins, 1976; van den Berghe, 1975) followed, including at least one (Leibowitz, 1978) that focused on sex and gender. As we shall see, sociobiology incorporates several lines of reasoning previously encountered in this chapter.

Sociobiology's General Assumptions

Sociobiology can be defined as "the analysis of social behavior as an outcome of organic evolution" (Boorman and Levitt, 1980). For our purposes, its essential features can be reduced to three:

1. The method is *evolutionary* and the time scale is large. This extension of the Darwinian theory of natural selection holds that all animals act so as to maximize the chances of their genes being propagated and surviving to maturity (Sayers, 1980). It is assumed that if any behavior has a genetic component, that behavior is adaptive. That is, it has developed so as to maximize the number of genes favoring that behavior being passed on to future generations (Lowe, 1978:119). Evolutionary arguments are offered for the inevitability of biological sex differences. Evolution is believed to have favored both physical and behavioral dimorphism because of the resulting advantage in attracting mates, producing and caring for offspring, and utilizing resources (Lambert, 1978:98). This statement will be expanded later.

2. Sociobiologists' primary means of determining whether human behavior is genetically or environmentally determined is to look for *cultural universals* (Lowe, 1978:121). It is assumed that behavior observable in all societies is determined primarily by the human genetic makeup. The male-female division of labor discussed previously under the heading, *The Anthropological Approach*, is seen to be one such universal.

3. A large part of sociobiology's data and principles is based on the behavior of the *lower animals*. Extrapolations to human social life are made from these nonhuman species (Kunkel, 1977:69). Sociobiologists are especially interested in the implications of sexual dimorphism (both anatomical and behavioral) among nonhuman primates, such as the baboons. The strategies of searching for universals in human behavior

and analyzing animal behavior are often combined. After a "universal" human behavioral trait has been identified, sociobiologists then attempt to find similar behavior in nonhuman primates, in order to strengthen the argument that human behavior has evolved through natural selection (Lowe, 1978:121).

"Parental Investment": A Brief Illustration of Sociobiological Analysis[3]

The sociobiological attempt to demonstrate that women's traditional role in child care is biologically determined is based upon an evolutionary viewpoint. In addition, it incorporates appeals to cultural ubiquity and the behavior of other species.

In *The Selfish Gene* (1976), Richard Dawkins argues that the domestic division of labor between the sexes is determined primarily by differences in the size of the female and male sex cells. From the moment of conception, females invest more in each offspring than do males. "Sperms and eggs too contribute equal numbers of genes, but eggs contribute far more in the way of food reserves; indeed sperms make no contribution at all, and are simply concerned with transporting their genes as fast as possible to an egg. At the moment of conception, therefore, the father has invested less than his fair share (i.e. 50 percent) of resources in the offspring" (Dawkins, 1976:153). According to Dawkins (1976:157), this greater initial investment by the female means that she will continue to invest more in her offspring than will the male. "Since she starts by investing more than the male in the form of her large, food-rich egg, a mother is already at the moment of conception 'committed' to each child more deeply than the father is." So, on this basis, "females can be expected to invest more in children than males, not only at the outset, but throughout development" (p. 158).

Also, females invest more in each child because they cannot produce as many offspring as can males. Although Hecuba, queen of Troy, was said to have had more than twenty children, in most societies six or seven children is considered a large family. By contrast, there is almost no biological limit to the number of children men can produce. A single male ejaculation produces enough sperm to fertilize every woman in North America. Ismail, a seventeenth-century king of Morocco, supposedly fathered 1,056 offspring (Barash, 1979:47).

As you might expect, feminist critics such as Janet Sayers (1980) remain unconvinced by these arguments. They charge sociologists with flawed reasoning because their position relies on the assumption that prior parental investment ensures future parental investment in offspring.

Evaluating Sociobiology

The controversial ideas of sociobiologists such as Wilson (1975) have received wide publicity and catalyzed an enormous critical literature, which varies from partisan enthusiasm to bitter invective. (See, for example, the May 1977 issue of *The American Sociologist*.) Speaking of this critical literature, Barash (1977a:67) says "rarely has so much been said by so many, about something they understood so little." It is both impossible and unnecessary to discuss here all of the issues involved, or to reiterate the cautionary points pertaining to the intellectual tactics shared by sociobiology and the theoretical perspectives treated earlier in this chapter. However, several problems must be dealt with before we move on to an illustration of sociobiology's basic argument, that sex-linked behavioral differences were functional for the evolution of *homo sapiens*.

To begin with, a compliment, and a significant one at that! Sociobiology has exercised a salutary influence on sociology by challenging certain received notions within the discipline. There is a new open-mindedness in contemporary sociological thought concerning the similarities between human beings and the infrahuman species (although the very terms *infrahuman* and *lower animals* reflect an egotistic elevation of *homo sapiens* above all other creatures). Until recently, the exaggeration of alleged human differences in language and culture went hand in hand with what van den Berghe (1977:75) calls sociology's "dogmatic environmental determinism"—the refusal to acknowledge any biological component in human social behavior. "[Sociology's] longstanding opposition to efforts to take biological factors into account in the study of human social systems has become an albatross. If we persist in ignoring or, worse yet, denying the powerful influence of genetic and biochemical factors, we jeopardize sociology's credibility in the scientific community" (Lenski, 1977:73).

With reference to sociobiology in particular, Barash (1977a:67) suggests that a rational response would be to give "for-the-sake-of-argument" credence to evolutionary biology, to see how much of the variance in human behavior it explains. To the sociology of gender relations, sociobiology offers the related advantages of a very long time-perspective and the potential integration of many diverse strands of thought.

The most serious criticism of sociobiology concerns the difficulty of subjecting its hypotheses to empirical test. Gathering evidence for events that occurred eons ago is a formidable task. The obstacles involved in circumventing the problem through cultural universals and animal studies have already been reviewed. Specifically, the keystone of sociobiology is its assumption that behavior with some genetic component is adaptive. Unfortunately, grave problems are involved in distinguishing empirically the genetic from the environmental effects (Lowe, 1978:119).

An example may help. Even where the role of genetic factors seems established beyond doubt, as in some male-female physical differences, recent research has shown that environmental influences can still be profound. In comparing arm strength in women and men, "several researchers have concluded that much of this difference is the result of society's encouraging the average man to be more active than the average woman. They feel that the social influences are so great that inherent physiological differences in strength cannot yet be estimated" (Lowe, 1978:120).

A difficulty related to the foregoing is worth a brief note. The fact that an observed behavioral trait can be shown to be adaptive cannot be taken as evidence that the behavior is biologically determined (Lowe, 1978:120).[4] It may well be that the behavior of "the helpless food-gathering child-breeding-feeding female in the hunting and gathering society who is both protected and victimized by the brute strength of the male" (Boulding, 1976:36) may have been adaptive on evolutionary grounds. However, the causation may be biological of sociocultural or some combination of these factors. Sociology's newfound fascination with biology and genetics should not lead to amnesia concerning its traditional emphasis on human learning, language, cultural accretion and planning.

A final criticism attacks sociobiology's conservative thinking and the implications of such thinking for the formulation of policy (Lowe, 1978:123-25; Tavris and Offir, 1977:266-67). This evolutionary approach assumes that social customs such as male supremacy exist because they work. This "we're here because we're here" conclusion both smacks of circular reasoning and suggests that any practice that has survived must be "good." For example, sociobiologist Barash (1977b:301) says, "Women have almost universally found themselves relegated to the nursery while men derive their greatest satisfaction from their jobs. . . . Such differences in male-female attachment to family versus vocation could derive in part from hormonal differences between the sexes."

Because feminists seek to ameliorate the *status quo*, they are irritated by the sociobiologists' endorsation of stability. If survival becomes the ultimate yardstick, then those in power can justify many questionable practices: "not only male supremacy but war, slavery, infanticide, and wholesale imprisonment, oppression, and slaughter of outgroups of every description" (Tavris and Offir, 1977:267). Moreover, if people believe that male/female inequality has a biogenic origin, they are unlikely to support social programs designed to eliminate such inequality. Such attempts to go against "natural law" would be deemed quite futile.

All these, as well as other criticisms, have been launched against Lionel Tiger's genetic explanation of why women are everywhere the "subordinate sex" (to use Boulding's [1976:35] term). A brief discussion of his famous, or infamous, argument follows.

Tiger's Male Bonding Hypothesis

Anthropologist Tiger's book, *Men in Groups* (1969), appeared six years before Wilson's (1975) inaugural definition of the discipline. However, it fits into the sociobiological mode of thought. Appeals are made to an evolutionary imperative, to cultural universals and primatology, as well as to a variety of other sources.

Tiger's (1969:27) argument focuses on the phenomenon of *male bonding*, which he defines as "a particular relationship between two or more males such that they react differently to members of their bonding unit as compared to individuals outside of it." These male bonds allegedly generate strong feelings that differ, in some mystic way, from the emotionality of female-female friendships and male-female love relationships. The biological propensity for males to bond resulted from the human evolutionary experience, according to Tiger, and is transmitted genetically.

Early hominids faced the double problem of bringing home the bacon and avoiding becoming someone else's bacon (van den Berghe, 1975:36). Males who bonded together and hunted in groups had a survival advantage over solitary hunters. In view of the nine-month gestation period and two-year lactation period, human females and their infants would be a hindrance on the hunt. Thus, the woman who stayed home had a greater chance for survival and transmission of her genes than her sister who joined the hunt. Bonded males were more successful hunters and, because they were better able to feed and protect their children, they were more successful in leaving offspring. Female bonding, on the other hand, was apparently not required for survival of the species.

Much of Tiger's book is devoted to tracing the consequences of male bonding. Male aggression, which strengthens group cohesion (according to Tiger), is one ramification. Hierarchical social organization involving male leadership is another. Groups formed for purposes of economics, war, religion, politics, etc., must have leaders and followers. Tiger says that males control these organizations because of their bonding capacity. Females, on the other hand, are not found in leadership positions; the fact that females do not bond with males means that females cannot trigger follower behavior in males. Instead, the presence of women in otherwise all-male groups is found to be sexually stimulating and hence disruptive. Although Tiger (p. 96) does acknowledge some of the sociocultural reasons for female subordination (the "complexities of the role of child-rearing, the legal propertylessness of females. . . . [their difficulty entering] professions such as law, and [the facts] that they are generally less well educated and have fewer broad opportunities for political experience") he maintains that their lack of bonding propensity is the main cause.

The major criticism launched against Tiger's arguments concerns the lack of empirical evidence for the existence of the male bond (Nielsen, 1978:98). He has been accused of offering "cross species analogy [with baboons] and cross cultural anecdote rather than valid evidence to support his claims" (Rosenblatt and Cunningham, 1976:78). Moreover, scientists have not identified a gene that is responsible for bonding. Tiger's delineation of the link between the biology of bonding and actual behavior is vague, as is his depiction of differences between male-male bonds and other sorts of friendship and love attachments. Most of his concepts are simply too nebulous to test. Indeed, this criticism may be expanded to sociobiology in general. Hypotheses concerning male-female differences, based on society's evolution, are extremely difficult to test scientifically. Thus, such hypotheses may be "more metaphysical than scientific" (Rosenblatt and Cunningham, 1976:78).

THE PSYCHOANALYTIC ARGUMENT

Overview of Freudian Psychology

Psychoanalytic theory, as formulated by the Viennese physician, Sigmund Freud (1856-1939), is another attempt to explain female-male differences. Segments of the psychoanalytic perspective (which is both a theory of the personality and a system of therapy) are of particular interest to gender relations specialists.

The Freudian view of women (1927-1975) was the first integrated and widely accepted modern theory of feminine psychology (Weyant, 1979:364). The wide-ranging ideas of this prolific thinker (see Brill, 1938) have had an enormous influence upon twentieth-century thought. Freud's notions of femininity have shaped clinical therapy practice, with consequences for the psychiatric treatment of women that have only recently been recognized (Chesler, 1972). Moreover, many of his ideas have become part of the folk culture. Whether or not they have studied Freud's theories, many Canadians are familiar with such Freudian terms as *repression*, *Oedipus complex* and *superego*. This tremendous impact upon Western culture in general and on the discipline of psychology in particular means that Freudian thought has been a basic ingredient in the conception of femininity.

The psychoanalytic theory of female and male personality reflects extreme biological determinism. (This is the reason for its discussion in this chapter rather than in the next.) Freud coined the phrase, "anatomy is destiny," and he argued that boys' possession of a penis and girls' possession of a clitoris inevitably produced sex differences in adult temperament and personality (Frieze et al., 1978:71). This type of thinking does not endear Papa Freud to the feminists. Nor are they pleased with his assessment of women's relative worth. He judged the penis to be by far the superior organ. Therefore, although Freud "neither advocated nor criticized the societal subjugation of women . . . [he simply] concluded that they are inferior—anatomically, psychologically, developmentally, and ethically" (Tauer, 1979:288). A brief description of the psychoanalytic theory of personality development is needed in order to clarify these cryptic remarks.

Key Assumptions

Psychoanalytic theory is based on a number of general assumptions (Mackie, 1980a:138-39; Lee and Hertzberg, 1978:29-30):

1. The roots of human behavior lie in the depths of the unconscious. Because Freud's ideas arose from his study of neurotic patients and because he objected to what he considered the excessive rationalism of his day, he placed heavy emphasis on the irrational, unconscious dimensions of the mind.
2. According to Freud, adult personality is the result of the child's early experiences within the family. This assumption may be expressed in terms of the old cliché that the "child is the father of the man" (and "mother of the woman").
3. Freud saw child development as a process of repression, a battle between the family (as agents of society) and the impulsive animal-like nature of the child. Essentially, the parental task is to tame and redirect the inborn urges of the child.
4. Central among these urges is sexuality, which Freud viewed as a primary motive for human functioning. He postulated the existence of a powerful sexual instinct both in childhood and throughout later life.

Stages of Personality Development

The psychological development of personality parallels the physical maturation of the child. This development from infancy to adulthood proceeds through a sequence of stages. Freudians hold that every child goes through this sequence in a fixed order. Each stage marks a preoccupation with a different part of the body, called an *erogenous zone*.

In the first two stages, which occupy the first four years of life, male and female experiences are undifferentiated. Indeed, Freud's androcentric bias led him to describe children of both sexes as "little men." During the *oral stage*, which lasts from birth to eighteen months, the infant is preoccupied with pleasures associated with the mouth (sucking and biting). The major outcome of this stage is the establishment of a predominant disposition to either trust or mistrust other people. The *anal stage* covers the period from eighteen months to three years of age. As the anus and buttocks are eroticized, the child becomes preoccupied with elimination of the bowels. Parental attempts at toilet training represent the first serious demands for self-control. Out of this conflict emerges the superego (conscience) in very amorphous form.

Movement into the *phallic stage* occurs when the child is about four years old. As erogenous gratification becomes focused in the genital area, children substitute masturbation for thumb sucking and begin to be curious about differences in sexual anatomy (Chafetz, 1974:14). During this stage, gender identity is established through resolution of the *Oedipus conflict*. This conflict involves the child's craving sexual possession of the opposite-sex parent, while viewing the same-sex parent as the rival who stands in the way of satisfaction of these erotic impulses. The key to personality development is the fact that boys possess penises and girls do not.

Male and female children experience the Oedipus conflict somewhat differently. Let us describe the male experience first. The boy's feeling of love for his mother becomes more sexual during the phallic stage. He becomes antagonistic toward his father, who is seen as the competitor for his mother's attention. The male child fears that his father will retaliate against him for his interest in his mother. The feared punishment takes the form of *castration anxiety*. Apprehension centers around the penis because that organ is the source of his lust for his mother. The castration anxiety inhibits the boy from consciously indulging in his incestuous fantasies. Instead, the boy begins to identify with his father and to emulate the gender behavior of this person who possesses both the "bigger and better" penis and the cherished object of the child's fantasies, the mother (Chafetz, 1974:15).

During the phallic stage, the female child is also sexually curious and preoccupied with masturbation. However, Freud regarded the clitoris as an inferior version of the male organ, an "atrophied penis," and wrote of the "momentous discovery which it is the lot of little girls to make. They notice the penis of a brother or playmate, strikingly visible and of large proportions, at once recognize it as the superior counterpart of their own small and inconspicuous organ, and from that time forward fall a victim to penis-envy" (Freud, 1927, reprinted in Unger and Denmark, 1975:131). Indeed, Freud referred to woman as "the mutilated creature" and said that the difference between the sexes "corresponds to the difference between a castration that has been carried out and one that has merely been threatened" (Freud, 1927). The male experience of castration anxiety suggested a correlative experience in the female, the experience of horror at the lack of a penis. If the boy fears the loss of his penis, the girl must suffer jealousy from never having had one in the first place (Tauer, 1979:288).

Such penis envy may indicate that children in Western culture have already assimilated a "bigger-means-better" mentality. However, a superior interpretation is that little girls associate the greater power and privileges of males with their conspicuous anatomical characteristic of maleness (Chafetz, 1974:15). Tauer (1979:289), quoting Elizabeth Janeway, says their deprivation of a penis stands for "the deprivation of things that a female as a person truly *should* have: autonomy, freedom, control of her own life . . . for women are social castrates."

The girl child eventually understands that her possession of a cavity, rather than a penis, is a fate shared with her mother and all other females. Therefore, the girl joins all males in disdaining women. The female blames her mother for her loss of penis. Her penis envy motivates her to renounce her love for her mother and to turn to her father. Her shift in love for the father derives from her desire to have a (preferably male) child by him (and eventually by a male peer) which symbolically represents attaining a penis. Some resolution of the Oedipus complex occurs through the girl's later identification with her mother as a symbolic means of possessing the father. She acquires her superego and feminine identity from her mother. However, because the female cannot completely repress her interest in her father (she simply lacks the powerful motive of castration anxiety), women cannot have as strong a superego as men (Lee and Hertzberg, 1978:31-32).

Freud made it quite clear that women's anatomical inferiority led to ethical inferiority:

> I cannot escape the notion (though I hesitate to give it expression) that for women the level of what is ethically normal is different from what it is to men. Their super-ego is never so inexorable, so impersonal, so independent of its emotional origins as we require it to be in men. Characteristic traits which critics of every epoch have brought up against women—that they show less sense of justice than men, that they are less ready to submit to the great necessities of life, that they are more often influenced in their judgments by feelings of affection or hostility—all these would be amply accounted for by the modification of their super-ego which we have already inferred. We must not allow ourselves to be deflected from such conclusions by the denials of the feminists, who are anxious to force us to regard the two sexes as completely equal in position and worth. [Weyant, 1979:361-62]

The phallic stage is followed by the relatively peaceful *latency stage* (which occupies children from six to twelve years). The function of this latter stage is to consolidate the achievements of the preceding three stages. Energy is desexualized and directed toward people outside the family, such as teachers and friends of the same sex.

The *genital stage* is the turbulent period of adolescence marked by a resurgence of sexual urges resulting from physiological maturation. Sexual intercourse with opposite-sex peers is the preferred activity, with the boy's erotic focus being the penis and the girl's, the vagina. According to Freud, the feminine identity is established when the wish for a penis is replaced with a wish for a child, and when clitoral orgasm is replaced by vaginal orgasm. (Incidentally, sex researchers such as Masters and Johnson [1966] have shown this distinction to be meaningless.)

The Triadic Elements of Femininity

Freud claimed that normal femininity embodied a triad of elements: passivity, narcissism and masochism (Laws, 1979:268-71). Here again, anatomy is destiny. First of all, his psychology of women rested upon the presumed passivity of the female in sexual intercourse. Assertion and ambition in women were frowned upon as inappropriate masculine strivings that reflected penis envy. Feminine masochism reflects Freud's perception of menstruation, defloration and childbirth as horrible, bloody events. According to him, to bleed is to be masochistic. Female sexuality means accepting, and perhaps even seeking, pain. However, the masochism is not self-destructive because females are also considered to be narcissistic. Narcissism results from the fact that in some ways the woman remains childlike and hence selfish and self-loving. Clearly, the implication is that men are psychologically the more healthy sex and therefore deserving of their superior social status (Nielsen, 1978:105).

Evaluation of Psychoanalytic Theory

Until recently, the response of female social scientists to the Freudian account of female psychology and gender development has been sharply critical. The most charitable critics have viewed it as whimsical speculation; the most harsh as a scurrilous execration. Nevertheless, the psychoanalytic framework continues to be influential within both clinical psychology and the psychology of child development. Moreover, several intellectuals (Chodorow, 1978; Mitchell, 1974) have urged reconsideration of the utility to feminists of at least some segments of Freudian thought. The fact that the following statement is included in a recent critique of Freud's theory is indicative of a more generous stance on the part of critics: "Freud recognized the limited, tentative nature of his formulations about women. . . . Addressing the women in his audience, he remarked in 1933: 'If you want to know more about femininity you must interrogate your own experience or turn to the poets, or else wait until science can give you more coherent information' '" (Lee and Hertzberg, 1978:33).

We too shall try to provide a balanced evaluation, on the assumption that both flattering and deprecatory criticism are richly deserved.

Freud made a number of important contributions to social scientists' understanding of childhood socialization. His emphasis on early family experiences stimulated research on child-rearing practices, especially on cross-cultural variations in these practices. Freud's solution to the problem of how society gets inside the individual, namely, the identification of children with their parents, was a major insight. His consideration of the roles played by the emotions, sexuality and the unconscious, covers aspects of human motivation that social science otherwise neglects.

Psychoanalytic theory has also been severely criticized by feminists, as well as others. The major flaw has been the significant lack of fit between certain Freudian ideas and empirical reality. Here, the skepticism of critics has been augmented by the problem that much of the theory does not lend itself to empirical testing. (A central criterion for judging the utility of any theory is its vulnerability. That is, it must be possible to discover whether a theory's tenets are true or false.) The specialized nature of Freud's "sample" partly explains why later research failed to support some of his hypotheses. His ideas were based on his experiences with middle-class Viennese patients during the Victorian era. Consequently, the applicability of his notions to normal populations, and to other cultures and historical periods, is often limited. For example, a child socialized in a society that treats toilet training very casually will hardly experience anal stage trauma. A related shortcoming is that Freud's speculations about children's behavior were based on his experience with adults, not with children.

Here are some examples of Freudian ideas that research does not document. Boys' possession of penises and their castration anxiety, and girls' "penislessness" and penis envy are essential to this theory. However, studies of children at the age level of the Oedipus complex find little evidence of castration anxiety in boys and even less evidence for female envy of male anatomy (Lee and Hertzberg, 1978:35). Although Freud argued that the female conscience is never as well developed as the male conscience, research suggests just the opposite (Baron and Byrne, 1977:357). For example, Hoffman (1975) presented children and their parents with a questionnaire asking about such acts as stealing, cheating and hit-and-run driving. Hoffman found that females more than males associated moral transgressions with feelings of guilt. In contrast, the males were more afraid of simply getting caught and being punished.

Other negative points can be dealt with more quickly. Investigation has shown that clinical therapy based upon psychoanalytic theory has only limited effectiveness. Eysenck (1952) reported that of a group of neurotic patients, the improvement rate of those who received psychoanalysis was 44%. Of those who received psychotherapy, the improvement rate was 65%. However, of the neurotic patients who received no treatment at all, the improvement rate was 72%. These results have *not* been subsequently refuted. (See also Eysenck, 1966.) To quote Peter (1977:413, cited in Nettler, 1980), psychiatry is "a way of correcting our own faults by confessing our parents' shortcomings." Goldberg, (1976:24-25) with incisive wit, says that the psychoanalytic approach is "a little like treating food poisoning by exploring early eating habits."

Another criticism, which is well taken, is that in emphasizing biological causation, the theory unduly minimizes the social context of behavior. Only the family grouping is acknowledged, while social class, culture, political organization, etc., are ignored. A related point is the inadequate conceptualization of the role of learning. For example, children's learning about the implications of gender involves considerably more than the simple observation of male-female genital differences, as Freud would have it (Chodorow, 1978:146). Finally, feminist displeasure was aroused by Freud's masculine bias, even misogyny. If we were to take women, rather than men, as the norm, perhaps the irony of the situation could be appreciated. Why not assume that the male is biologically inferior and describe his penis as a "bloated clitoris" (Lee and Hertzberg, 1978:34)? Why not emphasize "breast" and "womb" envy? (Apparently, anthropologists have found evidence for these phenomena in their studies of the *couvade*[5] and of male initiation rites [Tauer, 1979:290].)

Unfortunately, the space here is insufficient to consider in detail each and every significant attempt to establish the source of female-male differences. Therefore, the last three topics that we have chosen for discussion—studies of infant sex differences, studies of psychosexual abnormalities, and biology and cognitive skills—will be dealt with in summary fashion.

SEX DIFFERENCES IN INFANTS

One way of exploring biological influences on sex differences is to examine the behavior of very young infants, the rationale being that any effects of culture are at a minimum in infants (Frieze et al., 1978:73-79). Unfortunately, despite the invention of new research strategies (Scaife, 1979), the methodological difficulties here are formidable.

To begin with, cultural factors come into play at birth. From the moment the delivery-room nurses wrap infants in pink or blue blankets, a child's maleness or femaleness is constantly reinforced. In interviews, mothers have expressed the idea that male and female infants should be treated differently, according to notions of gender-appropriate behavior (though they are not attempting to cause such behavior) (Barfield, 1976:75). For example, while male infants are touched more, female infants are talked to and smiled at more.

A second difficulty arises when the researcher attempts to relate aspects of infant behavior to aspects of children's and adults' behavior. For example, newborn males are able to lift their chins higher than newborn females, when placed on their stomachs. To what later characteristic, if any, might this behavior relate? (Shaving, maybe?)

Third, the observers of infant behavior nearly always know the sex of the child they are studying. This knowledge means that the researcher's stereotypic expectations may influence his/her conclusions. Despite these and other methodological problems, some valid data have been accumulated on certain infantile characteristics that may act as precursors to the major stereotypic sex differences discussed in Chapter Two.

Attempts have been made to link later male aggressive behavior with infant behavior. One line of reasoning suggests that prenatal testosterone would produce male infants that are more active than female infants. Another suggests that male babies would be more irritable. Both hypotheses depend on a harsher parental response to male behavior to turn the active or irritable baby into an aggressive child. The evidence is complex. For example, males and females seem to show roughly equal amounts of total activity. However, males show more gross, vigorous bodily motion, probably because of their less well-developed nervous systems. Females show more restricted movements, such as lip twitching and eyebrow raising (Barfield, 1976:73). Although, when sex differences are found at all, it is the male babies who are the more active or irritable, researchers conclude that biology alone does not appear to account for boys' later aggressiveness.

If females are naturally more social and nurturant than males, they can be expected to smile more and earlier and to respond more positively to human faces than do males. Unfortunately, the sociability evidence based on infant behavior is equivocal and no conclusions can yet be drawn.

Popular stereotypes hold that males are more independent than females. One infant behavior associated with dependence is separation anxiety (distress when the child's parent is leaving or out of the room). Another is fear of strangers or novel situations. No consistent sex differences have been found in infant incidence of either of these behaviors.

Researchers (Frieze et al., 1978:78-79) conclude from studies such as the above that there are few, if any, distinct differences between male and female infant behavior. Biological factors operating in early infancy do not tell us much about later sex differences. However, the matter is more complicated than it first appears; a given sex difference need not show up in infancy for it to be biologically based. For example, the hormone system does not reach maturity until puberty, and sex differences in traits such as mathematical and spatial skills emerge at puberty. By then, however, separating the influence of socialization from the influence of biology is an almost insuperable task.

HORMONE AND GENE RESEARCH

It will be recalled that the few well-established sex differences included females' greater verbal fluency, males' greater visual-spatial ability and male aggressiveness (Maccoby and Jacklin, 1974). This section provides a brief description of the hormone and gene research that is concerned with the etiology of these differences.

To review, boys and girls have similar and low levels of testosterone and estrogen, respectively, during childhood. At puberty, the testes increase their production of testosterone and the ovaries increase production of estrogen. The result is the development of secondary sex characteristics and reproductive fertility. The question that interests us here is whether these hormones are responsible for psychological, as well as physiological effects (Tavris and Offir, 1977:110).

In human beings, the female ovum and male sperm each possess twenty-three chromosomes. The fertilized egg has forty-six chromosomes, aligned in twenty-three pairs. One of these pairs, the sex chromosomes, determines the sex of the embryo. It consists of an X from the mother, and either an X or a Y from the father. If the embryo has two Xs, it is female; if it has an X and a Y, it is a male. Some human traits are sex-linked. That is, the gene for the trait is carried on one of the sex chromosomes, usually the X chromosome. For example, hemophilia and color blindness are carried by the X chromosome (Tavris and Offir, 1977:100).

Much of the current effort to explain women's superior verbal ability and men's superior spatial ability centers on sex disparities in the brain. Although there appear to be no sex differences in brain size or structure, male and female brains seem to differ in organization (Bryden, 1979; Carter and Greenough, 1979; Goleman, 1978). The left hemisphere of the brain controls language, and the right hemisphere, spatial and nonverbal functions. *Lateralization* is the term used to label the specialization in the functioning of each hemisphere. The left side is normally dominant in both sexes. It has been proposed that this dominance is more complete in females, thus explaining female language superiority and male visual-spatial superiority (Barfield, 1976:101).

At the moment, the mechanisms responsible for the sex difference in lateralization and its precise impact on spatial and verbal skills are unclear. However, a number of hypotheses involving the sex hormones or genes are being explored (Frieze et al., 1978:91-94). For example, it has been suggested that functionally different brains in the two sexes might be the product of prenatal exposure to androgens (Barfield, 1976:101); however, the evidence is inconclusive. Another view is that sex differences in brains are genetically "wired in." It has been found that spatial ability seems to be inherited, that it is a skill transmitted by a recessive gene on the X chromosome; a finding that supports the biological theory. Nevertheless, there is still room for social experience. For example, anthropological evidence shows that sex differences in spatial ability can be large or small, depending on how children are raised. In cultures where females are not allowed to roam freely, their visual-spatial skills are very poor, compared to those of men. However, in cultures such as the Eskimo, where both sexes are given early independence, their visual-spatial abilities are nearly equal (Goleman, 1978:54-55).

Sex-difference experts Maccoby and Jacklin (1974:274) conclude that the evidence for greater male aggressiveness is unequivocal. This behavioral sex difference has been found in a wide variety of cultural settings and established by a wide variety of indices (p. 228). The dimension of aggression-passivity is related directly or indirectly to a wide variety of sex-differentiated behaviors. Therefore, it is a critical dimension for gender relations specialists. What is being suggested is that sex differences in achievement, competition, activity levels, dominance, personal and public power relations, as well as war and violent crimes, might be linked to the fact of differential aggressiveness between males and females (Weitz, 1977:11).

Maccoby and Jacklin (1974:242-43) further contend that the sex difference in aggressiveness has a biological foundation. Their reasons are as follows:

1. Males are more aggressive than females in all human societies for which evidence is available.
2. The sex differences are found early in life, before differential socialization practices have been brought to bear to "shape" aggression differently in the two sexes.
3. Similar sex differences are found in humans and primates.
4. Aggression in animals is related to levels of sex hormones.

Animal studies with, for example, rhesus monkeys, reveal that when male hormones are administered prenatally, the female offspring show elevated levels of malelike or aggressive behavior. In addition, a high testosterone level is correlated with aggressiveness in male animals. However, we have already remarked on the danger of drawing human analogies from animal behavior. The human evidence is meager and inconclusive. Although testosterone is related to animal aggressiveness, the implications of such findings for humans is unclear (Frieze et al., 1978:85).

In summary, although there does appear to be a biological foundation for sex differences in cognitive skills and aggressiveness, the exact mechanisms are as yet unknown. Neither genes nor hormones affect behavior in a simple, direct manner. The next section will give further consideration to the topic.

PSYCHOSEXUAL ABNORMALITIES[6]

Over the years, John Money and his colleagues at the Johns Hopkins Medical Center have published a series of classical studies on children's psychosexual abnormalities. Two topics have been chosen for brief treatment here, from among the many aspects of these researchers' work: one variety of female hermaphrodite and an interesting case of male gender reassignment. These sexual deviations, which to a certain extent function as "natural experiments," should provide some insight into the question of the relative importance of biological and social causation in the development of gender identity. However, extrapolation from these unique individuals to human beings in general must be made carefully. In addition to atypicalities in their hormones, chromosome structures and anatomy, these people differ from the general public in being part of a clinical population. That is, their unique experience, including their knowledge of their own abnormalities and the reactions they elicit from therapists and families, constitute intrusive influences upon any conclusions reached.

Hermaphrodites are organisms that possess both male and female characteristics. A hermaphrodite may have only one ovary and one testicle, the genitals may be ambiguous in appearance, or the sexuality of the external and internal organs may be contradictory. Of particular interest are genetic females (XX) who received heavy dosages of androgen prenatally, because of their own defective adrenal glands or because of maternal drug usage. The reason for the interest in these cases is that they appear to parallel animal experiments where female fetuses that are given androgens demonstrate masculinized effects in aggressive and sexual behavior (Weitz, 1977:46). If the human hormone imbalance that resulted in masculinized genitals also produced psychological effects upon these girls, the case of the biological determinists would be strengthened. As well, the orientation of the girls' gender identity (their deep-seated conviction that they are either masculine or feminine) is especially interesting.

Money and Ehrhardt (1972) interviewed and administered psychological tests to twenty-five hermaphrodites who had received corrective surgery on their genitals and who had been raised as girls. Their behavior and attitudes were compared with a control group matched by age, IQ, socioeconomic status and race (but not clinical experience). The researchers found that the fetally androgenized females were more interested in masculine clothing, games and toys. Although they regarded themselves as female, they were considered by their mothers and themselves to be tomboys. In comparison with the control group, these subjects were less interested in baby-sitting and future marriage as opposed to careers. Interestingly, no greater incidence of physical aggression was reported. Money and Ehrhardt concluded that the male sex hormone had had a masculinizing effect. However, critics such as Frieze et al., (1978:88), emphasizing the methodological limitations of the research, point out that their behavior is within the normal range for females in our society and, further, that female gender identity is not seriously disrupted by the presence of prenatal androgens.

Our second study, one of the most dramatic cases of Money and his associates, reinforces the importance of gender as *social* assignment. In the 1960s, a couple took their perfectly normal seven-month-old twin boys to a hospital to be circumcised. According to Money and Tucker (1975:91-92),

> the physician elected to use an electric cauterizing needle instead of a scalpel to remove the foreskin of the one who chanced to be brought to the operating room first. When this baby's foreskin didn't give on the first try, or on the second, the doctor stepped up the current. On the third try, the surge of heat from the electricity literally cooked the baby's penis. Unable to heal, the penis dried up, and in a few days sloughed off completely, like the stub of an umbilical cord.

Doctors recommended that the boy's sex be reassigned and that female external genitals be surgically constructed. The child's name, clothes and hairstyle were feminized, as the parents made every effort to rear twins—one male and one female. As the following anecdote about the twins at the age of four and a half shows, the parents and children all successfully developed "sex appropriate" attitudes and behavior. The mother, talking about the boy, reported, "In the summer time, one time I caught him—he went out and took a leak in my flower garden in the front yard, you know. He was quite happy with himself. And I just didn't say anything. I just couldn't. I started laughing and I told daddy about it."

The corresponding comments about the girl went this way. "I've never had a problem with her. She did once when she was little, she took off her panties and threw them over the fence. And she didn't have no panties on. But I just gave her a little swat on the rear, and I told her that nice little girls didn't do that and she should keep her pants on" (Money and Ehrhardt, 1972:119).

This case and others suggest that the sex of *assignment* outweighs biological factors in determining gender identity. In Money and Ehrhardt's words (quoted in Tavris and Offir, 1977:109), "to use the Pygmalion allegory, one may begin with the same clay and fashion a god or a goddess." The psychosexual abnormality evidence clearly contradicts Freud's insistence that possession of a penis or a vagina is a necessary or sufficient condition for developing a male or female gender identity (Kessler and McKenna, 1978:57). Instead, social labelling seems to be crucial.

The problems associated with sex reassignment are surmountable, provided, first, that the parents are not ambiguous about the child's gender, and second, that the reassignment is done early enough. According to a case reported by Robert Stoller (and described in Stockard and Johnson, 1980:125), at six years of age it is already too late. A genetic female was raised as a boy until the age of six, when she precociously entered puberty. The pediatrician recommended that the parents change the child's gender. The results were disastrous. In later years, the girl was "unable to progress in school, with a severe speech defect, no friends, clumsy, and grotesque-appearing in girl's clothes."

CONCLUSIONS

This chapter has explored the relationship between biology and gender. Though some conclusions are warranted, nearly every section of our discussion of the foundations of female-male differences has raised more questions than it has answered. All of the various biological perspectives that we dealt with—animal experimentation, anthropological and sociobiological approaches, psychoanalysis, research into infant behavior, on genes and hormones and on psychosexual abnormalities—will continue in the future to provide useful ways to search for answers.

What has been learned so far? First of all, it is obviously folly to search for *either* biological or environmental causation of gender patterns. To pose the question as "nature versus nurture" is misleading and simplistic, for the question is a complex one. Both nature and nurture are implicated. In Kunkel's (1977:71) words, "available evidence suggests that biochemical and genetic factors set the stage . . . but that culture and history provide the script for social life [emphasis omitted]." Biology seems to be directly involved in male aggressiveness and cognitive differences, and indirectly involved in male-female division of labor. Considerable research will be required to establish the mechanisms of the interaction of biology with sociocultural experiences.

Several observations about the field of sociology are also in order. In the long run, both sociology in general and gender relations in particular will benefit from abandoning their ideological opposition to biological explanations of social behavior. Feminist social scientists have shied away from a biological perspective because it has been used to justify male dominance, for example, in the popularized biologistic formulations of Tiger (1969) and Goldberg (1974). There are practical as well as academic implications involved, here. If the public believes that male-female social arrangements are rooted in biology and hence immutable, they will lack interest in social programs designed to eliminate inequalities. Nevertheless, sociologists of gender relations violate their mandate as social scientists when they adopt a dogmatic stance against all biological explanations. (The amount of truth contained in the biological perspective is, of course, a separate issue.)

4 Gender Socialization: The Social-Psychological Perspective on Sex Differences

WHAT, asks the nursery rhyme, are little girls made of? Double X chromosomes. A vagina, a clitoris and, eventually, a bosom. Passivity, verbal ability.

What are little boys made of? An X chromosome. A Y chromosome. A penis and related parts. Later, mustache, beard or five-o'clock-shadow. Aggressiveness. Mathematical and spatial ability.

Not sugar and spice and everything nice. Not snips and snails and puppy-dog tails. According to researchers, this short, unromantic inventory of male-female distinctions covers the essence of femininity and masculinity. The list proves longer when consideration is given to matters of fashion (long hair and pants are no longer reliable guides), etiquette and demeanor (who pays for dinner?) and social roles (maternal versus paternal aspirations).

The review of the evidence in the previous chapter established the significance of *learning* in the acquisition of gender. Most of the psychosocial differences between male and female are not innate but rather come about through socialization. Even where biology appears to play a causative role (in the production, for example, of male aggressiveness and certain cognitive differences), interaction occurs between biological and sociocultural influences.[1]

Psychosexual Abnormalities Revisited

As we saw in Chapter Three, social scientists find the experiences of people with psychosexual abnormalities useful in sorting out whether gender is a biological fact or a social fact. It will be recalled that children whose gender identity (personal conviction of being male or female) conflicted with their genetic sex acquired gender behaviors and attitudes that agreed with their gender identity, rather than with their genetic sex (Frieze et al., 1978:95). The following excerpts from the autobiography of the English writer, Jan Morris, *Conundrum* (1974), serve to remind us of two points: (1) the psychological and sociological definitions of gender may or may not be congruent with the individual's biological equipment; (2) masculinity and femininity involve both differentiation and evaluation.

Morris says, "I was three or perhaps four years old when I realized that I had been born into the wrong body, and should really be a girl" (p. 3) though "by every standard of logic I was patently a boy. I was James Humphry Morris, male child. I had a boy's body. I wore a boy's clothes" (p. 4). For twenty years, the secret of his transsexualism was not shared with a single soul. (According to Stoller [1968:89-90], "transsexualism is the conviction in a biologically normal person of being a member of the opposite sex. This belief is these days accompanied by requests for surgical and endocrinological procedures that change anatomical appearances to that of the opposite sex.") A celebrated foreign correspondent, author and father of four, Morris followed his "passionate, lifelong, ineradicable conviction" (p. 8) and underwent sex change procedures. Morris's account of the psychological and physiological shifts of living first as a man and then as a woman is most revealing:

> We are told that the social gap between the sexes is narrowing, but I can only report that having, in the second half of the twentieth century, experienced life in both roles, there seems to me no aspect of existence, no moment of the day, no contact, no arrangement, no response, which is not different for men and for women. The very tone of voice in which I was now addressed, the very posture of the person next in the queue, the very feel in the air when I entered a room or sat at a restaurant table, constantly emphasized my change of status.
>
> And if others' responses shifted, so did my own. The more I was treated as a woman, the more woman I became. I adapted willy-nilly. If I was assumed to be incompetent at reversing cars, or opening bottles, oddly incompetent I found myself becoming. If a case was thought too heavy for me, inexplicably I found it so myself. Thrust as I now found myself far more into the company of women than of men, I began to find women's conversation in general more congenial. . . . Men treated me more and more as a junior . . . my lawyer, in an unguarded moment one morning, even called me "my child"; and so, addressed every day of my life as an inferior, involuntarily, month by month I accepted the condition. I discovered that even now men prefer women to be less informed, less able, less talkative, and certainly less self-centered than they are themselves; so I generally obliged them. [Morris, 1974:148-49]

However, Ms. Morris admits to a frank enjoyment of the "small courtesies men now pay me, the standing up or the opening of doors, which really do give one a cherished or protected feeling" (p. 160).

Socialization Defined

Sociologists define *socialization* as the complex learning process through which individuals develop selfhood and acquire the knowledge, skills and motivations required for participation in social life. Although the learning that occurs in childhood lays the foundation for future development and is, therefore, especially critical, socialization is a lifelong process. The family is the major agent of socialization. However, its influence is augmented by that of peers, schools, the mass media and other institutions.

Socialization is the link between the individual and society and may be viewed from each of these two perspectives. From the point of view of the individual, interaction with other people is the means by which human potentialities are actualized. From the point of view of society, socialization explains how commitment to the social order is maintained over time.

The foregoing paragraphs briefly explain the meaning of socialization in general. *Gender socialization*, in particular, involves the processes through which individuals learn to become masculine or feminine according to the expectations current in their society.

Socialization is an abstract, umbrella concept that conveys a richness of meaning to those initiated in its use. Spelling out some of the implications of the term will help in understanding how "girls turn out girlish and boys boyish" (Tavris and Offir, 1977:164).

1. The fact that it is *learning* that is involved, not maturational "unfolding," constitutes the essence of socialization. Various theories have been developed to explain precisely how this learning occurs. This chapter will consider the most important theories of the mechanisms of gender socialization.

2. Each society has its "scripts" (Laws, 1979) for masculinity and femininity, and the emotions, thoughts and behavior of children are shaped in conformity with these scripts. Our first task will be to enumerate the content of the lessons of gender socialization within Canadian society.

3. Though for the sake of economy of language, sociologists speak of "society" socializing its constituents, "society" is not really a monolith that operates upon helpless individuals. Rather, influence is exerted upon people by the family, the peer group, the school, the mass media, etc. The next two chapters will discuss how gender socialization is carried out by these agencies.

   Some aspects of socialization are intentional, while

others are unintentional. Because society has given the family and the school a mandate to socialize youngsters, both of these agencies deliberately attempt to equip them with the knowledge and values required to fit into adult society. The influence of the peer group and of the media is, however, for the most part unintentional.

4. The fact that socialization is a *lifelong* learning process calls for some further definitional distinctions. The main point here is that there are proper times to learn to play marbles, to learn to flirt, to learn to wield a scalpel. Sometimes new lessons contradict old lessons.

Primary socialization is the basic socialization that occurs in childhood. The development of language and individual identity, the learning of cognitive skills and self-control, the internalization of moral standards and appropriate attitudes and motivations, and some understanding of societal roles are all involved in primary socialization.

Adult socialization is that which occurs beyond the childhood years. Although primary socialization lays the foundation for all later learning, it cannot completely prepare people for adulthood. For one thing, the meaning of gender varies by level of psychological and physiological development. Also, our age-graded society confronts individuals with new, gender-related role expectations as they move through life. People must learn how to be husbands and wives, how to be fathers and mothers, how to be widowers and widows.

Resocialization occurs when a new role or situation requires that a person replace established patterns of behavior and thought with new patterns (Campbell, 1975). Old behavior must be unlearned because it is incompatible in some way with new demands. An example of resocialization (which is more characteristic of adult socialization than of primary socialization) is learning new, nonsexist language forms such as "fisherperson" and "Ms."

Although Chapters Four to Six will be concerned with all three aspects of socialization, the major emphasis will be on primary socialization.

5. The term *socialization* carries value connotations. These considerations of "right" and "wrong," "ought" and "ought not" constitute a different category from those outlined above. Here, the sociologist acts as concerned citizen, not as scientist, in considering the desirability of differential socialization for girls and boys.

THE CONTENT OF GENDER SOCIALIZATION

The objective of this section is to establish the content of the lessons involved in Canadian gender socialization. Before we turn to specific content categories, some general remarks are needed in order to provide a context for our discussion.

Sex-typing may begin even before birth. During the last few months of pregnancy, an active fetus that kicks and moves a great deal is often defined by its mother as male. Similarly, folk wisdom relates a child's prenatal position to its sex. Boys are supposedly carried high and girls low (Lewis, 1972). From the moment of their entry into the world, female and male infants are handled differently. Girls are cuddled and talked to more, while boys are jostled and played with more roughly. Up to six months of age, boys are handled more than girls, but after that the amount of handling of male infants diminishes (Lewis, 1972).

Parents treat girls as if they were more fragile (Minton, Kagan and Levine, 1971; Pederson and Robson, 1969). Boys are more likely to be punished by spanking and other forms of physical punishment (Maccoby and Jacklin, 1974), while girls are more likely to receive gentle verbal reprimands (Serbin et al., 1973). Parents give boys of preschool and elementary school age much more freedom in the physical environment (freedom from special permission or adult accompaniment) than is the case for girls of the same age (Landy, 1965; Saegert and Hart, 1976). Parents are extremely upset by any sign that their boys are "sissies," while girls are encouraged to be neat and obedient and to be "feminine" in both behavior and dress. (Descriptions of these studies were compiled by Sidorowicz and Lunney, 1980.)

Fox (1977:809) concludes that early childhood studies of gender learning show that "even as infants, girls are expected to be, thought to be, and rewarded for being quieter, more passive, more controlled—in short, 'nicer' babies—than are boys."

Parents' choice of toys reinforces their gender expectations. Cultural norms, to a certain extent, determine which toys are "appropriate" for each sex. Toy manufacturers comply with these norms (Chafetz, 1974), and parents supply their children with sex-typed playthings. Ambert (1976:71) says that "boy toys . . . encourage rougher play, activity, creativity, mastery, and curiosity; girl toys, on the other hand, encourage passivity, observation, simple behaviour, and solitary play." Play has been described as children's "work." As their main occupation during the preschool years, play helps to create sex differences in taste, ambition, outlook and experience (Laws, 1979:246,248). A description of two studies of toy and activity preferences will serve to document the above points.

Sidorowicz and Lunney (1980) observed how adults interacted with

Baby X, an infant variously introduced as a boy, a girl, or without any gender information. The university student subjects were told that the study concerned the responses of infants to strangers, and were encouraged to talk with and touch the baby. In the room there were a small toy football, a doll and a teething ring (gender-neutral). When the baby was designated as male, 65% of the subjects chose the football. When it was designated as female, 80% of the subjects chose the doll. When no gender was assigned, 25% chose the football, 40% the doll and 35% the teething ring. These adults, then, acted in sex-stereotyped ways with the *same* infant, depending on the label provided.

Rheingold and Cook (1975) inventoried the contents of the rooms of children from one month to six years of age. Boys' rooms contained toys of more categories than girls' rooms (machines, sporting equipment, animal toys, vehicles, educational toys, etc.). The toys given to older boys encouraged activities away from home, while girls' toys encouraged domesticity.

Somewhat different conclusions about the impact of gender norms on activities emerged from Farley's (1979) analysis of the ways in which Toronto-area children used their leisure time. The author hypothesized greater participation in domestic work by girls, greater participation in employment away from home by boys, and more participation by girls in relatively passive, indoor activities, such as television watching and socializing. When the time spent on various activities was analyzed, the data failed to show strong relationships between sex and activity patterns. Boys spent 70-75% as much time on domestic work as girls did. Girls spent 60-70% as much time as boys on active recreation. Boys did not spend more time working away from home. However, girls reported more participation than boys in cooking, sewing, reading, listening to music and movies. Boys reported more participation in mechanical and electronic hobbies, sports and youth organizations. In general, Farley concluded that (a) sex-typing of activities has decreased in recent years, particularly in middle-class settings, and (b) the discrepancy between the time-budget results and self-reporting of activities may well reflect respondents' tendencies to give "sex-appropriate" answers when asked what pastimes they liked.

Over and over again, research demonstrates that activities associated with masculinity enjoy superior prestige. Laws (1979:248-49) cites research that found that boys avoided an attractive but "sex-inappropriate" toy to a greater degree than girls did, especially when the experimenter was present, and that boys showed more reluctance to play the role of a girl in a "pretend" telephone conversation. Similarly, a Canadian study (Berger and Gold, 1976) of problem-solving performance in young children reported that boys have a greater need to separate themselves from opposite-sex activities than do girls.

Very likely, the adoption of masculinity involved in tomboyism reflects girls' envy of boys' fun, freedom and superior position, rather than sexual abnormalities. Although the latter hypothesis sounds odd, the literature does contain the suggestion that tomboyism may be a precursor of transsexualism or lesbianism. However, Hyde, Rosenberg and Behrman (1977) tell us that 63% of a junior-high sample of girls reported being tomboys, and 51% of an adult women sample reported having been tomboys in their childhood. Can you imagine 60% or more of a sample of junior high school boys admitting to being "sissies" or expressing a preference for dresses, sewing and indoor games?

The discussion will now turn to a number of more specific categories of gender socialization content.

Societal Attitudes toward Women and Men

Children are socialized to fit into a society whose members hold various gender-related attitudes, covering such matters as the relative value of males and females, appropriate role definitions concerning division of labor within the family, in the work force and so on. Since Canadian society is not homogeneous, various subgroups adopt differing attitude positions, which could be represented on a continuum ranging from *traditional* to *egalitarian*. According to Boyd (1975a:155), the "traditional view generally sees women as belonging in the home and as responsible for child rearing," while the egalitarian view maintains that "women and men should participate equally in the home and in economic sectors."

Table 4.1, which contains nine questions taken from two Canadian studies (Boyd, 1975a; Gibbins, Ponting and Symons, 1978), provides us with a national sampling of gender attitudes.² The table describes the responses (expressed in terms of percentages) of the total sample, of females and males, and of Anglophones and Francophones. Since the questions were asked over a period of time, the year the information was collected has been indicated in parentheses after each question.

What does Table 4.1 tell us about Canadian gender attitudes? First, we must register some precautions. The issues dealt with in the table are hardly exhaustive. They represent only a sample of the attitudinal universe. (Table 4.2 deals with a different segment of this universe.) Also, because each measurement was made at one point in time, we cannot draw any conclusions about attitudinal changes over time. In general, Canadians adopt a relatively egalitarian position when the issue concerns the woman in the labor force, and the implications of her work for her family are left unmentioned (Items 1 and 2). This liberality, at the verbal level anyway, is also shown by two 1964 Gallup Poll items (Boyd, 1975:160) not included in the table. When asked, "If, in an emergency

TABLE 4.1
Canadian Attitudes toward Women

Attitudinal Item		Yes/ Agree/ Good %	No/ Disagree/ Bad %	Undecided/ Don't Know[a] %
1. In the business world more women should be promoted into senior management positions (1976)*	TOTAL	72	14	14
	Male	67	15	18
	Female	76	13	12
	Anglo	69	13	17
	Franco	76	15	9
2. Will you tell me if you approve or disapprove of this suggestion: that women who work should receive equal pay with men for the same kind of work (1971)**	TOTAL	86	11	2
	Male	84	14	2
	Female	89	9	2
	Anglo	89	9	2
	Franco	83	15	2
3. Although a wife's career may be important, she should give priority to helping her husband advance in his career (1976)*	TOTAL	69	19	13
	Male	65	21	15
	Female	71	18	11
	Anglo	68	18	14
	Franco	74	20	6
4. Would you consider a decline in the husband's importance [in the Canadian] family to be good or bad? (1973)**	TOTAL	20	63	17
	Male	23	58	19
	Female	17	68	5
	Anglo	23	59	18
	Franco	14	72	14
5. When children are young a mother's place is in the home (1976)*	TOTAL	81	10	9
	Male	83	9	8
	Female	80	11	9
	Anglo	83	8	9
	Franco	81	13	6
6. A woman should have the sole right to decide whether or not to have an abortion (1976)*	TOTAL	56	34	10
	Male	56	35	10
	Female	56	33	10
	Anglo	55	33	12
	Franco	54	37	8
7. If your party chose a woman as federal leader, and if she was qualified for the job of prime minister, would you vote for her? (1964)**	TOTAL	71	25	4
	Male	70	26	4
	Female	72	24	3
	Anglo	71	26	3
	Franco	72	24	5

Attitudinal Item		Yes/ Agree/ Good %	No/ Disagree/ Bad %	Undecided/ Don't Know[a] %
8. [Asked of women only.] There has been a great deal of discussion in the past two or three years about women's liberation. Have you found the average man's attitude toward women has changed because of this? (1973)**	TOTAL	37	63	[b]
	Anglo	30	70	[b]
	Franco	52	48	[b]
9. [Asked of men only.] There has been a great deal of discussion in the past two or three years about women's liberation. Have you found that your attitude toward women has changed because of this? (1973)**	TOTAL	13	82	5
	Anglo	15	80	4
	Franco	8	89	3

* Taken from Gibbins, Ponting and Symons (1978)
** Taken from Boyd (1975a)
[a] Because of rounding, some totals do not equal 100%.
[b] "Don't know" option not provided respondents to Item 8.

you had to call in an unknown doctor and it turned out to be a woman, would you have more or less confidence in her ability than in a male doctor?" 81% said "the same," 13% "less confidence" and 5% "more confidence." A parallel question regarding a woman lawyer elicited the following responses: 65% "same," 25% "less confidence," 8% "more confidence." Seventy percent say they are willing to accept a female prime minister (Item 7). However, the liberality melts away when women's work may conflict with family responsibility (Items 3 and 5). Opinions are polarized on the abortion issue (6). Finally, most agree that the weakening of husbands' importance in the Canadian family is unfortunate (4) and that the women's movement has not changed male attitudes (7, 8).

How does the sex of the respondent affect attitudinal position? Sex makes surprisingly little difference. The females are slightly more egalitarian on the work issues (1, 2) and slightly more traditional on the family-related items (3, 4). What about mother tongue? Although some of the differences are small, there is a tendency (which is supported by Gallup Poll data not included in Table 4.1) for Francophones to be more liberal about work issues (1) and less liberal about family-related issues (3, 4). Notice the discrepancy between the viewpoints of Francophone males and females regarding Items 8 and 9. What is a possible explanation?

TABLE 4.2
Calgary (Alberta) Attitudes toward Women and Men
N = 928

Attitudinal Item	Agree %	Disagree %	N/R %	Sex	Education	Age
1. A man with a family should be hired before a woman even if she has slightly better qualifications	38.4	57.9	3.7	N.S.	*	*
2. Children of employed mothers are not as well adjusted as those of mothers who stay home	44.2	5.16	4.2	*	*	N.S.
3. If a woman were offered a good job in another city, the husband should be willing to move there with her	28.4	66.3	5.2[a]	N.S.	N.S.	*
4. When a husband and wife both work, housework should be shared equally	85.8	11.3	2.8	N.S.	N.S.	*
5. It is only natural for little boys to want to be doctors and little girls to want to be nurses	35.3	60.9	3.9	*	*	*
6. People really should not give a boy a doll on his birthday	57.5	38.7	3.9	*	N.S.	*
7. A man should not feel embarrassed about crying if things go badly	85.0	11.8	3.1	*	*	*

Attitudinal Item	Agree %	Disagree %	N/R %	Sex	Education	Age
8. If a man does something considered traditionally as feminine, he should feel less of a man	11.5	84.6	3.9	*	*	*
9. Women should be encouraged to keep their maiden name in addition to their married name	23.7	70.8	5.5	N.S.	*	N.S.
10. Women should have the right to an abortion	63.0	32.7	4.2	*	*	*

NOTE: Data was taken from 1975 Calgary (Alberta) study of the relationships between the work and family institutions. Principal investigators were Merlin B. Brinkerhoff, James S. Frideres, Eugen Lupri, Marlene Mackie and Donald L. Mills, all of the University of Calgary.

a Columns may not total 100% because of rounding errors.
* One-tailed, chi square, <.05 (a statistically significant association exists between the attitudinal item and the demographic variable).

N.S.: The association between the attitudinal item and the demographic variable is not statistically significant.

Table 4.2 provides information about the gender attitudes of a Calgary (Alberta) sample that the author and her colleagues interviewed in 1975. There are several good reasons for devoting yet more space to this topic. The ideal method of establishing empirically the content of Canadian gender roles would involve systematic study of how girls and boys, men and women actually behave, as well as the reactions elicited by nonconformity. Because we do not have nearly enough information of this sort, the best available indicators are studies that describe how people believe men and women ought to behave. In addition, Table 4.2 tells us more than Table 4.1 about male norms. Finally, the table tells us whether or not these attitudes are statistically associated with sex, education and age.

First of all, let us take a look at the attitudes of the total sample. Although most agreed that housework should be shared in a family where both adults work (Item 4), the husband's work still takes priority over the wife's (Items 1, 3). The sample is divided over the fate of the working mother's children (2). A surprising amount of latitude is given to men (7, 8). In theory, they may cry if they feel so inclined. Sex-typed occupational ambitions are not supported (5). However, the majority feel that little boys should not play with dolls (6). More than 70% say that married women should not be encouraged to retain their maiden name (9). The findings of tables 4.1 and 4.2 on the abortion issue (10) are nearly identical.

How do sex, education and age affect Western Canadian gender attitudes? Although sex differences were significant on only six of the ten items, males were more traditional than females on every item except 10 (abortion). Further, the males took an especially conservative position on the items pertaining to males. For instance, 51% of the females and 64% of the males felt that a doll was an inappropriate present for a boy (6). With regard to education, on every single item low education was associated with traditionalism. People with junior high school or less tended to be the most conservative. Finally, as we might expect, increasing age was statistically associated with traditionalism; age "brings resistance to change because the individual has a longer investment in the traditional ways, and because of the personal difficulty in changing deeply ingrained habits and beliefs" (Staines, Tavris and Jayaratne, 1974:55).

Do Canadians differ from Americans in their family patterns and gender attitudes? This is a question of major importance to gender relations specialists in this country. Eichler (1977a:410), for example, warns against the faulty assumption that "the match between the two societies is so exact that theories and data are transferable without any alteration." Further, she says, "Feminist researchers in Canada are in fact overwhelmed by the mass of feminist research flowing into the country from the United States, which is distributed more widely within Canada than Canadian publications because of a more elaborate distribution system" (Eichler, 1977a:422). The literature emphasizes two major sources of Canadian-American familial differences: the French-English dualism and the ethnic diversity existing here, and Canada's allegedly greater traditionalism and inegalitarianism. The latter differences are seen to flow from the differing historical origins of the two countries (the United States was born of revolution, Canada was not).

What does the very scarce empirical research bearing upon this matter have to tell us? Williams (1975) found that Canadians, more than Americans, give priority to the rights of parents over those of children. Therefore, Canadian mothers are, according to Williams, more independent of their children, less "tyrannized" by them. Schreiber (1975) compared Canadian-American responses to four opinion poll questions that were asked in both countries. She found either no difference or somewhat *more* liberal attitudes among Canadians. Finally, Mackie and Brinkerhoff (1982) compared familial/gender attitudes of people born in Canada and people born in the United States. Not one of the fifty-five relationships examined proved to be statistically significant. Although we must be cautious in our conclusions because of the limited number of studies available, it does appear that American-Canadian differences are less extensive than previously suspected. Certainly, no support is provided for greater Canadian traditionalism. (For information on American gender attitudes, see Mason, Czajka and Arber [1976], Thornton and Freedman [1979], and Cherlin and Walters [1981].)

Stereotypes as Gender Socialization Content

Stereotypes, consensual beliefs about masculine and feminine qualities, are an important segment of society's gender attitudes. There is no need to repeat what was said about stereotypes in Chapter Two. Instead, we wish to place sex stereotyping in the context of lessons of socialization, and to point out the relationship of these societal definitions of masculinity and femininity to children's occupational aspirations.

The first of these objectives is quite straightforward. Evidence exists that Canadian children learn about stereotypes as part of the socialization process. Lambert's (1971) questionnaire study of the gender imagery of 7,500 Canadian children, ten to sixteen years old, established that the children were aware of differential societal expectations for females and males. He measured perception of gender role differentiation in terms of appropriate traits, behavior, tasks, and peer and authority relations. Although we do not really know whether it is so, stereotypes (as well as the other components of gender attitudes) presumably serve as abstract guides to behavior. Incidentally, Lambert reported that boys were considerably more traditional in their thinking about the sexes than girls. This opinion is congruent with the finding of Percival and Percival (1979) that Maritime male university students stereotyped more than their female counterparts.

Both gender attitudes in general and stereotypes in particular contain reference to what are appropriate major time and energy investments for women and men. According to this ideal division of labor, men are expected to work outside the home, marry and support their families, while women are expected to marry, carry the major responsibility for child rearing and rely on men for financial support and social status. Although the woman too may work outside the home, attracting a suitable mate and looking after his interests (and eventually those of her children) take priority over serious occupational commitment.

Occupational Sex-Typing

The sex-typing of occupations is a central element of the societal script for masculinity and femininity learned by children. Traditionally, women have been expected to engage in "female" occupations such as secretary, librarian, nurse or elementary school teacher, while men enter "masculine" fields such as plumbing, engineering and law. Olympic figure-skating champion Toller Cranston says that his father, who "couldn't quite believe what he had hatched . . . could never quite relate to [my] skating" (*Today*, 27 June 1981:4).

Schlossberg and Goodman (1972) discovered that five-year-old kindergarten children were already aware of these norms. When these children were asked to set occupational goals, 83% of the girls and 97% of the boys chose occupations consistent with the traditional gender norms. Barty (1971) (described in Kimball, 1973) found that when ten- to thirteen-year-old Vancouver children were asked to choose between being a doctor and being a nurse, 70% of the girls chose to be a nurse while 80% of the boys chose to be a doctor. (However, sex-typing did not occur when they were asked whether a boy or a girl would win a hypothetical university scholarship.)

Are these decade-old results outdated? Apparently not. Kalin, Stoppard and Burt (1980) asked 156 Queen's University students, who were allegedly taking part in a "person perception" experiment, to pretend that they were guidance counsellors. They were presented with descriptions of twelve fictitious students in their final year of high school and asked to rate each student's suitability for study in eight occupational fields. The sex of the fictitious students was varied by changing first names. Here is an example of one fictitious student:

Gloria (George) Rutherford is nineteen. She (he) has an IQ of 100 and maintains an average of 65%. Her (his) father works for a newspaper. Her (his) mother is actively involved in several social events and is presently organizing a church bazaar. Gloria (George) helps to run a youth program at the church and derives much personal satisfaction out of talking with varied sorts of people. She (he) also enjoys music and works at Dominion to make enough money to invest in a high fidelity stereo. She (he) is a member of the U.N. Club at school. Gloria (George) is a good student and is a reliable individual. She (he) is on the class executive and does a commendable job. She (he) is a friendly girl (boy).

The possible future occupations (male and female) were chosen so that they were all of similar social class level. The eight were: social worker (F), commercial traveller (M), surveyor (M), librarian (F), engineering technician (M), nursing (F), sales manager (M) and occupational therapist (F).

Kalin, Stoppard and Burt reported a number of interesting results. The fictitious female students were rated as more suitable for female than for male occupations, while the reverse was true for the male students. Although the authors say that blatant sexism is uncommon at the university, the women subjects were as likely as the men to make judgments along traditional sex lines. Finally, the suitability of all the fictitious high-school students, males as well as females, was rated to be higher for female than male occupations. The authors explain the last result as follows: "It is as if participants saw female occupations as easier and therefore thought that anyone could do them. If this impression is correct, participants showed a general devaluation of female occupations."

Masculine and Feminine Traits

The future adult activities of children require cultivation of appropriate skills, attitudes and comportment. A cross-cultural survey of sex differences in socialization among 110 nonliterate cultures (Barry et al., 1957) reported that most societies emphasize nurturance, obedience and responsibility in the socialization of girls, and independence and achievement in the socialization of boys. Greenglass (1973:110) suggests that attributes such as independence, aggressiveness and competitiveness are encouraged in boys because they are essential for their future occupational success. Girls, on the other hand, are expected to derive their self-esteem from heterosexual relationships. Although girls may not necessarily be encouraged to be dependent and passive, they are usually not encouraged to be independent and forthright (Freeman, 1971:131). Bronfenbrenner (1961:260), quoted in Freeman (1971:131), mentions that a difference in goals results in differential treatment of the two sexes: "With sons, socialization seems to focus primarily on directing and constraining the boys' impact on the environment. With daughters, the aim is rather to protect the girl from the impact of the environment. The boy is being prepared to mold his world, the girl to be molded by it."

In recent years, the men's liberation literature has argued that boys, as well as girls, have a sad socialization tale to tell. The traditional male role has placed greater restriction on men's behavior and actually grants them fewer choices in life-style than women have. Male socialization is the more stringent because more is expected of men than women, in adult life. Middle-class males, in particular, are permitted few options other than full-time employment, and are discouraged from expressing emotions and developing close relationships with other males (Baker and Bakker, 1980). The instrumental component of the male stereotype and the expressive component of the female stereotype reflect the personality traits associated with the traditional sexual division of labor.

Knowledge and Skills

If socialization in general were being considered, the knowledge instilled would cover everything required to function as a member of Canadian

society, including language, table manners, the meaning of role relationships, even geography. The specific process of *gender socialization*, on the
other hand, refers to the acquisition of the specific knowledge and skills
required to be female or male. Though more overlap now occurs between
male and female experience (Farley, 1979) and, consequently, less sex-
typed knowledge is needed today than in the past, some differentiation
still exists. Girls learn to apply mascara to their eyelashes and boys learn
to tie Windsor knots in their neckties. Girls cook and sew, while boys
engage in mechanical and electronic hobbies.

Try this exercise. Ask yourself what you would need to know if you
were to "pass" successfully as a member of the opposite sex. Another way
of phrasing this question is to inquire about the evidence you would use to
categorize a newcomer into your social circle as male or female. The "best
test" of gender supposedly involves the nature of the primary and secondary physiological sexual characteristics. However, "in terms of serving as
the basis for social relationships, there are very few occasions in which the
physiological test of gender is relevant, appropriate, or applied" (Lauer
and Handel, 1977:286). Remember, gender is a social matter.

Garfinkel's (1967:116-85) case study of "Agnes" provides insight into
the general question of how gender is socially established, as well as the
particular issue of gender-associated skills and knowledge. Agnes, who
had been raised as a boy, was equipped with a normal penis and scrotum.
However, "she" began taking estrogen at age twelve, probably because
"she" was a transsexual, who (like James Morris above) believed "she"
was a female trapped unfairly in a male body. Eventually she became
completely feminized in her secondary sex characteristics (breasts,
absence of body hair, shape of pelvic girdle). When Garfinkel encountered her, she had applied for a sex-change operation and was "passing" as a woman. Because Agnes became female abruptly, she did not
have the usual long period of gender socialization to learn the details
associated with femaleness. Instead, she had to suppress evidence of
masculinity and learn femininity as she went about portraying herself as a
bona fide, 120% female. Her femininity could be claimed only at the cost
of vigilance and work. Success in passing entailed hiding her ownership of
a penis. Consequently, she avoided driving a car lest an accident render
her unconscious and result in exposure. For the same reason, she avoided
solitary dating and drinking. More to the point, Agnes was serving a
secret apprenticeship to learn female skills. In the early 1960s, "acting like
a lady" involved learning about cooking, dressmaking, shopping and
home management skills. As well, Agnes was not to want her own way,
offer her opinions when she should be retiring, be sharp in manner when
she should be sweet, complain instead of taking things as they were, pro-
fess sophistication instead of being innocent, or demand services instead
of trying to give her male companion pleasure and comfort (Garfinkel,
1967:146-47).

The "appropriate" gender knowledge and skills will vary over the life cycle. Little girls learn to prefer dolls, not trucks, to attend to limb position and posture when wearing dresses, to converse and to get along nicely with peers and adults. Adolescent girls learn to flirt tastefully, to apply cosmetics and to fear mathematics. Women learn the gender-appropriate details of being a worker, mate, parent, divorcée or widow. The age grading of gender scripts sometimes involves painful resocialization. Old behavior must be discarded to make way for new patterns. (A two-year-old boy may cry when he is frightened, but a twelve-year-old boy who climbs into his mother's lap and whimpers is thought to be odd.)

FEMALE AND MALE SELVES

According to our definition, one of the products of socialization is selfhood. Since gender socialization is only a part of this learning process (and since the matter of the emergence and multifaceted development of the social self in its entirety is not at issue here), the relevant effects to be discussed include the development of gender identity and the impact of sex upon the self-concept, including self-imagery and self-esteem. However, our immediate task is to specify the meanings of all these interrelated concepts.

We begin with the most inclusive of the concepts, the *self*. Although we know instinctively what we mean when we say we have a self, the *self* is an elusive concept, difficult to define. Gordon (1968:116) says, "The self is *not* a thing; it is a complex *process* of continuing interpretative activity—simultaneously the person's located subjective stream of *consciousness* (both reflexive and nonreflexive, including perceiving, thinking, planning, evaluating, choosing, etc.) *and* the resultant accruing *structure of self-conceptions*" [emphasis in original].

The fact that the self is a "verb-like" process, not a "noun-like" thing, means that it forms and changes as a result of ongoing interaction. *Self-concept*, in turn, refers to the person's subjective cognitions and evaluations of himself/herself, to his/her self-image and self-esteem. *Self-image* refers to the kind of person one thinks one is, and *self-esteem* refers to how favorably one regards oneself (Lauer and Handel, 1977:176).

The term *identity* is a close relative of the term *self*. The existence of a separate word serves to emphasize the fact that the self is a social phenomenon. Every society has certain categories or ways of classifying its members, which are important to its functioning. The individual's placement in these categories determines how that individual is known or identified by other people and also by herself/himself. *Social identity* is more general than *gender identity*. About the former concept Goffman (1971:189) says, "By 'social identity,' I mean the broad social categories (and the organizations and groups that function like categories) to which an individual can belong and be seen as belonging: age-grade, sex, class, regiment, and so forth." After inspection of their genitalia at birth, infants are placed in one or another of two sex categories (or classes), and once again, quoting Goffman (1977:304), "Insofar as the individual builds up a sense of who and what he is by referring to his sex class and judging himself in terms of the ideals of masculinity (or femininity), one may speak of *gender identity* [emphasis in original]."

Gender Identity in Young Children

Though a child's adult socializers place it in a sex class at birth, it is a few years before the child responds to himself/herself in terms of gender. By the age of three, a child can accurately and consistently answer the question, "Are you a girl or a boy?" At the same age, children show preferences for either "girl" or "boy" toys and activities (Kessler and McKenna, 1978:101, 102). This timing seems to agree with researcher John Money's notion of *critical periods*. Hermaphrodites whose sex identifications were changed before the age of three or four displayed relatively little maladjustment (Yussen and Santrock, 1978:397). Children of this age do not have a clear understanding of the reasons for their self-attribution or toy preferences.

The fact that young children do not interpret gender in the same way that adults do is shown by studies that ask children to draw pictures of boys and girls, or to apply gender labels to such pictures. Researchers report that three-year-olds are considerably better than two-year-olds in attributing the correct gender, but one-fourth of the three-year-olds still make mistakes. One hundred percent accuracy does not come until they are five or six. Young children use hair length and clothing, not anatomy, as gender cues. Often their reasons for saying that a picture is of a boy or girl are even more peculiar. When six-year-old Jesse was asked what made the figure in his picture a girl, he answered, "Because there is a sun and girls go out on sunny days" (Kessler and McKenna, 1978:81, 103, 105).

Names, Self and Gender Identity

Names form a basis for the development of the self and remain an integral part of social identity, including gender identity (Mackie, 1977c). As a first step toward self-awareness, the child learns his or her name. (I am Simon. I am Suzy.) The reverse also holds true. Loss of name symbolizes loss of self, as Wolfenstein (1968:269) notes, in referring to Lewis Carroll's nonsense poem, "The Hunting of the Snark." The hero's name loss and consumable nicknames anticipate his eventual demise at the hands of a beast.

He had wholly forgotten his name.
He would answer to "Hi!" or to any loud cry,
Such as "Fry me!" or "Fritter my wig!"
To "What-you-may-call-um!" or "What-was-his-name!"
But especially "Thing-um-a-jig!"
While, for those who preferred a more forcible word,
He had different names from these:
His intimate friends called him "Candle-ends,"
And his enemies "Toasted-Cheese."

A given name individualizes the infant and classifies it by sex. Baptizing a child "Mary" simultaneously separates this infant from other infants and signifies its femaleness. A feminist's parable of a "Secret Scientific Xperiment" to undermine sex stereotyping tells the tale of a child named "X":

> Once upon a time, a baby named X was born. This baby was named X so that nobody could tell whether it was a boy or a girl. Its parents could tell, of course, but they couldn't tell anybody else. [Gould, 1972:74]

The tale also makes the point that gender "is almost wholly a social, not biological, consequence of the workings of society" (Goffman, 1977:303).

Given names, surnames and titles of address also communicate society's differential evaluation of the sexes. Consequently, they serve as one of the more subtle lessons of gender socialization. Name choice can signify the superior status of males. For example, *males* are stigmatized by the feminine connotations of bisexual names such as "Marion." Amy Vanderbilt (1967:187-88) advised that, "Giving a boy a name that could be mistaken for a girl's name is to put him at a psychological disadvantage. There are so many handicaps on the way up to adulthood, why add one more in a name?" Moreover, females often receive male diminutives (Erica, Andrea), but the reverse situation is rare. Other naming practices reflect the superior value placed on male children. Boys are more likely than girls to be named after relatives, and "boys' names are more traditional, less currently fashionable than girls' names" (Rossi, 1965:504). The fact that the family name is carried on by males also enters into this situation. Finally, female Victorian writers and even modern female painters have been forced to assume masculine names in order to have their work judged on its own merits (Rosenberg and Fliegal, 1971:660). Female impersonators are among the few males in history to adopt female pseudonyms.

Because the feminist movement is "a means to the end of self-discovery and identity" (Rosenberg and Bergstrom, 1975:9), its proponents' scrutiny of their own name-labels is not surprising. Most of their concern has focused on the custom (*not* a legal requirement) that women take their husbands' name on marriage. The fact that it is the women, not the men, who change their names upon marriage suggests that the married status effects more profound change in women's lives than in men's. In addition, this name change symbolizes the married woman's forfeiture of a portion of her social identity. According to early feminists (Friedan, 1963:41), the married woman exists for and through her husband and children. She becomes "Mrs." in all but the most personal contexts, thus advertising her marital status in a way not required of her husband. Incidentally, Amy Vanderbilt (1967:147) approved of professional women working under their own names, partly because the practice protected her husband "should she engage in any activities that might run counter to his own professional or business interests." The possibility of the husband's activities harming his wife's reputation was not considered.

Although more women are substituting "Ms." for "Mrs.," and retaining their maiden name, this practice does not really solve the identity problem. "When I divorced for the second time, I thought I should get back 'my own name.' What was that? My first husband's last name wasn't my name. My late father's last name wasn't my name. I thought of taking my mother's birth name, but realized that wasn't her name, but her late father's. I came to the conclusion that a woman has no name" (Lee, 1976:2). The fact that some radical feminists invented new names for themselves, such as Ann Fury, Dair Struggle and Ann Forfreedom, carried a clear message.

The Impact of Gender Identity upon Self-Imagery

Because sociologists (Kuhn, 1960) have argued that gender is an axis of self-definition that permeates the smallest details of everyday existence and shapes life opportunities, some fairly extensive gender differences in self-imagery might be expected. Although very little evidence is available, the literature tends to *assume* this relationship. For example, Yorburg (1974:vii) states that, "in any particular society, at any particular time, these learned, sex-typed role definitions and expectations typically result in differing basic self-images . . . for men and for women." McClelland (1965:182) says that "interpersonal relations define [women's] self-image." According to Erikson (1964), women's self-concepts are determined in particular by relationships with husbands or potential spouses.

This expectation was tested by a study (Mackie, 1978b) related to the one described in Chapter Two (Mackie, 1980b), which examined the relation between sex stereotypes and self-imagery. The self-imagery of a sample of 797 Calgary (Alberta) residents was measured by means of the Twenty Statements Test (TST). Four hypotheses were put forth.

The first hypothesis predicted that gender would be more salient for males than for females. Males have more prestige, power and freedom than females, and it was assumed that a status that is culturally esteemed will be prominent in the individual self-concept structure. Saliency was measured by the relative mention of gender in TST inventories. The data did not support the hypothesis, for gender was cited by 34.5% of the males and 34.3% of the females (chi-square, p. < .50). Comparing the relative level of gender mention with the same sample's mention of the statuses of religion, nationality and ethnicity helps interpret this result. One-third mentioned gender, 18% religion, 10% nationality and 4% ethnic background. Therefore, it appears that gender matters and, contrary to the initial hypothesis, it matters equally to both sexes.

The second hypothesis predicted that marital status would be more salient in female than in male self-imagery. According to traditional gender norms, the life goal of women is to establish and maintain a family. The fact that the wife's social existence and life-style derive from marriage to a particular male should be reflected in the more prominent place that marital status occupies in her self-imagery, compared to that of her husband. The results supported the second hypothesis. Marital status was mentioned by 80.8% of the women and 75.0% of the men (chi-square, p. < .05).

The third hypothesis predicted that parental status would be more salient in the self-imagery of mothers than in the self-imagery of fathers. This prediction rested on society's expectation that children are the particular responsibility of the mother. (When a baby is born it is the mother, not the father, who might decide to interrupt her career. When a couple separates, custody of the children is usually awarded to the mother.) The fact of parenthood was mentioned significantly more often by mothers (94.3%) than fathers (85.0%) (chi-square p. < .0005).

Finally, because traditional gender norms place emphasis on men's work outside the home, but not on women's, the fourth hypothesis predicted that work would be more salient in the self-imagery of men than in that of women in the labor force. The data supported the hypothesis: the male self-imagery contained significantly more work statements (p. <0005).

Though there are many other dimensions of self-imagery that might be explored, this study demonstrates that gender does have an impact on self-imagery.

Gender and Individual Self-Esteem

Theoretically, there are several reasons for expecting women to evaluate themselves less highly than do men (Whitehurst, 1979). For instance, the Freudian perspective would expect women to develop less self-esteem. After all, the "woman's self is one that is and only can be a 'poor version of a man'—a woman is like a man, but with something missing"

(Whitehurst, 1979:76). The *symbolic interactionist* perspective, which stresses that the self arises out of social interaction, would expect the cultural devaluation of women to result in lower levels of self-esteem. If the self mirrors society, how could it be otherwise? Nevertheless, despite the persuasiveness of these theoretical arguments, the empirical evidence in general fails to establish a sex difference in self-esteem (Maccoby and Jacklin, 1974; Whitehurst, 1979).

The Calgary study discussed in the foregoing section (Mackie, 1978) anticipated that Canadian society's differential evaluation of the sexes would have individual consequences. Therefore, female self-esteem was expected to be lower than male self-esteem. The Rosenberg (1965) Self-Esteem Scale, which records maximum esteem as ten, was used. When male ($\bar{x}$ = 8.86, S.D. = 1.46) and female ($\bar{x}$ = 8.82, S.D. = 1.34) mean reponses were compared, no sex differences in self-esteem were found (nonsignificant t of 0.44).

How can we explain the fact that women and men apparently have equally high self-esteem? A methodological reason sometimes advanced is that self-esteem is a difficult concept to measure. Therefore, the argument continues, the clumsiness of our present techniques is obscuring real sex differences. (For example, the numerically high scores on the Rosenberg Scale reported above strongly suggest that social desirability is implicated, that is, research subjects responded as though they had high self-esteem, because our society expects people to be self-confident.)

Deaux (1976:36-37) suggests that one possible explanation of why the literature fails to support H. L. Mencken's statement ("No healthy male is ever actually modest. . . . His conversation is one endless boast— often covert, but always undiluted"), is that both sexes accept their societal roles. Essentially, this argument suggests that men and women compare themselves to a different standard, and that self-esteem is relative to this standard of an ideal man or an ideal woman, rather than an absolute measure. We must conclude "that there are no differences between men and women in their overall level of self-esteem, though the basis for self-esteem may be somewhat different" (Deaux, 1976:38).

Gender and Group Self-Esteem

The fact that females as a group are valued less than males has led to the expectation that females despise their own sex. This belief is a long-standing one: " 'I never yet knew a tolerable woman to be fond of her own sex,' wrote Jonathan Swift, who wasn't terribly fond of either men or women. Indeed, many women throughout history have been willing to proclaim the inferiority of their own sex. 'I'm glad I'm not a man,' confessed Madame de Staël, 'for if I were, I'd be obliged to marry a woman' " (Tavris and Offir, 1977:187).

Frequently, the reason for this self-denigration has been attributed to women's minority-group status, a line of thought that draws parallels between women's situation and that of disadvantaged ethnic groups. The "minority group" label, of course, refers to the discriminatory treatment accorded females, not their numbers. In a paper published three decades ago, Helen Hacker (1951) was one of the first sociologists to consider systematically the implications of depicting women as a minority group. Among the implications was the notion of group self-hatred: "This feeling is exhibited in the person's tendency to denigrate other members of the group, to accept the dominant group's stereotyped conception of them, and to indulge in 'mea culpa' breast-beating. He may seek to exclude himself from the image of his group, or he may point the finger of scorn at himself" (Hacker, 1951:61).

Twenty years later, Freeman (1971) suggested that the "traits due to victimization" described in Allport's (1954) analysis of ethnic prejudice also applied to women. She says, "Included are such personality characteristics as sensitivity, submission, fantasies of power, desire for protection, indirectness, ingratiation, petty revenge and sabotage, sympathy, extremes of both self and group hatred and self and group glorification, display of flashy status symbols, compassion for the underprivileged, identification with the dominant group's norms, and passivity" (Freeman, 1971:125).

Although the above quotation encompasses a host of testable hypotheses (Do women, like blacks, have a special affinity for Cadillacs? [Akers, 1968]), the issue here is group self-hatred. (Chapter Seven considers the theoretical utility of viewing women as a minority group.)

Several studies of sex-linked bias in the evaluation of performance have provided empirical support for the proposition of female group self-hatred. Goldberg (1968) asked female college students to judge scholarly articles on architecture, law, city planning, etc. Identical articles were supposedly written by either Joan T. McKay or John T. McKay. Goldberg showed that females rated the performance of females lower than that of males. That is, the same article was rated more favorably when it was attributed to a male author. Labovitz's (1974) study of Western Canadian student response to fictitious names denoting ethnic group or sex (cited earlier) found sex bias to be far less serious than ethnic bias. However, some tendency was reported for female students to evaluate the article attributed to Edith Blake (vs. Edward Blake) less favorably than did male students. Another study (Pheterson, Kiesler and Goldberg, 1971), which required women to rate paintings attributed to either female or male painters, found similar results when the painting was described as an entry in an art competition. However, when the paintings were described as contest winners, no sex prejudice emerged.

Recent studies (Percival and Percival, 1979) do not find women prejudiced against women, possibly because it is now unfashionable to express such sentiments. Operation of the "social desirability effect" is suggested by yet another author-evaluation study (Starer and Denmark, 1974). Female subjects, when tested individually, were prejudiced against their own sex. However, when tested in groups, they discriminated against male authors. Before any hard-and-fast conclusions can be reached, we need information about women's reactions to women in a variety of contexts. "Change of name" studies provide us with very limited knowledge.

A recently unearthed variant of female antifeminism has been dubbed the "Queen Bee syndrome" (Staines et al., 1974). Again, group self-disapproval revolves around the issues of competence and success. However, in this case, women who have "made it" in the male professional world judge women who have not, and find them wanting. Although these successful women are in an excellent position to advance the cause of women, they do not identify with their own sex. "The true Queen Bee has made it in the 'man's world' of work, while running a house and family with her left hand. 'If I can do it without a whole movement to help me,' runs her attitude, 'so can all those other women.' " (Staines et al., 1974:55). Research has isolated several reasons for her attitude. As a token representative of a minority group, the Queen Bee has probably adopted a countermilitant stance as the price of acceptance in a male organization. The bargain likely was unconscious. The first women in the male arena had male colleagues and took on male attitudes toward women. As well, the successful woman may relish the fact that she is special; "it can be fun to be the rare, one-in-a-million woman at the top. Why let in the great unwashed and spoil it all?" (Staines et al., 1974:57). Finally, the Queen Bee who is successful in a male-dominated field feels little animosity toward the system that has permitted her to reach the top.

Though there is empirical confirmation of the existence of Queen Bees, the term has apparently received sufficient publicity to become an unjust epithet for any female boss. The successful man may be labelled "aggressive," the successful woman "bitchy."

THEORIES OF GENDER SOCIALIZATION

We have established the point that sex differences are mainly the product of socialization, not biology. However, simply to conclude that sex differences are learned still leaves a great deal unsaid. Exactly how does this learning occur? Three theoretical perspectives attempt to explain the detailed processes involved in gender socialization: the *identification*, *social learning* and *cognitive-developmental* theories. This section will describe and assess each of these theoretical approaches in turn. It is important to note that none of these theories was specifically developed to explain gender socialization. Rather, they are all general psychological theories about human learning and development, which are applicable to sex-typed behavior as well as other sorts of behavior (Stockard and Johnson, 1980:178).

Identification Theories

The various identification theories of the acquisition of sex-typed behavior originate in Freudian psychology, which has been described as "the most intellectually exciting theory of socialization known to modern social science" (Schellenberg, 1978:5). Be that as it may, psychoanalytic theory, as a biologically based theory of psychosexual development, has already been dealt with (Chapter Three) and only a brief reiteration is needed here.

Identification was Freud's term for the child's unconscious need to be like the same-sex parent. The child's need to mold his or her own "ego ideal" on the parent went beyond mere copying of parental mannerisms, to incorporating ("introjecting") the same-sex parent's personality. Thus, Freud saw identification as the means through which individuals conformed to societal demands, and uncivilized infants became transformed into responsible adults (Frieze et al., 1978:97).

According to Freud, the motivation for identification is biologically rooted in the ownership or nonownership of a penis. Moreover, the motivation is a dual one: it includes the fear of loss of love as well as the fear of retaliation. During the oedipal phase, the boy becomes afraid that his sexual interest in his mother will lead to his castration. This fear motivates the boy to identify rather than compete with his father. Since the girl has no penis, she cannot form a defensive identification with either parent. The result is a weak superego. Her penis envy is channelled into the wish to bear a male child. Fear of loss of her mother's love explains her continuing identification with the mother. Freud believed that the differing processes underlying male and female identification explained sex differences in personality (Frieze et al., 1978:97-99).

Contemporary identification theorists (e.g., Mischel, 1970; Mussen, 1969) de-emphasize the sexual motivation for imitating or modelling parental behavior. Instead, they hypothesize that children are motivated to imitate *powerful* models, or *nurturant* models or *similar* models. Evidence does show that, other things being equal, children will imitate the more dominant, powerful figure rather than the less dominant, and will imitate the more nurturant rather than the less nurturant model. The problem is that no theoretical reason is given to explain why the power or nurturance of a model should affect the two sexes differently.

The problem, to restate, is "why children of the two sexes should learn *different things*—sex-typed things [emphasis in original]" (Maccoby and Jacklin, 1974:287). Two explanations have been offered: (1) that the same-sex model is more available, and (2) when both same-sex and opposite-sex models are available, children select on the basis of perceived similarity. In neither case is the empirical evidence persuasive (Maccoby and Jacklin, 1974:286-90). With regard to similarity, Stockard and Johnson (1980:188) point out that while there is some evidence that older children tend to imitate selectively, it is difficult "to see how very young children who have not established a concept of their own sex could know which parent they were more similar to."

Despite the plausibility of the notion of "identification," social scientists have had difficulty in devising a test to determine whether or not identification has occurred (Tavris and Offir, 1977:169). One such test (which has logical deficiencies) proposes that if children turn out like their parents, then identification was responsible. For example, sociologists have suggested that the nature of the mother's occupation should influence the daughter's work aspirations. However, contrary to this hypothesis, Brinkerhoff's (1977) study of Western Canadian high-school girls found that the mother's work (whether or not she worked outside the home, whether or not she had a prestigious job) did not have much effect on the daughter's work ambition. Does this finding imply a failure of identification?

More generally speaking, although the discovery of similarities between child and same-sex parent would not prove that these similarities had occurred through modelling, finding *little* similarity would give us reason to question the entire modelling approach. "In fact, correlation studies of parent-child similarities find that children are not especially similar to their own parents, and that it is not at all clear that girls are more like their mothers and boys are more like their fathers. This is true for both young children and young adults, and for both non-sex-typed and sex-typed behavior" (Stockard and Johnson, 1980:188).

Finally, a major problem with identification theory is the concept of *identification.* Sanford (1955:107) was probably right when he said, "a term that can be employed in so many different ways . . . could hardly mean anything very precise." For some psychologists, identification means that a child wants to be like a parent; for others, that a child actually behaves like the parent; and for yet others, that the child feels closer to one parent as opposed to another. Additional problems arise in identifying the source of emulative behavior. Children are exposed to many models including parents, teachers, other adults, peers and television heroes and heroines. As Bandura (1969:215) observes,

> indoctrination into masculinity and femininity is diligently promulgated by adorning children with distinctive clothes and hair styles, selecting sex-appropriate play materials and recreational activities, promoting associa-

tions with same-sex playmates, and through nonpermissive parental reactions to deviant sex-role behavior. In view of the extensive discrimination training, peer modelling, and frequent maternal demonstrations of masculine activities at times when the father is absent, it seems highly improbable that a three-year-old child looks and behaves like a boy primarily as a result of identifying with a 35-year-old man whom he can observe for relatively brief periods mainly during leisure-time activities if the commuting schedule happens to be favorable.

In general, then, we can conclude that the proposition that girls learn to be feminine by identifying with their mothers and boys learn to be masculine by identifying with their fathers is far too simplistic (Tavris and Offir, 1977:169). Newer translations of identification notions into the language of learning theories (e.g., Bandura, 1969), offer more promise.

Social Learning Theory

Social learning theory constitutes the second general psychological theory that attempts to explain gender differences. Learning theorists have attempted to develop a set of principles that will explain how learning occurs in human beings as well as in lower animals. Learning to be feminine or masculine is of course only one aspect of learning.

Several major points of disagreement exist between social learning and identification theorists (Frieze et al., 1978:104-9). First, identification theorists imply that becoming male or female occurs at one fell swoop, once the crucial identifying link has been forged. In addition, they assume that this global process does not require reinforcement (rewards). Learning theorists, by contrast, see gender learning as occurring gradually, with individual components being reinforced. Identification theorists stress the importance of an emotional bond to the same-sex parent. Learning theorists posit that children learn appropriate gender behavior through the influence of a wide variety of models. Although nurturant models tend to be imitated, an emotional bond is not seen as necessary. Finally, social learning theorists do not assume the existence of internal motives of the subterranean Freudian sort, which cause the child to adopt appropriate gender behavior. Instead, incentives for learning come from the external social environment.

Learning theory has three very general aspects: behaviorism, associationism and hedonism (Deutsch and Krauss, 1965).

Behaviorism is the methodological position that psychology should deal only with "observables" and not with what goes on inside the organism. The stimuli (internal or external events that bring about changes in the behavior of an organism) impinging on an organism's sense organs and the responses or behavior elicited by these stimuli can be seen by any observer. It is unnecessary for the psychologist to speculate about how the organism experiences or interprets these stimuli. Since psychologists can easily agree on what they observe, the omission of the organism's internal experiences enables research to be objective and, hence, presumably more scientific than it otherwise would be. Behaviorists object to Freudian views on socialization, including identification, on the grounds that they are far too introspective (Frieze et al., 1978:104).

Associationism refers to the assumption that behavior can be explained by studying the associations or linkages between stimuli and accompanying changes in an organism's behavior, called responses. For example, if a mother rewards her little girl with a smile when she chooses to wear a frilly dress rather than blue jeans, the child is likelier than she otherwise would be to choose a dress in the future. The reward or positive reinforcement associated with a given response makes it more probable that that response will be repeated in the future. Responses that are unrewarded, those that are simply ignored, are less likely to be repeated. To learning theorists, complex behaviors are seen as chains of simple S-R (stimulus-response) associations.

Hedonism is the assumption that explains the motivation for behavior in terms of reward and punishments. In 1898, Thorndike phrased it this way: "Pleasure stamps in; pain stamps out." Thorndike's famous phrase is a shorthand way of saying that seeking reward and avoiding punishment is the basic explanation of all behavior. More recently, Homans (1961:13) argued that human behavior is a "function of its payoff; in amount and kind [human behavior] depends on the amount and kind of reward and punishment it fetches." If Daniel is scolded for crying when he goes broke playing Monopoly, his future stoicism reflects hedonism. Note that the strict behaviorist is uninterested in Daniel's feelings about losing his hotels on Boardwalk or being scolded.

Operant conditioning,[3] a major mechanism of social learning, is associated with the American psychologists, E. L. Thorndike (1898, 1913) and B. F. Skinner (1953). Walter Mischel (1970) is responsible for what is probably the best-known application of these learning principles to gender socialization. Since until recently most research in this area was done with infrahuman species such as rats and pigeons, we will illustrate the basic principles involved with lower animals. First of all, the organism must make a specific response. If that response is followed by a reward or a punishment, it then becomes (over time) a conditioned or learned response. In a hypothetical experiment, a hungry pigeon is placed in a cage equipped with four differently colored keys. It goes through a trial-and-error procedure of pecking at the keys and, eventually, pecks the red key. The red key, when depressed, releases food. Because this particular response was rewarded, the pigeon will, after a few trials, go directly to the red key when hungry. In avoidance learning, an animal would be exposed to a noxious stimulus, such as an electric shock. In that case, it would learn to prevent punishment by pressing a certain key. In general, though, punishment is not a very reliable way of shaping *human* behavior. It stops unwanted behavior for the moment but, for various reasons, its effect on human behavior tend to be somewhat uncertain.

Common sense suggests that children do learn many of their general socialization lessons through operant conditioning. (Parents positively reinforce desired verbal responses, such as "please" and "thank you." They punish unwanted behavior such as rude talk, selfishness or taking candy from stores without paying for it.) However, to be "a viable explanation of sex-role acquisition, it must be demonstrated that parents and other socializers differentially reinforce and punish boys and girls in accordance with sex-role standards (Frieze et al., 1978:107). Maccoby and Jacklin (1974) summarize findings about parental behavior toward boys and girls. They examined questions such as this. Since one of the firmly established sex differences is greater male aggressiveness, does parental reinforcement encourage this difference? According to the studies reviewed by Maccoby and Jacklin, parents and teachers reprimand boys more often than girls for aggression. For example, a study of the child-training values of English-Canadian and French-Canadian parents (Lambert, Yackley and Hein, 1971) reported a cross-culturally similar tendency on the part of parents of boys to be harsher than parents of girls in their reactions to temper. (Temper is a verbal form of aggression.) In general, Maccoby and Jacklin (1974) conclude that the sexes are not trained very differently when young. During the preschool years, parental behavior is controlled more by the age of the child than by her/his sex.

There are a few exceptions to the foregoing conclusion, however. Differential parental response is indicated by choice of toys and clothing according to current sex stereotypes. Children prefer what is familiar and find rewarding the sex-typed possessions that the parents have provided. According to this "canalization" process (Frieze et al., 1978:108), Sally finds dolls rewarding. Her environment contains dolls; it does not contain trucks. For instance, Fagot (1978), described in Stockard and Johnson (1980:184), found marked toy preferences in two-year-old children. Girls preferred dolls and soft toys, while boys preferred to play with blocks and manipulate things. Parents reinforced these preferences; they encouraged boys to play with blocks and discouraged doll playing. Generally, though, parents need not punish their children for sex-inappropriate toy choices if they canalize their children's environment.

Another exception to Maccoby and Jacklin's conclusion of "no sex difference" is the fact that from infancy on, boys are spanked and handled more roughly than girls. In the study cited above, Lambert, Yackley and Hein (1971) report a consistent tendency for both French-Canadian and

English-Canadian parents to be harsher with boys than girls. The authors suggest that "Canadian parents may be reacting to the stereotype that girls are not to be as severely reprimanded as boys, as though the latter were tougher." However, boys may need more punishment because they misbehave more.

Some of the difficulty here may arise from extrapolating conclusions from pigeon research to human beings. With the latter, the learning processes may be more subtle. For one thing, the complex language of humans offers an economical shortcut to tedious, on-the-spot reinforcement (Tavris and Offir, 1977:164). The mother can tell her daughter that she approves of her help in the kitchen instead of enthusiastically reinforcing her each time she loads the dishwasher or sets the table. In addition, anticipated rewards and punishments affect human behavior just as actual ones do. "As psychologist Walter Mischel . . . says, 'A man does not have to be arrested for wearing dresses in public to learn about the consequences of such behavior' " (Tavris and Offir, 1977:164).

In general, the role of operant conditioning in gender socialization may be evaluated as follows. Although the evidence of differential reinforcement of preschool children is weak, the principles may be more useful for explaining the *persistence* of gender-related behaviors once they have been learned. The last point rests on data that show that direct pressure to conform to such expectations increases as children get older (Frieze et al., 1978:109).

When we look closely at the processes involved in social learning, the theory's ineffectiveness in explaining sex differences is easily understandable. Operant conditioning is a tedious, trial-and-error process. Deliberately teaching a child the names of the provinces would require laborious shaping of every sound and syllable, and their proper combinations, (as well as meaning), after initial trial-and-error emission. Observation of children learning to talk suggests that they do not learn this way. They learn at a much faster pace. Parents do not abandon all other activities to give language instruction. Sex-typed behavior seems to be a similar phenomenon. It is learned far too quickly and is far too pervasive to be explained by a gradual shaping process (Nielsen, 1978:117). It seems, then, that neither identification theory nor social learning theory can adequately explain gender socialization. The final type of socialization theory to be considered is cognitive-developmental theory.

Cognitive-Developmental Theory

The third, and most promising, theoretical approach to gender socialization, cognitive-developmental theory, is primarily the work of one man, Lawrence Kohlberg (1966). Kohlberg has based his ideas upon Jean Piaget's (1928) theory of the general processes involved in the development of children's thought-patterns. As the word *cognitive* suggests, Piaget and Kohlberg are interested in thought processes such as reasoning, remembering and believing. The term *developmental* serves to indicate their interest in the systematic changes that occur over time in children's thought processes.

The theory's central assumption is that the child needs to make sense of his/her cognitive environment. The child's reality is qualitatively different from the adult's reality. This difference stems not from ignorance or improper teaching, but from a basic disparity in thought structure. Piaget's observations on the concept of *conservation of physical properties* provide us with an illustration of this difference. The intellectual operations of the child under six years of age rely heavily on what it can perceive in the here and now. There is difficulty in imagining changed circumstances. If liquid is poured from a short, wide container into a tall, thin container, the child will state that the latter contains more water. Only the higher water level is noticed. If asked to imagine that the contents of the tall container are poured once again into the short one, the child has difficulty handling this mental reversal. The child has not yet learned the adult rules for reality construction. The structure of children's thinking changes in discrete stages until eventually they do show an adult's "accurate" view of the world (Kessler and McKenna, 1978:96).

Kohlberg sees children's notions about gender as one dimension of their cognitive organization of their world. The child "gradually develops concepts of 'masculinity' and 'femininity,' and when he has understood what his own sex is, he attempts to match his behavior to his conception" (Maccoby and Jacklin, 1974:365). Kohlberg's theory implies that all human beings need a sense of gender identity in order to function at all (Stockard and Johnson, 1980:196).

The assumptions of the cognitive-developmental perspective contrast sharply with those of identification and social learning theories. First, cognitive-developmental theorists assume that the child is cognitively *active* in the selection and organization (structuring) of perception, knowledge and understanding (Mussen, 1969:724). Indeed, Maccoby and Jacklin (1974:364) describe Kohlberg's theory as a "self-socialization" theory. Motivated by a desire for competence and mastery over the world, the child actively seeks out relevant information (Frieze et al., 1978:116). (Social learning theory assigns the child a passive role in the learning process.)

A second difference concerns the assumed motivation for gender learning. Freudian identification theorists assume that the child imitates the same-sex parent to reduce fear. Social learning theorists assume that external reinforcement is responsible for learning. By contrast, cognitive-developmentalists assume that children are motivated to master the behavior that they consider appropriate in order to maintain a competent, positive self-image. Rewards serve as cues to the appropriateness of various behaviors for the formation of gender identity (Frieze et al., 1978:118). In Kohlberg's (1966:89) words:

> [In the view of social learning theorists], sex-typed behavior and attitudes are acquired through social rewards that follow sex-appropriate responses made by the child or by a relevant model. The social-learning syllogism is: 'I want rewards, I am rewarded for doing boy things, therefore I want to be a boy.' In contrast, a cognitive theory assumes this sequence: 'I am a boy, therefore I want to do boy things, therefore the opportunity to do boy things (and to gain approval for doing them) is rewarding.'

Third, Kohlberg takes exception to the Freudian view that the acquisition of gender is explained by biological maturation. Admittedly, sex-typing is universal; all cultures prescribe differential behavior for the two sexes. However, cultures differ dramatically in the kinds of behavior associated with males as opposed to females. Therefore, such learning is assumed to be culturally, not biologically, determined (Brophy, 1977:250).

Finally, the cognitive-developmental theorists argue that the other theories have overstressed the socialization role of parents relative to that of peers and the media. Because children positively value the acquisition of sex-related characteristics and behavior, gender learning occurs with very little direct instruction from parents or anyone else (Brophy, 1977:251). Kohlberg also criticizes the importance assigned to parents by psychoanalytic theory, which asserts that appropriate behavior results from identification with the same-sex parent. However, Kohlberg cites research that indicates that children are already "sex-typed" in their behavior at an age (four years) when, according to psychoanalytic theory, both boys and girls are identified with their mothers (Kressler and McKenna, 1978:97). He does acknowledge though, that "a family climate of warmth, expressiveness, security . . . and high social perception" may facilitate gender socialization because it "allows for the explanation and interpretation of the new and the problematic" (Kohlberg, 1966:156).

Gender development begins with sex labelling. Children learn the words "boy" and "girl" and they hear others label them this way. By the age of two or three, they know their own self-labels. Often they can label others accurately. However, according to Kohlberg, gender is a physical category based on anatomy, and until children have grasped the concept of conservation despite transformation (described above), they do not have permanent gender identities. Until they understand that the amount of water does not change when poured from one kind of container to another, they also do not grasp that a boy does not become a girl when he abandons trucks for dolls. At the age of six or seven, the child develops the concept of conservation, including the idea that gender is invariant. "Just as the amount of water remains the same when it is poured from a short, fat glass into a tall, thin one, a woman remains a woman when she wears pants" (Tavris and Offir, 1977:167). Not only does the child now know that she is a girl, she knows that she will always be a girl (Kressler and McKenna, 1978:96-97).

Once the child has discovered the difference between the sexes and developed an interest in the implications of the difference, the self-categorization as "boy" or "girl" becomes a major organizer and determinant of many attitudes and activities. Though some modelling and some reinforcement are probably involved, the primary motivating mechanism for gender learning seems to be the development of the insight, "I am a boy, and therefore I should act like a boy and do the things that boys do," or "I am a girl and therefore I should act like a girl and do the things girls do." Evidence does show that *after* discovery of sex differences and self-labelling, children begin to prefer same-sexed playmates, toys, games and clothes characteristic of their own sex. They also begin to show an aversion for things associated with the opposite sex that they once happily accepted (Brophy, 1977:250).

Because of the higher prestige males enjoy in our society, the socialization process as described by cognitive-developmental theorists works out more clearly for boys than for girls. Six-year-old girls know they are girls and want to be like their mothers. However, girls are not as sex-typed in their preferences as boys, because they identify with their fathers too. "In the reality of the young child, 'male' is identified with 'big' and synonymous with 'more powerful' " (Kessler and McKenna, 1978:97). Consequently, both boys and girls identify to some extent with maleness.

How should the cognitive-developmental theory be judged? Although the approach is not without some problems (which we will get to in a moment), it has provoked enthusiastic appraisals. For example: "Kohlberg's presentation is intriguing, thoughtful, stimulating, and plausible. It cites relevant, supportive evidence and emphasizes a number of important problems neglected by other theories of sex-typing" (Mussen, 1969:726). Empirical support for Kohlberg's ideas derives mainly from data demonstrating that the timing of gender learning is closely associated with the timing of cognitive development (Brophy, 1977:250). Gender learning involves mastering a set of concepts concerning sex differences and the role differences associated with them. Kohlberg and Zigler (1967) have shown that gender learning is more closely associated with children's general brightness than with chronological age or similarity to the same-sex parent. Children who are cognitively more mature than their age-mates show earlier awareness of gender differences. However, while strong sex-typing is associated with high intelligence in young children, it is associated with low intelligence in adolescents. Therefore, cognitive growth involves acquiring less rigid notions of gender roles (Stockard and Johnson, 1980:196).

Cognitive-developmental theory does present some difficulties.

Cognitive development as such is not really explained. Because the underlying mechanisms are not specified, it seems to "just happen." Also, the perspective fails to give adequate attention to individual differences in gender learning and gender-related behavior. Kohlberg's explanation in terms of rate of cognitive growth is not really satisfactory. As Mussen (1969:726) notes, "in any group of boys of the same age and equal intelligence, there are wide variations in degrees of masculinity of interests, activities and behavior." Nevertheless, we must remember that cognitive-developmental theory is quite new, and many of the hypotheses derived from it have not yet been tested.

Which of the three theoretical approaches to gender learning is correct? A great deal of research is needed before a proper assessment can be made. Meanwhile, the ideas of the identification theorists, learning theorists and cognitive-developmental theorists all contribute to our understanding of gender socialization. Kessler and McKenna (1978:101) tell us that, "theories may be more or less useful, more or less aesthetically pleasing, more or less in vogue, but their claim to truth is, in some sense, a matter of faith in their basic assumptions." Therefore, all three should be seen as complementary rather than competing systems of thought.

Kohlberg's ideas are useful in explaining *childhood* gender behavior. Imitative learning (the modern version of identification theory, which rejects its Freudian ancestry) seems on the other hand to explain how children acquire *adult* behavior, which appears later (Brophy, 1977:251). Only the social learning theorists explain the precise mechanisms involved at either stage. However, a limitation exists in all three approaches. All of them offer more complete and satisfactory explanations of male than of female development (Kessler and McKenna, 1978:100).

After evaluating all of the relevant evidence, Maccoby and Jacklin (1974:365) arrived at this conclusion: "We believe that the processes of direct reinforcement and simple imitation are clearly involved in the acquisition of sex-typed behavior, but that they are not sufficient to account for the developmental changes that occur in sex typing. The third kind of psychological process—the one stressed by cognitive-developmental theorists such as Kohlberg—must also be involved."

Sex Differences in the Costs of Socialization

Which sex suffers the most, in undergoing gender socialization? To anticipate the end of the story before it is even begun, the answer depends upon the phase of gender socialization in question. Boys can legitimately complain about their difficult childhood and girls about their difficult adolescence.

The ideas of David Lynn (1959, 1969) serve as an introduction to this debate. He postulates that because of the greater availability of the mother and the relative absence of the father during early childhood, little girls easily develop their gender identity through imitation and positive reinforcement. However, little boys must shift from their initial identification with the mother to masculine identification. Since male models are scarce (being away at work), boys have greater difficulty than girls in achieving gender identity. According to Lynn, males must learn by intellectually piecing together the problem of definitions of masculinity. Some of this learning comes from peers and from media presentation of sex stereotypes. Some results from punishment for displays of feminine behavior. Hartley (1959:457) points out that for boys, "the desired behavior is rarely defined positively as something the child *should* do, but rather, undesirable behavior is indicated negatively as something he should *not* do or be [emphasis in original]." Consequently, males remain anxious about gender throughout life. As adults, they are more hostile toward both the opposite sex and homosexuals than are females. Nevertheless, a boy learns to prefer the masculine role to the feminine one. "He is rewarded simply for having been born masculine through countless privileges accorded males but not females" (Lynn, 1959).

Professor Lynn, then, tells us that gender socialization demands more from boys, at least during childhood, and that as adults, males cherish their superior status. Their gender identity remains, however, less secure than that of females. Although their theoretical reasons differ, many social scientists agree with Lynn's key points. Chodorow (1971:285) argues that because of the cultural devaluation of feminine qualities, young girls are allowed to dress and act like boys. Their feminine identity, nevertheless, remains firm. During childhood, the male role is the more inflexible one. More pressure is placed on boys to act like boys, than for girls to act like girls. Girls' problems start with adolescence.

Bardwick and Douvan (1971:227-28) put it this way:

> Since girls are less likely to masturbate, run away from home, or bite and draw blood, their lives are relatively free from crisis until puberty. Before that girls do not have to conform to threatening new criteria of acceptability to anywhere near the extent that boys do. When boys are pressured to give up their childish ways it is because those behaviors are perceived as feminine by parents. Boys have to earn their masculinity early. Until puberty, femininity is a verbal label, a given attribute—something that does not have to be earned.

However, cognitive-developmental theorists argue that maleness is more clearly spelled out for children than is femaleness. They emphasize male prestige, while identification theorists like Lynn emphasize the availability of parental role models.

The volatile period of adolescence is marked by pressure to solve the problems of "Who am I?" and "What shall I become?" As adolescents mature into creatures with sexual urges, masculinity/femininity becomes an increasingly more fundamental component of their identity. The salience of gender is also reinforced from without. Teenagers are exposed to more complex and more precisely defined norms of sex-appropriate behavior than are young children (Kohlberg, 1966). Moreover, the decisions they make at this time carry lifelong consequences, and these decisions are made within the context of societal gender expectations.

In *The Second Sex*, published "when feminism was no longer and not yet a live issue" (McCall, 1979:209), Simone de Beauvoir wrote a sensitive account of the discontinuity between childhood and adolescence, experienced by the "girl-child." Her basic thesis is that man conceives of himself as "the essential, the Self, and made of woman the Other." Women "have internalized the alien point of view that man is the essential, woman the inessential" (McCall, 1979:210). However, according to de Beauvoir, and her contemporary disciple, Judith Laws (1979), the young girl resists her future, which entails a "yoke of sexual bondage" (Laws, 1979:233), a fate as the "passive prey of man." (de Beauvoir, 1952:332) (These emotionally loaded words signal these analysts' sympathy with the distaff side of the melancholy socialization tale.) On the subject of women's "erotic dependence" on men, Laws (1979:233-34) says, "Reading the literature on female socialization reminds one of the familiar image of Cinderella's stepsisters industriously lopping off their toes and heels so as to fit into the glass slipper (key to the somewhat enigmatic heart of the Prince)—when of course it was never intended for them anyway. As Cinderella and the Prince fade into the Happily Ever After, our attention is diverted from the leftover and mangled stepsisters. However, I think of them a lot."

De Beauvoir (1952:328-33) suggests that the adolescent girl's masochistic defiance may take many forms, all of them symbolic but ineffective: flaunting of a crude vocabulary, whimsical food habits, self-mutilation, kleptomania. The eating disorder, *anorexia nervosa*, is another form of metaphoric revolt by females that is appearing with greater frequency (Boskind-Lodahl, 1976; Orbach, 1978). The adolescent victims of this syndrome—90% of them female—starve themselves, become emaciated and, in some cases, die of malnutrition. This bizarre behavior reflects an ambivalence about femininity. On the one hand, starving destroys the curvy, full woman's body. Anorectics do not menstruate. On the other hand, self-starvation expresses an exaggeration, as well as rejection, of femininity. "This bird-like eating is a reflection of a culture that praises thinness and fragility in women" (Orbach, 1978:167).

Some observations concerning juvenile delinquency should serve to rectify the impression left by the preceding paragraphs that socialization is painful only to girls. In addition, the topic provides some insight into young people's changing reactions to gender socialization. Adolescent trouble with the law seems to partially reflect problems in establishing gender identity. Sex differences in both the amount and type of delinquency are relevant here (Ghitan, 1979). Around the turn of the century, the ratio of male to female juvenile delinquency was approximately fifty to one (Halleck, 1972). In the early 1970s this ratio had been reduced to three to one in Canada, the United States and England (Landau, 1975). The larger *amount* of male delinquent activity, as well as the *type* of activity engaged in, have been interpreted by sociologists as male attempts to establish "their 'masculine' prowess and independence" (Chafetz, 1974:63). For example, Clark and Haurek (1966) note that male offenses involving risk and aggressiveness increase until mid-adolescence, perhaps because these acts are seen as a testimonial to masculinity, and then decrease as the anxiety surrounding masculine identity lessens somewhat in later adolescence. Traditionally, female offenses, as opposed to male offenses, have more often offended society's propriety rather than its property (Ghitan, 1979:3). When the offenses involved a victim, it was usually the girl herself. While girls appear in court for sexual immorality, truancy or "unmanageable" behavior, boys are charged with burglary, car theft and vandalism (Landau, 1975). Though larceny is the most frequent offense for both sexes, girls tend to shoplift. In the past, females' more law-abiding behavior has been explained by gender expectations that emphasize passivity, dependency, nonaggressiveness and noncompetitiveness. In addition, females have been subject to more home and school supervision and regulation than males, and their peer group associations have differed (Ghitan, 1979:8-9). Now the gap is closing. Female involvement in all aspects of delinquency, including the more serious offenses, has increased dramatically (Adler, 1975).

Although the precise reasons for this change are not yet clear, they do seem to reflect changes in gender socialization (Adler, 1975). Regardless of the specific etiology, this new tendency for females to turn their anger outward against the world, instead of inward against themselves, is a most interesting development.

In summary, the socialization process seems to be traumatic for both sexes. The male is often left unclear about his gender identity. According to one viewpoint (Kessler and McKenna, 1978:100) the higher incidence of "gender disorders," such as transvestism, transsexualism and paraphilia (preference for unusual sexual practices) among men indicates the precarious nature of male development. The woman need not prove her gender identity either to herself or to society. However, her "problem is that this identity is clearly devalued in the society in which she lives" (Chodorow, 1971:286).

CONCLUSIONS

Chapter Four is the first of three chapters to treat the development of femininity and masculinity from the social-psychological point of view.

In the social-psychological perspective, interest centers simultaneously on the individual and on the social context in which the individual operates. Social, as opposed to biological, influences are emphasized.

Three topics were considered in this chapter: the definitions of general socialization and gender socialization; the content of socialization lessons (society's gender attitudes, occupational sex-typing, knowledge and skills, and male and female self-imagery/self-esteem); and the major theories of gender socialization (identification theory, social learning theory, and cognitive-development theory).

The next two chapters will consider the various socialization agencies, possibly the most thoroughly researched area within the sociology of gender relations.

5 Family and Peer Group: Primary Sources of Gender Socialization

CHAPTER Five continues the discussion begun in the last chapter, on how girls and boys learn to be female and male. The main topic for consideration here is the contribution of *agents of gender socialization*. Where do children and adolescents get their ideas about gender? What influences impinge upon them to shape their attitudes and behavior in accordance with societal notions of femininity and masculinity? Obviously, children being socialized are confronted by specific human beings, not by an amorphous blob called "Society." Similarly, gender is an umbrella concept encompassing a myriad of details concerning our particular culture's interpretations of masculinity and femininity. The business of this chapter is to explore the sources of socialization.

The discussion will focus on the two major primary group-agents of socialization; the family and the peer group. The *primary* versus *secondary* relationship is a long-standing distinction in sociology. "Primary relationships involve frequent close contact and a high degree of personal involvement, and generally take place in small, informal groups. Secondary relationships involve infrequent and impersonal contact with a low degree of personal involvement, often in large formal organizations" (Curtis and Lambert, 1980:106).

Family and friendship groups are the prototypical primary groups. People are valued as total personalities (not as the segmented selves involved in such secondary relationships as customer-sales clerk or patient-doctor), and intense feelings are often aroused. Both family and friendship groups are potent agents of gender socialization. Discussion of *secondary* group gender socialization agents (such as the school and the church) and of the *symbolic* agents (language, literature and the mass media) will be reserved for the next chapter.

THE FAMILY

The family's impact upon the child transcends that of all the other agents of socialization. In Clausen's (1968:132) words, "the 'widening world of childhood' spirals out from the parental home." Learning occurs rapidly during these crucial years of early childhood, during which the family has almost exclusive control. Children are physically dependent on adults, and out of this material dependency develops psychological dependency (Tolson, 1977:23). Therefore, learning takes place in the context of close emotional bonds. Moreover, the family touches every sphere of the child's existence. The early immersion of the child within the family guarantees that that institution lays the foundation for the later and lesser influences of the other socialization agents, which are considerably more specialized.

There is a second reason for sociologists' assigning primacy to the family. Various characteristics of the family orient the child to specific configurations of experiences, values and opportunities. By being born into a particular family, the child automatically becomes part of a larger family of grandparents, aunts, uncles and cousins. Also, the family's social class position means that the child will learn a particular set of values. Moreover, the opportunities of a child born into an upper-middle-class family are considerably different from those of a child born into the working class. The family's geographic location is also the child's. Growing up in Toronto is a quite different experience from growing up in rural Saskatchewan.

Most gender socialization theories also see the family as the primary agent of feminine and masculine socialization. (The exception here is cognitive-developmental theory, which stresses "self-socialization" and the peer group.) Learning and identification theorists emphasize the function of the parents as either providing same-sex and complementary models to their children, or as direct reinforcement agents, meting out rewards and punishments for appropriate gender behavior.

Weitz points out that the parental attitude is one of compromise between the deeply ingrained patterns of their own childhoods and challenges to sex-typing in the contemporary world. "Parents provide a conservative link to the past in that many of their behaviors are shadows of a distant socialization experience of their own" (Weitz, 1977:81). Although space limitations preclude an extended discussion of gender socialization of adults in later years, a person's family of procreation (the family that he/she establishes through marriage) continues the teaching of masculinity and femininity begun by the family of origin. Specific types of attitudes and behavior are expected from the husband and father, as opposed to the wife and mother.

Siblings, too, play a role. Indeed, Goffman (1977:314) calls the household a "socialization depot" because "family life ensures that most of what each sex does is done in the full sight of the other sex." Further, "it is as if society planted a brother with sisters so women could from the beginning learn their place, and a sister with brothers so men could learn their place" (Goffman, 1977:314).[1]

Same-Sex and Cross-Sex Parent-Child Relations

What difference does it make to gender socialization if the influential parent is the same sex as the child, or the opposite sex? Although same-sex/cross-sex effects constitute yet another "underdeveloped" research area, the question has both theoretical and practical significance.

The sex of the parent and that of the child are relevant to *modelling* (or imitation) theories of gender socialization, whether the process is Freudian identification or social learning. Although the motivation differs according to theoretical orientation, the boy child, for example, learns to be masculine partly by imitating his father's masculinity and partly by observing and complementing his mother's femininity. Further, parental influences (mother's or father's) are certainly not interchangeable during what psychoanalytic theory calls the oedipal phase. However, same-sex/cross-sex effects do not enter into cognitive-developmental theory (Chapter Four).

Because most of the relevant research has involved observation or interviews with mothers only, until recently, cross-sex/same-sex effects have rarely been assessed (Maccoby and Jacklin, 1974:346-47). However, some interesting findings do exist concerning parental response to aggression directed toward them by their children. Fathers are more tolerant of aggression from their daughters, mothers from their sons. Why should cross-sex favoritism result from shows of temper and insolence (Lambert, Yackley and Hein, 1971)? Perhaps the oedipal mechanism is the explanation; the father would be interpreting his son's aggression as a threat to his dominance, and his daughter's as coquettish flirtation.

There are also practical reasons for being interested in the consequences of the fact that women are the primary socializers of children. Single-parent females are a case in point (Schlesinger, 1975). Although most Canadian children grow up in the traditional two-parent nuclear family, separation and divorce have contributed to an increasing proportion of single-parent families since 1966 (Wargon, 1980:23). The 1976 Canadian census found that 9.8% of Canadian households were headed by lone parents. Eighty-three percent of those lone parents were female (Wargon, 1980: Table 2.13).

Even in the traditional "intact" home, it is mainly mothers who bring up children. An analysis of the time budgets of several hundred married couples in the greater Vancouver area done by Meissner et al.

(1975) reported that only a small proportion of husbands with a child under ten years contribute to child care. Overall, the wives spent an average of 3.3 hours a week and the husbands an average of 0.9 hours a week on child care. The amount of time devoted by fathers to child care does not depend very much on whether the mother is employed outside the home, or on the number of children in the family (Walker, 1970). According to Rowe (1977:173), "Only in Scandinavia and Cuba have top government leaders systematically asserted equal rights for men in the home and with children and equal sharing with women of social responsibility for reproducing and socializing the human species. Nowhere does that equal sharing appear yet to have taken place."

When the biological mother is unable or unwilling to parent, other women, rather than men, nearly always take her place. Even in societies where nonfamilial child care is widespread—Israel, China, Soviet Union, Cuba—it is the women who provide this care (Chodorow, 1978:3, 216). Moreover, until children reach high school, the overwhelming majority of their teachers are women.

"Momism"

For decades, the mass media have caricatured maternal power and paternal decline: "On television, in movies, and in comic strips of the 1940s and '50s, fathers were often made to appear as fumbling incompetents, 'a kind of living fossil, a creature trying to ape some of the manners of a bygone era.' Dagwood Bumstead, for example, blustered and fussed in front of Blondie and the kids, but the reader knew that Dagwood could not control anything, not even the family dogs" (Dubbert, 1979:257-58).

The following description of a 1967 program about the FBI reveals the other side of this dreary tale—television's vulgarization of wonderful mom:

> An exceptionally ugly middle-aged woman is led into the office of the FBI hero (Efrem Zimbalist, Jr.). Her expression at first suggests no more than a liver complaint, but the dialogue quickly establishes that her son is dead. It looks to her like foul play: a policeman is accused of the murder. The mother says she knows her son was a bad boy, but, but . . . (breakdown, racking sobs, contorted features). Zimbalist, Jr., strokes the left side of his nose with his left thumb. He is embarrassed by the mother's instability, he would like to get on with the rational business of proving the policeman's innocence.
>
> After several seconds of this noisy stalemate, Zimbalist, Jr., conducts the mother to the door. Through it, he tells an unseen secretary to get Mrs. Distraught a glass of water and a cot to lie down on. The genuine relief which is felt with her departure from the scene constitutes a rare moment of rapport with the FBI. But the point is thought to be still clouded. A second FBI man therefore spells it out: Here was a dreadful

son—a junkie, a pimp, a firebug, etc. Yet This Woman, His Mother, Loved Him. Zimbalist, Jr., waggles his head (mystified awe of maternal feeling). The solution of the case gets under way. [Ellman, 1968:133]

A final circa 1981 media illustration. In the past, women spun their "web of dependence" by catering to male family members and by holding complete power over children. Now, the women's and men's movements both have allegedly produced an army of wounded males (Collison, 1979). Male power has been further eroded by female competition and by the "mortification of masculinity" that is a crucial concern of the men's liberation literature. "Purging oneself of nasty male qualities—or at least taking on gentleness and passivity as if one were being annointed at some sort of androgyne prince's coronation—is the major cathartic experience involved in becoming a Liberated Man" (Collison, 1979:29). The "Hi and Lois" comic strip family is being affected by these developments. Lois, the intrepid mother of four, has a part-time job as a real estate saleswoman. A cartoon shows Hi and Lois chatting over a cup of coffee. Hi glumly listens to Lois's monologue: "A rich couple is really interested in this house I'm showing—and you know what? If I sell it, I'll make in one *day* what *you* make in a third of a year." After Hi leaves Lois sitting alone at the table, she says, "Gee, it used to be the *wives* that went into the bathroom and pouted."

Writers ranging from pop sociologists to scientists have speculated about the impact of strong matriarchal influence upon boys. Unfortunately, imaginative accounts exceed empirical data. The most dramatic theme of this literary genre concerns the emasculation of males. Many psychoanalysts locate the etiology of male effeminacy in the quality of early mother-son interaction. In such situations, fathers are "if not *physically* absent from family interaction, at least *dynamically* absent [emphasis in original]" (Stoller, 1968). However, Green's (1974:239-41) explanation of how effeminate boys get that way also incorporates peer group interaction. The first component of his etiological sketch involves a mother who considers her infant male child to be unusually attractive and responsive to being held. Her emotional (and time) commitments are such that she has few other avenues for channelling her feelings of love. As the child begins exploring his environment for play objects, he finds available his mother's accessories: shoes, cosmetics, jewelry. He imitates the person with whom he is primarily in contact, his mother. This early "feminine" behavior is considered to be cute or funny. If the father is present, he is a much less significant figure in the boy's life than his mother. Usually the boy prefers the calmer domestic activities of the mother to the rough-and-tumble play of the father. Similarly, the boy likes to play with girls because boys "are too rough." As time goes on, the emotional distance grows between father and son, while the mother continues to respond positively to the boy's interest in improvising feminine costumes. As might be expected, his displays of feminine gestures, walking style and vocal intonations increase social stigmatization. The child is labelled a "sissy" and teased by his rejecting peers.

Another hypothesized consequence of the fact that women are the primary socializers for boys is men's subsequent "dread of women" (Chodorow, 1971:274ff). This notion originated with the psychoanalyst Karen Horney (1932). Initially, the mother has complete power over the child's satisfaction of its needs. Also, it is the mother who first forbids "instinctual" activities, thus creating enormous anxiety in the child. "[One] way of coping with dread is to glorify and adore women—'There is no need for me to dread a being so wonderful, so beautiful, nay, so saintly'— or to debase and disparage them—'It would be too ridiculous to dread a creature who, if you take her all round, is such a poor thing' " (Chodorow, 1971:275). The devaluation of what women do and are creates an enormous pressure on males to conform to prescribed goals and behavior. Male inexpressiveness may be one result, as boys "learn early not to exhibit feminine personality traits—to hide emotions and pretend even to themselves that they do not have them" (Chodorow, 1971:277).

Sons' obsessive attachment to their mothers, and mother's attachment to their sons—the "elevation of motherhood into a divine mission"— represents a significant strand of the glorification of women mentioned above (Dubbert, 1979:17). Victorian poetry and prose contain "endless accolades for mother, 'synonym of all that is good,' surrogate of God" (Bernard, 1975:138). Although the following poem begins like a rousing limerick, it is a tribute to motherhood written by J. Echegaray, a Spanish poet and 1904 Nobel laureate (This translation, one of several, is by Jean Richepin.)

> There was a young man loved a maid
> Who taunted him. "Are you afraid,"
> She asked, "to bring me today
> Your mother's head upon a tray?"
>
> He went and slew his mother dead
> Tore from her breast her heart so red
> Then towards his lady love he raced
> But tripped and fell in all his haste.
>
> As the heart rolled on the ground
> It gave forth a plaintive sound.
> And it spoke, in accents mild:
> "Did you hurt yourself, my child?"
>
> [J. Echegaray, "Severed Heart," from Bernard (1975:138)]

During the post-World-War-II era, adoration of "Mother" became transmogrified into contempt for "Mom." In part, the change represented a reaction to the excesses of the "motherhood cult." The phenomenon of "Momism" signalled the plight of middle-class women caught in late motherhood with nothing "meaningful" to do. The Jewish supermother, the self-sacrificing martyr who "devoted" her life to her ungrateful children is an anachronistic caricature of Momism (Bart, 1971a). (This purveyor of unwanted chicken soup whines to her daughter, "How is it that you can't come see me on weekends when all I've ever done is be your mother?" [*Time*, 26 February 1979:65])

The epithet, "Momism," referred to the obsessive devotion of sons for their mothers and mothers for their sons, and particularly to the unwillingness of mothers to let their sons develop a sense of masculine independence (Dubbert, 1979:240).[2] Mothers refused to let their nests stay empty; thus, this "monument of love, sacrifice, tenderness had become a viper" (Bernard, 1975:138). Philip Wylie's 1955 *Generation of Vipers* argued that such women "raped the men, not sexually, unfortunately, [*sic*] but morally, since neuters come hard by morals."

The temptation for mothers to suffocate their children (or, to use more trendy language, to "overinvest" in them) was socially caused (Boyd, Eichler and Hofley, 1976). Some of these factors are still at work, though their effect is attenuated. Post-World-War-II women acquired laborsaving devices that served to give them more time to spend with their children. However, at the same time, housework became a more solitary endeavor. In addition, societal perceptions of maternal responsibilities became sharper, with the proliferation of child-care experts and child-care manuals. "Mothers are being told that they are indispensable for the care of their young children; at the same time it has been suggested that they can produce near perfect children if they adopt the right socialization techniques. Problem children are no longer identified as naturally bad or imperfect children, as may have been the case in the past, but are identified as a result of poor parental performance, especially on the part of the mother" (Boyd, Eichler and Hofley, 1976:14).

Mothers were charged with almost exclusive responsibility for these potentially perfect children. The intellectual atmosphere surrounding proper motherhood was set by Bowlby's famous treatise, *Maternal Care and Mental Health* (1952), commissioned by the United Nations. Child-care experts interpreted his notion of "maternal deprivation" to mean that mothers who fail to lavish 100% of their time and attention on their children are neglecting their offspring. The "maternal deprivation" notion was congenial to the era of the 1950s, which idealized home and family. A final reason for excessive mother-child contact was (and is) the physically inhospitable urban environment (Boyd, Eichler and Hofley, 1976:15). Because of heavy traffic and other hazards, small children could not be allowed to play unsupervised. At the time under discussion, day-care centers were rare.

The attacks on Mom have ceased. One reason is that we are no longer quite so enthusiastic about motherhood, nor do we idealize motherhood to quite the same extent. When Ann Landers asked her readers if they would produce children if they had it all to do again, 70% of the 10,000 parents who wrote her said no. During the 1950s, attitudes favored elaborate housekeeping and the production of many children. In part, adulation of home and family represented a reaction to the disruption of domesticity occasioned by Second World War experiences. The demise of "Momism" is also attributable to social change that has opened horizons beyond the home. A world that contains jobs and other interesting things to do mitigates against excessive concern with offspring.

In general, current evidence recommends a balanced view of maternal effects on male gender socialization. The deleterious effects suggested are hardly universal. Most experts do agree with Green's (1976) belief that "two adults involved in the upbringing can counteract each other's more bizarre tendencies and complement each other's talents and blind spots." For instance, since both men and women are more lenient toward children of the opposite sex (as we mentioned earlier), and since both control and indulgence are required for childrearing, adults of both sexes should be involved in child care. These adults need not be biological parents (Maccoby and Jacklin, 1974:372-73). However, at least one recent study takes a contrary position. Shepard (1980) claims that fathers and mothers are interchangeable agents of gender socialization, that is, that the sex of the parents doesn't particularly matter. Moreover, several studies (Barclay and Cusumano, 1961; Hetherington, 1966) indicate that the absence of the father (through death, divorce or separation) has little influence on the sex-typed behavior or masculine identification of sons after the age of five.[3] Biller (1971) presents many interesting ideas on this subject, which warrant the attention of future researchers. He points out the importance of variables such as mothers' attitudes toward the absent fathers, peer group interaction and the length and timing of the father's absence.

Optimism also prevails so far as the father's *relative* absence is concerned. Colley (1959) (quoted in Green [1974]), proposes a "parthenogenic" approach to the emergence of gender:

> Our theoretical plan allows for the total absence, physical or psychological, of one parent without disturbing the child's [gender identity], provided there is one appropriately identified parent with whom the child experiences close interaction. One parent may supply sufficient differential response to the child . . . even in a father's absence . . . mother will respond to a boy 'as if' he were a male and will expect him to treat her as a male would treat a female.

Also, Maccoby and Jacklin (1974:348) submit that the sheer amount of time spent in the presence of a particular socialization agent may not be the most important index of that agent's influence. The suggestion is that fathers can be very effective agents despite the fewer hours they spend in the home.

This proposition sounds possible in principle. However, in practice, fathers' impact upon children is unlikely to rival mothers' impact. First of all, society holds *mothers* responsible for children. The domestic power is theirs. In addition, though "parenthood," as an abstraction, evokes a sentimental response, the actual, concrete jobs involved in parenting are hardly popular. In this connection, the child-rearing expert, Dr. Benjamin Spock, once tried to persuade women that it was "much more creative to rear and shape the personality of a fine, live child than it is to work in an office or even to carve a statue." Sociologist Mirra Komarovsky (1976:254) retorted that women cannot be made to believe Spock's message unless men believe it too. And "if men believed for a moment that the rearing of children is as difficult and important as building bridges, they would demand more of a hand in it too" (p. 255).

Mothers and Daughters

But what about girls? They have not been heard from since the second paragraph of this section. Their neglect here reflects their neglect in the literature as a whole. Until the feminist movement's recent interest in the topic (especially one aspect of it, to be considered below) cross-sex effects were considered mainly in the context of the Freudian oedipal complex, and same-sex effects in the context of the greater availability of the maternal model. (You will recall Professor Lynn's ideas here. Essentially, his argument was that because children grow up around women, being feminine makes more sense than being masculine, to boys as well as girls.) However, exceptional interest in the psychodynamics of girls' socialization was shown by Helene Deutsch (1944) and by Simone de Beauvoir (1952). According to the latter, girls' self-esteem suffers as they move from the female-dominated home to the male-dominated society:

> If the little girl at first accepts her feminine vocation, it is not because she intends to abdicate; it is, on the contrary, in order to rule; she wants to be a matron because the matrons' group seems privileged; but, when her company, her studies, her games, her reading, take her out of the maternal circle, she sees that it is not the women but the men who control the world. It is this revelation—much more than the discovery of the penis— that irresistibly alters her conception of herself. [de Beauvoir, 1952:267]

Despite accusations that the women's liberation movement disparages motherhood, the movement has stimulated both scholarly (Chodorow, 1978) and popular (Friday, 1977) analyses of mother-daughter relationships. According to *Time* magazine (26 February 1979), this "knotty" relationship has been kept in the "feminist closet" because the movement preferred to focus on the "abuses of male power rather than on what women do to each other." Concern with the issue seems widespread: Nancy Friday's mother-daughter memoirs, *My Mother/My Self* (1977) sold a quarter of a million copies in hardcover and more than two million in paperback (*Time*, 26 February 1979). Although the two books cited here (as well as others) argue that girls have more difficulty liberating themselves from their mothers than boys do, the putative villain is male-dominated society, not mother (and most decidedly not "Momism").

As the title suggests, Nancy Chodorow's book, *The Reproduction of Mothering: Psychoanalysis and the Sociology of Gender* (1978), is ambitious in its intellectual scope. Her intriguing analysis makes excellent use of Parsonian sociological theory and of psychoanalytic ideas and case studies. However, empirical evidence is needed before her ideas can be accepted as "gospel truth."

Briefly, Chodorow contends that because current societal arrangements leave most of the parenting to women, many mothers "overinvest" in their children and dominate their emotional lives. For "a girl, just as for a boy, there can be too much of mother" (p. 177). She shares the identification theorists' viewpoint that because of the physical availability of mothers, boys are taught to be masculine more consciously than girls are taught to be feminine. ("Males tend to identify with a cultural stereotype of the masculine role; whereas females tend to identify with aspects of their own mother's role specifically" [Lynn, 1959:130].) However, according to Chodorow, the pubertal transition is more difficult for girls than boys. Though as children, girls had little difficulty in identifying with their mothers, in adolescence, they have trouble in differentiating themselves from their mothers. Consequently, daughters have "insufficiently individuated senses of self" (p. 212). Mothers are ambivalent: they desire both to keep their daughters close and to push them into adulthood (p. 135). Friday (1977:199) dramatically expresses this *folie à deux*:

> Daughters fear they will anger their mother so much that mother will desert them. Mothers fear they will anger their daughters so much that daughters will desert them. Both women call it guilt. Every woman speaks of it. It is not guilt. It is terror. The terror of losing each other. It makes them cling even harder, tightens the claustrophobia between them even more. In the end, the ironic truth is that if you have the courage to let each other go, you may be friends for life.

Bernard (1975:151) claims that friendships with middle-aged daughters *do* constitute the major relationship in older women's lives. Old hostilities are mastered as women of both generations grow older.

New Avenues of Parenting

Contemporary feminists attribute the blame for disturbed mother-daughter relations to Western social arrangements that isolate mothers and fail to hold fathers responsible for half the parenting. Chodorow (1978:213) hypothesizes that mother-daughter relationships in which the mother is supported by a network of women kin and friends, and has meaningful work and a sense of self-esteem, will produce daughters with a capacity for nurturance and a strong sense of self. Similarly, she argues that men will face inevitable problems so long as parenting is almost exclusively women's jurisdiction: "the very fact of being mothered by a woman generates in men conflicts over masculinity, a psychology of male dominance, and a need to be superior to women" (p. 214). If parenting is equally shared, mothers are less likely "to overinvest in and overwhelm" the relationship, and children are better off where love is "not a scarce resource controlled and manipulated by one person only" (p. 217). Presumably, fathers would benefit from being in the center of the family, rather than at the periphery.[4]

Mike McGrady left his job as newspaper columnist to be a house-husband and housefather, while his wife went out to work. In his book, *The Kitchen Sink Papers* (1975), he says that through the years, he had missed quite a bit by being no more than a father. (He also learned some of the disadvantages of parenthood). He cites the day he took his sixth-grader son, Liam, to catch a 4:00 A.M. bus for an overnight trip sponsored by the school. All the other chauffeurs that morning were mothers. His own wife was home in bed. It is important that breadwinners face the new day with a full night's sleep.

" 'You going to eat all your food down there?' I asked Liam.

'Sure,' he said.

'What if you don't like it?'

'Well, I made five sandwiches just in case,' he said. 'Peanut butter. I've got them in the suitcase.'

'Peanut butter? Inside the suitcase?'

'Don't worry about them,' he said. 'I wrapped them up in the shirts.'

'Liam . . .'

'Just kidding, Dad.' "

As he watched his son climb onto the bus, there was a lump in his throat that couldn't be swallowed. There he was. Liam McGrady, "carrying camera and overnight bag and maybe some peanut-butter sandwiches, openly enthusiastic about his debut in the world" (McGrady, 1975:200-201).

Nontraditional Family Structure and Maternal Employment

Identification theory assumes that children pattern their ideas of appropriate gender behavior upon the parental behavior they observe. If their home is organized along traditional lines, children will in all likelihood regard this organization as perfectly "normal." In other words, children's minds reflect the gender patterns that their parents have established.

Ronald Lambert's (1971) study of children's images of masculinity and femininity was based on this very point. A major premise of his research was that "if sex makes a difference in the organization of the family, then it will make a difference in the thinking of the children [emphasis in original deleted]" (p. 43). Because this study will be cited in subsequent sections, some details on the conduct of the inquiry are worth mentioning. Children's beliefs about the psychological distinctiveness of the two sexes were measured by means of questionnaires administered to 7,500 children between ten and sixteen years of age, a third of them French-speaking from Quebec, a third English-speaking from Ontario and a third English-speaking from British Columbia and Nova Scotia. (Two-thirds of their mothers also completed questionnaires.) Four dimensions of "sex-role differentiation" (SRD, the study's dependent variable) were measured: *SRD-Traits* (psychological distinctiveness of male-female characteristics); *SRD-Behavior* (whether certain types of conduct are suitable for males and females); *SRD-Jobs* (possible sex-typing of occupations); *SRD-Relations* (sex-appropriate ways of relating to peers and adult authority figures). A major hypothesis was that the "more sharply parents' roles were determined according to sex, the greater would be the children's SRD" (p. 31). Says the author:

> If sex is a basis of differentiation of each person's duties and rights within the family, then we suppose children's attitudes toward the sexes will reflect this fact. And if sex is unimportant as a basis of role assignment in the family, then children will think in 'modern' or non-differentiated ways. Thus, we make the assumption that mind is a derivative of social structure, in this case, family structure. We make the further assumption that children extrapolate from these experiences to the world in general. [p. 31]

Professor Lambert's major finding confirmed this assumption: children who perceived the sexes as quite different came from homes organized along traditional sex divisions in terms of discipline, caring and power.

Some additional findings were that boys tended to sex-type more than girls, except in the authority dimensions of SRD-Relations. Second, imagery did not become more differentiated with age. The youngest and oldest age groups differentiated the sexes more than the intermediate age group (p. 27). We will have occasion to refer to the Lambert study later on.

Though a number of criteria could be used to diagnose family structure as "nontraditional," most research here has focused on mothers' employment outside the home, which theoretically parallels fathers' absence. However, it was "maternal deprivation," never paternal deprivation, that caused Bowlby (1952) and his sympathizers to fret. Mothers who did not devote themselves full time to motherhood were threatened with the possibility that their children would be psychologically or socially maladjusted. The timing of the "maternal deprivation" notion may not have been coincidental:

> The idea gained currency just at the time when men were being demobilized at the end of World War II, and began to displace women from the jobs they had occupied during the war. . . . Child care facilities, provided to induce women to enter employment, were disbanded. Women were being pushed out of the paid work force by men, at the same time they were having full responsibility for child care 'restored' to them. The 'maternal deprivation' thesis provided a convenient rationale for these changes. [Laws, 1979:126-27]

Both situations represent departures from the traditional family setup, namely, "father out coping with the external world, mother at home creating a haven of warmth and comfort within which father can shelter and children grow" (Rapoport and Rapoport, 1977:327). Since we have already dealt with paternal absence, this section will confine itself to the impact of mothers' employment upon the socialization of children.

A substantial and increasing proportion of Canadian homes are potentially affected by the phenomenon under discussion. In 1973 (the last date for which information is available), 35% of the women in the Canadian labor force had children under age sixteen (Statistics Canada, 1977:22). The labor-force participation of Canadian mothers increased steadily between 1967 and 1973, at an annual growth rate of 8.1%. Although women with no children are much more likely to participate in the labor force, one-third of mothers with preschool children *are* in the labor force (Boyd, Eichler and Hofley, 1976:28-30).

Research suggests three reasons why more mothers are not in the labor force. As we noted earlier, a strong norm proscribes maternal employment outside the home. (Eighty-one percent of a national Canadian sample agreed that "when children are young a mother's place is in the home" [Gibbins, Ponting and Symons, 1978:23].) In addition, some mothers of preschool children stay home because they feel personally responsible for their children's care (and, in many cases, derive pleasure from providing such care) (Bruce, 1978). Finally, lack of suitable alternative child-care arrangements discourages some mothers (Bruce, 1978; Spencer and Featherstone, 1970). Very likely, the social attitude has something to do with both maternal attitudes and scarcity of day-care facilities.

A thoroughgoing review of the research pertaining to effects of maternal employment upon children is a complex endeavor. (See Etaugh, 1974; Hoffman, 1974; Nye and Hoffman, 1963.) Many "effects" on children have been considered: their mental health, social adjustment (including independence) and juvenile delinquency. Here, our attention will be confined largely to children's conception of gender, particularly femininity. Similarly, researchers have found a number of family-related variables to be relevant, including (1) family size, (2) age, sex and ordinal position of children, (3) social class and (4) child-care arrangements. Finally, the nature of the work the mother does (e.g., full-time or part-time/professional or nonprofessional) and her attitude toward working are centrally involved. Because of space limitations, our discussion will be limited, (1) to research's general conclusions on whether the overall effects of maternal employment are beneficial or detrimental, and (2) to data that pertain to impact on children's gender imagery.

It is necessary first to be more specific about the reasons for supposing that the mother's outside work alters the family social structure. Before the sociological experts are consulted, a somewhat optimistic letter to Ann Landers (1981) will be cited. (In addition to the fact that Ann Landers's material is more amusing than most social scientists', her own assessment of her credentials seems reasonable. "Yes, it's a different world out there, and as one who has closely witnessed the shifting of scenery over the past twenty-five years, I feel as if I'm sitting in the catbird seat. For my mail faithfully reflects what's happening at every economic, intellectual and social level. My readers tell me *everything*" (emphasis in original, Landers, 1981:14).

Here is the sanguine letter:

> Dear Ann Landers:
>   I'm not writing about a problem. I just want to tell a few million people what a healthy thing it can be for the whole family when the wife is forced to take a job outside the home.
>   My husband and I are both in our middle 30s. We have three boys, ten, eight and seven years of age. When they were babies, Jim never lifted a hand to help with the kids. Fortunately, my mother lived next door. Without her help, I would have wound up in the loony bin. To be fair, it wasn't all Jim's fault. He worked hard at his job and it never occurred to me to ask him to give me a hand with the kids.
>   Two years ago, when our youngest son started kindergarten, Jim and I talked it over and decided the only way we could keep up the mortgage payments, buy groceries and pay heating bills was for me to go back to work. . . .
>   Today I can honestly say, Ann, that my going back to work was the best thing that could have happened to our family. Circumstances have forced Jim to get to know his sons. Also, he has a better understanding of what it's like to keep house and raise children, because he's doing it right

along with me. Jim and I are closer now than we've ever been. And, oh yes, the kids are terrific about pitching in. They've really shaped up since I've had to go to work (Mandy). [Landers, 1981:18-19]

Several changes in the traditional family organization are implicit and explicit in this letter. (We will set aside for the moment the question of whether this lady's happy experiences can be generalized to all working wives.) First, the very fact of the mother's going out to work means that she provides her children with a novel conception of femininity. Women are seen as people who have jobs and earn money. The husband, in the letter at least, also provides a different model. A second suggested consequence of the mother's employment outside the home concerns changes in the familial division of labor. "Jim" now lifts a hand to help, so "Mandy" no longer fears the loony bin! Do families indeed become more egalitarian or do women simply try to cope with the combined load of domestic and external employment obligations? Meissner et al.'s (1975) study of the time budgets of Vancouver couples (cited earlier), as well as their evaluation of previous research, allows us to assess the relative merits of these two conflicting possibilities.

As Meissner et al. (1975:425) note, research projects in America (Blood and Wolfe, 1960), Sweden (Gendell, 1963), France (Michel, 1970b) and Britain (Young and Willmott, 1973) have reported extensive husband-and-wife sharing of household tasks when wives hold paying jobs. However, the way these social scientists designed their research very likely influenced their findings. The wives being interviewed were either asked if their husbands helped with housework, or given a list of chores and activities in order to indicate whether they were always done by the wife or the husband, more by one spouse than the other, or equally. This approach is open to perceptual misinterpretation, memory lapses and to social desirability.

Time budget studies, on the other hand, tend to support the opposite position. Here, researchers ask for detailed information on how time is used.

The time budgets of some 30,000 people in twelve countries show that married women with paying jobs are overworked in comparison to employed men and to housewives (Szalai, 1972. . .). A study of American women (Walker, 1970) has demonstrated that women's overall workload and housework hours are dramatically affected by their paid work and the number and ages of children, while their husbands' hours remain unchanged except in the extreme case when their wives worked for pay *and* they had either five or more children or the youngest was under two. [Meissner et al., 1975:427]

The results of the Canadian study were consistent with those of time budget studies done elsewhere. The total weekly workload of employed wives increases by eighteen hours over that of full-time housewives. In couples without a child under ten, husbands increase their 3.3 hours of weekly housework by six minutes when the wives go out to work. In couples with a young child, the husbands' five hours of weekly work around the house increase by one hour a week when their wives work for pay (Meissner et al., 1975:436).[5] All these figures are averages, of course. Overall, the data support the conclusion that "Mandy" is unusually lucky, because most women still bear most of the burden of household tasks.

A third possible consequence of the wife's employment is an increase in her power within the family. Although Mandy's letter does not make specific reference to this outcome, her newfound delight in her situation implies getting her own way more often. "Getting one's own way" is very close to the technical definition of *power* as "the ability in an interpersonal situation, to get what you want" (Turk, 1975:238). An upswing of interest in family power developed during the 1950s. Out of this research emerged questions concerning what the concept of "family power" really meant and how it could be measured (Turk, 1975:237). Perhaps the most influential views on the subject of conjugal power were those associated with "resource theory" (Blood and Wolfe, 1960).

Resource theorists make the assumption that the balance of power depends on the relative resources that each marriage partner contributes to the marriage. Possible resources include the social status of a prestigious occupation, distinguished lineage and money. When a wife is employed, she can contribute to the family income. Therefore, the argument goes, her power within the family increases and she is in a better bargaining position to suggest or to demand a more egalitarian marital division of labor (Brown, 1978:6). Studies conducted in a number of different cultures do support these predictions (e.g., Heer, 1958; Lupri, 1969; Michel, 1970b; Richmond, 1976; Safilios-Rothschild, 1967; Scanzoni, 1970). However, a few studies have failed to find a relationship between the wife's employment and family power (Centers, Raven and Rodrigues, 1971; Kandel and Lesser, 1972).

Despite the pattern of consistent findings, the question of what *familial power* means exactly began to be debated. Eventually, critics reached the conclusion that "what family researchers have found out about power is more influenced by the measure than by the family being studied" (Turk, 1975:238).

This methodological point was forcibly made by Turk's and Bell's (1972) study of 211 Toronto families. Nine different measures of power, drawn from previous studies, were used to assess the power relations within each of these families. For example, one procedure replicated Blood's and Wolfe's (1960) questionnaire, which sought wives' answers as to who made decisions in the family: "husband always," "husband more than wife," "husband and wife exactly the same," "wife more than husband," "wife always." Eight areas of decision making were tapped (Turk, 1975:239): What car to buy? (husband always). Whether or not to buy life insurance? (husband and wife exactly the same). Where to go on vacation (husband and wife exactly the same). What house or apartment to take? (husband and wife exactly the same). Whether or not the wife should go to work or quit work? (husbands always!!). What doctor to have when someone is sick? (wife more than husband). How much money the family can afford to spend per week on food? (wife more than husband). According to this decision-making measure, the family would be classified as egalitarian.

A more recent Alberta study (Brinkerhoff and Lupri, 1978) reiterates the criticism that researchers using the Blood and Wolfe measure are assuming that all decisions are of *equal importance* within a family and that all decisions are made with *equal frequency*. Their findings were slightly different than Turk's. Brinkerhoff and Lupri found wives to be slightly more powerful than their husbands in making decisions. Wives' power was increased when items relating to children were included ("childrens' spending money," "childrens' discipline," "childrens' clothes"). Moreover, they report that the wives' desire to change jobs is now an egalitarian decision. However, contrary to resource theory's initial prediction, Brinkerhoff and Lupri state that working wives report slightly lower power scores than nonworking wives.

Since the other measures of conjugal power that Turk and Bell (1972) replicated are not as popular as the first one, they can be more quickly described. The second procedure involved asking married couples to indicate who usually won when there was a disagreement between them. (In 39% of the couples, both said "husband" and in 12%, both said "wife." The remainder of the responses were distributed between one or both saying "neither partner winning.") A third measure assessed power by asking "Who is the real boss in your family?" Only wives replied. (Seventy-six percent said their husband was boss, 11% claimed themselves to be boss and 13% said it was shared equally between husband and wife.) The remaining measures replicated were observational measures of how the family behaved in an observed task. One task asked families to decide how they would spend a gift of $300. They could do with it what they pleased as long as they did not save it or spend it on something they had already decided to buy. Whoever suggested what the family eventually decided to buy was seen as the more powerful person. (Husband and wife power was about equal here, but for the first time, children were seen to have power.) The other measures were labelled "interactional" measures because they were based on various aspects of group behavior in the course of spending the $300 or resolving differences. For example, the relative number of interruptions each person initiates is a measure of power.

What conclusions did Turk and Bell reach about conjugal power? The main conclusion was that the measures were not very highly related to each other. When questionnaire techniques were used, husbands seemed dominant. When observational techniques were used, the power between spouses was more balanced. Obviously, the whole concept of power requires rethinking. A second conclusion was that the findings depend on which family member is treated as the key informant. Although wives have, in the past, been the more accessible informants (to the point where Safilios-Rothschild [1969] criticized the sociology of the family for being "wives' sociology"), wives, husbands (and children) have their own particular perceptions of what goes on in their family. Finally, Turk and Bell concluded that the results from their Canadian sample showed no substantial differences from other, mainly American, samples. In short, while power measures are reliable, their validity is suspect. Before sociologists can properly decide whether outside employment truly enhances the mother's power, more refined conceptualizations and measures of power have to be devised.

Meanwhile egalitarianism within the family does carry richer connotations than equality in the decision-making process. Eichler (1975b:223), for example, defines an egalitarian family "as a family in which both husband and wife have equal rights and duties." Equality under the law constitutes one aspect of family equality. According to Eichler, an egalitarian family style, i.e., a nontraditional gender socialization environment for children, might be possible *if* wives had access to jobs superior to the low-paying, low-prestige jobs where employed women tend to cluster. That is a big "if", since the labor market is resistant to change. At the moment, we can hypothesize that dual-career, professional families are most likely to provide an egalitarian atmosphere. However, British and American studies of dual-career families support Meissner et al.'s (1975) general finding of limited change in division of domestic labor—"the wife in dual-career families is still the one *responsible* for the well-being of the children and the household, although commonly the husband will *help* [emphases in original]" (Eichler, 1975b:226). A second possible solution, which is yet more utopian, involves allowing *either* partner the choice of staying home to raise children or entering the labor market, with the government compensating the efforts of the partner who stays home. In that way, the efforts of both partners would be compensated, and economic dependence on the working spouse would be avoided (Eichler, 1975b:230). Eichler, then, agrees with Chodorow (1978) that parenting should not be the exclusive responsibility of the mother.

To return to the main consideration, namely, the impact of maternal employment on the children, the first question to be answered is whether the impact is beneficial or detrimental. Despite existing societal opinion, the working mothers themselves do not seem to be unduly perturbed by this consideration (Mackie, 1976). While 21% of a Western Canadian sample of working mothers agreed with the attitudinal statement, "I worry that I'm not a good mother," 25% of a comparable sample of full-time housewives responded in the same fashion to this item. Sixty-eight percent believe that working makes them better mothers. (This was especially so for those women working for intrinsic job satisfaction [76%], as opposed to those working primarily for money [35%].) Eighty-five percent of the working mothers enjoyed the time away from their children.

The conclusions reached by a review of the effects of maternal employment on children (Etaugh, 1974) are presented here according to children's age. Apparently, young children can form as strong an attachment to a working parent as to a nonworking parent, provided that that parent interacts frequently with the child in the time that is available. Stable substitute care arrangements are important for the normal personality and cognitive development of preschool children whose mothers work (p. 75). Similarly, the adjustment of elementary-school children is not adversely affected by the mother's working (p. 77). "Mothers who are satisfied with their roles—whether working or not—have the best-adjusted children" (p. 80). Finally, the mother's working has little effect on the adjustment of adolescents, though lower-class children may have some trouble adjusting to full-time maternal employment (p. 90). We can conclude, then, that mothers who work are not harming their children. Maternal employment does not necessarily imply maternal deprivation.

Our second question inquired into the relationship between maternal employment and gender behavior. Considerable evidence exists to demonstrate that maternal employment does influence children's perception of gender. For instance, working women's daughters have been found to have higher career aspirations than do daughters of nonworking women (Etaugh, 1974:85).[6] Perception of father's approval of mother's employment is an important factor in the daughter's intention to pursue role-innovative occupations (Baruch, 1972).

In a similar vein, working mothers' children are less likely to endorse a traditional or stereotypical view of women. For example, students with employed mothers perceived significantly smaller differences between male and female roles, with the women being more affected by maternal employment than the men (Hoffman, 1974). An interesting finding here concerns the evaluation of other women's competence by daughters of employed versus nonemployed women (Baruch, 1972). The study was of the kind mentioned in the previous chapter; subjects were asked to evaluate professional articles that differed only with respect to the sex of the author. Half the articles were given female authors, half male authors. Daughters of nonemployed women devalued the professional competence of female authors more than did the daughters of employed women. Maternal employment has been found to be positively related to favoring social equality for women. However, curiously enough, the relationship between maternal employment and gender ideology (beliefs concerning kinds of behavior appropriate for females and males) is not clear (Etaugh, 1974; Hoffman, 1974). Some studies find the expected, positive relationship, while others find no relationship.

For girls, maternal employment is related to greater admiration of the mother and a higher evaluation of female competence (Hoffman, 1974). Although researchers had expected that this, in turn, should imply a more positive self-concept for daughters of working mothers, the results are somewhat confusing. For example, Kappel and Lambert (1972), (described in Hoffman [1974]), having administered a questionnaire measure of self-esteem to 3,315 nine- to sixteen-year-old Canadian children, found that the daughters of nonworking mothers were lower in self-esteem than were the daughters of mothers working part-time but higher than were the daughters of mothers working full-time. However, the daughters of mothers working full-time had higher self-esteem than did those of nonworking mothers, when the mothers worked because of a desire for self-actualization or were professional.

Finally, three Canadian studies report that some effects of maternal employment are influenced by social class. Gold's (1976) study of ten-year-old children found that while children of employed mothers generally had more egalitarian gender concepts than those of nonworking mothers, gender distinctions were especially salient for the sons of employed mothers in working-class families. The other two pieces of research suggest that in working-class homes, the mother's employment signals to the child that the father is an economic failure (Hoffman, 1974). In the study cited above, Kappel and Lambert (1972) found that the nine- to sixteen-year-old sons of full-time working mothers in the lower class evaluated their fathers lower than did the sons of other full-time working mothers and lower than did the sons of part-time or nonworking mothers in any class. That processes of gender socialization may differ in working-class and middle-class homes receives further support from Propper's (1972) survey of Toronto high-school students. She reports that fewer sons of working-class employed women chose their father as the man they most admired, than sons of nonworking mothers from the same social class. A decade has passed since these last two studies were done. Lower-class devaluation of the father's capacity as a breadwinner may well have diminished with the increasing prevalance of employed mothers.

To summarize, when the mother works outside the home she provides a different role model for her children. Benefits accrue particularly to daughters. Although the division of labor and the distribution of conjugal power are not altered as dramatically as analysts had originally supposed, we can describe the resulting home atmosphere as "non-traditional," if not "egalitarian." Since an increasing number of married women are in the labor force, we would expect substantial numbers of Canadian children to be exposed to experiences that may lead to some blurring of gender distinctions. Nevertheless, radical changes cannot be predicted from this source alone. Children observe parental behavior in the home, not in the workplace, and women still bear most of the burden of household tasks. Another likely consequence of the fact that maternal employment is becoming the norm rather than the exception is that in the future, working mothers may no longer be nontraditional models. Finally, the fact that maternal employment does not imply maternal deprivation merits emphasis.

Siblings as Agents of Socialization

Approximately one-half of Canadian families have two or more children (Kalbach and McVey, 1979), thus making possible socialization by siblings. Because brothers and sisters play an important role in the gender socialization of one another, we would also expect gender socialization to involve sibling-sibling as well as parent-child influences. Unfortunately, sibling influences are quite difficult to isolate (Yussen and Santrock, 1978:379). The number and sex of siblings, as well as the number of years separating them in age, have to be considered.

Although much more research is needed before firm generalizations can be stated, such data as do exist suggest that siblings act as surrogate parental models for gender behavior (Weitz, 1977:84). Rosenberg and Sutton-Smith (1968) report that girls with sisters scored significantly higher on the Gough Scales of Psychological Femininity than girls with brothers. Similarly, Brim (1958) found that five- and six-year-old boys with older brothers displayed more of the traits than have traditionally been thought of as masculine than did boys with older sisters. He also found that girls with older brothers displayed more traditionally masculine traits than girls without older brothers. These girls did not substitute masculine for feminine traits. Instead, their repertoire included characteristics that have traditionally been attributed to both sexes. Vroegh (1971), however, found little evidence that the presence of older like-sex siblings reinforces appropriate gender identity.

A closely related matter for which even less evidence is available is the possible effect of birth order upon traditional gender behavior. Kammeyer (1967) found firstborn girls to be more traditional than girls born later. Though at this point we can only guess at the causal mechanisms involved, the older children in a family do tend to be more intensely and thoroughly socialized. Parents have more time and energy to devote to older children. In addition, older children tend to be more socially conventional and more like their parents than are other children (Brophy, 1977:260). (However, Rosenberg and Sutton-Smith [1968] reported that birth order did not affect femininity scores.)

Demographic Variations in Gender Role Socialization

Canadian society is a heterogeneous one, and there are ethnic, social class and regional differences in family processes that might well influence gender socialization. Though the work on how various Canadian subcultures interpret and teach gender relations has barely begun, we do have some preliminary indications of the relationship between gender socialization and social class (along with education), rural versus urban residence, and ethnicity.

Social Class

Canadian society, like all other large societies, is socially stratified. When sociologists talk about *social stratification*, they are referring to the arrangement of a "group or society into a hierarchy of positions that are unequal with regard to power, property, social evaluation, and/or psychic gratification" (Tumin, 1967:12). The occupations of the parents provide the best indicator of a Canadian family's social class position, which will influence the child's socialization experiences and consequent opportunities.

Members of different social classes, by virtue of experiencing different conditions of life, come to see the world differently and develop different conceptions of social reality (Gecas, 1976; Kohn, 1977). Theorists suggest that working-class parents are more traditional in their values and experience greater role division by sex than do middle-class parents (Romer and Cherry, 1980:249). Middle-class fathers tend to be warmer, more expressive and less authoritarian than working-class fathers. Working-class mothers are seen as more traditionally feminine, more family-oriented and (in many cases, by definition) less well-educated than their middle-class counterparts. Male and female roles are expected to be less sharply differentiated in middle-class homes than in working-class homes.

Social class variation exists in styles of socialization, as well as in content of socialization lessons. In general, middle-class parents tend to be more permissive than lower-class parents in their child rearing (Gecas, 1976). Lambert (1981:68) elaborates upon his observations in this area:

> The outstanding finding then is that Canadian parents of working-class backgrounds are decidedly more demanding and more punitive than middle-class parents in their child-rearing values. . . . We can only

speculate about the reasons for these parental differences in outlook. It could well be that working-class parents train their children with more security and exigence, as a means of preparing them for the world these parents know well, a world where, because of one's lower status in society, one must be prepared to suffer, to be humiliated, and especially, to be prepared to do what one is told.

The available Canadian studies support the theoretical sketch of class differences given above.

Lambert's (1971) study of gender imagery in Canadian children, which was mentioned earlier in another context, found parents' social class (as measured by the Blishen [1967] scale) to be strongly related to their (the parents') perception of gender. Greater traditionalism was found among working-class respondents. This finding accords with Mussen's (1969:711) views. The latter contended that lower-class children are aware of gender patterns earlier and also conform to these preferences more clearly than do middle-class children.

In order to test the hypothesis that the working class is more conservative than the middle class in its ideology about women, Gaskell (1975) conducted a questionnaire study of 243 Boston high-school girls. Four dimensions of what she labelled "sex-role ideology" were measured: descriptions of femininity and evaluation of the importance of being feminine; beliefs about division of labor within the home; beliefs about proper power relations between the sexes; and beliefs about the desirability of change in "sex role" relationships through the women's liberation movement. Gaskell found in general that girls from working-class homes were more traditional in their views. Although only two of the four relationships were statistically significant, the direction of the relationship was always the same. That is, the working-class girls were more conservative. The effect of social class background was more pronounced on beliefs about division of labor within the home and the desirability of change in "sex roles." Social class was a less important influence upon the belief in male supremacy and the importance placed on femininity.

The result that lower-class people tend to hold more conservative views on gender seems to be well established. Why is this so? Working-class children grow up in homes that provide more traditional role models than do middle-class children, but this observation fails to explain how the homes got that way in the first place. Kohn (1977) speculates that the parental values apparent in socialization of their children are extensions of modes of behavior that are functional for them in their occupations. He argues that the white-collar work of the middle class enunciates values of self-direction, such as freedom, individualism, initiative, creativity and self-actualization. Blue-collar work, on the other hand, is more likely to involve values of conformity to external standards, such as orderliness, neatness and obedience (Gecas, 1976:44-45). From these conjectures, several lines of reasoning about gender can be extrapolated. For instance, lower-class people may be more resistant to innovation in male-female relations. Perhaps they are less concerned about the actualization of female potential. And so on.

Rural-Urban Differences

Very little attention has been paid to the differences, if any, in the way gender relations are defined by the 5% of the Canadian population who live on farms (Statistics Canada, 1980:92). To date, most commentary has focused on farm women, rather than farm children. However, if we wish to make a prediction about the relationship between a family's location (rural versus urban) and its children's socialization, there is some reason to expect farm families to be more traditional. For one thing, agricultural work is closer to blue-collar work than to white-collar work. Therefore, Kohn's (1977) analysis of occupational value orientations (discussed above) would lead to a prediction of more conservative gender patterns in rural areas. This hypothesis is also supported by the conclusions drawn by a National Farmers Union report, prepared with International Women's Year funding, entitled *Farm Women in Our Society* (Carey, 1978-79), that male dominance prevails in agriculture and women are viewed as "helpers."

However, the fact that farm children see their mothers engaged in activities that are a far cry from traditional "women's work" might lead, on the contrary, to a prediction of blurred gender definition. A study of Ontario farm families (Abell, 1975) reported that farms most often depended entirely on the labor contributed by the farmer, his wife and children. Ninety-seven percent of the farm wives said they did one or more farm tasks, such as "operating farm machinery, driving a truck or tractor, keeping farm accounts, handling eggs and feeding livestock, as well as some field and garden work" (Abell, 1975:370). In the words of Norma Taylor (1976:151), who lives with her husband and three of their five children on a sheep and grain farm near Biggar, Saskatchewan, "Economic necessity has made the farm wife an integral part of the entire family operation. It has always been difficult to afford hired help, and she is the cheapest possible source of labour. She is cook, baker, gardener, accountant, part-time butcher, seamstress, hired man and mother. And all this for three-and-a-half per day. (No not dollars—three meals and half the bed.)"[7]

We can cover our bets and argue either way. What does the evidence tell us about the relationship between gender socialization and growing up on a farm? The one relevant piece of research that we were able to locate did *not* support rural traditionalism. When Lambert (1971) analyzed gender imagery in terms of rural-urban residence, he found "no hint of any relationship." Therefore, he concluded that, "the mass media and centralized schooling have presumably urbanized even the nominally rural, so that there is no sign that people outside the cities cling to traditional conceptions of the sexes" (Lambert, 1971:26). Though the impact of these nonfamilial agents of socialization may indeed be responsible for this finding, Lambert's correlational data cannot of course pin down the precise causation involved. Our suggestion of nontraditional role models may also be a factor. Although repetition may become tiresome, we must once again say that more research is required before firm conclusions can be drawn.

Ethnicity

Canada is frequently described as an ethnic mosaic. According to the 1971 census, 45% of the population had a British background and 29% a French background. The ethnic origins of the remaining 26% were extremely diverse, with thirty-five other groups being listed by the census.

Because Canada is not a melting pot that culturally homogenizes its people, ethnicity is presumed to exert a major influence on many families (Ishwaran, 1980). Indeed, social scientists view the family as the "cradle of ethnic consciousness." Although most Canadians share a common core of experiences and values, both their general socialization and their gender socialization may reflect ethnic differences in values, norms and identity. The matter is further complicated by the fact that ethnic background and social class position are frequently related. Both John Porter's *The Vertical Mosaic* (1965) and the Royal Commission on Bilingualism and Biculturalism emphasized "the manner in which the fact of ethnic affiliation is interwoven with the structure of social class" in this country (Blishen, 1973:162). Regional variations produce further complexity. Driedger (1978:14) tells us that "the political and economic power elite . . . are still largely British. The British elite . . . dominate the Canadian economic system with a strong influence in urban industrial Ontario, with emerging strength in Alberta but declining strength in the Maritimes. The French dominate the political structure in the province of Quebec, the British dominate in Ontario and the East, and other ethnic groups are increasingly becoming politically influential in the West."

No one has even begun to untangle the ways in which gender socialization is influenced by the interacting effects of ethnicity, social class and region. Unfortunately, too, systematic information is sparse concerning the nuances of gender socialization in nearly forty different ethnic groups. However, our discussion below of the three types of relevant studies that have been carried out will serve to alert the reader to the fact that "the Canadian family" necessarily represents an abstract oversimplification of reality (Ishwaran, 1976).

One fragmentary source consists of scattered references to gender relations in descriptions of specific ethnic groups. Two examples of this type of research will do to illustrate this type of work. In his observations on the acculturation of Italian immigrant children, Danziger (1976) reports that, "whether it is a question of role specialization or individual autonomy, traditional patterns affect the girl more than they do her brothers." He attributes this to the "special importance that the immigrant group attaches to the maintenance of strong and reliable family ties" (p. 211). Our second example is Susan Mackenzie's (1978) ethnographic study of Hutterite women. She sought answers to questions such as these: How do Hutterite women fill their days? How are their work groups and alliances formed? What importance does the colony attach to women's work? What social control techniques preserve the subordination of Hutterite women? Although the answers to these questions are too complex to describe here, Mackenzie's work does signal new developments in anthropological research. Previous studies of the Hutterites (an Anabaptist sect living communally in Western Canada and the Northeastern United States) focused almost exclusively on male behavior and male definitions of the situation.

The second type of research on the relationship between ethnicity and gender consists of English-Canadian/French-Canadian comparisons. The evidence here shows that French-Canadian attitudes have moved toward increased egalitarianism over time. In his study of gender imagery (mentioned above), Lambert (1971) found French-Canadian parents to be more traditional than English-Canadian parents.[8] French-Canadian children, however, had less differentiated views of appropriate gender behavior than did English-Canadian children. Lambert suggested that the parental difference might be partially attributable to the higher average educational level of his English-speaking sample. This interpretation accords with his finding of greater traditionalism in the working class.

Somewhat later studies showed that although some changes were occurring, French-Canadians remained quite traditional about those aspects of gender relations that concern the family. For instance, Boyd's (1975a) analysis of Gallup Poll results (cited above) found that French-Canadians entertained two attitudinal complexes with respect to women. They supported equality between the sexes, but only when the Gallup questions did not evoke maternal or wifely imagery. When these roles did become salient, French-Canadians tended to become more traditional in their attitudes toward women.

More recently, Hobart's (1981) study of university and technical students across Canada reported that Anglophone men now have the most traditional attitudes about marriage, followed by Francophone men, Anglophone women and Francophone women, in order of increasing egalitarianism. Although all four categories increased in egalitarianism between 1968 and 1977 (years in which data were collected), the Francophone increases for both sexes were very much greater. Egalitarian stances were adopted in formerly sensitive areas such as authority within marriage, child rearing, household management and women's work outside the home. According to Hobart, these data signal that recent changes have been more dramatic in Quebec families than among families in the rest of Canada. However, we suspect that the older generation of both ethnic groups remains relatively traditional in its gender attitudes.

The third category of work consists of the one Canadian study known to the author that comprehensively examines the relationship of ethnicity to familial/gender patterns, for a range of ethnic groups (Mackie and Brinkerhoff, 1982).

Despite the fact that it would be difficult to exaggerate the significance given to ethnicity by Canadian scholars, mass media and ethnic group spokespersons, some doubt has been expressed about the extent to which ethnicity really matters to many Canadians. For instance, Anderson and Frideres (1981) claim that ethnicity "has been carelessly overemphasized in the literature of sociology and other social sciences" (p. 45) and ask, "what proportion of the claimed members of a given ethnic group are actually aware of, interested in, or readily identifiable by their ethnic identity?" (p. 46). According to one study of an Alberta community (Mackie, 1978a), the answer seems to be "very few." Under research conditions that do not focus the respondents' attention on their ethnic heritage, this consideration apparently does not occupy a significant place in their consciousness.

Nonetheless, it is important to realize that whether or not ethnicity is "social reality" or "social fiction," it quite likely varies with the regions of the country. This issue is particularly interesting with regard to the prairie provinces because of two features that distinguish the region from the rest of the country. First, the prairie region is the most ethnically diverse part of Canada. Approximately half of the population is composed of people whose origin is neither British nor French. Second, the prairies have a much lower percentage of foreign-born residents than do Quebec and Ontario. Moreover, most of the present foreign-born arrived prior to World War II. Therefore, the major problem is the maintenance of ethnic identity among the established groups rather than assimilation of newcomers (Mackie, 1981a).

Mackie and Brinkerhoff (1982) categorized their Alberta respondents according to these birthplaces: Canada, Britain, Eastern Europe, Western Europe, Southern Europe, United States. The dependent variable, familial/gender attitudes, used eight types of items (wife's work status—work versus no work; division of labor within the family; tasks regarding children; socioemotional activities; decision-making power; decisions concerning children; womens' rights and mens' rights). The country of birth turned out to have surprisingly little to do with family/gender attitudes. (Of 825 statistical comparisons, only 2.4% were significant.) When various controls were applied (e.g., year of immigration, social class, education, religion), the relationship between birthplace and attitudes became even weaker. However, a pattern did emerge for those few items that were significant. People from Southern and Eastern Europe tended to be traditional, while the British, Canadians and Americans fell on the modern end of the scale. (Western European responses were mixed.)

As a check on the above findings, ethnicity was operationalized according to people's replies to a question as to whether or not they claimed ethnic identification with their ancestors who first came to this continent. The familial/gender attitudes of people who claimed British, French, German, Ukrainian and Italian identification were compared. Once again, ethnicity appeared to have little bearing upon familial/gender attitudes. However, the fact that this research involved a Western Canadian sample is obviously quite pertinent. Exaggeration of the "ethnic fact" is most likely to occur in the prairie provinces, where non-British, non-French elements predominate and are separated by three generations from homelands elsewhere. It remains to be seen whether similar results would be found in regions other than Alberta, such as Eastern Canadian cities that have experienced heavy immigration recently.

This discussion of ethnic variation concludes our analysis of the family as an agent of gender socialization. We now turn to the role played by the peer group in shaping femininity and masculinity.

THE PEER GROUP

The Importance of Children's Peer Groups

Until very recently, the influence of psychoanalytic theory led social scientists to consider childrens' relationships with peers and other relatives to be rather trivial in comparison with their relationships with their parents (Rubin, 1980). Increasingly, researchers have come to appreciate the intricacy of childrens' relationships with other children (and with other adults, both inside and outside the family, such as grandparents, neighbors, cousins and playmates' parents). The growing tendency for mothers to be employed outside the home may partly account for this new focus. The extent to which these other people are replacing the mother in childrens' lives is an interesting question.

The peer group is unquestionably a potent socialization agent. Bensman and Rosenberg (1979:80) define a peer group: "*By definition, such a group is an association of self-selected equals who coalesce around common interests, tastes, preferences, and beliefs.* Peer groups use informal criteria for membership, confer informal rewards, and impose informal sanctions. Friendship, acceptance, and belongingness are staples of the peer group in which roles remain loosely defined to cover a wide range of attachments" (emphasis in original). For children (but not necessarily for adults), peers are other children of approximately the same age. Because modern societies are age-graded, the impact of peer socialization upon children is increased. People in similar age categories tend to be segregated in schools, neighborhoods and various recreational settings. Propinquity (simply being in the same place at the same time) tends to facilitate friendships. Although children do not consciously set out to socialize one another, their need for companionship and approval results in mutual learning of a variety of information. Gender-related "knowledge" constitutes one such variety.

Friendship permits people of all ages "to escape the too close bonds of the family" (Bensman and Lilienfeld, 1979:57). The amount of time spent with friends provides an indicator of the importance of peer relations. One study of American sixth-grade children found that, over a weekend, these children spent more than twice as much time with their peers as with their parents (Condry, Siman and Bronfenbrenner, 1968, cited in Yussen and Santrock, 1978). This alternative to the family is particularly important for children; interaction with friends provides the first major social experiences outside the family circle. Peer relations allow children to begin to separate themselves from the family's all-encompassing influence and to develop other facets of their identity. One of the goals of socialization, remember, is the eventual ability to function independently of the family. Another point worth stressing is that children share a relatively equal status with their peers. This equality contrasts sharply with the low-status position of the child vis-à-vis the parents.

There are some things that can be learned only from equal-status peers. Sexuality is a case in point. "Combatting the fears of failure in sexual relations, celebrating success, and exchanging information, accurate or not, are all means for providing social support for universal biological drives that are either not deeply supported or denied at family and public levels" (Bensman and Lilienfeld, 1979:60).

In general, children interpret the world for one another in a manner that adults cannot possibly duplicate. In addition to sensitive topics more easily discussed with peers than with adults, there are many aspects of the world that matter greatly to children, of which adults are ignorant. The fact that much of this peer information might be the wildest misinformation is beside the point.

Friendship Over the Life Cycle

Peer influence is not of course confined to children. Friendship is important to people of all ages (Brenton, 1974). Even young infants stare at each other with fascination. By the age of two, children play alongside one another. By three or four years, this parallel play becomes shared play. Most parents know that companionship with other children is a necessity, not a luxury. They take pains to find little companions for their child and worry if their offspring does not seem to make friends. Within a few years children are able to relate to groups of children.[9] By eight or nine years, most children are concerned with having one special friend. For some of us, being rejected by a best friend was one of the poignant tragedies of childhood.

Researchers' newfound appreciation of the importance of early peer relations has led to interest in how children think about friendship. Rubin (1980) tells us that children have friendships that are more sophisticated than they can explain. Apparently, children have their own original "theories" of friendship. Selman and Selman (1979), who studied the "friendship thinking" of 250 subjects, aged three to forty-five, claim that children's understanding develops in a relatively universal, but overlapping, sequence of five stages. These investigators called *Stage 0* (ages three to seven) the stage of *momentary playmateship*. Here, friends are valued for their material and physical attributes—"she is my friend because she has a doctor kit with real candy pills." Friends are those who are close by. *Stage 1* (ages four to nine) is the stage of *one-way assistance*. Although the child can differentiate between his/her own perspective and that of others, the notion that relations with other people involve give-and-take is not yet understood. Hence, Milly regards Billy as a good friend because Billy does what Milly wants him to do. *Stage 2* (ages six to twelve), the stage of *two-way fair-weather cooperation*, involves some conception of friendship as a two-way street. However, the purpose of friendship is seen as serving separate self-interests, rather than mutual interests. *Stage 3* (ages nine to fifteen) is the stage of *intimate, mutually shared relationships*. Friends share secrets, plans, feelings and activities. Close friendship is both intimate and somewhat possessive. *Stage 4* (age twelve and older), the stage of *autonomous interdependent friendships*, characterizes the friendship theories of adolescents and adults. There is an appreciation of the need to provide a friend with both autonomy and psychological support. Freedom is granted to form other friendships.

Adolescence seems to mark the peak of peer group influence. The teenager's orientation to the companionship, opinions and tastes of age-mates helps to bridge the gulf between childish dependence on the family and adulthood. In the words of Bensman and Lilienfeld (1979:66), "some friendships, especially the friendships of adolescents, are likely to reach considerable depth, intimacy, and mutual involvement. The common vulnerability of adolescents and the lack of sharp barriers to their sense of self enables others who are sympathetic to their aspirations to reach them." Peer relations continue to matter a great deal to people in the middle adult years and also in old age.

We now turn from the general discussion of the influence of age-mates to a consideration of the relationship between friendship and gender socialization. These questions are addressed: Does the predominant pattern consist of same-sex friendship groups or mixed-sex groups? What evidence exists to support Lionel Tiger's (1969) contention that males "bond," that male friendships differ in quantity and quality from female friendships? How do cultural definitions of gender influence relations with the opposite sex in adolescence and adulthood? Here, we focus briefly on platonic and romantic relationships. We remain concerned with the overriding issue: What gender-relevant lessons are learned from peers?

Prevalence of Same-Sex Friendships

The research literature pertaining to our query, whether people are more apt to have same-sex or opposite-sex friends, is unequivocal. Throughout the life cycle, same-sex friendships predominate. Preschool age children choose playmates of the same sex, regardless of the nature of play activities (Fagot and Patterson, 1969). The same pattern prevails among elementary-school children. In a sociometric[10] study of American children in the fourth to sixth grades, Hallinan (1979) reported that only 5% of the friendship choices were cross-sex choices. Friendship patterns follow same-sex lines through adolescence into adulthood, though cross-sex dating and mating occur, of course (Frieze et al., 1978:96). Some mates are also friends!

Why do same-sex friendships completely overshadow cross-sex friendships? Our answer relies not on firm data, but on extrapolation from related areas and commonsense speculation. Although this observation does not seem very instructive, same-sex friendships occur partly because society views same-sex friendships with approval. Barbara's parents are more comfortable when she plays with Arabella than with Bruce. With regard to older people, Chafetz (1974:164) argues that, "the one way in which neither sex is taught to view the other is as potential friends and peers. Thus in any platonic relationship there is a built-in dynamic encouraging one or both participants to redefine the situation by 'falling in love.' Generally, either both do, in which case TRUE LOVE results, or one alone does, in which case the relationship becomes uncomfortable and is usually abruptly terminated."

Though Chafetz's case seems a bit overstated, some of the findings of a *Psychology Today* survey on friendship (Parlee et al., 1979) support her point. Seventy-three percent of the 40,000 readers who voluntarily mailed in questionnaires (the number indicates that the subject interested many people) felt that friendships with someone of the opposite sex were different from same-sex friendships. The major reasons given for this position were that sexual tensions complicate such relations and that society does not encourage them. Almost half these respondents had had a friendship turn into a sexual relationship. This report refers to adults. However, even children are teased about having a "little boyfriend" or "girlfriend" when they play with children of the opposite sex.

The choice of same-sex friends is a specific case of the well-documented general relationship between interpersonal attraction and similarity. People are attracted to people who resemble themselves. Think about your closest friend. How old is that person? How tall? What eye color? Ethnicity? What is your friend's occupation? If a student, what course of studies is he/she involved in? What kind of music or books does he/she prefer? Would you describe this person as religious or not religious? Politically liberal or politically conservative? In all likelihood, many of your friend's characteristics match your own. Research (Rubin, 1973:136-37) shows that friends are similar in terms of religion, economic background, occupation, education and political allegiance. (Matching physical features like eye color and height might indicate the same ethnic background.)

Why similarity? In a famous proposition (which does have exceptions), George Homans (1950:112) predicted that, "If the frequency of interaction between two or more people increases, their degree of liking for one another will increase." Interaction provides opportunities for rewards. Familiarity with others like ourselves is apt to be particularly rewarding. Similarity provides a basis for shared activities, in this case, doing "boy things" or "girl things." To take the opposite case, it is sometimes difficult to predict how people who differ from us are likely to behave, and this absence of shared frames of reference can be punishing. In general, then, similarity leads to liking, and liking in turn leads to increased similarity as friends influence one another. Children's same-sex peer groups tend to reflect the containing culture and reinforce sex stereotyping (Chafetz, 1974:79).

The Quality of Male versus Female Friendships

It will be recalled from Chapter Three that Lionel Tiger (1969) argued that males' biologically based propensity to "bond" was responsible, in part, for male dominance over females. Although Tiger is vague, even mystical, about the precise nature of this bonding, he does imply that all-male associations are superior in quality and quantity to all-female associations.

First, are males more likely to form groups? Three studies negate Tiger's contention. In Hallinan's (1979:46) sociometric study of children's friendships cited above, no sex differences were found in the number of friendship choices made or received. (The average child chose about five best friends.) A 1972 study carried out by Booth (and described in Deaux [1976]), involved interviewing 800 Nebraska adults. Males reported an average of 3.9 best friends, versus 3.6 for females (an insignificant difference). Contrary to Tiger's position, men reported more opposite-sex friends than women (15% for males and 9% for females). When he investigated voluntary organization membership, Booth found that women did belong to somewhat fewer organizations than did men. However, the average number of hours spent working for these organizations was higher for women. Finally, a national survey of volunteers in Canada (Carter, 1975:16-17) found volunteers to be 44.4% male and 55.6% female, a finding in opposition to Tiger's bonding hypothesis.

Tiger's argument contradicts traditional wisdom, which depicts females as the sociable sex. Maccoby and Jacklin (1974:211) tested the accuracy of "the view of female personality as involving 'greater interest in people, and greater capacity for the establishment of interpersonal relations.' " Although, as subsequent sections will demonstrate, males and females differ in the *expression* of their sociability, Maccoby and Jacklin's (1974:225) survey of the research found little sex differentiation in need for affiliation or sociability.

Tiger is not alone in his belief that male and female friendships differ in quality. The "flawed" friendships of females have been the subject of considerable comment (Brenton, 1974:142). André Maurois (not known as a feminist) claimed that a woman "will always give first place to the man she loves physically, and if he insists, will renounce the most perfect friendship for him." Even Simone de Beauvoir (1952), a pioneer champion of women, entertained ideas about women's friendships that seem odd today. However, she attributed the problem to women's status as "the second sex," not to biological predisposition.

> Women's fellow feeling rarely rises to genuine friendships. . . . Women feel their solidarity more spontaneously than men; but within this solidarity the transcendance of each does not go out toward the others, for they all face together toward the masculine world, whose values they wish to monopolize each for herself. . . . Woman's mutual understanding comes from the fact that they identify themselves with each other; but for the same reason each is against the others. [p. 513]

What do social scientists have to say about allegations such as these? Although it is sometimes difficult to untangle conjecture from empirical evidence, it is clear that sex differences in friendship do indeed exist and, second, that these differences are shaped by sex stereotypes. Therefore, friendship with people of the same sex serves as a gender socialization vehicle; it aids in learning how children of one's own (and the other) sex are supposed to behave. Also, adherence to appropriate gender norms may constitute a criterion of acceptance into the same-sex peer group (Ambert, 1976:78). However, sociologists cannot respond directly to the pejorative content of statements such as the above, which contrast jolly masculine camaraderie with feminine jealousy and antagonism. In the last analysis, assessing the desirability of male versus female friendships involves value, not scientific, judgment. [11]

A recent study (Gibbs, Auerbach and Fox, 1980) set out to test Tiger's (1969:261) hypothesis that "men have a genetically determined propensity, culturally reinforced to form non-erotic bonds with other males, and that these bonds are stronger and more stable than female ties." Accordingly, a questionnaire was developed to assess similarities and differences in women's and men's same-sex friendship, in terms of these three components: (a) *empathy* (the "sharing of one's innermost thoughts and feelings with a trusted other"); (b) *altruism* (the "selfless consideration of another's welfare"); (c) *companionship* ("doing things together"). Although Gibbs, Auerbach and Fox felt that women's capacity for friendship was as great as men's, they hypothesized that women's friendships would have a higher altruistic and empathic component than men's, while men's would have a higher companionship component. The sample was made up of American college students. The results showed a "remarkable similarity" between male and female subjects in what they looked for in same-sex friendships. So far as the findings were concerned, both sexes valued empathy most highly. Contrary to Tiger's hypothesis of male bonding, it was the males who showed greater unfriendliness toward their own sex. Gibbs, Auerbach and Fox concluded that women have a greater capacity for friendship than cultural stereotypes would suggest.

According to evidence from several surveys, women's friendships (as opposed to men's) tend to be more intimate and to involve more exchanging of confidences. The relative emotional depth of these relationships is shown, for example, by the freedom women feel in speaking of themselves as "loving" their female friends. Men say they "like" their male friends (Rubin, 1973:221). In addition, research on self-disclosure shows that men typically reveal less personal information about themselves to others than do women. Moreover, women are the recipients of more disclosures than men (Jourard, 1964:47-51). Self-disclosure, love and trust are all tied together. Rubin (1973:221) suggests that, "Loving for men may often be channeled into a single opposite-sex relationship, whereas women may be more able to experience and express attachment, caring and intimacy in other relationships as well." This point receives support from Lowenthal and Haven's (1968:28) finding [cited in Chafetz, 1974] that while wives were *most* frequently designated as confidants by husbands, husbands were *least* frequently mentioned as confidants by wives. In this respect, widowhood is easier for women than men (Lopata, 1979). Also, males who expect marriage to provide their exclusive source of friendship place a tremendous burden on the marriage. One person simply cannot serve all the needs of another.

Women's friendships stress expressiveness, while males' stress activity. According to Chafetz (1974:182), "males will usually be found doing something together (fishing, bowling, tinkering with machinery, working). Men do not, of course, carry out these activities in total silence." Unfortunately, studies of sex differences in conversational topics are either dated or involve women who do not work outside the home. For example, the authors of a 1924 study (Landis and Burtt) [cited in Thorne and Henley, 1975:267], wore rubber heels and cultivated an "unobtrusive manner" in order to overhear conversations in Columbus (Ohio) public places. The most frequent topics of male-male conversations were business and money (49%), sports or other amusements (15%) and other men (13%). Women talked to other women about men (22%), clothing or decoration (19%) and other women (15%).

A 1962 study (Komarovsky) of American blue-collar couples reported that husbands and wives had very little to say to one another. In social situations involving couples, conversation was sexually segregated. "The women talked to other women about family and interpersonal matters; the men talked to male friends about cars, sports, work, motorcycles, carpentry, and local politics. The men ridiculed female conversation ('dirty diapers stuff,' one called it), a derogation the women were aware of, but did not apparently reciprocate" (Thorne and Henley, 1975:21). It would be very interesting to replicate these studies with contemporary Canadian samples of various social classes. (The relationship between language and gender is further discussed in Chapter Six.)

Why do same-sex friendships take on these patterns? Once again we see the impact of the expressive/instrumental dimension of sex stereotypes, which encourages female intimacy and discourages male intimacy. The specter of homosexuality prevents demonstrations of tender feelings in male friendships. If such feelings are not choked off completely, they sometimes reemerge as effusive displays of backslapping and arm punching. Also, women and men (but especially the latter) are in competition against their own kind. Until recently, occupational competition has been mostly a masculine "game"; one is reluctant to reveal weaknesses to a competitor (Chafetz, 1974:182). Also, since both sexes compete in the marketplace of love and marriage, some suspicion creeps into same-sex relationships.

Disparagement of same-sex friendships is unfortunate. For one thing, some benefits, such as deep understanding, can only be derived from persons of the same sex.

No matter how sympathetic or empathetic we may individually be, men toward women, women toward men, we cannot 'know' each other as essentially as men can know men and women can know women. Men can 'understand' the capacity for childbirth and to some extent feel it, but not really; males can't really know what it is like to have that kind of body. . . . Similarly, an empathetic woman can understand the special accountability that always accrues to the man during the sex act because the penis, unlike the vagina, is a visible symbol of performance success or failure, but she can't truly feel that accountability. [Brenton, 1974:184]

And shared gender is at least as equally profound a foundation for friendship as shared sex.

Finally, is there any truth to André Maurois's charge that the woman will give "*first place*" to the man she loves and, if he insists, will "renounce the most perfect friendship" for him? Although "perfect" friendships are hard to come by for sociological study, some research has been done on the effects of marriage on women's friendships. In 1963 Babchuk and Bates studied the initiation and maintenance of friendships by both husband and wife in middle-class Nebraskan suburbs. These researchers found that males dominate the couples' friendships, with the friends of the husband becoming the friends of the couple. Similarly, Babchuk (1965) found that during the engagement, the woman orients herself away from her friends and the man determines the majority of the couples' activities, which tend to involve his friends. Contradicting these findings is research by Simon, Crotts and Mahan (1970), who studied a sample of middle-class and working-class Illinois women. According to these researchers, both classes of women initiated about half the couples' friendships. White's (1974) study of friendship, performed in the University of Calgary married student housing complex, supported Simon, Crotts and Mahan. She reported husbands to be the source of only 17% of their wives' friends. Other sources were equally or more important (community or school, 26%; the neighborhood, 18%; work, 15%).

The adult friendship patterns described above have their roots in childhood. However, before turning our attention to that topic, we want to look at the views of those who believe that the peer group is especially important in male socialization.

The Male Peer Group as Refuge from Women

Ruth Hartley's classic article on male socialization (1959) is based on the assumption that gender is learned through the process of identification. Since fathers are not at home as much as mothers are, boys' paternal identification objects are often unavailable as models. (These ideas are shared by others, notably David Lynn [1969], mentioned in Chapter Four.) More stringent demands are made on boys than on girls and masculinity is negatively rather than positively defined.

As a reaction to the relative absence of fathers and the vagueness of parental demands, the young boy looks to his peers for specific guidance in being masculine. Unfortunately, his peers are likely to be no better informed than he is. Therefore, "the picture they draw is at once oversimplified and overemphasized." Physical strength and athletic skills are exaggerated. There is no place for tender feelings or responsibility for those who are weaker.

Julius Lester's (1975:54) account of "Being a Boy" communicates the grief children experience when they fail to match peer group specifications.

> As boys go, I wasn't much. I mean, I tried to be a boy and spent many childhood hours pummeling my hardly formed ego with failure at cowboys and Indians, baseball, football, lying, and sneaking out of the house. When our neighborhood gang raided a neighbor's pear tree, I was the only one who got sick from the purloined fruit. I also failed at setting fire to our garage, an art at which any five-year-old boy should be adept. I was, however, the neighborhood champion of getting beat up. "That Julius can take it, man," the boys used to say, almost in admiration, after I emerged from another battle, tears brimming in my eyes but refusing to fall.

Hartley goes on to argue that the male peer group, in addition to teaching "proper" masculine behavior, functions as a refuge against women. The growing boy faces a conflict between society's insistence that he eschew all things "womanly," and his placement by the same society under the almost constant jurisdiction of women. In other words, the boy who is warned to be strong and disdain "sissies," "is forced into close contact with the epitome of all sissy-things—women—for most of his day and he is commanded to obey and learn from them." The company of boys his own age provides some protection against the danger of turning out a "sissy," as well as a shield against women's power. Stockard and Johnson (1980:241) add that a concomitant of the male peer group's protection against the dangers of females and femininity is the peer group's promotion of "the sex objectification of women, making women not human beings but objects to be possessed and used sexually."

If these commentators are right in their assertion that the peer group serves to validate masculinity through avoidance of what is feminine (Stockard and Johnson, 1980:241) then we have here yet another reason for the scarcity of cross-sex friendships. Although these arguments appear to have face validity, systematic study of the more subtle peer group functions hypothesized above still needs to be done. However, there is some information on boys' attitudes toward girls, and girls' attitudes toward boys (Maccoby and Jacklin, 1974:211). As one would expect, these cross-sex attitudes change over time. During the preschool years, children prefer their own sex. For example, four-year-old boys more often tried to attract the attention of other boys, while girls directed their attention-getting activities to other girls. In the fifth grade (and probably earlier as well), girls like boys better than boys like girls. After the age of ten, the situation begins to change. Girls' attitudes toward boys remain stable, while boys begin to become more positive about girls. During the sixth and seventh grades, both boys and girls become more favorable toward one another, but the boys change at a faster rate. As well, their peer groups are not sex-segregated to quite the same extent.

The reasons for the development of more charitable cross-sex attitudes have not been clearly established. Perhaps the hormonal changes associated with the onset of puberty coincide with the establishment of a more secure masculine identity, and with encounters with social norms that encourage more mingling of the sexes. In other words, little Julius no longer despises girls, because the juices are flowing, because the definition of masculinity now requires contact with girls (not isolation from them) and because he now finds himself at social occasions where girls are present. Since Professor Homans (1950) informs us that increased interaction enhances attraction, Julius should eventually be able to tolerate girls. However, according to his reminiscences, Julius Lester (1975:55-57) was no happier during this stage of gender socialization than he was with the last one:

> Through no fault of my own I reached adolescence. While the pressure to prove myself on the athletic field lessened, the overall situation got worse —because now I had to prove myself with girls. Just how I was supposed to go about doing this was beyond me, especially because, at the age of 14, I was four foot nine and weighed 78 pounds. (I think there may have been one 10-year-old girl in the neighborhood smaller than I.) . . . I wasn't a total failure in high school, though, for occasionally I would go to a party, determined to salvage my self-esteem. . . . no one marked my talent for standing by the punch bowl. . . .
>
> After several hours of wondering whether I was going to die ("Julius Lester, a sixteen-year-old, died at a party last night, a half-eaten Ritz cracker in one hand and a potato chip dipped in pimento-cheese in the other. Cause of death: failure to be a boy"). . . . Now, of course, I know that it was as difficult being a girl as it was a boy, if not more so. While I stood paralyzed at one end of a dance floor trying to find the courage to ask a girl for a dance, most of the girls waited in terror at the other, afraid that no one, not even I, would ask them.*

* From "Being a Boy" by Julius Lester in *Sex: Male—Gender: Masculine* by John W. Petras, by permission of Mayfield Publishing Company. Copyright © 1975 Alfred Publishing Co.

Sex Differences in Children's Friendships and Play

Researchers studying children's experience with age-mates have discovered that boys and girls have different friendship patterns and different forms of play. Consequently, they acquire different sorts of social skills, which have implications for their later adult behavior. Two studies (Eder and Hallinan, 1978; Lever, 1978) of this aspect of gender socialization will be described below.

A sex difference exists in the *size* of children's play groups (Eder and Hallinan, 1978). Girls tend to play in small groups, especially the *dyad* (two-person group). Boys, on the other hand, prefer to congregate in larger groups. The size of the group is explained by the different types of play activities preferred. Sutton-Smith and Rosenberg (1971) asked children between the ages of nine and fifteen to indicate which games they liked best. The games selected by boys tended to require a larger number of participants than the games selected by girls.

This sex difference in the type of preferred play explains a somewhat divergent conclusion arrived at by Maccoby and Jacklin (1974:205-7). Their survey of the affiliation literature reports that while boys tend to be more affiliative in the sense that they engage in more social interaction with their peers, girls are more likely to report that they like the people with whom they interact. In part at least, the greater amount of male interaction derives from the fact that girls focus their play on intensive relations with one or two "best friends," while boys play in larger groups. Also, "for much of the interaction that occurs in boys' play groups, liking and disliking one's playmates is essentially irrelevant" (Maccoby and Jacklin, 1974:207). Since the game is what matters, the choice of participants is likely to be made on the basis of game skills.

Another implication concerns the relative exclusiveness of girls', as opposed to boys', play groups. The requirement of a larger number of participants for male games encourages male dyads to expand. There is no similar pressure on female dyads. The girls, who tend to engage in more intimate behavior than boys (telling secrets, for example), protect their exclusive groups against the advances of newcomers. Little girls probably blame themselves for the greater trouble they have in making friends.

Does having only one or two "best friends" make girls especially vulnerable to peer pressure? Are girls more likely than boys to side with their friends when peer values conflict with parental values or their own position? (Maccoby and Jacklin, 1974:210). Surprisingly, one study (Hollander and Marcia, 1970) of this question reported boys, not girls, to be more susceptible to peer influence. Ten-year-old children were required to resolve dilemmas that pitted peer values against either their own or parental values, and to identify classmates on items such as these: (a) this is a classmate who does things independently; (b) this is a classmate who gets other children to do things; (c) this is a classmate who goes along with what other children are doing; (d) this is a classmate who does what grown-ups think is right; (e) this is a classmate who gets along with other children (Maccoby and Jacklin, 1974:488).

Related to the sex difference in the size of children's play groups, mentioned above, is a sex difference in the complexity of their play. Lever (1978) observed the play of fifth-grade children, interviewed them and asked them to complete questionnaires and to maintain a diary record of their leisure activities. On the basis of these data, boys' play was found to be more complex than girls' play. Boys tend to play competitive games involving teams of interdependent players with definite roles. Such games are played according to specific rules. Hockey is a good example. In comparison, girls prefer to converse or to play games such as hopscotch, which require few participants. Playing dolls or hopscotch does not require the coordination of effort that hockey or baseball does. One result is the learning of different types of skills, which very likely carry over into adulthood.

Boys' games, particularly team sports, provide a learning environment for the cultivation of the kinds of skills later demanded by bureaucratic work organizations. In principle, at least, boys learn to deal with a diversity of roles, to coordinate their actions, to cope with impersonal rules and to work for collective as well as personal goals. Sports provide experience in leading and following, and in coping with criticism. Being able to depersonalize attacks, and to maintain self-control in the face of criticism, is an especially important aptitude (Lever, 1978:480-81).

Girls' spontaneous, imaginative, mostly rule-free play teaches quite different skills. Since activities such as skipping rope often have no explicit goals, girls experience less interpersonal competition. Leadership is less relevant. Girls often prefer to talk rather than play formal games, and thereby develop the ability to converse with other people and to empathize with them (Lever, 1978:481).

Extrapolations suggest that childhood play equips adult females to deal with people in primary group settings, such as the family, but not in secondary group settings where power is wielded and the business of the world conducted (Lever, 1978:482). Women's facility in socioemotional matters is indicated by the finding that people of both sexes disclose intimate things about themselves more easily to women than to men (Rubin, 1973:39). Here, we are speculating that there is a causal link between children's play and adult skills. It would be nice to have evidence, for example, that those women who have succeeded in bureaucratic organizations *also* played the complex games in childhood from which girls have traditionally been excluded.

Some supporting data are provided by Hennig's and Jardim's (1976) study of twenty-five American women in top management positions. Apparently, team games played in childhood were important to all of them (p. 111). One woman comments upon the contribution in her life of both competitive games and her special relationship with her father (another typical experience of outstanding women):

> It's funny how to this day, I really enjoy hard physical activity and physical competition of any kind. I think this goes back to my days of tennis playing with my dad. He taught me when I was very young and he always told me that when I set foot on the court, I should play to win— that was the name of the game, to win. One of the most exciting feelings in the whole world is to work or play so physically hard at winning that you think you are about to collapse and then, at that last second before desperation, you win. [Hennig and Jardim, 1976:103]

Organizational skills can of course be learned in other places besides competitive team sports. Business administration schools and on-the-job training socialize adults very effectively. Finally, our intention is not to denigrate the type of interpersonal skill at which women excel. Expressive *and* instrumental skills would be valuable for both sexes to have.

Sport and Gender

There is reason to believe that the picture of males engaged in sweaty camaraderie on the playing fields and watched by a coterie of admiring females reclining in the shade is somewhat anachronistic.

So far as children are concerned, Eder and Hallinan (1978:247) cite evidence that over the past forty years, girls have been showing an increasingly greater preference for the games preferred most by boys.

Some conclusions about adult leisure can be drawn from Statistics Canada material. Unfortunately, trend data on this subject are difficult to find, so that we cannot really tell whether male/female physical activities have changed over time. When sports and athletic activities are lumped together, the sex differences in participation rates are not very substantial. In 1976, Statistics Canada conducted a national survey on Canadian participation in fitness, physical recreation and sport. According to this report (Statistics Canada, 1978:7), men participated in sports to a slightly greater degree than women (54% of men versus 46% of women). The sex difference was even less marked for exercise activities, 60% of men and 58% of women participating. ("Participation" meant doing the activity at least once in the twelve months prior to the survey.)[12]

When particular sports and physical activities are considered, however, gender does seem to matter. A 1973 survey of 5,200 Ontario residents illustrates this point (Statistics Canada, 1977: Table 7.5). ("Participation" was again defined as doing the activity at least once in the twelve months preceding the survey.) Participation in the following activities accords with the gender comparisons made in the previous section: baseball/softball (male 63.8%, female 36.2%); golf (male 78.0%, female 22.0%); hockey (male 85.6%, female 14.4%); football (male 83.2%, female 16.8%); curling (male 62.0%, female 38.0%). But badminton and volleyball involve both sexes almost equally, as do the less-structured activities of swimming and horseback riding.

Though the operation of traditional gender norms can still be detected in national surveys, the more sedentary leisure pursuits occupy both sexes. Television viewing is the single most popular activity (Statistics Canada, 1977:133). In 1978 English-speaking Canadians watched an average of twenty-two hours of television a week, with males watching an average of twenty-one hours and females, twenty-three hours (Statistics Canada, 1980:Table 8.20). Seventy-two percent of Canadians read at least one book in 1977 (65.8% males versus 77.6% females) (Statistics Canada, 1980:Table 8.1). Finally, in 1975 at least one movie per year was attended by 58.8% males and 55.5% females. However, classical music concerts drew 12.5% females (versus 8.5% males) and ballet performances 4.7% females (versus 2.4% males) (Statistics Canada, 1977:Table 7.13).

In the past decade, two influential movements have exerted pressure against gender norms in physical activity and against sex discrimination in sport. The first is the women's movement. The second is the physical fitness craze. Sports have not been a high-priority issue for feminist groups. Indeed, many feminists have "dismissed discriminatory sporting practices as being unimportant compared to the real issues underlying the sexist nature of our society" (Hall, 1980:51). However, others have argued the importance of sport on the grounds that participation in athletics brings about a sense of mastery and accomplishment that carries over into other areas of life. (Rohrbaugh, 1979:41). Some women have inveighed against differential socialization practices in the home and the schools, and against discrimination against female athletes in the wider community. The Royal Commission on the Status of Women (1970:187) recommended that the provinces and territories review their policies and consider practices to motivate girls to engage in athletic activities and to provide them with equal sports opportunities in the schools. Among the pieces of evidence cited by the Commission was a University of Toronto physiologist's report suggesting that "lack of activity and consequent poor heart-lung fitness is a more serious problem in girls than in boys" (p. 186). Unfortunately, the Report has so far provoked little government action (Batt, 1978). Physical fitness advocates exhort us all to exercise regularly.

Many people, who a few brief years ago felt that the best exercise of all was a good, brisk sit, are now munching their bran and jogging along city streets.[13]

Not everyone is persuaded. The Statistics Canada (1978:7) national survey mentioned above lamented that although almost 93% of Canadian adults were physically capable of participating in some activity, only 59% did exercise at least once during the month prior to the study. Other social analysts have had difficulty deciding whether Canadians in general (and women in particular) are indeed becoming less sedentary over time. Milton (1975:31) poses this general question in terms of an "active society" versus a "sedentary society" model. Evidence for the former is the "stay fit movement," with the "new popularity of bicycling, jogging, hiking, camping, sports 'house leagues' in work places, health clubs" (p. 31). The "sedentary society" model holds that spectatorship is a problem for Canadians, who prefer "to sit and watch rather than actively participate in leisure activities" (p. 31). Alas, Milton's evidence, based on a national survey of adult Canadians, tends to support the "sedentary society" model. He found males, regardless of age or education level, to be considerably more involved in sports activities than females (p. 79). However, the situation may well have changed since the mid-1970s, when these data were collected.

How did these distinctive play patterns for males and females come about? Historically, in Europe as well as North America, the definition of sport as a masculine endeavor (Lever, 1978:480) and the presumption of the physical inferiority of girls and women relative to boys and men were used to restrict female participation in many sports (Hudson, 1978). These beliefs led turn-of-the-century educators to reserve competitive athletics for boys and gymnastic exercises and dance for girls. This policy was reinforced by the view that "sport served as the training ground for future soldiers ('the battle of Waterloo was won on the playing fields of Eton')" (Lever, 1978:480).

In an article entitled "They Who Risked Their Delicate Organs," Griffiths (1978:11) tells us that the story of adult Canadian females in sports is barely 100 years old.

> Prior to that time the early pioneers were busy carving out communities in the new world. The small rural towns, moreover, were notorious for their strict moral code. Frivolity in the guise of sport was often frowned upon for men, let alone for women. Leisure was rare and women's enjoyment of it rarer. There were a few heroines of those rough and ready days who shot straight as a die and could ride like the wind but they were the exception and their image has been romanticized by modern literature.

As the population multiplied, so did the leisure class, but sport was out of the question for the female members of this small group. Vigorous activities were ruled out by propriety and by the "stylish clothes that kept women flounced, drawn in, upright and padded" (Griffiths, 1978:11).

Traditional values eventually crumbled in the face of urbanization and industrialization. The years 1920-35 were a golden era of sports for Canadian women (Cochrane, Hoffman and Kincaid, 1977). A Canadian contingent of six women was assembled under great difficulty for the 1928 Olympic Games in Amsterdam. They brought back to Canada two gold, two silver and four bronze medals for track-and-field competition. A women's basketball team called the Edmonton Grads became "the most successful team in the history of the sport" (Griffiths, 1978:13). In the 1920s and 1930s, there were national championships in women's ice hockey (Hoffman, 1976:7). Unfortunately, the aftermath of World War II, with its resurgence of emphasis on traditional femininity, brought a decline in women's sports. Although a few individual athletes, such as Barbara Ann Scott, were public figures, mass participation in sports and women's team sports became almost unknown. Other relevant factors were the growth of professional men's teams (along with media coverage of their games) and the lack of facilities (leagues, teams, coaches) for females (Cochrane, Hoffman and Kincaid, 1977). The old myths about female athletes regained currency.

Credence is still given to three sets of beliefs about female athletes. The first myth holds that women athletes are physically unattractive and muscle-bound. Sports allegedly masculinize women and make them uninteresting to men. This myth is portrayed by a character in the "Peanuts" comic strip, Peppermint Patty, "tomboy and serious athlete, who is not above trading her friends to strengthen her baseball team and who is often referred to as 'Sir' in deference to her unfeminine interest" (Birrell, 1978:143).

The second myth views females as physiologically inferior and, hence, ill equipped for athletics. Dr. Creighton J. Hale, executive vice-president of research for Little League, mounted his case for the exclusion of American girls from baseball on the basis of this myth (Hudson, 1978:19-20). He (falsely) contended that female bones were especially susceptible to fracture, that females had slower reaction time than males and that blows could produce cancerous lesions upon female breast tissue.

The third myth denies that there are social barriers to women's involvement in sports and holds that the relatively small number of participants is the result of lack of desire to participate (Hoffman, 1976:7). The "Peanuts" character, Lucy Van Pelt, embodies this myth. After her attempts to kick a football end in utter failure, she walks off without "visible distress or embarrassment," muttering, "I'm too feminine for this game." Lucy "doesn't care about sports, she isn't any good at sports, and her failure in sports is inconsequential and excusable because she's a girl" (Birrell, 1978:143).

Although girls' differential socialization may well make them less enthusiastic than boys about sports, enhancing their motivation will not solve such problems as lack of facilities and out-and-out discrimination. A growing number of complaints of alleged sex discrimination in sport are being filed under human rights legislation (Greaves, 1978). The Little League baseball cases in the United States have counterparts in Canadian hockey, soccer and softball disputes. These cases arise when girls who are qualified to make boys' teams are denied the opportunity to compete because they are female. The attempts to seek remedy in the courts are sometimes successful, sometimes not. However, the publicity surrounding this litigation serves to exert some pressure on traditional gender norms. Should society continue to be "enthralled by the athletic skill and prowess of a few women," but reject sport for most women? (Spears, 1978:3). An equally pertinent question (which also falls outside the boundaries of social science) is whether society should insist on a modicum of athletic skill and interest in its men and boys. Both Gail Cummings, an eleven-year-old crackerjack hockey player who was denied the right to play on the Huntsville (Ontario) all-star team (Greaves, 1978), and Julius Lester (1975), the boy who failed the boyhood tests of masculinity, were gender misfits.

In order to restore the balance between the sexes, we end this section with Julius's reminiscence of his summer holidays:

> Each morning during the summer, as I cuddled up in the quiet of a corner with a book, my mother would push me out the back door and into the yard. And throughout the day as my blood was let as if I were a patient of 17th-century medicine, I thought of the girls sitting in the shade of porches, playing with their dolls, toy refrigerators and stoves. [1975:54]

We will now consider various implications of gender for friendships in adolescence and adulthood. Cross-sex friendships and same-sex friendships will be discussed in turn.

Cross-Sex Relations in Adolescence and Adulthood

Our question is: How are male-female primary relationships influenced by gender? Our basic contention is that a dual influence is at work. Cross-sex friendships are shaped by societal definitions of masculinity and femininity. In addition, the way that such relationships are played out serves to reinforce gender norms. Earlier we noted that cross-sex friendships are rarer than same-sex friendships, and that in adulthood there is a tendency for such relationships to either turn into love affairs or to dissipate. In the following paragraphs we will examine, first, platonic relationships,[14] then romantic relationships.

Platonic Friendships

These relationships tend to be short-lived, tentative and unstable. Why should this be so? Three interrelated factors seem to be responsible and all of them boil down to one basic reason: constricted cultural definitions of the male-female situation.

First, if either person in the cross-sex friendship pair has romantic attachments to a third person, the third party may well be suspicious. Our culture encourages us to treat love as a zero-sum game, to assume that each person has only a finite quantity of that emotion available to give (Chafetz, 1974:162). Our reasoning often goes like this: If Person A loves Friend B, then Person A has less love left over for Lover C. Indeed, *Roget's Thesaurus* lists "jealous" among the synonyms for "loving," and the *Webster's Third New International Dictionary* offers this Freudian-inspired definition of "platonic love": *A close relationship between two usually opposite-sexed persons in which an element of sexual attraction or libidinal desire has been either so suppressed or so sublimated that it is generally believed to be absent.* The tendency for the friendship to turn romantic is clearly implied.

Male jealousy, in particular, has a long tradition. Wives have been viewed as husbands' property, and trespass upon this property (adultery) has been grounds for divorce. Accusing a man of being a cuckold is a supreme insult in most societies (Chafetz, 1974:164). (The sociological emphasis given here to the gender norms for jealousy does not deny its psychological impact, for it is surely one of the nastier emotions. Moreover, jealousy is not limited to males, though the law has supported their claims. In short, jealousy hurts and both sexes are at risk.)

A second cultural reason explains why adult platonic relationships rarely develop in the first place and why they tend to be fragile if they do. The second reason is closely related to the first reason. The popular image of cross-sex relationships is limited to sexuality, perhaps romance, but does not extend to friendship. According to Chafetz (1974:164), "Females are taught to view males primarily as potential mates or husbands, name-ly, the objects of TRUE LOVE. Males learn to view females primarily as sex objects to be exploited if possible, married if necessary." Similarly, Brenton (1974:15) argues that, "when women and men see each other in stereotypical roles, as has historically been the case to now, only expecta-tions based on 'You're a man' and 'You're a woman' are easily possible. Every encounter between a woman and a man then becomes heavy with unspoken demands: confirm that I'm desirable, acknowledge my virility, my orgasmic capacity, prove to me that I'm a sexual being—that's your role, that's your job." Although these views may be exaggerated, they do make the point that men and women have not been taught to regard one another as peers. Which brings us to the third reason.

The inequality of males and females is a recurring theme of this book. Reiteration of the point is not really required here. As noted earlier, similarity of important attributes predicts interpersonal attraction and friendship. The superior status of males and the inferior status of females constitute dissimilarity of the first order. Although women and men may well come to recognize their basic equality once they have become friends, the three cultural norms outlined above make unlikely the initial establishment of friendship.

Though cross-sex friendships remain the exception, they seem to be happening a bit more frequently now, particularly among teenagers and among professional workers. Friendship in these quarters reveals something of the content of gender socialization.

Teenage Platonic Friendships

Peer relations of all types are especially important to teenagers, who are striving to differentiate themselves from their families, to solve the problems of "who am I?" and "what shall I become?" Partly for this reason, cross-sex friendships appear to form more easily in adolescence than at other periods in the life cycle. After talking with teenagers and with observers of the "teenage scene," Brenton (1974:163) concluded that there is a growing incidence of nonsexual, nonromantic friendships between adolescent girls and boys. To this author, such platonic friendships seem more possible now than in the 1950s, for example, when girls faced strong pressure to "go steady," to wear someone's (anyone's) fraternity pin, and when breaking up was a "mini-divorce." Although the pressure to establish exclusive relationships may have lessened, the pressure to engage in sexual activity has not. Perhaps platonic friendships constitute a reaction to this pressure to perform sexually (Brenton, 1974:163). Or, alternatively, teenagers' more open acknowledgement of their sexuality may free them to form cross-sex relations on other bases.

That contemporary young people entertain more liberal ideas about sex is supported by Hobart's questionnaire survey of sex attitudes and behavior of students at the University of Alberta, the Northern Alberta Institute of Technology, the University of Waterloo, the Université de Montréal and a trade school in Montreal. Professor Hobart (1976b:418) says, "of course, a certain proportion of young people have experimented with sex in every generation, but the cultural inducements and encouragements to do so in Canada, and indeed throughout North American and other capitalistic industrial societies, are more explicit and widespread than at any other time in the last two thousand years."

His data justify this statement (Hobart, 1976a). Among the Anglophone students, 50% had experienced intercourse (56% of the males, 44% of the females). Among the Francophone students, 47% had

had intercourse (63% of the males, 30% of the females). After comparing these findings with previous information, Hobart (1976a:158) concluded that these data point to "erosion of the grip of the old morality," namely, "the expectation of premarital virginity among women." (The rates of male intercourse experience were comparable with those found in studies carried out fifteen to twenty years earlier.)

What gender lessons emerge from teenage friendships? The boy and the girl are testing "their emerging maleness and femaleness against each other" in a "safe" (nonsexual) environment (Brenton, 1974:163). They are learning how to be male and female, and what to expect from, and how to interact with, a member of the other sex. A female friend can be particularly useful to the male. Since male competitiveness discourages disclosure of anxieties and weaknesses to other males, female friends can serve as safe confidants (Chafetz, 1974:165).

Perhaps, with the demystification of sex, adolescents are able to devote more attention to unravelling the intricacies of gender. When sex is treated with more straightforwardness, its possibilities need not suffuse every female-male encounter. If today's teenagers are truly more sexually liberated than their elders, adult platonic friendships may become more common in the future.

Professionals' Platonic Friendships

Collegial relationships among professional workers constitute a second type of cross-sex friendship that seems to be flourishing. The importance of informal relationships at work has long been recognized by sociologists. Indeed, close identification with colleagues is one of the distinguishing attributes of professional workers. For the most part, the collegial group is still trusted by the public as the only competent arbiter of work performance. Moreover, fellow practitioners act as sources of professional identity and useful information. This function is crucial for beginners in a profession. (Becker's 1972 article is titled, "A School is a Lousy Place to Learn Anything.") A normal professional career without colleague support is unthinkable. (Here, we are talking about occupational socialization, not gender socialization. Bear with us, for the moment.)

Until very recently, there was a consensus that women in male-dominated professions were excluded from the circles of collegueship. In Theodore's (1971:30) words, "Discrimination of a more subtle nature is also evidenced in the exclusion of females from the informal networks of cliques, clubs, and other peer relationships where professional decisions are made, knowledge shared, and favors exchanged in terms of clients, consultantships, grants, and research collaborations."

In seeking the reason for women's unacceptability, analysts (Epstein, 1970), a decade ago, took the lead from Hughes (1958), who declared that *female* and *professional* are incongruent statuses, and women are simply the wrong kind of people for admission into the masculine "brotherhood" or "inner fraternity." Caplow (1954:238) claimed that sex segregation of work is based on the fundamental cultural premise "that intimate groups, except those based on family or sexual ties, should be composed of either sex but never of both." Those sentiments may well recall Tiger's (1969) notions about male bonding. When the gender stereotype and professional stereotype conflict, male workers find interaction unpredictable and hence punishing.

If women were indeed totally rejected by their peers, the consequences would be devastating. They would be powerless, improperly socialized and beyond colleague control, denied access to expertise, resources and clients. But the situation does not seem to be quite this grim. For one thing, women, like minority groups, have mitigated this situation by finding clients of their own kind, as well as choosing feminine occupational specialties. (For example, female physicians tend to be overrepresented in pediatrics and gynecology and underrepresented in surgery.) Moreover, women who have come to appreciate how efficiently the "old-boy networks" function for men are beginning to establish "old-girl networks" of their own. Books (Welch, 1980) are being written and colloquia and extension courses offered on the subject of "networking." Finally, there are indications that females are experiencing some acceptance from their male colleagues.

Much of the literature cited above was written before the impact of the feminist movement. Though it would be foolish to suggest that the sexists have all been converted, the treatment of women in the 1980s is not what it was a decade or more ago. Also, the increase in the number of women in the workplace is another factor promoting platonic relations (Brenton, 1974:159).

In order to test whether women in male-dominated professions are in fact excluded from informal collegial circles, the author (1977b) carried out an analysis that focused upon female sociologists. The amount of collaborative publishing in fourteen major sociology journals provided the indicator of collegial acceptance. Comparisons were made between 1967 (the year the Constitution of the American Sociological Association was revised to improve the status of women) and 1973. The results are given in Table 5.1. This table shows us that the proportion of articles published by mixed-sex teams increased from 5.9% in 1967 to 9.8% in 1973 (a difference that is statistically significant). Collaborative work among males remained stable. Although this study examined only one indicator of cross-sex friendships on the job, it does suggest that analysis of the professional women's plight cited above may be overly pessimistic.

TABLE 5.1
Authorship of Article in Fourteen Sociology Journals

| | 1967 | | 1973 | | Significance |
	N	%	N	%	Level[a]
Single author, male	331	58.8	285	49.1	.005
Single author, female	52	9.2	73	12.6	.05
Male teams	144	25.6	158	27.2	.35
Female teams	3	0.5	7	1.2	.14
Mixed teams	33	5.9	57	9.8	.01
Total publications	563	100.0	580	99.9	

SOURCE: Mackie (1977b:286).

[a] One-tailed, chi-square, one degree of freedom.

These adult opposite-sex friendships have implications beyond the work-oriented examples discussed above. From a personal point of view, work provides the opportunity for women and men to relate to one another. The gender socialization by-products would seem to be similar to those accruing from teenage friendships. Such relationships provide information concerning the "nature of the opposite sex beast" and experience in dealing with "it." Moreover, "a friendship without sex is not a sexless friendship"; opportunity is provided to "test" oneself sexually and to enjoy "being considered attractive by one's platonic friend" (Brenton, 1974:159). The reciprocal nature of male/female roles, then, implies both gender and sexual socialization.

Romantic Relationships

Emerging social relationships tend to be interpreted in terms of the repertoire of relationships that are culturally available (Forgas and Dobosz, 1980). As already noted, in our society heterosexual relationships, from puberty on, acquire romantic connotations. The topic of romantic relationships offers considerable insight into the workings of gender. During intimate encounters, females are especially feminine and males especially masculine. This section will concentrate on dating, courtship and their contemporary alternatives, especially as they occur among young people. Although "falling in love" is not limited to people in their teens and twenties, the latter are both more constrained by pressures for sex-appropriate behavior and vulnerable to and impressed by the lessons of gender socialization.

Dating and *courtship* can be analytically distinguished. Dating is the more frivolous pastime that occupies the rather long period in our society between puberty and marriage. It has "its own routines and norms, and is a recognized way for single persons to meet and relate" (Laws and Schwartz, 1977:105). Courtship, on the other hand, has the goal of permanent mate selection.

In a pioneering study, Mirra Komarovsky (1946) described how the gender norms of that era constrained women's behavior in dating situations. Her paper, "Cultural Contradictions and Sex Roles," is also interesting because it stimulated other sociologists (Dean et al., 1975; Gove, Hughes and Geerken, 1980; Wallin, 1950) to replicate her work. (Replication, a basic feature of scientific endeavor, provides assurance that what is accepted as "truth" is indeed true. However, sociologists "sometimes seem reluctant to challenge previous findings, preferring endless citation without replication" [Dean et al., 1975:207].)

Komarovsky concluded from her study of American college women that their exposure to incompatible cultural definitions of their situation constituted a role conflict between the "feminine" role and the "modern" role. The "feminine" role requires women to be more emotional and less aggressive than men. The "modern" role, on the other hand, expected women to display the same virtues, attitudes and behaviors as men of the corresponding age. According to Komarovsky, both sets of demands were present in the same social environments at the same time. For these college women, the role conflict centered on "academic work, social life, vocational plans, excellence in specific fields of endeavor, and a number of personality traits" (p. 185). One aspect of this conflict was the inconsistency of goals set for the woman by her family. For example, a bewildered student wrote:

> I get a letter from my mother at least three times a week. One week her letters will say, "Remember that this is your last year at college. Subordinate everything to your studies. You must have a good record to secure a job." The next week her letters are full of wedding news. This friend of mine got married; that one is engaged; my young cousin's wedding is only a week off. When, my mother wonders, will I make up my mind? Surely I wouldn't want to be the only unmarried one in my group. It is high time, she feels, that I give some thought to it! [Komarovsky, 1946:185]

Komarovsky also implies that the personality traits required for career success conflict with those required to attract men. Accordingly, 40% of the women in her sample said that they occasionally "played dumb" on dates. "Playing dumb" entailed concealing academic honors, pretending ignorance on some subject, allowing the man to "win" intellectual arguments or athletic games. Interviewees made the following comments:

> I am better in math than my fiance. But while I let him explain politics to me, we never talk about math even though, being a math major, I could tell him some interesting things.

On dates I always go through the 'I-don't-care-anything-you-want-to-do' routine. It gets monotonous but boys fear girls who make decisions. They think such girls would make nagging wives.

When my date said that he considers Ravel's *Bolero* the greatest piece of music ever written, I changed the subject because I knew I would talk down to him. [Komarovsky, 1946:187-88]

In a subsequent study, Wallin (1950) also found "inferiority playing" and conflict between traditional and modern roles among university women. However, he regarded the problem as "less momentous" than Komarovsky. For example, he suggested that women's occasional pretense of inferiority was a dating "line" that could be dropped when the relationship became more serious (Wallin, 1950:292). For a quarter of a century, the Komarovsky-Wallin observation was widely cited in the sociological literature as "evidence of the pervasive and detrimental effect on women of their lower status in modern society" (Gove, Hughes and Geerken, 1980:89).

However, recent replications of the Komarovsky-Wallin thesis have arrived at entirely different conclusions. Among several methodological problems of the original studies was the fact that men were excluded from their samples. When Dean and his colleagues (1975:212) looked at a college sample of both sexes, they found that "men reported playing inferior to their dates in roughly the same proportions as women!" As well, neither sex plays dumb very frequently. Finally, Gove, Hughes and Geerken (1980) examined a national probability sample of Americans and found that about a quarter reported ever playing dumb and that, overall, men were more likely to play dumb than women. Thirty-one percent of the males and 23% of the females reported ever pretending to be less intelligent or knowledgeable than they really were. More to the point, 9% of females and 8% of males reported playing dumb with dates. (However, 10% of the females and 6% of the males report playing dumb with spouses!) So far as dating is concerned, it appears that playing dumb is an impression-management strategy that is infrequently, but about equally, used by men and women.

In 1973, Komarovsky provided a final footnote to the above controversy with her study, "Cultural Contradictions and Sex Roles: The Masculine Case." One-third of her sample of Ivy League college Americans find themselves caught in conflict between the traditional norm of male intellectual superiority and the modern norm of intellectual companionship between the sexes. One form that this conflict took was intellectual insecurity on dates. For instance, one said, "I may be a little frightened of a man who is superior to me in some field of knowledge, but if a girl knows more than I do, I resent her" (p. 874). Perhaps the point to be stressed here is that 70% reported no such problems, partly because intellectual prowess is no longer considered unfeminine.

Traditionally, social scientists have viewed courtship (and dating) in terms of exchange theory (e.g., Goode, 1966; Murstein, 1970; Waller, 1938). To explain further, "these theories posit a marriage market, somewhat analogous to the market in which economic goods and services are exchanged, in which females offer characteristics desired by males in exchange for the characteristics and the status they desire from males. The greater the desirability to the opposite sex of the characteristics the person has to offer, the more in the way of desired characteristics he or she will be able to obtain in a spouse" (Taylor and Glenn, 1976:484). Theorists using this market metaphor have traditionally assumed that women offer their physical attractiveness in return for the social status men have to barter.

Physical attractiveness constitutes a central criterion for both sexes in judging other people. Beauty is especially important in determining favorable first impressions. Even children as young as three prefer pretty children to less attractive children (Dion, 1977), and already dislike fat bodies, for instance. From nursery-school age onward, surprising agreement exists on how well other people meet our cultural standards of beauty (Dion and Berscheid, 1972, cited in Middlebrook, 1974). Also, inferences are made about trait linkages, and the assumption is made that what is beautiful is good. Attractive people are rated as more sensitive, kind, interesting, sociable, outgoing, strong and exciting than less attractive people. Moreover, student samples expect more attractive people to be more likely to find good jobs and good mates and to live happily ever after (Dion, Berscheid, and Walster, 1972). Expectations such as these can become self-fulfilling prophecies. Studies show that good looks are related to the happiness, self-esteem and emotional adjustment of *women* but not of *men* (Al-Issa, 1980:289; Mathes and Kahn, 1975). This observation brings us to the main point of this discussion.

Though no one, male or female, wants to be ugly, beauty (and youth) are more critical for women. The studies relating attractiveness to happiness (cited above) involved people in their teens and twenties. Women who were exceptionally attractive when young have been found to be poorly adjusted to life in their forties. Since in our society, beauty is seen to fade with age, these women had more to lose as the years went by. However, no such relationship between attractiveness and happiness in later life was observed for men (Al-Issa, 1980:290; Berscheid and Walster, 1974).

According to de Beauvoir (1952:505), women who "endeavor to preserve themselves as others preserve furniture or canned food" are embarked upon a lost cause. "Good meals spoil the figure, wine injures the complexion, too much smiling brings wrinkles, the sun damages the skin, sleep makes one dull, work wears one out, love puts rings under the eyes, kisses redden the cheeks, caresses deform the breasts, embraces wither the flesh, maternity disfigures face and body."

The following excerpt from Alice Munro's novel, *Lives of Girls and*

Women (1971:177), shows that gender socialization for girls, such as the fictional Del, involves learning complex beauty rituals:

> Sometimes I did wash my hair, and did it up on horrible steel curlers that prevented me from sleeping; in fact I could spend hours, now and then, in front of a mirror, painfully plucking my eyebrows, looking at my profile, shading my face with dark and light powder, to emphasize its good points and minimize the bad, as recommended in the magazines. It was sustained attention I was not capable of, though everything from advertisements to F. Scott Fitzgerald to a frightening song on the radio—*the girl that I marry will have to be, as soft and pink as a nursery*—was telling me I would have to, *have to*, learn [emphasis in original].

To be sure, adolescent boys also worry about the impression their appearance makes on girls. Bill Cosby (1975:58) gives a hyperbolic account of his preparations for a Monday morning encounter with Rosemary, who is also in the fifth or sixth grade. "OK, Monday. So now, I take four baths Sunday night: six times I grease my hair; I brush my hair 982 times—I'm getting these little curls I got down pat; and, like, I wash my face so good —I don't want to get anything that looks halfway like a skin blemish or anything and I clean my toes; everything, man."

Nevertheless, physical appearance is of greater continuing importance to women (Mathes and Kahn, 1975). Male value in the courtship "marketplace" is influenced by the power and prestige they derive from their occupation and from simply being male. "Women, however, must rest their case largely on their bodies. Their ability to attain status in other than physical ways and to translate that status into sexual attractiveness is severely limited by the culture" (Bell, 1970:75). Therefore, it is women who show primary (though not exclusive) interest in makeup, fashionable clothing, cosmetic surgery for wrinkles and jowls, health spas, diets and Weight Watchers meetings. Apparently, all this effort "pays off." A woman's physical appearance and frequency of dating are strongly correlated (Berscheid et al., 1971). *Psychology Today* (Tavris, 1977) readers described their "ideal man" and their "ideal woman" in terms of a series of traits. Twenty-six percent of the men and 29% of the women said that it was "very important" or "essential" for the ideal man to be physically attractive. By contrast, 47% of the men and 32% of the women felt it "very important" or "essential" for the ideal woman to be physically attractive (p. 37).

Marcia Millman's (1980) three-year study of the lives of overweight people concluded that being fat is a different story for women than for men. In our society, being fat has a pervasive effect upon women's self-image, social identity and treatment by others. Even men who were 200 pounds overweight told Millman that they didn't think very much about being fat and that it didn't cause them suffering at work or in their private lives. For instance, in comparison with obese women, obese men did not find eating in public embarrassing. One man often goes into restaurants to compete with a friend in eating desserts. ("We would sit there for two hours eating every dessert on the menu. I didn't care what people in the restaurant thought of me" [p. 218].) By contrast, a woman had this to say about her compulsive eating: "There were about five or six delicatessens near where I lived, and usually I would stop at all of them, buying something different so it wouldn't look so bad. I usually would try to buy something normal, like bananas or chicken, along with the ice cream, the cookies and the candy." Unlike women, men didn't "psychologize" about their weight or see it as indicative of personal problems. The men's concern about weight was in terms of health problems. However, Millman does suggest that younger men *are* now beginning to worry more about their appearance.

Gender roles during dating and courtship dictate that the male does the choosing, and the female makes herself as "choosable" as possible (Laws and Schwartz, 1977:42). Here we come up against an admixture of *gender* socialization and *sexual* socialization. Learning how to be masculine or feminine includes learning how to be male or female. However, because of differences in male/female *sex* socialization, "looking nice" carries different connotations for adolescent boys and girls. Alice Munro's Del (reluctantly) wanted to look pretty, but not sexual. Her ultimate goal was marriage. For the present, romantic dating was enough. On the other hand, Bill Cosby's goal was achieving status with his peers and this entailed sexual activity. Rosemary's allure was her unsavory reputation. These conflicting male/female goals can produce considerable confusion. In early adolescence, at least, the female may be oblivious to the sexual signals she transmits by "looking nice." In the traditional "script," girls intended to be alluring, but not "bad," because men marry only "nice" girls (Wilson et al., 1977).

The distinction between "good" girls and "bad" girls is a product of the "double sexual standard" (Kleinman, 1978:101). While almost any sexual contact enhanced a male's reputation with his peer group, the one traditional exception was premarital intercourse with the woman he intended to marry. Women, on the other hand, were expected to remain virgins until marriage (and any sexual contact detracted from females' reputation with their peer group [Laws and Schwartz, 1977:108].) The double standard created two classes of women: the "bad" women whom men slept with but did not marry, and the "good" ones, with whom they refrained from sexual intercourse and whom they did marry (Kleinman, 1978:101). All of this sounds very old-fashioned in these sexually liberated times. However, even though more women are sexually involved than in previous times, research (Kleinman, 1978:115) shows that these women feel "marginally deviant" and are concerned "about the projected and/or actual responses of others toward their behavior."

Our society values youth at least as highly as beauty, and nearly everyone dreads the prospect of old age. However, the external symptoms of aging—dulling hair and skin, crow's-feet around the eyes, sagging breasts—are particularly devastating for women. This "double standard of aging" (Sontag, 1972) stems from the fact that traditionally, appearance has been women's major asset. Williams (1977:356) says, "Woman especially has had good reason to fear the passing of youth. Her most socially valued qualities, her ability to provide sex, attractive companionship, and to have children and nurture them, are expressed in the context of youth, which is endowed with physical beauty and fertility." On the other hand, money, power and worldly experience make men's grey hairs seem dignified, even virile, and certainly not drab and dowdy. Thus, men become more satisfied with their bodies as they age, while women become more anxious (Posner, 1980:86). All of this explains why women are coy about their age and lie about it more frequently than men (Bell, 1970:192).

The double standard of aging is also reflected in norms regarding appropriate ages for marrying. John (thirty-eight years) marrying Jane (twenty years) arouses a different societal reaction than Jane (thirty-eight) marrying John (twenty). " 'Robbing the cradle' is not nearly so extreme an affront to society as 'being old enough to be his mother' " (Posner, 1980:85). In the past, at least, a youthful bride was not only at her prettiest, but able to embark on a long career of childbearing. Also, the younger woman is more likely to be impressed with the worldliness of an older man and, therefore, perhaps more amenable to his control.[15] The young-bride–mature-groom combination does not benefit either partner, in terms of the criterion of sexual performance. The erotic responsiveness of women increases as they get older, while men's tends to decline (Wilson et al., 1977:234).

Differential age norms make remarriage more difficult for a divorced or widowed woman than for her male counterpart (Bell, 1970:76). Suppose divorce occurs when a fictional couple are in their mid-thirties. (In 1975, the average age of divorcing Canadians was thirty-five for women and thirty-eight for men [Ambert, 1980:34].) To exaggerate only a little, the man can find a new mate among women from eighteen years old to his own age. This includes many women under twenty-five who have never married. The woman, by contrast, is limited by custom to men her own age or older. Most men in this age bracket are already married. The divorcée is therefore restricted mainly to men who have returned to the marriage market through divorce or widowhood. A woman's likelihood of remarrying drops dramatically after age thirty. At that age, the probability of remarriage for women is .62, for men .93. By age forty, it is .34 for women and .63 for men. (However, this lower incidence may express both lack of opportunity and unwillingness to remarry [Boyd, Eichler and Hofley, 1976:25].)

The classified personal columns in urban newspapers offer a fascinating source of sociological data. The following preliminary observations emerged from a reading of several weekend *Calgary Herald* personal column ads related to mate seeking among the divorced and widowed:

> (a) Men place ads more often than women. Given the greater availability of women, why might this be so? Are men less concerned about potentially dangerous consequences?[16]
>
> (b) Women's letters tend to advertise their own attractive appearance and seek financial security in males; men's letters are the reverse. To illustrate, these letters are taken from the 8 May 1981 *Calgary Herald* personal columns:

> > Lady, European, very attractive, new in Calgary. Intellectual interest, fond of sports. Divorced, no dependents, would like to meet unattached, professional businessman, age 40-55.
> >
> > Bachelor would like to meet tall slim woman 25-35, nonsmoker. She should consider herself to be attractive and desirable. Let's go to lunch to see if we're interested in going out to dinner.

Although courting occurs at various points in the life cycle and romantic relationships "the second time around" are becoming increasingly common, most courtship in our society occurs when potential partners are in their late teens and early twenties. This is a time "when, on biological grounds, the female maximally fits commercial ideals regarding sexual attractiveness" (Goffman, 1977:309). Both men and women are likely to find the early stages of the traditional courtship ritual traumatic. She has to bide her time until he chooses to take the initiative (if he ever does). He has to risk rejection. In Goffman's (1977:309) words, "The strategic advantage of the male in courtship derives from his ability and right to withdraw interest at any point save perhaps the last ones, that of the female from control of access to her favors. . . ." If the courtship is successful, "he obtains exclusive [not necessarily "first claim"] rights of access [to her "favors," to use Goffman's euphemism] and she gets a social place" (Goffman, 1977:310). Although in conventional wisdom, it is the women who are most eager for domestic felicity, men tend to fall in love more readily than women, and women tend to fall out of love more readily than men. Contrary to stereotypes about romantic and sentimental women, women appear to be more practical about mate selection (Hill, Rubin and Peplau, 1976:150).

Does the empirical evidence support the exchange theory of courtship? Do women "trade" their beauty for prospective husbands' status-conferring ability? One major study (Taylor and Glenn, 1976) of a United

States national sample found that wives' attractiveness did *not* correspond highly with husbands' occupational prestige. Two reasons are suggested (p. 495) for failure of these data to support the exchange theory of courtship. Other sorts of assets may outweigh female attractiveness and male status-conferring ability on the marriage market. These may include, for both sexes, warmth of personality, ability to provide humor, emotional support, ego support, relaxation or stimuli for diversion. The physical attractiveness of prospective husbands may also be more important to wives than was expected.

In general, the evidence tends to support the "matching hypothesis" (Murstein, 1972; Silverman, 1971), which holds that people tend to relate to others of approximately equal beauty. Here, we have a particularization of both the similarity principle (discussed earlier) and the exchange theory of the marriage market. Murstein (1972:11), one of the earliest researchers of this "matching hypothesis," talks about the association of individuals "with *equal market value* for physical attractiveness [emphasis added]." This means that though each of us might ideally prefer to date and mate with an extremely beautiful person, we tend to be realistic enough to "settle" for someone reasonably close to our own level of attractiveness. Goffman (1952:456) put the more general idea rather cynically: "A proposal of marriage in our society tends to be a way in which a man sums up his social attributes and suggests to a woman that hers are not so much better as to preclude a merger or partnership in these matters." In sum, there is a good deal of evidence that dating, engaged and married men and women (and even same-sex friends [Cash and Derlega, 1978]) are similar to one another in degree of physical attractiveness (Berscheid and Walster, 1978:85).

This section has considered various ways in which gender (and sex) socialization are related to romantic relationships. It may occur to the reader that words such as "courtship," and "marriage proposals" and "going steady" have an old-fashioned ring to them. (Are males to be found down on their knees proposing marriage only on the late, late movies on television?) Nevertheless, because of the limited repertoire of social scripts at people's disposal, the trendier forms of relationships such as group dating, cohabitation and trial marriage closely parallel the traditional forms (Laws and Schwartz, 1977:117). The lessons of gender socialization remain the same, in pattern if not in detail.

This concludes our consideration of the peer group as crucible of gender identity. Social scientists are increasingly coming to appreciate the importance of the wide variety of social transactions between peers. We expect that in the years to come, theoretical explanations of gender socialization will be amended to give the peer group a more prominent position. Its contribution has been overshadowed too long by the family.

CONCLUSIONS

Chapter Five continued the discussion of gender from the social-psychological perspective, begun in the previous chapter. It addressed, once again, the central question: How do people learn femininity and masculinity? However, the focus of this chapter shifted to the *source* of socialization lessons, and to the family and peer group as primary group agents of socialization. These are the sources stressed in the theories of socialization dealt with in Chapter Four. Although *primary* socialization was emphasized, some attention was also given to adult socialization.

The following were some of the particular topics considered within the context of family and peer group: same-sex/cross-sex parent-child relations; siblings as agents of socialization; nontraditional family structure; demographic variations in gender socialization (social class; ethnicity); sex differences in play; women and sport; same-sex and opposite-sex friendships; romantic relationships and platonic relationships.

The next chapter will conclude our discussion of gender socialization with an analysis of secondary and symbolic socialization agents.

6 Secondary and Symbolic Agents of Gender Socialization

CHAPTER Six is the last of three chapters to explore the acquisition and reinforcement of gender identity from the social-psychological perspective. To reiterate, our problem is to explain how people develop masculine or feminine personality traits, behaviors and attitudes. Our approach is social-psychological; that is, we explore how the social environment impinges upon the individual. Our concern in this chapter is *not* with biology, psychology or social structure, but with the various *secondary* and *symbolic* agents of socialization. Attention will be given to the school and the church (secondary agents) and to language and mass media (symbolic agents). Once again, the focus is mainly upon the sources,[1] rather than the content, of gender lessons.

The previous chapter dealt with the family and peer group, which are *primary* agents in several senses of the word. First, the strength of the emotions aroused in family and friendship groups are not rivalled by the more impersonal contexts of school and church. For instance, the primary relationship of parents and children may be contrasted with the more secondary relationship of teachers and children (Lightfoot, 1977). The latter is not characterized by the "chaotic fluctuation of emotions, indulgence, and impulsivity" found in the association of parents and children (p. 396). "Even those teachers who speak of 'loving' their children do not really mean the boundless, all-encompassing love of mothers and fathers, but a very measured and time-limited love that allows for withdrawal" (Lightfoot, 1977:396). Intense affectivity bespeaks influence.

Another way of saying all this is that parents have *particularistic* expectations for their children (and friends for their friends), while teachers (and preachers) have *universalistic* expectations (Lightfoot, 1977:396). Parents and friends attend to individual qualities and needs. By contrast, teachers and preachers try to judge everyone by the same objective standards and hold out generalized goals for all children.

Second, the primary influences occur early in life when the child is most impressionable. The child moves beyond the family circle to confront the peer group, the school, perhaps the church, youth groups, etc. Research evidence shows that timing is important, that gender identity, for example, is "very solidly entrenched before children even enter public school" (Richer, 1979:198).

Third, the primary agents are particularly important because they determine the child's exposure to subsequent agents and interpret the meaning of these secondary influences. The family's "channelling function" is obvious. Most generally, "the child confronts different constellations of values, beliefs, people, and opportunities depending on where his family is located socially, geographically, and temporally" (Clausen, 1968:136). The family determines which school and which church (if any) the child will attend. It may influence what mass media the child may consume. Both the family and the peer group act as "reference group" filters for the meaning of these alternative sources. For example, the Jesus movement appealed to adolescents caught between parental and peer expectations and troubled about the latter's permissive attitudes regarding drugs and sex (Heirich, 1977). Some teenagers will receive parental and peer support for adherence to a conservative Christian view of masculine-feminine demeanor. Implicit in this example is another important point. Although children's exposure to socialization agents is cumulative, the depiction of gender by those agents may be far from coherent. Children may have to learn to reconcile conflicting expectations. Ishwaran (1979:17) says that "the internal pressures of the different agencies make it virtually impossible to socialize the child to order, according to any preconceived plan."

The symbolic and secondary agents have both common and unique characteristics. The mass media and, to a certain extent, verbal and nonverbal communication forms share with the school and the church the differences from the primary socialization agents enumerated above. However, these symbolic sources are characterized by some distinctions that require emphasis at the outset. The school, the church (and the family) deliberately set out to equip children with the knowledge required to fit into adult society. Although much of the impact that these agencies have upon children's gender socialization is unintentional, their socialization aims are still more clearly articulated than those of the symbolic agencies. The mass media—television, radio, newspapers, magazines, books, movies, records, tapes—are impersonal communication sources that exist to entertain, to inform, to sell products. For most people, the fact that the media are also in the business of gender socialization is beside the point.

The part played by language and nonverbal communication is more subtle and perhaps more profound. Language is the major means by which all socialization agents socialize. Yet it is more than just the means. We assume, as do many scholars (Sapir, 1933; Whorf, 1949; Berger and Luckmann, 1966; Schutz, 1967; Cicourel, 1970), that "reality" is constructed and perpetrated through symbols, and through language as a specific set of symbols. Thus, to a considerable extent, what people think and know and do is determined by the language categories at their disposal. Since language and sex are linked in many complex ways, children's linguistic lessons are also lessons in gender relations. Many involve the "semantic derogation of women" (Schulz, 1975:65). Consider, for example, the connotations of *bachelor* compared with those of *spinster* or *old maid*, and the insult delivered by applying the latter terms to a man, as opposed to labelling a woman a "bachelor." Language is a ubiquitous socializer, which also serves as the vehicle for all socialization agents. *Nonverbal* communication, too, is a potent agent; children learn about masculinity and femininity through observing others communicating nonverbally (and by doing so themselves). There are sex differences in touching people and in maintaining eye contact, for example.

THE SCHOOL

Industrialized nations such as Canada assign to the school a major role in preparing children for adulthood. The knowledge and skills required to function effectively in urbanized, industrialized societies are too extensive and too complex for parents to convey to their offspring. According to Parsons' (1959) classic statement, the educational system performs two major functions for society. The *socialization* function involves the child's internalization of commitment to broad societal values and to the tasks that the society requires done. The *allocation* function refers to the channelling of people through programs of occupational preparation into positions in the socioeconomic structure. Since gender is related in one way or another to societal values, tasks and occupational roles, the school also teaches the child about femininity and masculinity.

Although Canadian schools may be public or private, religiously committed or secular, they all come under government jurisdiction. The curriculum guidelines issued by provincial departments of education represent our society's most conscious attempt to structure systematically the content of socialization (Pratt, 1975). But though the school is the most deliberate socialization agent, much of its actual impact on children has very little to do with the academic curriculum. Most of the content of gender socialization is incidental to the school's stated goals.

Enrolling in school represents for children a significant step beyond the family and the neighborhood. For most, elementary school is the first formal institution they encounter. These young pupils are confronted with impersonal rules for behavior, which are not rooted in parental or peer authority. Moreover, each child is treated not as a unique individual, but simply as one member of a cohort. One indication of the education system's probable impact is that a child spends approximately 7,000 hours in school from kindergarten to the sixth grade (Ishwaran, 1979:23). Although school continues to be a socialization source through high school and postsecondary education, our emphasis here is on early schooling, for its influence on children is greatest. However, we must reiterate that the school is a *secondary* socialization agent, which reinforces and elaborates the basic ideas about gender acquired by a child from the primary sources.

In this section, we will examine the role played by teachers and text-books in gender socialization. (Although the child is socialized as well by other pupils, this influence is an aspect of peer socialization, which was discussed in the preceding chapter.) In 1970, *The Report of the Royal Commission on the Status of Women in Canada* expressed its concern that there had not been equal educational opportunity for females in this country. Has the situation changed?

The Teacher

The topic of teachers as gender socialization agents will be approached by describing Richer's (1979) excellent observational study of the kindergarten classroom in an Ontario urban school. This classroom was observed (and videotaped) for two months by three field-workers. Unlike many social scientists, who take for granted the gender socialization role of the teacher, Richer documented these socialization processes. Moreover, his observations were guided by theory. Therefore, his research serves as a useful review of learning theory, cognitive-developmental theory and identification theory (discussed in Chapter Four).

The basic premise of *learning theory* is that learning occurs largely through systematic encouragement or discouragement of particular behavior via the manipulation of rewards and punishments. Regarding gender learning, the argument is that important people in the child's life positively reinforce girls for "feminine" behavior and positively reinforce boys for "masculine" behavior. At the same time, cross-sex behavior is negatively reinforced. This theory leads us to look for instances of teachers rewarding or punishing gender-related behavior.

The *cognitive-developmental* approach emphasizes the active role of the child in seeking to impose order and coherence on the environment. Unlike learning theory assumptions, this perspective does not view the child as reacting to external stimuli or responding to external agents as motivating forces. Instead, the child is a processor and interpreter of incoming stimuli, which must be interpreted consistently with his/her constantly developing image of external reality. Gender learning, like all other learning, requires a grasp of certain fundamental (and consistent) concepts. Children must first learn that gender is invariant and then discern "appropriate" behavior for their own gender. The cognitive-developmental perspective led Professor Richer to look for recurring patterns in the classroom experience that reflect gender differentiation and that could sharpen the child's classification scheme of concepts concerning gender-related behavior.

Finally, *identification theory* indicates that learning takes place through imitation of adult models. External rewards are not necessarily needed for learning to occur. This approach suggested to Richer the possibility of the teacher's acting as role model, that is, providing personal cues for pupils' behavior and attitudes.

Before commenting on Professor Richer's theory-related findings, it is worth repeating a point made earlier: by the age of four, children are already well aware of their own gender and are acting appropriately. Two types of classroom observations supported this statement. The first was *voluntary seating patterns*, for example, when the children gathered every morning around the piano for "Good Morning Time." This consisted of a teacher-led discussion of the weather or approaching holidays and several songs. In the typical seating arrangement (on this and other occasions) the girls sat together close to the teacher, while the boys formed a group at the back further away from the teacher.

Sex homogeneity also characterized friendship preference in the game, "Farmer in the Dell." First of all, the teacher would choose one child to be farmer. Then the child would stand in the middle of a circle, while the nursery rhyme was sung. During the singing, the farmer would choose a wife, who would choose a child, who would choose a nurse, who would choose a dog, who would choose a cat, who would choose a rat, who would finally choose a cheese. The researchers observed four games of "Farmer in the Dell." Of the twenty-eight choices made, twenty-five were same-sex choices. The male "farmers" even chose male "wives." In general, the same-sex friendship pattern (noted in the previous chapter) characterized the children's play.

Richer (1979:199) interprets these behavioral indicators to mean that, "Any role the school might play in such socialization is likely to be minimal, confined to reinforcing or failing to reinforce patterns already well underway." We gain some appreciation of the function of the school, in general, and of the teacher, in particular, from his theoretical analysis of the observational data.

First, then, do teachers reinforce sex-appropriate behavior as learning theory suggests they should? Two examples of such reinforcement were found. The first example concerned teacher response to aggression. Of the fifty-five male acts of aggression, only eleven (20%) resulted in explicit punishment. However, of the eight female aggressive acts, over half (five) produced some kind of punishment. This observation suggests differential teacher tolerance for aggressive acts. The second example was the fact that the teacher was more likely to choose boys to move chairs and athletic equipment. Since four-year-old boys do not excel in muscular strength, this teacher was following her idea of sex-typed behavior. (Other instances of teachers reinforcing traditional gender behavior have been reported by Fagot and Patterson [1969] and Serbin and O'Leary [1975]. However, other researchers have found that teachers reinforce feminine behavior in both sexes.)

Cognitive-developmental theory proposes that the child learns early that girls and boys belong in different and invariant categories. To what extent does the teacher provide cues that could enable the child to "properly" classify the two sexes? Richer looked for recurring situations where boys and girls were treated differently in interaction, or spatially segregated or alluded to verbally as different social units. All three types of behavior were found. As we saw above, teachers treated aggression and helping behavior differently. When teacher-pupil interactions were coded, 65% of all teacher interactions with the boys were discipline-related commands (e.g., "Sit down and be still"; "Don't fight"). Only 40% of the teacher interaction with girls was of this type. (Incidentally, the high percentage of discipline-related commands was partly due to the fact that the coding was done during the first two weeks of school, when social control demands were urgent.) In addition, the teacher found sex to be a practical basis on which to organize the children. For example, children lined up by sex to move from one activity to another—going to the library or the gymnasium, retrieving food from their lockers, preparing to go home. Also, sex was used to motivate participation activities— "The girls are ready, the boys are not" or "Who can do it the fastest, the boys or the girls?" Richer (1979:201) cites this illustration of organization and motivation:

> In the coordination exercises, where the children were asked to respond quickly to changes in directions regarding hand movements, the commands were invariably given by sex: "Boys, put your fingers on your nose; girls, put your hands in your laps; boys, touch your toes, etc." When someone slipped up here, the teacher's admonishment sometimes took the following form, "Are you a girl? I thought all along you were a boy." This kind of reference, which in this case left the child squirming a little in embarrassment, served not only to accentuate further the sex differences in the class, but also to put a negative value on behaviour inconsistent with one's own sex.

Parenthetically, we ask whether the embarrassment described in the quotation above stemmed from sex inconsistency per se, or from loss of status associated with the "demotion" from boy to girl? Be that as it may, the teacher was reinforcing gender identity, as predicted by cognitive-developmental (and learning) theory.

Finally, identification theory directed the researcher to seek evidence of pupil identification with the teacher. Such identification was found to occur in three stages. During the first stage, the girls (but not the boys) were actively engaged in creating an *affective* bond between themselves and the teacher. The girls sat closer to the teacher and they initiated physical contact with her—hand holding, caressing and leg hugging. This behavior began on the first day of school. About three weeks later the second stage, teacher *imitation*, was initiated. Once again the behavior was limited to the girls. The performance went this way: one of the little girls sat on the piano stool (the teacher's territory), book in hand, and pretended to read to an imaginary class of children. Gradually, this "surrogate teacher" drama moved on to the third, or *identification*, stage, as the child adopted teacher attitudes and behavior, and other children formed a real audience. For example, the "teacher" would realistically portray anger over acts of "deviance" detected in her audience. This drama was observed at least nineteen times. Richer concludes that through this identification (which occurs because of shared sex), the girls' gender identity is reinforced and appropriate behavior and attitudes toward school are learned. At the end of this section we will return to the implication that females find school to be an especially congenial place.

Meanwhile, we conclude that the teacher as human agent in the educational institution reinforces and embellishes the gender identity that children have developed in their home and neighborhood. Very likely, the emphasis given to gender in this first formal institution they encounter, adds additional, impersonal dimensions to their notions of gender. Perhaps there dawns, in these early school years, some realization of gender as a major societal axis of differentiation, and some sense of being a member of a large, abstract category. Although parental admonishments, such as "boys don't cry" or "girls don't sit with their legs apart," make reference to boys-in-general and girls-in-general, actually being among many children lends reality to membership in the category.

Textbooks

A second major way in which the school socializes is through textbooks. Their content augments the information conveyed by teachers, and as pupils advance through the educational system an increasing proportion of their new knowledge is obtained through this impersonal source.

Sociologists have been very interested in how texts affect students' attitudes (Pratt, 1975). This concern has its source partly in the nature of young readers. Particularly during the formative elementary-school years, textbooks make up the bulk of the reading material of many children. In addition, this assigned reading carries the cachet of authority; it is "official" school reading. One of the observations of the cognitive-developmental theorist, Jean Piaget, is that children do not develop the intellectual ability to be critical about what they read until their later school years. Therefore, for better or worse, texts have considerable potential for conveying social attitudes along with factual material. The current interest in textbook treatment of gender parallels an earlier concern with the treatment of racial groups.

The Report of the Royal Commission on the Status of Women in Canada (1970) analyzed the gender imagery in a representative selection of Anglophone and Francophone elementary-school textbooks. Versatile characters who have adventures are invariably males. In French-language textbooks, the girls "are preparing to be only mothers and housekeepers, and are portrayed as passive, self-sacrificing and submissive" (p. 175). A series of readers used in Ontario featured a stereotypical family. The kind, understanding father takes his children on interesting expeditions, while the mother stays home to prepare meals and to tell the children "what is best for them." The sex-typing even appeared in arithmetic books, with children being presented with problems such as this: "A girl can type about 48 words per minute. She has to type 2,468 words. Can she do this in 45 minutes?" (p. 175). Although the elementary-school curriculum is similar for girls and boys, the textbook models provide children with clearly differentiated gender imagery. From this content analysis, the Commission concluded that "A woman's creative and intellectual potential is either underplayed or ignored in the education of children from their earliest years" (p. 175). Therefore, they recommended "That the provinces and territories adopt textbooks that portray women, as well as men, in diversified roles and occupations" (p. 175). Has progress been made?

One answer to this question is provided by an analysis of discriminatory content in nine series of grade one readers most frequently used in Montreal's Anglophone Protestant schools, done by the Montreal YWCA Women's Centre (1977). This study of thirty-eight books was undertaken to determine how males and females are presented in the material that is used to teach reading skills to young children. The researchers examined the numerical distribution of the sexes, the sex of the central characters and the activities of females and males.

The statistical analysis demonstrated that all nine series reinforced cultural myths concerning males and females. "Instead of helping children to explore their capabilities and potential, grade one readers are contributing to a socialization process which channels girls and boys into restricted roles" (p. 7). Boys appear in the stories far more frequently than girls. (Females comprise 50.1% of the Canadian population, but only 37% of the fictional population.) Since the main character is by definition more important than the others, the sex of the central character is perti-nent. The researchers found that 177 stories centered on boys and 68 on girls, 35 on men and 15 on women. Therefore, the females' image "as passive participants or adjuncts to males, the central actors, is per-petuated" (p. 7). The boys in the stories are the active, competitive, prob-lem solvers, while the girls are passive and preoccupied with domestic chores, but sensitive to others' problems. Those adult women not por-trayed as homemakers were restricted to eighteen occupations, largely traditional and often supportive. Men, on the other hand, were represented in seventy-eight different occupations ranging from profes-sionals to manual workers. Fictional women were librarians, teachers, nurses and cooks, while fictional men were clowns, kings, astronauts, lumberjacks, stevedores, pirates and drum majors. In general, boy-girl activities were less caricatured than men-women activities.

Textbooks are not the only teaching material found (by earlier critics, at least) to be infected with sexism. A former teacher describes a social studies film called *Big People, Little People*:

> It was very careful to reflect a racial mix, showing a lot of children play-ing adult roles with a black boy playing the mayor. But apparently the idea of female roles had never occurred to the filmmakers. Throughout the entire eight minutes, females appeared twice; the total time they were on screen was thirty-eight seconds; and each time they were carrying mops. The committee viewing this film dissolved into hysterics. If it had been prepared deliberately as a satire on sex stereotyping it couldn't have been done better. [Nelson, 1976:173]

Although most studies of gender socialization in the schools have focused on elementary-school texts (and rightly so, considering the im-pressionable nature of beginning students), high school and university texts have not been completely slighted. Critics have complained that in senior literature and history texts, women are either given tiny roles as mothers, wives, daughters, or lovers, or are totally invisible. "Men's lives, at least in literature and history, *seem* more interesting than women's" (Howe, 1974:127). Awareness has grown that male lives and male creative work appealed to the male scholars who dominated (in numbers, power, or both) these learned professions. As pointed out in Chapter One, contemporary scholars are now attempting to overcome these biases. (See for example Trofimenkoff and Prentice, *The Neglected Majority: Essays in Canadian Women's History* [1977].)

As mentioned in an earlier chapter, the treatment of gender in sociology textbooks has become a continuing concern (Schneider and Hacker, 1973; Nett, 1979). Introductory texts in particular are scrutinized for their treatment of the roles of women and men in society, for sexist language (e.g., the use of the generic term *man* for *people*), for the sex composition of pictures, for the inclusion of the topic of gender relations. According to the newsletter, *Society* (February 1981 issue), the Social Policy Committee of the Canadian Sociology and Anthropology Association (CSAA) actively promotes the idea of "non-gender-specific language" with publishers, and encourages members to raise this issue when promoting books. All in all, gender is probably treated in a more balanced fashion in educational materials at the university level than at the primary or secondary levels.

The publicity received across the country by the Royal Commission on the Status of Women and by activist groups such as the Montreal Women's Centre and CSAA Social Policy Committee has made teachers, parents and publishing companies aware of the problems discussed above. Attempts are being made to improve the quality of teaching materials.

Despite the foregoing, the *causal link* between the exposure of children to biased textbooks and their subsequent sex-typed behavior remains conjectural. Establishing causality would require pre- and postmeasurement of gender-related knowledge and attitudes, as well as control groups. As Richer (1979:203) points out, "researchers cannot have such a free reign in our schools." However, in the absence of such controlled experiments, the argument being made by American scholars for the causal link does sound plausible (Laws, 1979:258-59). Achievement tests are a case in point. [The items on these tests depict stereotypic situations much like those found in elementary readers (Saario, Jacklin and Tittle, 1973).] Testing materials are much more exciting and interesting to boys than to girls. It is reasonable to expect that this "relevance" factor would enhance boys' attention and motivation to perform well. Whether or not the same situation exists in Canada is not known. The difficulty of empirically establishing gender socialization effects will be discussed at some length in connection with the mass media. Meanwhile, we must consider the hotly debated topic: "Who is more comfortable at school, boys or girls?"

Congeniality of the School Atmosphere

Though classrooms are usually not segregated by sex, school does not seem to be the same psychological or social environment for girls as for boys. As we have just seen, elementary school is a place where women rule and approve of the girl students, who identify with them, where the energetic fictional boys have fun and adventures, and where the boy students are scolded for being rambunctious. The issue here is whether school provides a hospitable environment for girls and an alienating one for boys (Fink and Kosecoff, 1977). Further, if school is indeed a "feminized" environment, why is the long-term "payoff" for girls so meager?

During the early years of school, girls are more successful academically than boys. The fact is incontrovertible. Girls beginning school are, on the average, two years ahead of boys, developmentally. This intellectual advance is reflected in girls' academic achievement. They begin to speak, read and count before boys do. In the early grades, girls are at least equal to boys in mathematical skill (Fink and Kosecoff, 1977). Two to three times as many boys as girls have reading problems. Boys also seem to have a more difficult time adjusting to elementary-school classroom demands for obedience, order and neatness (Howe, 1974:124). Female students progress through elementary and secondary school faster than male students. Canadian data show that only 19% of the female students versus 26% of the male students at the elementary educational level during 1968-69 were older than the modal age (i.e. the most frequently occurring age) for that level (Martin and Macdonnell, 1978:212).

Are there factors other than girls' precocity in physical development that are responsible for their early success? Several explanations have been put forth (Richer, 1979:203). Girls' greater verbal ability would predict greater success, since the earlier grades are concerned largely with the transmission of verbal material. As well, "feminine" behavior seems more appropriate to school. It is possible that girls have already learned at home to be obedient and quiet, while boys have been reinforced for "bouncing about, questioning, being curious or aggressive" (Howe, 1974:124). This position is supported by a longitudinal study of middle-class Anglophone Montreal children from kindergarten through grade five (Lester, Dudek and Muir, 1972). These authors suggest that girls' superior academic achievement is related to male/female personality differences, as measured by the Cattell Personality Questionnaire. Girls were more obedient, dependent, sober-minded, quiet, practical and realistic; boys were more assertive, independent, excitable, happy-go-lucky and freethinking. Finally, the female authority figure in the elementary grades makes it easier for girls to identify with their teacher and "hence with the general values of academic commitment and performance" (Richer, 1979:203).

The advantage to girls of having the same-sex teacher (and the "modelling effect" that results) does not mean that there is any greater tendency on the part of boys to dislike their teachers, or that teachers take less interest in their boys' performance (Maccoby and Jacklin, 1974:135). Elementary teachers tend to give *more* attention to boys, in fact. They talk with them more and listen to them more; they have more interaction, both approving and disapproving, with them (Sears and Feldman, 1974). The "modelling effect" serves to elaborate the *attitudinal* advantage of girls, which likely began in the home. Since girls do not obtain higher scores on aptitude or achievement tests, their superior grades in school must reflect "some combination of greater effort, greater interest, and better work habits" (Maccoby and Jacklin, 1974:135).

Although some observers have feared that the "feminized" school atmosphere would "feminize" boys, boys seem to manage (though at the cost of considerable confusion) to remain boyish. Studies show that female teachers (and sometimes male teachers) reinforce both sexes for feminine behavior (Fagot, 1981; Fagot and Paterson, 1969). However, for boys, the reinforcement from peers and family serves to counter teachers' influence and thus maintain masculinity. Richer (1979:202) may also be right in suggesting that perceived similarity (common sex) between socializer and "socializee" (teacher and student, in this case) is a prerequisite for identification.

Though the idea that American schools were turning boys into sissies aroused some outrage south of the border (see Laws, 1979:260-62), from the author's point of view the situation presents an interesting puzzle, namely, that of explaining how girls' initial advantage in the education system becomes dissipated.

The "Reversal of Success" Phenomenon

At issue is the complex matter of sex differences in educational and occupational aspirations, which has been characterized as "reversal of success" between the sexes. One dimension of this situation is that, despite the superior academic achievement of girls from primary through high school, proportionately more of the boys continue their education beyond high school (Hunter, 1981). Although the general problem for girls is "not achievement at all, but attrition" (Howe, 1974:124), women's participation in postsecondary education has improved greatly over the past fifteen years. In Canada, in 1962-63, females made up 38% of the enrollment in postsecondary institutions (university and nonuniversity). In 1974-75, this figure rose to 51%. There has been a steady increase in the number of females in universities (27% in 1962-63 versus 39.5% in 1974-75) and a decline in females in other postsecondary institutions (70% in 1962-63; 47% in 1974-75) (Statistics Canada, 1977:92, 99). However, the apparent rise in female university enrollment mentioned above is somewhat misleading. In the view of Robb and Spencer (1976:86):

> The past few decades have witnessed an enormous expansion in enrollment in education at all levels. This increase has been shared by both males and females.
>   Even so, at the more advanced levels the enrollment rates of women remain substantially below those of men. Moreover, women in postsecondary education continue to enrol mostly in "traditional" fields, such as arts, education, and nursing. At the same time, the number of women enrolled in such traditionally male-dominated fields as law, medicine, and commerce has increased sharply, though the numbers remain small relative to males.

Sex-typing of occupations (an issue raised in Chapter Four) continues to occur.

A second aspect of the "reversal of success" phenomenon refers to the school's function of allocation into the occupational structure. While females are the sex most comfortable in school, they end up doing less well in the occupational structure. Although occupational choice is more egalitarian now than it was in the past, girls still aspire to a constricted range of "female" occupations that have characteristics congruent with sex stereotypes, "social-emotional, nurturant, and person-centered (Klemmack and Edwards, 1975:511). Most girls want to be teachers, social workers, nurses or secretaries, not chartered accountants, engineers, architects or firemen. Not only are fewer occupations chosen, but even in traditionally female occupations, the administrative positions are dominated by men. The pattern is one of male chiefs and female Indians (Sutherland, 1978). We should emphasize that our intent is not to denigrate female occupations. Rather, the complaint is that many women, by charting their destiny according to traditional gender patterns, are not developing their human potential. In concrete terms, most of the Canadian women who work outside the home are concentrated in a small number of low-skilled, poorly paid jobs (Armstrong and Armstrong, 1975). Although in this section our concern is with ambitions and intent, sex differences in adolescents' occupational aspirations do reflect the reality of sex segregation in the occupational structure (Marini and Greenberger, 1978).

The continuation of the pattern of relatively low female aspiration beyond high school is documented by Sutherland's (1978) survey of nearly 1,000 Canadian university students. Of all men in the sample, 28% intended to take one degree, 48% two degrees and 23% three degrees. By comparison, twice as many women (59%) expected to leave the university after one degree, 31% intended to take two degrees and 10% said they aimed for three degrees. Thirty-eight percent of the men (versus 7% of the women) aspired to one of these professions: engineer, dentist, doctor, lawyer, architect, veterinarian, economist, accountant, church leader, professional psychologist. The largest number of women (36%) intended to be school teachers.

Sex differences in occupational aspirations are a complex problem, for it is difficult to isolate the influence of education from other influences. To what extent are the official and the unofficial curricula of the school responsible for the depression of girls' aspirations? Aside from educational influences, the jobs that people end up with depend on factors besides their sex, such as academic ability, personal attitudes, ethnicity, social class and labor market conditions, as well as sheer chance and other imponderables.[2] This means that despite the myth of egalitarianism that prevails in North America, not everyone enjoys equal opportunity for success.

The problem of social and attitudinal barriers to educational and occupational aspirations has been explored by social scientists such as Robert Pike in *Who Doesn't Get to University and Why* (1970), John Porter in *The Vertical Mosaic* (1965)[3] and Jill Vickers and June Adam in *But Can You Type?* (1977). According to their analyses of the Canadian situation, the system of privilege is "stacked" against full participation by the poor, by members of some races and ethnic groups, and by women (Vickers and Adam, 1977:33). Obviously, girls who are from poor families, from Indian or Inuit families and from remote regions of the country will be even more disadvantaged. Indeed, such studies as are available (Marini and Greenberger, 1978) tell us that gender constitutes a more formidable barrier to women's occupational achievement than does a lack of resources (in academic ability or socioeconomic background). From his study of Western Canadian high-school students, Brinkerhoff (1977:300-301) concluded that "Sex-typing of occupations serves as only one of several barriers to 'women wanting to work in a man's world.' Being a woman is one strike against her—perhaps the most important. This barrier, when combined with the others [mentioned above] operates to funnel girls' choices into traditional occupations and to continue the sex-role segregation currently pervasive in the work world."

In summary, an explanation is required as to why women's academic and occupational achievement drops below that of males, given the facts that, (1) females and males have equally good intellectual potential, (2) similar achievement motivation exists throughout the school years (Maccoby and Jacklin, 1974:164) and (3) the school atmosphere is "feminized." Though women's career goals appear to be broadening somewhat now (Garrison, 1979; Maxwell and Maxwell, 1981; Robb and Spencer, 1976), their occupational aspirations are still quite sex-typed, and their hopes modest. What happened to females' initial advantage?

Why Are Females' Ambitions So Modest?

The social-psychological reasons for the "reversal of success" phenomenon can be found in the cultural and personal definitions of gender. (The biological and social-structural explanations are of course somewhat different.) Society expects men to commit themselves to their occupation and women to their family. As they reach adolescence, males take school, which is the avenue to the breadwinner role, more seriously. Men's occupational ambitions are loftier than women's because work is a major ingredient of masculine self-esteem and because men expect to spend a lifetime in the labor market. Women too must prepare themselves for some occupation. The decision they face now is not between family and work, but between family and *demanding* work. Not so long ago girls gave priority to attracting a suitable husband and viewed work as a short-run diversion until the first baby came along. The roles of wife, mother and homemaker were assumed not to require special occupational preparation (Vickers and Adam, 1977:71). To the extent that housewifery and motherhood were the girls' destiny, heavy investment of time, energy and money for a short sojourn in the labor market did not make economic sense. Therefore, it is not surprising that a national U.S. survey (Douvan and Adelson, 1966) showed that while male-female attitudes were similar in early adolescence, within a few years boys were focusing on occupational success and girls on social success. We can also appreciate why parents (both mothers and fathers) have more often expressed the hope that their *boys* would go on to higher education (Robb and Spencer, 1976:74), and why families provide only niggardly support for capable daughters in university but continue to underwrite the university expenses of their less able sons (Sutherland, 1978:782).

In attempting to explain women's constricted work ambitions, psychologists have examined sex differences in various motivations and attitudes. The achievement motive, in particular, has been heavily researched. At first it was hypothesized that males had a greater need to achieve than females. After all, society seemed to reward males for achievement, while achievement was not expected in females. As an extension of this argument, school achievement in general and/or mathematics performance in particular eventually becomes defined as masculine (Laws, 1979:265). Although the last point is as yet insufficiently researched, measures of achievement motivation show no real sex differences. However, the evidence available does support the proposition that though women and men have similar needs for achievement, differences exist in the activities and goals on which these achievement needs are focused. To some degree, while work, sports and academic pursuits represent achievement for males, social situations provide achievement for females (who can aspire to be "the hostess with the mostest") (Deaux, 1976:49). Along with achieving in homemaker and interpersonal roles, the woman sometimes chooses to achieve vicariously, through her husband and children, rather than directly for herself (Frieze et al., 1978:240). Nonetheless, as we pointed out earlier (Chapter Two), the highly publicized "fear of success motive" (Horner, 1969) is not confined to women. Under certain circumstances, both sexes are wary of the negative consequences of success. However, at least one study (Deaux and Emswiller, 1974) suggests that success is sex-typed as masculine: male success was explained as ability, female success as luck (especially if the activity was a "masculine" task).

Although the causal attribution discussed in the last paragraph seems unfair to women, the same situation can be turned around to reveal a masculine dilemma. If men manage to succeed, they are rewarded with money, respect and power. But what if they blow it? (Deaux, 1976:33). Rigid sex stereotypes exact a price from men, too. (And the expectations for men are more rigid than for women. Commentators such as Goldberg [1976] believe that the price is premature death. In this view, the traditional male gender expectations are responsible for the higher male incidence of ulcers, heart attacks, suicides and accidents.)

The school is only one of many agents that markets sex stereotypes and depresses women's ambitions. However, the school reflects the values of the environing society, and consequently its teachers, curricula (official and hidden), textbooks and guidance counsellors (Russell, 1979) are engaged in the business of gender socialization. However, things are slowly changing. Because of the influence of the women's movement and the exigencies of the economic climate, women's lives are now less determined by the family cycle. Concomitant with later marriage, later initiation of childbearing, reduced family-size expectations, and the rising number of female-headed families is the growing occupational commitment of women (Garrison, 1979). Even women who would prefer to be full-time housewives and mothers are remaining in the labor market because their families need two incomes. The school, along with other social institutions, is being challenged to uncover and abandon sex-typing, and to prepare people of both sexes to meet the demands of a changing world. Steps are being taken to adopt gender-neutral teaching materials and to alert teachers to the problem. However, Richer (1979:203) warns us that the fact that "sex-role identity is so solidly developed in preschool children implies that those viewing the school as a possible vehicle for combatting sex-role stereotypes are overestimating its relative potency vis-à-vis exposure to family and other early childhood experiences."

RELIGION

This section considers the gender socialization role played by the church,[4] our final example of an institution that deliberately teaches people. The church, like the school, is a secondary socialization agent in the sense that its influence is mediated by family and peers, and exposure to it occurs later in the child's life. Our discussion of religion bears to some extent on the symbolic sources of gender socialization (our next topic), because the *content* of religious thought is central to our purposes. This dual emphasis reflects the fact that the churches accomplish gender socialization both directly, through the explicit efforts of human agents, and indirectly, through the permeation of the culture by their ideas. Although not everyone is exposed to direct religious conditioning in childhood, each of us has been influenced to some extent by religious traditions.

Religiosity in Canada

Some idea of the importance of gender socialization within the religious context may be gained from data on the prevalence of religiosity in this country. Bibby's national survey (1980) reported that Canadians exhibit relatively high levels of belief, practice, experience and knowledge. Only 2% say they do not believe in God, just 17% dismiss altogether the possibility of life after death and only 18% claim never to pray.

According to the 1971 census, fewer than 5% of Canadians indicated that they had no religious preference. (1971 religious affiliations were 46% Roman Catholic, 43% Protestant, 1% Jewish, 6% other [Statistics Canada, *1971 Census of Canada*, Bul. 1.3-3, Table 11].) (Incidentally, a Western Canadian study of 708 young people found that 75% were socialized to belong to the denomination of their mother [Currie, 1976:467].)

When we look at religious attendance, as opposed to religious preference, Canadians seem less enthusiastic. According to Gallup Poll findings, weekly attendance of national samples has dropped from 67% after World War II to 35% in 1978 (Bibby, 1980:402). This latter observation is confirmed by Bibby's (1980:402) statistical survey. While 74% of the respondents claimed to have attended religious services weekly while growing up, fewer than 31% said they were presently doing so. Finally, Currie's (1976:470) study reported the presence of a strong religious atmosphere in only 37% of the homes.

Functions of Religion

Until modern times, religion was found in every human society. Sociologists of the functionalist persuasion assume that religion persists because it benefits individuals and social systems (O'Dea, 1966:4-7). According to this line of reasoning, its primary function for the individual is meaning. Religion helps people to adjust to the "brute facts" of the human condition—death, suffering, failed plans, scarcity of resources. At these "breaking points," where ordinary techniques of adjustment falter, deprived, frustrated souls ask, "Why?" Religion allays cognitive frustration by fitting the "here and now" into a "beyond" (O'Dea, 1966:6). A second major benefit of religion, posited by functionalists, is that it offers emotionally satisfying relationships with supernatural beings. Religion facilitates emotional adjustment to life's existential conditions by "enabling men [and women too?] to enter into relationships with God, gods, or other sacred forces, and to act out responses and feelings involved in those relationships" (O'Dea, 1966:7). Religious affiliation provides emotionally satisfying relationships with earthly beings, as well. It is also a source of "normative closure" (Robbins and Anthony, 1979:78), that is, socially supported standards of right and wrong. Finally, religion provides various direct rewards, such as organizational experience and positions of status and power (and sometimes even clothing, food and shelter) (Stark and Bainbridge, 1980).

Two questions concern us. First, how does religion shape children's notions of femininity and masculinity? (Gender socialization was *not* among the functions of religion enumerated above.) Second, are the benefits of religion affected by the sex of the believer? That is, does it matter if the consumer of religious teaching is male or female? (Sarah, in Marian Engel's novel, *Sarah Bastard's Notebook* [1974:59], describes her childhood as "a competition to see who would make the best Lady Jesus.") Are the rewards of organizational experience equally available to both sexes? Many of the functionalists' views about religion remain conjectural; their general hypotheses (Cheal, 1978; Mackie, 1981b), as well as the application of those hypotheses to gender, require empirical testing.

This section will consider religious influences upon gender socialization under these major headings: the content of religious teaching; religious social organization; the feminist critique of the religious institution. Since it is the Judeo-Christian tradition that predominates in Canadian culture, discussion will be confined to that religious tradition. However, it is worth noting that Western religions are less prejudiced against women than Eastern religions (Andreas, 1971:69).

Gender in Religious Teachings

Many feminists worry about the manner in which gender is interpreted in the teachings of the Judeo-Christian (and other) churches and presented to young people. For instance, Ruether (1974:9) claims (perhaps extravagantly) that religion is "undoubtedly the single most important shaper and enforcer of the image and role of women." Partly because these religions developed historically out of patriarchal societies, their theologies continue to convey an androcentric world view, which gives divine sanction to traditional gender patterns. For example, Martin Luther taught that men and women are equally called to life in Christ, but that "the 'natural' order of the universe decrees women's lesser status and obedience to her husband" (Langdon, 1980:38). "Just as the snail carries its house with it, so the wife should stay at home and look after the affairs of the household, as one who has been deprived of the ability of administering those affairs that are outside and that concern the state" (*Lectures on Genesis, Luther's Works*, I:202-3). Children seem especially vulnerable to religious teachings. One scholar argues that:

Socialization of the young is etched deeply. The messages of the religion are carved into vivid scenes by the child's literal interpretations of Heaven and Hell, God and Satan, Good and Evil. The childhood literalness may be finally rejected by the adult, but the feelings and imagery initially associated with those learnings tend to linger. Questioning the moral authority of the church or its spokesperson, therefore, raises the deep-seated childhood images and fears of the transcendental, as well as whatever concerns about the transcendental the adult carries. [Walum, 1977:126]

An excerpt from *Children's Letters to God* makes the same point. " 'Dear God,' wrote a little girl named Sylvia. 'Are boys better than girls? I know you are one but try to be fair' " (Miller and Swift, 1977:70). The impact of early religious training is enhanced by the fact that the child is not confronted by a disembodied set of religious teachings. Religious ideas are typically sponsored by family, relatives and friends, and hence carry the primary group's "stamp of approval."

A brief survey of the contents of Judeo-Christian theology demonstrates why troubled feminists of both sexes feel that Sunday School lessons are not fit for little children. The male image of God and the fact that Jesus Christ is his son, not his daughter, buttress male supremacy on earth. If God is male, how can women be made in his image? In the words of feminist theologian[5] Mary Daly (1975:156), "If God in 'his' heaven is a father ruling 'his' people, then it is in the 'nature' of things and according to divine plan and the order of the universe that society be male-dominated." Critics (e.g., Miller and Swift, 1977:64) are not reassured by the counterargument that sacred metaphors must not be taken literally, that the symbolization of a masculine godhead does not mean that God really *is* male. If God is always presented as father, judge, shepherd, king, how can women (never mind children) believe that God is both male and female and yet transcends all sexual differentiation (Squire, 1980:35)?

The depth of this male imagery of God is shown by some unpublished research conducted by Diamond and described in Walum (1977:133). Using charades as a research vehicle, Diamond required his subjects to act out the word "God." He reports that "male charaders tend to take on Godlike qualities (such as puffing out their chests, looking stern and pointing a mighty finger down from on high) whereas female charaders assume the supplicant role by kneeling before and praying to God." The male actors can imagine themselves as God, but the female actors cannot.

Feminists do not feel that giving Jesus Christ a human mother solves their problem. No matter how revered she is, the Virgin Mary remains human and, as such, subordinate to the masculine Trinity. In addition, she symbolizes women's inferiority. She incubates and brings forth a God, infinitely superior to her, just as other women incubate and bring forth males superior to themselves (Poelzer, 1980:37).

Some attempts are being made to eliminate patriarchal imagery from religious language. Following her call for "the death of God the Father," Daly's latest book, *Gyn/Ecology* (1978), does not use the word "God" at all. However, according to a University of Ottawa professor of religion, Naomi Goldenberg (1978), a fundamental dilemma is involved. While feminists are right in their conviction that female equality is not possible in religions that maintain an exclusively male image of God, she argues that altering such imagery might spell the end of Judaism and Christianity. More specifically, Goldenberg believes that replacing the masculine image of God with either a feminine image of the divinity or with an "impersonal, shadowy, and abstract principle" would destroy the psychological impact of these religions (as interpreted by Freud and Jung).

The Book of Genesis contains two versions of the story of creation. Many feel that the fact that the church has downplayed the nonsexist version has provided scriptural justification for the inferiority of women. "And God said, Let us make man in our image, after our likeness: and let them have dominion . . . over all the earth. . . ." "So God created man in his *own* image, in the image of God created he him; male and female created he them" (Genesis 1:26-27). This latter version of the creation of humankind emphasizes that male and female were created simultaneously, and that God is either simultaneously male and female, or neither (Walum, 1977:127).

At any rate, it is the creation story quoted below that is usually taught to children. (Some religionists interpret it as simply an elaboration on the one discussed above.)

> And the Lord God formed man of the dust of the ground, and breathed into his nostrils the breath of life; and man became a living soul. . . .
> And the Lord God said, It is not good that the man should be alone; I will make him an help meet for him.
> And out of the ground the Lord God formed every beast of the field, and every fowl of the air, and brought them unto Adam to see what he would call them. . . .
> And Adam gave names to all cattle, and to the fowl of the air, and to every beast of the field; but for Adam there was not found an help meet for him.
> And the Lord God caused a deep sleep to fall upon Adam, and he slept; and he took one of his ribs, and closed up the flesh instead thereof;
> And the rib, which the Lord God had taken from man, made he a woman, and brought her unto the man.
> And Adam said, This is now bone of my bones, and flesh of my flesh: she shall be called woman, because she was taken out of man.
> [Genesis 2:7, 18-23]

Tradition depicts Woman as a creature made to assuage Man's loneliness, to serve him. God created her when the animals, created first, failed to be adequate company for Man. Some churches have used the sequencing of creation—the "fact" that Eve was made *after* Adam—to justify women's subordination. (A feminist commentator replied dryly, "If it's a matter of orderly progression then man ought to be subject to monkeys!" [Wallace, 1976:118].) The trajectory of her career thus established, Eve went on to become the "first sinner" and responsible for the couple's eviction from the Garden of Eden.

Ancient Judaic tradition includes stories of Lilith, Adam's first wife. Although her name does not now appear in Genesis, some scholars (Rivlin, 1972; Weiner, 1979) believe that the first creation story refers to Lilith. Mythology has it that when Lilith demanded equality with Adam (and objected to lying beneath him during intercourse), she left Eden rather than accept second place. She became a vampirelike demon, a whore and a killer of children. There is a feminist moral to Lilith's story. Banishment from paradise was the price of asking for equality.

The Christian tradition emphasizes two major images of women, both of which are "symbolic representations of male ideas about sex": "the sexual purity of the virgin, the sexual procreativity of the mother"—Mary—and the "sexual evilness of the temptress"—Eve (Hole and Levine, 1971:380-81, quoted in Walum, 1977:128). Neither the "virgin mother" nor the "sinner" have any resonance in the experience of contemporary women.

Even though Jesus was the son of God and his apostles were all male, feminists acknowledge that his attitudes toward women were unusually egalitarian for his time and culture. Jesus "violated Judaic law by touching menstruating women, by speaking alone with a woman not his wife, by allowing women to witness and to testify to his resurrection" (Walum, 1977:129). He reminded men, eager to stone an adulterous woman, of their own shortcomings. Jesus and his disciples were "men of emotion—they cry, fear, and agonize; they are able to be weak . . . and to demonstrate compassion . . . and humility" (Walum, 1977:129).

Indeed, Dubbert's *A Man's Place* (1979:136-39) (one of the few gender relations books written from a masculine perspective to mention religion) describes how the U.S. turn-of-the-century "bull moose mentality" found Jesus' personality wanting. A statement by Theodore Roosevelt, who modelled this masculine ethos, is typical of the period: "There is no place in the world for nations who have become enervated by soft and easy life, or who have lost their fibre of vigorous hardiness and masculinity" (p. 122). Accordingly, an attempt was made by several writers of this time to turn an "effeminized Christ" into a virile, energetic "he-man." These critics claimed that the noble ideas of Christianity had been emasculated by women, who emphasized the meek, humble, passive side of Christ. Moreover, complaining that modern art portrayed a "very mild-mannered Jesus, with dreamy eyes, long hair, and a resigned expression," they found Biblical evidence for a Jesus with strong masculine facial expressions and a domineering, courageous, angry, self-made-man image.

In general, the Scriptures degrade women and celebrate male supremacy. Indeed, some authorities argue that the Bible was written exclusively for men. For example, the Ten Commandments teach that "Thou shall not covet thy neighbor's *wife*." During the exodus, the Israelis made a pact with God, which required *circumcision* (Walum, 1977:130). ". . . I thank thee, Lord, that thou hast not created me a woman" (Orthodox Jewish prayer). "If a woman have conceived seed, and born a man child, then she shall be unclean seven days; . . . But if she bear a maid child, then she shall be unclean two weeks. . . ." (Leviticus 12:2, 5).

The Leviticus quotation comes from the Old Testament, where a wife is her husband's possession, where a woman gains status in the community only by bearing sons, where a man can get a divorce (if his wife is insane or barren) but a woman cannot, where daughters inherit only when there are no male heirs (Wallace, 1976:122). In Hebrew scripture, "one must look closely to find mention of women at all" (Driver, 1976:436).

So far as the New Testament is concerned, in de Beauvoir's (1952:89-90) view, "Christian ideology has contributed no little to the oppression of woman. . . . Through St. Paul the Jewish tradition, savagely antifeminist, was affirmed." These New Testament verses illustrate her point:

> Let the woman learn in silence with all subjection. But I suffer not a woman to teach, nor to usurp authority over the man, but to be in silence. For Adam was first formed, then Eve. And Adam was not deceived, but the woman being deceived was in the transgression. Notwithstanding she shall be saved in childbearing, if they continue in faith and charity and holiness with sobriety (1 Timothy 2:11-15).
>
> Wives, submit yourselves unto your own husbands, as unto the Lord. For the husband is head of the wife, even as Christ is the head of the church. . . . [The Epistle of Paul to the Ephesians 5:22-23]

While it is true that the symbolism and mythology of the Bible are rooted in a patriarchal time, modern translations and sermonizing have emphasized male-centered religious imagery and minimized egalitarian aspects of Biblical teachings. The central point is that the Judeo-Christian tradition has fostered the doctrine of feminine inferiority.

The Social Structure of Religion[6]

Church organization has traditionally assigned different roles to women and to men. The hierarchy of church structure is consistent with both religious teaching and the fact that most of the major prophets and leaders of Western religions have been men. With a few exceptions, men are the authority figures—deacons, priests, clergymen, bishops, cardinals, popes. The church tends to be a social organization "controlled by men to service women" (Walum, 1977:132). Ceremonial ties with the deities are maintained by men. When women are permitted a role beyond that of member of the congregation, it is usually a service role. For example, in the Roman Catholic church, the nuns teach and nurse, while priests celebrate mass, perform marriage ceremonies and ordain other priests. In Conservative and Orthodox Jewish synagogues, the women are seated separately from the men and they are not involved in official prayers and ceremonies (Stockard and Johnson, 1980:16).

Leadership in the Jewish and Christian churches has been overwhelmingly male. Said Samuel Johnson (1709-84): "Sir, a woman's preaching is like a dog's walking on his hind legs. It is not done well; but you are surprised to find it done at all." Although Reform Jews have ordained a few female rabbis, Orthodox and Conservative Jews refuse to accept women in that role. The latter groups associate intellectual activity with men and expect women to be family-oriented (Wallace, 1976:123). The Roman Catholic church rejects the idea of female priests, its latest official statement on the matter being the Vatican's 1976 Declaration on the Ordination of Women. A few years earlier, St. Joan's International Alliance (the world's oldest international feminist group, founded in 1911) was angered by the exclusion of Catholic women from the Second Vatican Council. Held in Rome from 1962 to 1965, the Council invited representatives of all the other major religious denominations, as well as non-Christians, atheists and Communists. At the instigation of the St. Joan's Alliance, the world press printed stories, ". . . about the bishop who, when asked why women had not been invited, looked blank and said, 'We never thought of it'; about the woman journalist in Rome asked to leave a gathering 'lest her presence defile the Pope' who was expected at any time" (Wallace, 1976:97-98).

Although many of the large Protestant denominations, such as the United Church, have agreed after much deliberation to ordain women, the numbers involved are very small (an estimated 2% in 1975). Often these female clergy remain marginal professionals (Bock, 1967), and are deflected from ministerial roles into teaching (Walum, 1977:131). In past years, women who wanted an active role had two options. They could join a sectarian religion that did accept women, e.g., Quakers, Salvation Army, Seventh-Day Adventists, Christian Scientists, or they could practise their old religion in a new setting by becoming a missionary (Zikmund, 1979).

Missionary life has been described as women's "earliest form of escape" from the monotony of conventional roles at home. The nine-

teenth-century women who chose this option often exchanged a hum-
drum existence for danger, loneliness and primitive conditions in outposts
across Canada, as well as in foreign service:

> Elizabeth McDougall, the wife of a Methodist missionary in various
> Canadian Indian settlements before the turn of the century, got her first
> taste of danger as a bride. One of her husband's responsibilities in the
> border town where they lived was to confiscate illegal cargoes of liquor
> from bootleggers, a task that repaid him with many scars from broken
> bottles wielded by lawbreakers seeking vengeance. Since tribal wars used
> to flare up and subside without warning, the fate of Mrs. McDougall and
> their five children, especially during her husband's frequent absences, was
> always precarious. Moreover, like many early pioneers and missionaries,
> she lost first a child and then her husband. [Bassett, 1975:22]

How has the exclusion of women from church leadership positions
been justified? As we might expect, many of the arguments have been
theological. The "sequencing argument" is an obvious choice: because
Eve was created after Adam, women should remain secondary. In forbidding the ordination of women as priests, Catholics have cited Thomas
Aquinas's logic that priests must exercise authority and a woman cannot
exercise authority because, according to Genesis, she is in a "state of subjection" to man (Wallace, 1976:102). Moreover, the Vatican's 1976 decision against women's admission was based on the grounds, first, that in
selecting only males as apostles, Christ intended church leadership to be
male (Walum, 1977:132), and second, that "the ministerial representation of Christ requires physical masculinity" because Christ himself was
male. Less ethereal arguments have also been put forth. The "schismatic"
position claimed, for example, that introduction of female clergy into the
Anglican church would motivate significant numbers of dissenting
members to leave the church. (Indeed, after the Canadian Anglican
bishops voted in 1975 to ordain women as priests, 350 Anglican priests
signed a manifesto calling for total boycott of any women who might
be ordained [Wallace, 1976:117].) Last, both Catholic and Anglican
churches rejected female priests on the ground that men are easily aroused
to lust. Said one authority, "in public worship men are less likely to
distract and stimulate the congregation sexually . . . because men are
more quickly aroused than women and respond to a wider variety of symbolic stimuli" (Wallace, 1976:112). This fear that women's sexuality
threatens men's salvation echoes the early Christian leaders' view of
women as temptresses and seducers of men. By contrast, good women,
idealized in the Virgin Mary, are not interested in sex (Frieze et al.,
1978:214).

Although the situation is changing, women's marginal position in
the churches has serious implications, direct and indirect, for gender

socialization. While children might encounter female Sunday School teachers, they (once again) see important roles as a male prerogative, and experience only males making ceremonial contact with the Deity. Other consequences are more indirect. As long as women remain outside the church's inner circle, the feminine intellectual perspective is missing. Therefore, male-constructed religious doctrine is more likely to go unchallenged. Religion's image of women is only one example: "Woman as temptress, the eternal Eve, the gateway to hell, and woman as virgin, pure, undefiled keeper of hearth and home are . . . impossible extremes of evil and good that leave no place for a real person" (Miller and Swift, 1977:74). Moreover, churches ignore women's point of view on matters of considerable concern to them, e.g., the Roman Catholic church's teachings on abortion and birth control (Ambert, 1976:107). One reason that feminists have sought the ordination of women is to give them a voice in policy formation (Walum, 1977:133).

Much that has been said up to this juncture is quite ironic in view of the significance of religion to women. Out of religion grew women's first organizational experiences. For instance, the nineteenth-century Woman's Christian Temperance Union became one of the strongest women's organizations in Canada. The WCTU later brought to the suffrage struggle a wealth of organizational experience (Mitchinson, 1981). (See Chapter Eight.) Furthermore, study after study shows contemporary North American women to be more religious than men. Women in all religions except Judaism and Mormonism tend to be more pious and to attend religious services more regularly than the men. Among Canadians over fifteen years, 5.7% of the males responded "no religion" to 1971 census takers, as opposed to 3.3% of the females (Veevers and Cousineau, 1980). A national study of churchgoing in Canada (Mol, 1976:Table 2) reported these differences in regular church attendance (one indicator of religiosity): United Church: males, 18%, females, 27%; Anglican church: males, 10%, females, 28%; English Catholic: males, 60%, females, 75%; French Catholic: males, 85%, females, 91%.

Considerable speculation surrounds the sex difference in religiosity. Women are allegedly attracted to the church because they experience more guilt than men, because the male deities appeal to them, because they have more time than men (Mol, 1976:244-45). Also, society has expected women, as guardians of the family and traditional values, to be more conventional and pious than men (Veevers and Cousineau, 1980:204). At the same time, the church often provides extrafamilial, but "safe," outlets for women's sociability (Walum, 1977:131). Another intriguing attempt to explain women's religiosity is grounded in the diagnosis of the church as a feminine social institution, a "place where feminine values are sanctified" (Walum, 1977:134). Accordingly, we may think about "both religion and women in Western societies as traditionally preoccupied with conflict-resolving, emotionally healing, integrative, and expressive functions, whereas men are more involved in competitive, differentiating, and instrumental activities" (Mol, 1976:245). However, the *deprivation hypothesis of religious commitment* (Glock, 1964) has probably been the most popular. Unlike the others, it has been tested. This hypothesis posits that deprived social categories such as women, the aged, the poor, and members of devalued racial or ethnic groups find compensation for their unsatisfactory statuses in religion. Marx's and Engels's (1964:134) version is famous: "Religion is the sigh of the oppressed creature, the heart of a heartless world, just as it is the spirit of a spiritless situation. It is the opium of the people. . . ."

Despite the intuitive appeal of the deprivation hypothesis, recent research (Hobart, 1974; Mackie, 1981b; McNamara and St. George, 1978) indicates that religion does *not* cushion the effects of negative feelings or lack of well-being among the deprived (when "deprivation" is operationally defined according to demographic categories). Instead, religion serves to enhance the happiness of those who are already status-advantaged. It adds "still more frosting to an already rich cake" (McNamara and St. George, 1978:318) for men, the young, the financially advantaged and so on. In short, women do not turn to religion because they are downtrodden. What women do get out of religion is not yet clear.

The Effects of Religious Gender Socialization

Do empirically demonstrable gender-related consequences flow from the exposure of young people to religious socialization? The preceding review of the literature would lead us to expect religious training to be associated with traditional gender attitudes. We might also hypothesize that the patriarchal form of religious teachings and the churches' male-dominated leadership structure would impair the social-psychological functions of organized religion for females as opposed to males. That is, women should find in religion a less satisfactory source of answers to existential questions, normative closure, leadership experience, etc.

Despite the surface plausibility of ideas such as these, research findings on the gender-related consequences of religiosity are scarce, as well as difficult to interpret. Disentangling the effects of religion from other social effects is not an easy task. For one thing, religion and family influence interact. Sometimes ethnicity and social class also enter into the mixture. Another reason why it is hard to establish religion's unique consequences is the fact that Judeo-Christian ideas are part of our general culture. Therefore, in Berger's (1961:41) words, we would expect people who have had religious socialization to embrace "the same values as everybody else, but with more emphatic solemnity."

Be that as it may, two major findings emerge from the few empirical studies that have been done. First, women who are more involved with religion are also more traditional in their gender attitudes. Second, women's religious affiliation is related to their gender attitudes. Jewish women and women without religious affiliation are relatively untraditional. Catholics and fundamentalist Protestants are quite traditional. Mainline Protestants fall somewhere in between (McMurry, 1978). In general, we conclude that religious socialization augments and reinforces other sources of gender socialization.

THE MASS MEDIA

The mass media are impersonal communication sources, which reach large audiences. As such, they function as secondary and symbolic socialization sources. If you try to imagine what a week spent without any of the media would be like, you will gain some idea of the important part they play in the lives of most Canadians. According to Statistics Canada, 98% of Canadian households have radios, 96% have television sets and 72% have record players.

Within the past twenty-five years, the introduction of television into Canadian homes has profoundly altered family activities. Canadians spend an average of twenty-three hours a week watching television (Statistics Canada, 1980:Table 8.20). By the age of eighteen a child will have spent more time in front of the television than anywhere else, including school (Liebert and Poulos, 1972). However, the school too makes extensive use of television and other media as teaching devices. Indeed, the activities of all the socialization agents—school, family, peer groups—are affected by the media.

The media have been described as the "cement" of modern social life and the coordinator of other societal institutions (Tuchman, 1978b:30). Their characterization as "a community of discourse" captures their real impact upon society: individuals, regardless of age, social class, religion or political predilection, can discuss "As It Happens," "Front Page Challenge" and *Maclean's*. "A community of discourse is comparable to a language: It integrates and controls; it provides common elements for strangers to use when they meet and creates strictures for what can be noticed or said" (Tuchman, 1979:540).

The possible influence of the media upon people's attitudes and behaviors has been a perennial worry. The saying, "the pen is mightier than the sword," has been updated by the claim that "the mass media are more powerful than the hydrogen bomb" (Klapper, 1960:12). Does the movie fare at the local theater include subliminal instructions to "Eat popcorn! Eat popcorn!"? Does a diet of comic books ruin the child's eyes and morals? Do children suffer psychological damage from fairy tales such as "Hansel and Gretel," which features a father who, at the behest of a stepmother, tries to lose his children in the forest? What about televised violence? Waters and Malamud (1975) claim that by the time the average child is sixteen, that child will have witnessed more than 13,000 television killings.

Since the advent of the women's movement, a parallel concern has been voiced over the impact of the media on the development of gender attitudes and behavior. Indeed, Friedan's *The Feminine Mystique* (1963) (often used to date the beginning of the movement) was partially motivated by the author's annoyance with frothy women's magazines.

Similarly, the Royal Commission on the Status of Women in Canada (1970) complained that the media perpetuated sex stereotyping. It was especially critical of the "degrading, moronic" depiction of women in advertisements, and argued that although men as well as women are stereotyped, "the results may be more damaging for women since advertising encourages feminine dependency by urging women not to act but to be passive, not to really achieve but to live out their aspirations in the imagination and in dreams" (pp. 14-15).

These charges against media advertising were expressed by other early critics. Komisar (1971) described an IBM ad: " 'Your wife's office is probably better equipped than yours' and pictures of a youthful housewife surrounded by the shining implements of her trade: wall oven, electric stove with grease hood, blender, rotisserie, four-slice toaster, and electric coffee pot" (p. 306). This same housewife is shown as a "nasty, sneering individual making caustic remarks to or about her neighbor just because she doesn't use a certain brand of soap" (Komisar, 1971:315). Automobile advertisements appear to be "fertility rites": one wonders whether "the final act of love will be between boy and auto, girl and auto, or attain the ultimate in some kind of intercourse among the three" (p. 310).

Farrell (1974:105) objected to masculine images in advertising, where the counterpart to the "housebound-mother-wife-maid-mistress is the infallibly successful, accomplished, virile male." Certain products, such as tobacco, automobiles and alcohol, seem to sell masculinity. A Seagram's V.O. Canadian Whisky ad headed, "For people who really know how to live," was accompanied by "a picture of a ruggedly handsome man, drink in hand, with a beautiful woman literally hanging around his neck" (Farrell, 1974:111). Marlboro cigarette ads featured tough cowboys with "leather chaps, leather face" (p. 108). An ad for boys' clothing superimposed this poem over a photograph of three boys frolicking in a meadow:

I'm Glad I'm a Boy
I don't like girls, I do not, I do not,
I know I didn't like them when I was a tot,
Girls hate lizards and rats, and snakes, bugs and mice.
And all the other things that I think are nice.
I sing a gay song and jump up for joy,
For I'm very happy that I'm a boy.*

[Farrell, 1974:113]

The main conclusions of these impressionistic accounts—stereotyping of both sexes and the "symbolic annihilation" and trivialization of women (Tuchman, 1978a)—have been corroborated by systematic research. In fact, media content is one of the most heavily researched topics in the field of gender relations. Two related questions are addressed by these studies. First, how do the mass media depict gender? Second, what effects flow from this media portrayal of gender? The second question is less easily answered than the first. A brief summary of findings from this voluminous research follows.

Television

A great many studies have explored how television, which is certainly the dominant media influence upon North American popular culture, stereotypes women in both broadcast programming and advertising. Since radio was eclipsed by television just at the time when large-scale media content studies were coming into existence, analysts spent their energies on the newer, more controversial medium. Therefore, no current data are available on radio's portrayal of gender relations (Butler and Paisley, 1980:92).

In both children's and adult programming, males dominate the television screen (Pyke and Stewart, 1974), with the exception of soap operas, where males constitute a "mere majority" (Katzman, 1972). Television presents twice as many males as females (Sternglanz and Serbin, 1974; Tedesco, 1974). This "symbolic annihilation" of women characterizes prime-time adventures, situation comedies and even children's cartoons (which include fewer females among the "anthropomorphized foxes or pussycats") (Tuchman, 1978a:10-11). A recent content analysis (Dominick, 1979) of 1,314 television programs and 2,444 starring characters appearing on prime-time television from 1953-77 revealed that the number of females in starring roles has remained relatively constant over the past twenty-five years. On the average, three out of ten starring roles have been filled by females, most of them in situation comedies.

* From a collection of poems by fifth-graders, published by the Creativity Center of Fordham University.

The presentation of the sexes is unbalanced in terms of function as well as numbers. While fewer women are shown as housewives or housekeepers now than in the 1950s, the makeup of the television labor force has consistently shown little relationship to the real-life employment patterns of women (Dominick, 1979). Males are represented as occupying a disproportionately high percentage of the work force, a greater diversity of occupations and higher status jobs. Despite the existence of women police officers and detectives, female characters rarely work outside the home. Since 1954, about 20% of the people shown on television as members of the labor force have been women (Tuchman, 1979). They are likely to occupy a low-responsibility position when they are employed (McGhee and Frueh, 1980). One reason for the relative scarcity of female characters on TV is the constricted range of roles seen as "appropriate" for women. Even when women work, they are often portrayed as incompetent or inferior to male workers (Tuchman, 1978a:13). Female detectives require rescuing by their male colleagues. Male physicians engage in surgery, while female physicians file official forms.

The behavior and personal characteristics of television personalities are often sex-typed (McGhee and Frueh, 1980). The females tend to be younger than the males and are more likely to be married or about to be married. As mentioned earlier, females are cast in comedy roles, while males assume the serious roles. Females tend to be "more attractive, happier, warmer, more sociable, fairer, more peaceful, and more useful," while males tend to be depicted as "smarter, more rational, more powerful, more stable, and more tolerant" (McGhee and Frueh, 1980:180). Nonetheless, television denies women their traditional edge in socio-emotional leadership. In the soap operas, men take the initiative in solving personal problems (Tuchman, 1978a:14). In the symbolic world of violence, women occupy a subordinate position: "Whether they have been knocked to the floor by a villain or are helped from the floor by a male colleague, vis-à-vis men, women are still on the floor" (Tuchman et al., 1978:42-43).

The 1978 briefs to the Canadian Radio and Telecommunications Commission by the National Action Committee on the Status of Women, concerning the Canadian Broadcasting Corporation's portrayal of women in programming, reiterated many of the above points (Canadian Advisory Council on the Status of Women, 1978). The briefs contended that women are shown in "a narrowly limited range of roles which is completely unrepresentative of the wide spectrum of interests, concerns and behaviours of women in Canadian society today" (p. 6). Moreover, they complained about the "negligible" coverage of women's achievements and concerns in news, public affairs programming, in documentaries and sports. While some Canadian programs were singled out as praiseworthy in their portrayal of women, the overall impression was that they are "peripheral to the cultural expression of and issues of importance to the society" (p. 7). This final conclusion is shared with the U.S. Commission on Civil Rights report, entitled *Window Dressing on the Set: Women and Minorities in Television* (1977).

An analysis of the existing research on advertising, sponsored by the Canadian Advisory Council on the Status of Women (Courtney and Whipple, 1978:13), concluded "that women are portrayed in extremely limited roles" and that this portrayal "has not changed significantly during the 1970s." With regard to television advertising:

> — Men predominate as announcers, voice-overs and other authority figures.
> — Men dominate as product representatives during prime-time hours.
> — Women predominate as product representatives for household and personal hygiene products. They are underrepresented in ads for "big ticket" products and services.
> — Women are shown in the home as housewives and mothers, while men are shown in a wide variety of occupational roles.
> — Older, intelligent males tell younger, scatterbrained females what to do and why.
> — Women are often portrayed as sexual objects. They are shown to have a great need for personal adornment in order to attract and hold men. [Courtney and Whipple, 1978:13-14]

These examples illustrate the offensiveness of many ads:

> — the woman who begs the male announcer not to take away her bleach.
> — the male announcer who convinces the hapless housewife that the peanut butter (or detergent, or deodorant or soap . . .) she has been buying for ten years is not as good as The Advertised Brand.
> — the woman whose self-confidence is shattered by spotty glasses.
> — the women who scrub away in mopping contests as the male announcer looks on.
> — the woman who cannot read a pet-food label.
> — the woman who feels more like a woman because she is wearing the right bra. [Courtney and Whipple, 1978:45]

Do television programming and advertising produce "real life" effects? For example, do advertisements that picture women as either "mindless domestics" or "creatures of sexual usage" reinforce the notion of men as naturally dominant and women as naturally subordinate? Do children (or adults, for that matter) take their cues about gender behavior from the image of that behavior projected by television and the other media? (Gornick, 1976). Although the general question of media effects is deferred until the end of this section, it is important to note that there has been a shift in recent research interest from television *content* to *effects*. For instance, children's attitudes about women can be influenced by traditional versus nontraditional depiction of women in television advertisements (Pingree, 1978). The nontraditional commercials included women physicians, truck and tractor drivers, accountants and golf professionals. (The conclusion of Pingree's research is somewhat restricted by the artificial laboratory situation.)

A Canadian study (Courtney and Whipple, 1978:32 ff.) evaluated the marketing efficiency of traditional versus liberated commercials. For example, the traditional breakfast food ad portrayed a full-time housewife preparing and serving breakfast for her husband and children. A male voiceover was used. The liberated version of this ad showed the same family cooperating in breakfast preparations as the mother prepared to go to work. A female voiceover was used. The results indicated that the liberated advertising was at least as effective as traditional advertising. Designing nonsexist ads that are both believable and inoffensive is apparently quite a challenge. (Is it really "bad business" to show two men "chatting about waxy buildup on a kitchen floor"? [Tuchman, 1978:15]) However, the above study does serve to indicate the new avenues that research is taking.

Magazines

If you were designing a comparative study of media presentation of gender, would you expect magazines to be more "liberated" than television? There is a basic difference between these media that supports such a prediction. Commercial television is a monolith, whose messages must appeal to the lowest common denominator. The cost of television time must surely encourage conservatism among advertisers and producers. By contrast, observe the variety of magazines available on the newsstand! Magazines are designed to appeal to particular segments of the population. Advertising congruent with reader characteristics is solicited. This advertising, and not the price paid by individual purchasers of the magazine, underwrites the costs of publication. Although high-circulation magazines cannot afford to be whimsical about changing their formats, magazines must keep pace with readers' changing interests. "To sell, magazines must reflect the dominant contemporary ethos" (Geise, 1979:52).

Consider women's magazines (the type on which researchers have focused). *Seventeen* appeals to teenagers, *Chatelaine, McCall's, Ladies' Home Journal* and *Good Housekeeping* to middle-class homemakers, and *Family Circle* and *True Story* to working-class women. Until recently, publishers and advertisers viewed women as a much more homogeneous, easy-to-reach mass market than men. Magazines for men covered a gamut of interests: *Sports Illustrated, Popular Mechanics, Fortune, Car and Driver, Esquire* and *Playboy* (Phillips, 1978:117). Women were homemakers, period. This statement by a former *Life* magazine editor carries implications for both sexes: "The most financially successful magazines of the past ten years have been designed to appeal to highly particularized intellectual, vocational, and avocational interests and are run by editors who know precisely what they are saying and to whom they are saying it" (Phillips, 1978:117).

In 1965 Helen Gurley Brown created *Cosmopolitan*, a woman's magazine that would go beyond homemaking hints and beauty advice to help contemporary women "get through the night" (in the words of its editor). Within the past few years, *Ms.*, *Playgirl*, *Viva*, *New Woman*, *Working Woman* and *Working Mother* have appeared to capitalize on the changing roles of women. *Ms.*, the most political of the magazines, takes a strong stand for women's liberation and against ads "insulting or harmful to women." *Playgirl*, on the other hand, promotes "healthy sexuality" and a male nude centerfold (*Bestsellers* Staff, 1978). *New Woman* preaches that any determined woman can become an economically successful "gray-suited upwardly mobile corporate woman" (and, according to critic Ehrenreich [quoted in Tuchman, 1979:537], thereby undermines feminist criticism of the status quo. Then there are magazines connected more specifically with the "fashion-food-home mold" of women's interests (Phillips, 1978:117), e.g., *Glamour*, *Vogue*, *Gourmet*.

The diversity of content in today's women's magazines is illustrated by these article titles chosen at random from various summer 1981 issues: *Ms.* ("A Day in the Life of a Woman Miner," "Some Cheerful Words about Men" from Gloria Steinem); *Working Mother* ("How to Sneak Out of the Office without Losing Your Job," "Why Some Mothers Feel Guilty and Others Don't"); *Chatelaine* ("Violence in the Home," "What Will Unions Do for Women in the 80s?" "Who Speaks for Women?"—an editorial on women, politics and power); *New Woman* ("You Want to Be Creative, But Are You Too Old? Too Busy? Too Dumb?" "Sticks and Stones Might Break Your Bones—But What They Say Can Hurt You Even More"); *Family Circle* ("Easy as Pie Main Dish Pies," "The Cruelest Mistake—the Story of a Woman's Agony Due to a Misdiagnosis That She Was Dying of Cancer"); *Cosmopolitan* ("What's the Difference between Marriage and Living Together?" "Nice Girls Do . . . And Now You Can Too"). Notwithstanding this tantalizing content, illustrations do not prove the point. What do empirical studies have to say about the depiction of gender relations by magazines?

Magazine research (which is less extensive than television research) has concentrated on variations upon one central theme: the portrayal of the female role in magazines with high female readership. The assumption is made that magazines transmit cultural prescriptions of female role performance and, at least by implication, of male role performance (Ferguson, 1978:98).

To begin at the beginning, Ferguson (1978) analyzed the covers of the three largest British women's magazines, *Woman*, *Woman's Own* and *Woman's Weekly*, covering the twenty-five-year period, 1949-74. A magazine cover functions to identify a particular magazine (at the minimum, to differentiate a "Her" magazine from a "His" magazine) and of course to sell it. Ferguson argues that by identifying with the photograph on the cover, readers are encouraged to model themselves upon this "mugshot of perfect woman." And this image is not very realistic. The professional models are invariably young and beautiful and middle-class. The author concludes "that the covers of women's magazines present the face of 'femaleness' as the face of the traditional woman —the smiling pleaser our culture defines" (p. 113).

Is the content of magazine fiction similarly traditional? Although the relevant studies answer yes, they are already dated. For example, Franzwa (1975) analyzed the roles played by female characters in 122 short stories drawn from *Ladies' Home Journal, McCall's* and *Good Housekeeping* over the years 1940 to 1970. These stories represented four major roles for women, each defined by her relationship, or lack of a relationship, with a man: the young single, the wife-mother, the widow-divorcée, the spinster. Several themes were associated with each role. For the young, single woman, "Marriage is inevitable for every normal female" and "To catch a man you must be less competent than he, passive and virtuous." For the married woman, "Married women don't work" and "To keep your man you must . . . be passive, less competent, virtuous, and have another baby." The widow/divorcée thinks she is independent and competent; however, she is incompetent in comparison with men and before the end of the story she finds herself remarried. The spinsters are depicted as "lonely, useless creatures who are unhappy because of their failures in love." They do not derive much satisfaction from their high-status jobs. According to Franzwa, the women in these stories are "half persons" who need a man for completion and fulfillment. Similarly, Flora's (1971) comparison of fiction in middle-class (*Redbook* and *Cosmopolitan*) magazines versus working-class (*True Story* and *Modern Romances*) magazines found female passivity and dependence to be positively regarded in fiction for both classes.

More up-to-date studies of *nonfiction* report that women's publications are reflecting societal changes in gender relations. Geise (1979) examined the imagery of women projected by *Redbook* and *Ladies' Home Journal* between 1955 and 1976. In general, she found that magazines are not so much rejecting traditional gender patterns as giving flexible consideration to nontraditional alternatives. For instance, in the 1955-65 period, love, marriage and family were the overriding female goals. In the 1966-76 period, the idea that a career could be equally important found support. In neither magazine was the "typical" woman portrayed as working outside the home. Sharing by spouses of household tasks received a "slight rise" in support. Sex discrimination received more attention as time went on. However, Phillips's (1978) comparison of the type of role models presented in *Family Circle* and *Ms.* reminds us that magazines vary considerably. While the women featured in *Ms.* articles and biographies are "culturally important, politically engaged, economically productive, and socially active," *Family Circle* women remain tied to "homespun activities" (pp. 124-25).

Our last topic here is the depiction of gender in magazine advertisements. Research done in the early years of the women's movement found that ads distorted reality. For example, Courtney and Lockeretz (1971) examined April 1970 ads in eight American general-interest magazines, such as *Life, Look* and *Newsweek*. Women in general, and working women in particular, were seriously underrepresented. The women shown had limited responsibility. Capable of caring for themselves and their homes, they needed male accompaniment when major purchases were contemplated. Similar results were reported by Venkatesan and Losco (1975) and Wagner and Banos (1973), whose time periods also ended in the early 1970s.

Kent's (1981a) more recent exploratory study points out that, because advertising studies of all media have emphasized discrimination against women, "only by implication and comparison do we see that men are also portrayed in a discriminatory manner." While media mothers are numerous, for example, media fathers are virtually invisible. Her study suggests that Tuchman's (1978) accusation that the media practise "symbolic annihilation of women" should be extended to families. When April 1981 issues of magazines were analyzed for ads portraying families, only magazines aimed at the traditional homemaker, such as *Ladies' Home Journal*, contained familial ads. None of the magazines for the "liberated woman" or those aimed at a general readership carried any ads showing families. In the very few ads that did show both parents, the mother was usually taking physical care of the child, while the father played with it or simply looked on.

Erving Goffman's monograph, *Gender Advertisements* (1976), assembles magazine and newspaper photographs in order to illustrate what he calls "themes of genderism." Series of pictures are grouped to concentrate on how gender is depicted by minute physical expressions and postures. Here are some of Goffman's conclusions. In advertising, a woman is taller than a man only when the man is her social inferior. When a photograph of men and women illustrates instruction of some sort, the man is always instructing the woman (and male children instruct female children). When an ad requires someone to sit or lie on the floor, that someone is hardly ever a man. There is repeated usage in advertisements of "women posed as children, acting like children, looking like children: utterly devoid of the natural sobriety which one associates with adult mien" (Gornick, 1976:viii). In short, these magazine ads are selling subtle, but traditional, "genderism."

To summarize, research tends to show that magazines have been more responsive to change than television. Magazines today show a "gentle support" for the women's movement (Tuchman, 1979). Although the image of women is less rigid now than a decade ago, it is still somewhat limited (Tuchman, 1978:24). However, because of the sheer variety of magazines and the distinctions among fiction, nonfiction and advertising treatments of gender, any generalization must be cautiously put.

Newspapers

Sociologists' commentary on newspapers and gender (which has been more discursive than empirical) is based on the proposition that *news is a social process* (Molotch, 1978). When a friend you meet on the street asks, "What's new?" you may be unclear about the type of information wanted. Does she want to know whether another postal strike is likely to occur, or how strong the Canadian dollar is this morning? Is she more interested in your personal life than in your version of world affairs? Even that topic is quite open. Does she want to know about your job, your family, mutual friends? Would she consider it news that your gas tank took thirteen dollars' worth of gas for the first time, or that you just discovered that a tablespoon of ketchup contains a teaspoon of sugar? In addition, the definition of "news" depends on who is talking to whom. Your friend and your daughter have different news needs from your own (Molotch, 1978).

In everyday life, men and women "do news" differently because of women's inferior position relative to men. Fishman (1978), who taped the everyday talk of couples at home, found that women tend to ask more of the questions, including "what's new?" and that men tend to give the answers. Women invite conversation, which is then male-dominated. Drabble (1980:47) describes a fictional dinner party: "The Swede aired his views on the justification for testing new contraceptive drugs in the Third World, Ted contributed an account of the economics of curing river blindness, Kate as expected asked bright and intelligent questions on both topics. . . ." Men's talk, then, is contingent on women's news needs to only a limited degree. "Being asymmetrically dependent upon the male for interaction/confirmation, she must take pretty much what he gives and find interest in it" (Molotch, 1978:179).

As in everyday talk, there are asymmetrical relationships in the mass media news process. News is a man's world:

> It is essentially men talking to men. The women's pages are a deliberate exception: Here it is the case that women who work for men talk to women. But in terms of the important information, the news pages, women are not ordinarily present. Women are not present either as news producers or as persons for whom news is intended. Those who

publish news perceive women as being in the kitchen, just as they have traditionally been whenever men have important things to discuss with one another. [Molotch, 1978:180]

The charge that news is a "men's world" rests upon these arguments:

1. The news business is controlled by men: publishers, wire service executives, editors and reporters are mostly men (Molotch, 1978:181). As the Canadian journalist, Eve Drobot (1978:3), says, "The public might think, seeing our names in the newspapers, our faces on television and hearing our voices on radio, that the battle has been won. But we know who is sitting behind the desk in the editorial offices, who is in charge of the television control room and who is running the radio news-room. It isn't one of us." We repeat that those who control the social definition of "news" are those in power.

2. Women are seldom news makers because few women hold dominant positions in society. For instance, Miller (1975) analyzed news photos in two large American newspapers. Men clearly dominated the photo coverage on the first page, in inside news and editorial sections, business, sports and entertainment. Only the life-style section contained more photos of women than men.

3. Several studies have found sex bias in newspaper coverage. Archibald et al. (1980) examined the way in which the press treated women candidates for political election in Canada's twenty-four largest municipalities, in the period 1950-75. When coverage of female and male candidates was compared, more frequent mention was made of the female candidate's marital and parental status, and of her husband's or father's status in the community. "Women candidates, much more than men, are judged by who they know, and less by what they know, in the Canadian press" (p. 183). Similarly, in samples of Texas newspapers, coverage of women was more likely to include mention of age, personal appearance, marital status, spouse and children (Forfeit et al., 1980). The authors suggest that criteria of newsworthiness for men and women are rather different. When women appear at all in the newspapers, it is from a man's perspective of what is interesting (Molotch, 1978:185).

4. Newspapers concentrate on the news needs of men (political events, sports, finances) and either ignore, or relegate to the women's pages, the events of daily life with which women traditionally deal. Omitted from the news pages are "the

processes of life and death involving diapers and suffering, vomit and dirt, serious intimacies and personal horrors [emphasis in original]" (Molotch, 1978:181). This gender distinction in what is news implies that men have no interest in events having to do with human concerns. "Ghettoizing" discussion of matters other than sports and politics and work, in the women's pages, reinforces "outmoded views that men should not be concerned with families and their own and others' emotional needs" (Epstein, 1978:221).

5. Newspaper treatment of the women's liberation movement reflected the masculine perspective. Reporting of the movement's early history was distorted. Morris (1973) compared the coverage of the women's liberation movement in two American and twelve British newspapers with the actual occurrence of events. Concluding that all of these newspapers underreported women's rights activity, she wondered whether this blackout constituted social control. However, one explanation was that the movement's political emphasis upon *issues* was difficult to report, when "hard" news stories were socially defined as dealing with *events*. Moreover, newspapers reported on women's movement issues selectively, according to male interests. Coverage in the early years centered on the alleged burning of bras (Molotch, 1978:184). Which sex is intrigued with bras?

6. Placing news about women on women's pages (recently renamed "people's pages" or "family living" because of feminist pressure) reinforces the view that the material is less serious and important than the news highlighted as general news (Epstein, 1978:217). The mixture of "news" on the women's pages further trivializes women's interests. Articles about rape laws and discrimination in access to jobs and credit are intermingled with cheesecake recipes, fashion advice, Ann Landers columns and reports of engagements, marriages and fiftieth wedding anniversaries. Items about women and of concern to women have become "non-news, almost oddities" (Tuchman, 1978b:26).

There are two reasons why newspapers convey a distorted image of gender relations. First, newspapers are more similar to television than to magazines when it comes to flexibility in serving local or particularized needs (Tuchman, 1978b:25). The reliance of local newspapers on national news services makes them components of a national medium. Unlike women's magazines, newspapers seek to appeal to entire families. They attempt to reach women through separate women's pages, much of whose content comes from national or even American sources. Once again, we see men being treated as the norm and "women as the deviation from the norm" (Eichler, 1977a:410). This monolithic structure encourages rigid treatment of gender relations.

Second, broadcasting and publishing organizations (along with universities and schools) can be viewed as "the ideological institutions of the society" (Smith, 1975), as well as important socialization institutions. They organize society symbolically. However, according to Smith (1975:354), "women have been largely excluded from the work of producing the forms of thought and the images and symbols in which thought is expressed and ordered. There is a circle effect. Men attend to and treat as significant only what men say." And further, "it is men who produce for women . . . the means to think and image" (p. 357). These facts have profound implications. We will return to them later on.

Novels

Fictional portraits of men and women provide a source of informal learning for children and adults. Social scientists as well as humanities experts have commented upon the gender effects of storybooks. For example, Weitzman et al. (1972) reported that in storybooks, females were numerically underrepresented, insignificant and passive. Pyke's (1975) survey of 150 Canadian children's books found few women shown in salaried occupations. Women's trademark was the "perennial apron," worn "even by female squirrels" (p. 68). The English professor, Modleski (1980), laments the social conditions that motivate women to "escape" into what commercials call "the wonderful world of Harlequin Romances." This fictional world (which expands at the rate of twelve new titles each month), bears an uncomfortable resemblance to the female readers' real life—"the heroine of the novels can achieve happiness only by undergoing a complex process of self-subversion, sacrificing her aggressive instincts, her 'pride,' and—nearly—her life" (p. 435).

Novels often provide caricatured heroes for male identification. In *Kiss Me Deadly*, Mike Hammer, Mickey Spillane's private eye, "plunges into the night hunting two killers, and when he finds them in a bar he hits one from behind 'like a kid snapping worms' and kicks the other's face so hard that 'the things that were in Charlie's face splashed all over the floor.' It was all part of a night's work, done with cool precision, followed by a respite in bed with another passionate dame" (Dubbert, 1979:264).

Although this section is confined to novels, commentary is available on other forms of culture, popular and "high." See Haskell (1974) and Mellen (1973) for movies,[7] O'Kelly (1980)[8] and Sydie (1980) for art, Ringwood et al. (1978) for the theater, and Bernard (1981) for popular songs. The commentators' emphasis on novels may partially reflect feminist pride. Female scholars have been delighted to discover a rich, complex literature by women that goes back to the Middle Ages, a literature "of diaries, of autobiographies, of letters, of protests, of novels, of poems, of stories, of plays" (Goulianos, 1973:xi). Novels represent one area of culture where women have been "remarkably successful" (Bernard, 1981:417). The first novel about Canada, *The History of Emily Montague* (1769), was written by a woman, Frances Brooke. Today, Canadian authors such as Margaret Laurence, Margaret Atwood, Alice Munro, Gabrielle Roy and Marian Engel often dominate the publishers' lists (Woodcock, 1977). Most of the analysis of novels done from a gender relations perspective treats male authors only by implication.

Are women's stories really different from men's stories? Two conflicting viewpoints, current in literary and feminist circles, were dealt with in Miners's (1976) study of the images of women in English-Canadian novels. One side is related to Smith's (1975) argument, mentioned above, that men have traditionally regulated the formation and evaluation of ideas. In her words, men "control what enters the discourse by occupying the positions which do the work of gatekeeping and the positions from which people and their 'mental products' are evaluated" (p. 357). This means that acceptance of the male standard becomes a prerequisite for success in artistic and intellectual pursuits. In the case of novels, the successful female writers are those whose work most closely resembles the work of successful male writers. Therefore, female writers would adopt male conventions, rather than relying upon their own special knowledge to create believable female characters. In other words, according to this point of view, women authors have internalized prevailing stereotypes of their own sex and their characters reflect this fact.

The alternative proposition maintains that female writers, because of their more intimate knowledge of their own sex, create more realistic female characters than do male writers (Miners, 1976:123-24). In this connection, Goulianos, the editor of an anthology of six centuries of women's literature, *By a Woman Writt* (1973:xi), says that, "When women wrote, they touched upon experiences rarely touched upon by men, they spoke in different ways about these experiences, they often wrote in different forms. Women wrote about childbirth, about housework, about relationships with men, about friendships with other women. They wrote about themselves as girls and as mature women, as wives, mothers, widows, courtesans, workers, thinkers, and rebels."

In order to test these conflicting hypotheses, Miners examined the presentation of women characters in sixteen selected English-Canadian novels[9] (eight by female and eight by male authors) with copyright dates from 1954 to 1972. Information concerning all female characters was recorded according to a scheme of basic information designed by Lefkowitz (1972) and a list of stereotype traits developed by Broverman et al. (1972). (See Table 2.2.) Miners's results failed to support the contention that male authors would present more stereotyped female characters than female authors. However, female authors tended to provide more information about their characters. Although her conclusion does lend credence to Smith's (1975) argument, it does not, of course, eliminate other explanations.

The literary imagery of women portrayed in twenty-six Canadian novels written in English by women during the 1970s was analyzed by English professors Gottlieb and Keitner (1979). According to them, the literary presentation of Canadian women underwent a "dramatic metamorphosis" toward the end of the decade. (Their finding does not disagree with Miners's, taking into account the time trends.) The more recent novels present "innovative images of women," which respond to the challenges of the women's movement in being "radical, searching, complex, . . . feminist" (p. 525). Novels such as Engel's *Bear* (1976), Van Herk's *Judith* (1978) and Barfoot's *Abra* (1978), "explore new constellations of woman and man, woman and nature, woman and woman; and they imagine creative new roles for woman alone" (Gottlieb and Keitner, 1979:523). These heroines have often rejected the painful world of men and "chosen instead to establish themselves in entirely new, and often isolated or remote settings where, finally, they can be in control of their own destiny" (p. 523).

Fritz and Hevener (1979) ask how female detectives are portrayed. Female detectives certainly do exist. (See Ellery Queen's *The Female of the Species* [1943], an anthology of stories about female detectives.) However, of the most famous female writers of detective novels, Josephine Tey, Ngaio Marsh, Marjorie Allington and P. D. James, only Agatha Christie produced a memorable female sleuth—the frail, elderly Miss Marple. Nonetheless, Fritz and Hevener managed to locate fifty-two female detectives in novels dating from the 1920s to the 1970s. Like Gottlieb and Keitner (1979), these researchers found the fictional depiction of women to mirror developments in gender definitions over time. Novelists writing before the 1960s and 1970s exercised one of two options in their portrayal of women detectives: "1) they could depict them as stereotypically feminine, in which case they were not effective as detectives and had to be rescued by a male, or 2) they could use them as the detective and unsex them as women by making them old or peculiar" (p. 123). By contrast, recent female detectives are attractive, happy career women of all ages, on an equal footing with their male partners. However, these fictional detectives do not combine marriage and career.

Our final example of current research on gender and fiction is Whitehurst's (1980) content analysis of twenty-six Hugo-award-winning science fiction novels. This study is interesting because it focuses on the images of women *and* men. Science fiction is also the novelistic genre with the greatest potential for exploring innovative roles for both sexes. In the past, few women wrote science fiction, and female characters appeared only sporadically. Today, 10-15% of the writers are women. The explanation seems to be science fiction's relationship to scientific and technical extrapolations and the assumption that science and technology are masculine domains. Ironically, the first piece of science fiction, *Frankenstein* (1818), was written by Mary Shelley (Sargent, 1974). According to Whitehurst, science fiction until very recently has not only *not* been futuristic so far as gender relations are concerned, it has actually lagged behind actual societal changes in this area. Science fiction has traditionally given women low status and low visibility as homemakers, wives and glamourous sidekicks. Pamela Sargent, editor of a book of science fiction stories by women about women (1974:xxxvii), elaborates: "Women, in their limited roles, served a practical function for the writer. In his story he could have a character explain the workings of a gadget or a scientific principle to an ignorant girl or woman, and by extension to the reader. Women could also serve as rewards for some heroic deed, could be rescued from danger, could sometimes be dangerous (or devious) enemies that the hero had to defeat." However, "Men are also heavily stereotyped, usually as the conquering hero, strong, all-powerful and all-knowing. . . . Men are expected to be the leaders, to make the decisions, and to be right; male characters who fail to do this are ridiculed" (Fritz and Hevener, 1979:328). Science fiction has finally begun to change, as witnessed by the manner in which books such as Ursula Le Guin's *The Left Hand of Darkness* (1969) treat gender.

For gender relations specialists, the central issue is the type of role models that novels present to impressionistic young people and to adults. Their uneasiness rests on the assumption (to which we will later return) that fictional portraits of femininity and masculinity influence readers' own attempts to be female or male according to the dictates of our society. Women novelists sometimes resent the pressure placed upon them by "fundamentalist" feminist critics. This exasperation is nicely expressed by Margaret Atwood (1979), who has been described as "Canada's first true woman of letters" (Woodcock, 1977:5). Atwood cites a female critic's review of Marian Engel's *The Honeyman Festival*:

> . . . The heroine of this novel is Minn, a very pregnant woman who spends a lot of her time reminiscing about the past and complaining about the present. She doesn't have a job. She doesn't have much self-esteem. She's sloppy and self-indulgent and guilt-ridden and has ambiguous feelings about her children, and also about her husband, who is away most of the time. The reviewer complained about this character's lack of initiative, apparent laziness and disorganization. She wanted a more positive, more energetic character, one capable of taking her life in hand, of acting more in accordance with the ideal woman then beginning to be

projected by the women's movement. Minn was not seen as an acceptable role model, and the book lost points because of this. [Atwood, 1979:31]

Atwood continued by pointing out that the world holds a lot more "Minn-like" women than ideal women. On another occasion, Atwood (1976:340), responding to two erudite articles on the feministic and theological significance of her novel, *Surfacing*, said, "my novel is not a treatise at all, but a novel . . . it does not exist for the sake of making a statement but to tell a story." Fair enough.

The Effects of the Mass Media

Our review of the evidence shows that despite some slight change in recent years and some differences from one medium to another, in general, the media distort both women and men. Furthermore, the media diminish women's status by defining women in terms of men, as sex objects or as wives and mothers (Tuchman, 1979:531).

Why are the media sexist? Scholars have come up with three explanations (Tuchman, 1979:533 ff.). First of all, few women hold positions of responsibility in the media industries. For instance, the Canadian Advisory Council on the Status of Women (1978) indicted the CBC for the "severe underrepresentation of women in management and production roles having decision-making functions regarding programming and policy" (p. 9). In 1978 12% of the managers and 19% of the producers were women (p. 11). (According to Clement [1975:332], women represent only 3.8% of the membership of the media elite.) This explanation for media sexism implies that the situation would improve if more women occupied creative and decision-making positions. Unfortunately, things don't seem to work out this way. Studies show that it is difficult for women in the media "to resist ideas and attitudes associated with sexism in their profession, even if those ideas disparage women" (Tuchman, 1979:535). Once again, there is evidence of Smith's (1975:367) proposition that successful female professionals have pleased male gatekeepers and have been thoroughly schooled in male-developed criteria of proper professional performance.

The second explanation is an economic one: the media are sexist because sexism is profitable to advertisers and, derivatively, to the media (Tuchman, 1979:536). Television, radio and newspapers all seek to deliver as many consumers as possible to their advertisers. (Magazines, however, can cater to more specialized consumer markets, and novels have little to do with advertisers.) Apparently, advertisers and media respond to changing circumstances when change makes money. With the first wave of the baby boom now approaching its late 30s, manufacturers and their advertising companies are challenged to extend the Pepsi generation and to make their formerly youth-oriented products appeal to mature consumers. Proctor and Gamble are now manufacturing "Attends" for incontinent adults, in addition to Pampers. Levi Strauss is constructing jeans for broader beams. Gerber is running a print campaign, showing a jar of its strained peaches nestled among potato chips and labelled "the unexpected snack" (Span, 1981). Some people would dearly love to get a handle on the factors that might eventually render sexism uneconomical.

The third explanation for the sexism of the media invokes Albrecht's (1954) *reflection* and *influence* hypotheses about the links between literature and society.[10] The *reflection* hypothesis holds that the media are sexist *because* they mirror cultural notions about gender. The *influence* hypothesis, which is more difficult to test, holds that the media shape and strengthen societal norms. So far as the individual is concerned, the influence hypothesis would predict that media content provides raw material for children's gender development. Both the reinforcement and modelling theories of child development would support this prediction.

The ability of the media to influence children has become an extremely important issue. If children can learn to read from educational television, if they pressure parents to buy heavily advertised toys and breakfast cereals and, worse, if they learn to solve problems through violent means by watching crime shows, and pick up constricted gender roles from their storybooks, then the media constitute a socialization agent whose power is almost beyond imagination.

Unfortunately, as we have repeatedly found, tracing the direct effects of any given socialization source is a difficult research task. When the media operate in the natural environment (i.e., outside the laboratory), their influence is one influence among many. For example, if Peter behaves chauvinistically, is it because of the type of television programs he watches, or his family, or his nasty temperament or some combination of factors? Further, most of the field studies of media effects done outside laboratories are correlational. "The studies demonstrate that two kinds of behavior are found together, but cannot state whether one behavior causes the other or whether both are caused by a third characteristic of the children studied" (Tuchman, 1978b:32). On the other hand, experimental studies that attempt to control for variables other than media content become so artificial that their conclusions may not hold outside of the experimental situation. Also, can you imagine the difficulty researchers would face in trying to place children in a long-term, "no television" control group, for example?

A major factor reducing media influence deserves emphasis. Twenty-five years ago, the persuasive power of the media was greatly feared by governments and social agencies. Social scientists, in keeping with this perspective, adopted the "hypodermic needle model" of media effects, which posited a direct relationship between the messages of the media and the subsequent actions of audience members. Later, however, the role played by primary groups in mass-communications effects began to be appreciated. (See Miall, 1972.) Children are exposed to media content in a social context. What they see and hear is monitored, at least to some extent, by parents. Similarly, their interpretation of media content is molded by the opinions of parents, friends and teachers. The points of view of these other socializers may or may not agree with the media's perspectives. (See Rickell and Grant [1979] below.) In short, the media have an impact on children but this impact is just one of the influences that shape a child's attitudes and behavior.

To date, studies of media impact on children's ideas about gender are relatively scarce. Most involve television or videotape. Researchers have reasoned that, since television portrays stereotyped females and males, children who consume a great deal of TV should hold more traditional attitudes about gender than children who watch little TV (Butler and Paisley, 1980). Beuf (1974) talked to girls and boys, three to six years of age, about what they would like to be when they grew up. About 70% chose occupations stereotypically appropriate for their sex. However, when Beuf compared "heavy" and "moderate" television viewers, only 50% of the moderate viewers versus 76% of the "heavy" viewers chose a sex-typed career. Freuh and McGhee (1975) report similar findings. Although these studies are persuasive, they show only correlation, not causality. "It could indeed be that media use *causes* children to become more stereotyped. Or it could be that those who are traditional expose themselves more to the media *because* they find TV compatible with their goals and values. It could even be that neither of these causes the other. Another factor, such as parents' attitudes, income, or intelligence, could cause children both to be more traditional and to use more media content [emphasis in original]" (Butler and Paisley, 1980:292).

Another series of studies suggests that nonstereotyped presentations of gender can make inroads into stereotypes (Butler and Paisley, 1980:294). For example, McArthur and Eisen (1976) read nursery-school children stories about a girl and a boy in which, (a) the girl achieved while the boy stood around and watched (reverse stereotype); (b) the boy achieved while the girl watched (stereotyped behavior); or (c) no achievement-related behavior occurred (control). As expected, the girls achieved more after hearing the story about a girl achieving, and boys achieved more after hearing the story about a boy achieving. Both Atkin and Miller (1975) and Pingree (1978) (mentioned earlier) have had some results in changing children's beliefs about women through nontraditional videotaped or televised commercials. Though experimental studies such as these do not leave causality in doubt, there have been inconsistencies in the findings. Some nonstereotypic messages influenced children, while others "mysteriously" did not. Age and sex of the children appear to affect results in ways only partially understood (Butler and Paisley, 1980:296-97). The "hypodermic needle model" fails to explain either adults' or children's media responses. With children, varying levels of cognitive development within the same age group tend to complicate matters.

Whether children receive consistent or differing messages about gender from their various socialization agents is a matter of some importance. Rickel and Grant (1979) reanalyzed previous studies to determine consistency of messages presented in the mass media and the schools. They conclude that these two sources, which occupy a major proportion of children's time, concur in presenting five stereotyped patterns: (a) women are numerically underrepresented by the media and the school curriculum; (b) women are portrayed frequently as "victims, butts of jokes, targets of direct insults, and perpetrators of self-deprecating remarks"; men are overrepresented as perpetrators of violent crimes; (c) these messages show boys as active and achieving directly, while girls are passive and achieve indirectly as helpmates to males; (d) the tendency is to consider men and their activities as important and to ignore or trivialize women and female-dominated activities. If children are indeed having traditional gender ideas reinforced by the schools and the media, family influences become all the more crucial.

Finally, studies of the effects of televised violence are relevant in this context. Because a variety of research methods have been used to tackle this question, we can have some confidence in the near consistency of the results. For example, both the report of the Ontario Royal Commission on Violence in the Communications Industry (Thatcher, 1978) and the United States Surgeon General's Advisory Committee report, *Television and Growing Up: The Impact of Televised Violence* (1972), express grave concern about violence in the media. Therefore, it seems reasonable to predict by extrapolation that children's media consumption can reinforce stereotyped gender images.

VERBAL AND NONVERBAL COMMUNICATION

Language and nonlingual communication forms make up the last gender socialization source to be discussed in this chapter. It is almost impossible to exaggerate the importance of language in human affairs. "Communication holds society together," since language supports the "intricate workings of our social institutions" (Miller and McNeill, 1969:666). A languageless human being is a contradiction in terms: the utilization, interpretation and creation of high-order signs distinguish human beings from the lower animals and give them characteristically human qualities (Lindesmith and Strauss, 1956:131 ff.). The significance of language in children's socialization is nicely expressed by Lindesmith and Strauss (1956). Their language is no doubt meant to refer to girl children, as well as boy children.)

> Language puts the child in touch with his parents and playmates in new and significant ways. . . . Through learning language he learns of the rules and standards that regulate social relations and develops ideas of morality and religious matters. Language is also the means whereby he is gradually prepared for and later inducted into the roles which he is destined to play and through which he learns to grasp the viewpoints and understand the feelings and sentiments of other persons. By means of language he becomes aware of his own identity as a person and as a member of groups in which he seeks status, security, and self-expression and which in turn makes demands upon him. [pp. 159-160]

An increasing appreciation is developing among scholars and the general public of the significance of nonverbal communication. The size and nature of personal territory that one commands, head- and bottom-patting, ogling, smiling and grimacing all convey messages relevant to gender socialization.

Even children are aware of the potential of language for insult: "We chant in childhood, 'Sticks and stones can break my bones, but words can never hurt me,' yet we carry the psychological scars from words long after the bruises and scrapes have healed" (Martyna, 1980:492). Properly socialized people know that polite discourse forbids addressing others on the basis of a physical deformity ("fatso," "gimpy") or national origin ("paki," "wop").

It is only within the past ten to fifteen years, however, that the sexism in language has been recognized. Since then, research has shown that the English language (among others) denigrates women, while it asserts male superiority. In addition, the language is inadequate for expressing the depth of female experience, which puts women at a disadvantage in understanding themselves. For example, since males have had the "power to name," women's own sexual experience is often described in a misogynous language of dirty jokes and offensive expressions for women (tramp, piece of ass, pig, pussy). Women lack their own colloquial words for vagina, for clitoris, for orgasm (Bernard, 1981:376 ff.). Nonverbal forms of communication also help to "keep women down." Children unwittingly imbibe sexism as they learn verbal and nonverbal forms of communication. As Davy (1978:47) points out, "since language categories are internalized at an early age, we tend to think of them as 'given' and truly representative of the order of things in the objective or natural world."

Some general comments about the connection between language and gender as a research area are in order before we delve into particularities. In the 1960s, sociolinguistics emerged as an interdisciplinary field of interest. At that time, however, the study of language as a social phenomenon was confined to social class, race and social setting. It took the impetus of the women's movement in the late 1960s to encourage study of sex differences in the English language. One reason for the vitality of the current research on language and gender is the variety of backgrounds of the practitioners (linguists, speech physiologists, anthropologists, psychologists, sociologists, novelists, literary critics). However, because of the newness of the field, "the questions are endless; the answers are few" (Thorne and Henley, 1975:31). Many exciting leads await systematic inquiry. For example, not much is known about these basic issues: How do females and males learn the speech styles associated with their respective sexes? How does the acquisition of sex-typed language fit into the overall pattern of gender socialization? (Thorne and Henley, 1975).

This section will consider verbal and nonverbal communication forms under five headings: sex differences in the structure and content of language; similarities and differences in female/male language usage; humor; nonverbal communication; prospects for change. Although we shall take this opportunity to explore some of the fascinating avenues of linguistic and paralinguistic behavior, our major emphasis remains the effect of language upon children's developing conceptions of gender.

Sex Differences in Language Structure and Content

A pervasive theme of the English language is that males are more important than females; indeed, that "all people are male until proven female" (Eakins and Eakins, 1978:111).[11] As children learn language, then, they unconsciously learn something about the relative value of the sexes.

Definition by Sex

Words are used to label people and things. In addition to naming, these labels often imply hidden messages about their referents. Emotionally charged verbal labels can also control behavior. Male children can be chastised by being called "girls" or "sissies." Similarly, the expletive "bitch" carries the connotation that the woman has failed to observe traditional gender standards. Terms of address (a topic that came up in Chapter Four) have aroused feminist ire. People feel free to be more familiar semantically with women. Observations of males and females in parallel positions in various companies and public places showed that women were more often addressed by first names or nicknames, while men were generally dealt with more formally, by title or last name (Eakins and Eakins, 1978:116). Usually men are at the top of work hierarchies and women are at the bottom. Men call the women by their first names, and the women address the men by last name plus title (Thorne and Henley, 1975:16). Until recently, women lost their surname upon marriage, while men not only kept their last name for life, but passed it on intact to sons. (A childless couple reportedly adopted a baby girl. When asked why they chose a girl, they explained "that if she did not live up to their expectations because of her genetic heritage, 'at least she won't carry on the family' " [Miller and Swift, 1977:5, 11].) Women get labelled in terms of the men with whom they are associated—"Mrs. Jones," "Bill Staubs's daughter," "Jack's wife." The importance of the neologism, "Ms." has been described as follows: "First, it separated women from their relationships to men both as daughters and as wives, and established 'woman' as a linguistic category in its own right. The new privacy regarding marital status symbolically elevated women to personhood from their previous commodity status in the marriage market where 'Miss' meant 'for sale,' and 'Mrs.' meant 'sold'" (Davy, 1978:47).

Occupational Titles

Occupational titles also establish males as primary, females as secondary. The majority of the titles for occupations are male (pilot, physician), and it is assumed that males occupy them. A few titles (nurse, prostitute, housekeeper, maid) belong to females. When either sex moves beyond its traditional sphere, special markers are needed—*female* physician, *male* nurse—which often cast negative connotations over the term. (Miller and Swift [1977:26] tell the story of the children who were disappointed to discover that "the dog doctor" was only a human being.) Another type of feminine marker is the addition of suffixes such as *-ess* or *-ette* (authoress, usherette, waitress, stewardess). "Adding appendages to words reduces women to appendages or extensions of males. It singles out a woman as a special case or exception to the rule, something that does not ordinarily belong" (Eakins and Eakins, 1978:115-16). Also, in English, the *-ette* suffix suggests imitation ("flannelette") or denotes small size ("dinette"). The implication is that "farmerettes" and "usherettes" are frivolous little people, who need not be taken seriously (Miller and Swift, 1977:142). Incidentally, Bem and Bem (1973) report that job advertisements that are free from sex bias encourage more high-school females to apply for "male" jobs.

Another way in which language treats the sexes differently is by regarding the female as a *sex object*. The assumption is conveyed that women's sexuality completely defines them, while male sexuality is only part of their identity as well-rounded human beings. A male "professional" is assumed to be a doctor or a lawyer. A woman "professional" is assumed to be a prostitute. Research on sexual terms produced ten times as many for females as for males. Women are labelled "nympho," "hooker," "tramp," "whore" and (most devastating of all) "slut." Similar terms for men carry more positive associations and reflect, perhaps, the "morality of machismo and the prevalence of the double standard": "Casanova," "Don Juan," "letch," "stud." Women are often defined sexually in terms of specific portions of their bodies: "pussy," "tail," "honey pot." Parallel terms for males are rare. Even when a male is called a "prick," it is a comment on his personality, akin to "creep" or "jerk," not on his sexuality (Eakins and Eakins, 1978:121-22, 136).

Perhaps the most revealing sexual metaphor likens women (and sometimes men) to food:

> Women are often compared to food in a manner that defines them as something to be consumed or enjoyed as good things—"delicious," "a dish," "good enough to eat." They may be fruits or vegetables: "tomato," "peach," "plum," "a peaches-and-cream complexion." Or they may be desserts and sources of sweets: "cookie," "honey," "sweetie-pie," "cheese cake," "cream puff," "cupcake." Males may occasionally be labeled as "big cheese," "meathead," "hunk of meat," "honey," or called a "fruit" but they are generally not . . . "laid out on a buffet." [Eakins and Eakins, 1978:122-23]

Margaret Atwood's character, Marian, in the novel, *The Edible Woman* (1969), becomes convinced that her engagement to Peter means that he plans to consume her. She becomes unable to eat until she rejects him.

Language's Evaluation by Sex

The English language also appraises the sexes. For example, *masculine connotations* tend to be strong and positive, while *feminine connotations* tend to be negative, weak or trivial. All references to God are masculine: Father, Lord, King. Mother Earth (the land to be cultivated, used) is feminine. Within the past year or so, threatening forces such as hurricanes and tornadoes have become masculine. Their strength makes this change easy to accept. The negative connotations attached to the word "woman" become obvious when we compare taking defeat "like a man" and taking defeat "like a woman." The *order* of word usage also communicates differential evaluation: "men and women," "boys and girls," "males and females," "husbands and wives." Another illustration of this phenomenon is *reverse devaluation*. Here, what is admirable in one sex is disdained in the other. Probably men fare worse in this trade-off of stereotyped traits. Labelling a woman "mannish" is less insulting than labelling a man "womanish." Indeed, "there are surely overtones of praise in telling a female she runs, talks, or, most especially, *thinks* 'like a man.'"

Then there are *praise him/blame her* pairs of words. He is a "bachelor" (romantic, eligible, free), she is a "spinster" or "old maid" (poor thing!). He is a "chef" and expert, while she is merely a "cook." He is "master" of all he surveys, she is a "mistress" cohabiting without benefit of marriage. She "chattered," he "discussed." She "nagged," he "reminded." She "bitched," he "complained." She is "scatterbrained," he is "forgetful." She has "wrinkles," he has "character lines." Finally, there are *euphemisms*, which substitute a soft term for an offensive term. "Woman" apparently carries sexual implications that need to be toned down. "Lady," connotes propriety and politeness. "Girl" carries not only connotations of youth, but implications of immaturity and irresponsibility. The office "girl" may be eighteen, thirty-eight or fifty-eight years old (Eakins and Eakins, 1978:125-34).

Language's Exclusion of Females

The "he/man" problem shows yet another way in which the English language fails to speak clearly and fairly of both sexes (Martyna, 1980). Here, language excludes and subsumes women through generic masculine terms that are supposed to refer to people in general: "he," "mankind," "man, the social animal," "man of good will." (Or even, "Man, being a mammal, breast-feeds his young" [Martyna, 1980:489].) The grammarians' claim that the generic masculine implies "woman," "she," "her," and that "man" embraces "woman," is countered by the feminists' claim that the generic masculine is both ambiguous and discriminatory. Empirical evidence shows that people of both sexes interpret generic masculine terms as *exclusively* male. For example, Schneider and Hacker (1973 [described in Miller and Swift, 1977]) showed college students pictures that were to fit under chapter headings for a hypothetical sociology text, headings such as "Social Man," "Industrial Man," "Political Man." Analysis of the pictures selected revealed that these chapter titles invoked images of males only, thus "filtering out recognition of women's participation in these major areas of life" (Miller and Swift, 1977:19). Similarly, "Marguerite Richie (1975) surveyed some 200 years of Canadian law and discovered that the ambiguity of the generic masculine has allowed judges to include or exclude women, depending on the climate of the times and their own personal biases. As she concludes: 'Wherever any statute or regulation is drafted in terms of the male, a woman has no guarantee that it confers on her any rights at all'" (Martyna, 1980:490).

Underlying our discussion of sexism in language is the assumption that as girls and boys learn a language, they learn something about women's place and men's place. Bernard (1981:376) puts the issue very strongly. According to her, English is a "hostile language" that expresses the "misogyny of the male world." Of course, English is not the only language that does this.

Sex Differences in Language Use[12]

Comparison of the ways in which females and males speak is a less well-established topic than sex differences in language structure. Speculation outruns solid evidence. Also, there has been a tendency for findings of "difference" to be emphasized while findings of "no difference" have been underplayed (Kramer, Thorne and Henley, 1978). In the English language, most sex differences are a matter of *frequency*. That is, various forms occur in both male and female speech, but they occur more often in one case than the other.

Sex is only one of many social factors that impinge on language use. Others are social class, geographic locale, ethnicity, race, age. Much of the research done so far deals with white, middle-class Americans. Little work has been done on the interaction of variables such as sex and social class, or on Canadian-American differences. A final complication is that "speakers may also shift speech styles, depending on situation, topic, and roles" (Thorne and Henley, 1975:10). Our interest is in establishing male-female differences. However, it may well matter whether the men being studied are young, WASP, middle-class businessmen, or older blue-collar workers who are first-generation immigrants to this country. As well, males may speak differently at work or on dates, in an all-male group, or a mixed-sex group. The challenge is to arrive at commonalities that distinguish males in general from females in general.

Our objective here is to briefly communicate some of the more interesting findings. Males are more likely than females to use *-in*, rather than the full *-ing* ("runnin" versus "running"). Females use the intensifiers "so" and "such" in an expressive way, more often than males ("I am *so* bored"). In general, though, the female style of speech is less obtrusive. There is less speech intensity, more nodding of the head and "mm-hmming," (rather than an emphatic "yes" or "no"). Women use tentative questions instead of declarative statements ("I'm going to go out, okay?"). As we mentioned in Chapter Five, men's and women's different interests lead to different conversational topics. A related and obvious finding is that women are more likely to know "the terminology of sewing, fabric, cooking methods and utensils, and child care, while men more frequently use and understand the vocabulary of sports and auto mechanics" (Thorne and Henley, 1975:22). Women differentiate colors more than men and their style is more descriptive. Moreover, women use significantly more words implying feeling, emotion or motivation. Females tend to "use a wider range of pitches and more variable intonation than male speakers and, in general, males have been found to speak louder and with less fluency and more filled and unfilled pauses" (Kramer, Thorne and Henley, 1978:639). Fifteen years ago, at least, in French Canada, men were more likely to be bilingual than women (Lieberson, 1965).

One aspect of the issue that has received considerable attention is the tendency for female speech to be politer and more correct than male speech. It has been argued that females' more circumspect speech behavior signals their subordination. An example may help to explain this: "Goffman . . . observed that in hospital staff meetings, the doctors 'had the privilege of swearing, changing the topic of conversation, and sitting in undignified positions,' while attendants were more careful and less relaxed in demeanor" (Thorne and Henley, 1975:18). Analysis of the speech of single-sex pairs suggests that while men tend to argue with one another, women acknowledge the other's speech, building upon it rather than disputing it.

Men are more likely to use profanity. Swearing and sex talk among men often function to exclude women (Coyne et al., 1978). The role played by this particular language difference in the failure of many women to succeed is emphasized in Ross's (1979) study of businesswomen in Montreal (Quebec), Delhi (India) and Sydney (Australia). Many of her respondents said that their male colleagues acknowledged their womanhood by "cleaning up their language" or "refraining from telling crude jokes" (p. 428). As a result, "businesswomen . . . may be excluded from their male colleagues" groups because they impose restrictions on men's freedom of expression, and thus interfere with one of the main functions of informal groups—that of providing a milieu in which tensions can be relaxed and people can converse freely without monitoring their language" (Ross, 1979:428). (In Chapter Five we discussed the importance of collegial relations for career advancement.)

Studies of mixed-sex conversations have produced some interesting (though often tentative) findings. In mixed conversations, men are more likely to interrupt women than vice versa and women, indicating submission, are more likely to allow interruption. Other studies of who interrupts whom suggest that differences in power and status are involved, which are more pervasive than gender alone (Kramer, Thorne and Henley, 1978). In taped university faculty meetings, high-status males interrupt low-status males and high-status females interrupt low-status females. In tapes from a physician's office, adults interrupt children. Also, in mixed gatherings, men talked more than women (Thorne and Henley, 1975:16). Smith (1975:364) describes some related conclusions reported by West (1973) in an unpublished master's thesis: "[West] observed a variety of different 'devices' used by men apparently with women's consent which serve to maintain male control of the topics of conversation. For example, men tended to complete women's sentences, to give minimal responses to topics initiated and carried by women, and to interrupt without being sanctioned."

Many of West's points are corroborated by Fishman's (1978) taped conversations of three male-female couples in their homes. Fishman believes that her work illustrates the expression of power in daily experience. (Here, power is defined as "the ability to impose one's definition of what is possible, what is right, what is rational, what is real" [Fishman, 1978:397].) Women asked three times as many questions as men. Women used some version of the conversational opening, "D'ya know what?" twice as often as men. (Children use this strategy to insure their right to speak.) Men often displayed minimal responses, indicating lack of interest. Men produced over twice as many statements as women, and they almost always got a response. For example, many times one or another of a couple were reading, then read a passage aloud or commented on what they were reading. "The man's comments often engendered a lengthy exchange, the woman's comments seldom did" (Fishman, 1978:402). Fishman concludes that women do more of the interaction work than men; they keep the conversation going. However, "the definition of what is appropriate or inappropriate conversation becomes the man's choice" (Fishman, 1978:404).

Is there a special "women's language"? Although the idea still requires corroborative evidence, Lakoff (1975) (as well as others) argues that females in childhood acquire a special style of speech. (Boys initially learn female language but allegedly switch styles around age ten.) These distinctive linguistic usages are later used to keep woman "in a demeaning position, to refuse to take her seriously" as a grown-up person. Women can also learn to switch from women's language to "neutral language" under certain circumstances, such as job interviews and university classroom discussions.

According to Lakoff's (1975:53-57) conjecture, "women's language" takes these forms:

1. Women have a large vocabulary of words related to their own interests, which men use tongue-in-cheek, if at all, e.g., precise terminology for colors, sewing and cooking, such as "puce," "placket" and "sauté."
2. Women use "empty" adjectives such as "divine," "sweet," "cute."
3. Women use question intonation where the declarative would be expected. Examples are tag questions ("It's nice out, isn't it?") and rising intonation in statements ("My name is Greta Laing?").
4. Women use "hedges," which suggest that the speaker is un-

certain and apologetic about what she is saying, e.g., "I guess," "kinda," "sort of."

5. Women use hypercorrect grammar and superpolite forms. They tend to speak properly and do not use off-color or indelicate expressions.

6. Women don't tell jokes and they don't "get" jokes. (More about this later.)

7. Women speak in *italics* to make sure that *someone* pays *attention*.

Lakoff argues that "women's language" is inferior to "men's language," which allows for more forceful statements. Furthermore, she feels that a woman is in a double bind. If she does not learn to speak "women's language," she is ostracized in traditional society as unfeminine. On the other hand, if she does use "women's language," she is considered to be less than a real person—"a bit of fluff" (p. 61). Remember, though, that intriguing as they are, some of Lakoff's claims (such as 2 and 6 above) remain quite speculative. We now turn to a more detailed consideration of sex differences in humor.

Humor

Social scientists take humor quite seriously. Though laughter and joking might seem frivolous, an analysis of humor can reveal interesting information about societies and groups. Jokes provide an "unobtrusive measure" of public opinion, since jokes have to have some relevance in order to be funny. Jokes provide a vehicle for the expression of feelings for which there is no other socially acceptable outlet (Winick, 1976). In the United States, a panel that has been in operation for twenty years reports on jokes heard in ordinary social interaction. During 1970-75, the most frequent categories were sex (15%), ethnic-racial (12%), politics (7%), alcoholic beverages (5%), family roles and relationships (4%), occupations (4%) and death/illness (2%). The list constitutes a not very surprising catalog of human concerns.

Many of the above topics are connected with intergroup attitudes and relations. Just how do people feel about mothers-in-law, Newfoundlanders, psychiatrists, the leader of the Conservative Party and the opposite sex? Humor is thought to serve a variety of group functions. Superiority "theories" build on Hobbes's (1651) assertion that laughter is occasioned by "a sudden glory arising from some sudden conception of some eminency in ourselves; by comparison with the infirmity of others, or with our own formerly" (Berlyne, 1969:800). Laughing at an outgroup also serves to strengthen the bonds of the ingroup. "We" are people who share common attitudes, as well as the freedom to express them. "Gallows humor" helps people to cope with difficult situations, such as long-term hospitalization (Coser, 1959). Humor is one way of bringing overwhelming problems down to manageable size (Winick, 1976).

What does humor disclose about gender relations? Supposedly, most women choose not to tell jokes (Lakoff, 1975). The few who try do not tell jokes well. They fumble and repeat themselves, mix up the order of happenings and kill the punch line. (Eakins and Eakins, 1978). They don't have the wit to laugh at jokes men find funny. Indeed, the women's movement has been charged with lacking a sense of humor (Walker, 1981).

Is there any truth to these allegations? Although we do not know whether women really do mistell and misunderstand jokes, fortunately, we do know something about the appreciation and production of humor. Most of the available research on sex differences in humor focuses on the type of jokes preferred. Males appreciate aggressive humor more than females do (Groch, 1974), while the reverse pattern holds for absurd humor (Brodzinsky, Barnet and Aiello, 1981; Terry and Ertel, 1974). Consistently, men have been reported to find sexual humor funnier than do women (Brodzinsky, Barnet and Aiello, 1981; Groch, 1974; Terry and Ertel, 1974.) Why men and women should react differently to types of humor is not entirely clear. Even in childhood, boys are more responsive than girls to hostile aggressive humor (although no overall difference exists in their appreciation of humor per se) (McGhee, 1976). Perhaps the difference here stems from the sex difference in aggressiveness, which we noted earlier. So far as sexual humor is concerned, some of the difference may reflect the tradition that "ladies don't joke about sex." However, some part of the explanation seems to be that women are turned off by sexual jokes that derogate women. In an English study, Chapman and Gadfield (1976) measured the responses of men and women to fifteen cartoons. The men enjoyed sexist sexual humor (e.g., themes of rape and female masturbation), but the women did not. No sex difference was found for nonsexist humor or for sexist humor that deprecated males (e.g., castration or male impotence themes).

Cantor (1976) asked female and male respondents to judge how funny these situations were:

> A movie actor, soon after his autobiography was published, was approached at a party by an actress who said, "I saw your new book . . . Who wrote it for you?" "I'm so glad you enjoyed it," came the reply, "Who read it to you?" [male-dominates-female version]
>
> A movie actress, soon after her autobiography was published, was approached at a party by an actor, who said, "I saw your new book . . . Who wrote it for you?" "I'm so glad you enjoyed it," came the reply, "Who read it to you?" [female-dominates-male version]

Cantor found an antifemale bias: respondents of both sexes found the situation funnier when the main target of ridicule was female. Females showed this bias to a greater extent than males.

Levine (1976) analyzed popular comedy recordings of four male and four female comics, including Bill Cosby, David Steinberg, Phyllis Diller and Lily Tomlin. Her principal finding was that females used self-deprecatory humor much more frequently than males. For example, Phyllis Diller despairs about her Living Bra—"it died of starvation." Totie Fields claims that happiness is getting a brown gravy stain on a brown dress, and adds, "Why am I such a slob? Maybe it's 'cause the target's so big." To explain the genesis of this self-deprecatory humor, the author surmises that "comediennes are echoeing the values of their social milieu in order to attract and keep a mass audience."

Although information about less contrived situations is scarce, one field study reveals the effects of the male-female hierarchy upon joking behavior. Coser (1960) recorded instances of humor and laughter in the staff meetings of a mental hospital over a three-month period. She found that higher-status people, such as psychiatrists, were much more likely to make jokes than lower-status people, such as paramedicals. A witticism was never directed at anyone present of higher rank. Even though a considerable number of women were at the meetings (including two female psychiatrists), men made 99 out of the 103 jokes. Nevertheless, the women often laughed harder. This sexual division of humor-related behavior reminds one of Fishman's (1978) conclusions (mentioned above) about the sexual division of interactive work in general.

The criticism that feminists lack a sense of humor has provoked rebuttal. Walker (1981) argues persuasively that women do have a tradition of humor, a gentle, self-mocking humor rather than a retaliatory humor. She cites Nora Ephron (*Crazy Salad: Some Things About Women* [1975]) and Judith Viorst (*How Did I Get to be Forty and Other Atrocities* [1976]) as authors who satirize overzealous feminists. (Viorst refuses outright to join a group of feminists who want to picket a men's clothing store "on the grounds that it only sold men's clothing.") Walker feels that contemporary feminist humor is not just another case of humble-pie, "do unto yourself before they do unto you" humor. Rather, in her view, "Feminist humor, even when it has featured women as its targets, has attacked the very qualities which the women's movement deplores in women: silliness, dependence, susceptibility to dubious or malevolent influences. The ideal woman who emerges by implication is gutsy, self-determined, clear-eyed" (Walker, 1981:8).

Dorothy Parker's "Indian Summer" (1973:107) illustrates the type of woman Walker has in mind:

In youth, it was a way I had
To do my best to please,
And change, with every passing lad,
To suit his theories.

But now I know the things I know,
And do the things I do;
And if you do not like me so,
To hell, my love, with you!*

Although Kaufman and Blakely, editors of *Pulling Our Own Strings: Feminist Humor* & Satire (1980), share aspects of Walker's characterization of feminist humor, they emphasize its satirization of the "oppressive" world at large. In her Introduction, Kaufman says that feminist humor is a "humor based on visions of change." Further, it is didactic, as it demonstrates human folly. Feminist satire "exposes realities not merely out of love for truth but also out of desire for reform." However, it treats men rather gently. For example, a cartoon shows a couple in a cocktail lounge. The woman says, "Melvin, I am self-supporting, articulate, and I have never spit up on you. So why do you call me 'baby'?"

Two satirical treatments of rape, of all things, illustrate feminist humor. The July 1974 *Saskatoon W L Newsletter* carried advice on "How to Avoid Rape." "Don't go out without clothes—that encourages men. Don't go out *with* clothes—any clothes encourage some men. Avoid childhood—some rapists are turned on by the very young. Avoid old age—some rapists prefer older women. Don't have a father, grandfather, uncle, or brother—these are relatives who most often rape young women. Don't marry—rape is legal within marriage. To be *quite* sure, don't exist!" (Kaufman and Blakely, 1980:108).

The protagonist of Atwood's "Rape Fantasies" (1977:101) complains that every magazine she opens has a column entitled "RAPE, TEN THINGS TO DO ABOUT IT, like it was ten new hairdos or something." Because a magazine insists that all women have rape fantasies, she dutifully contrives some to share with the women in the lunch room:

> "All right, let me tell you one," I said. "I'm walking down this dark street at night and this fellow comes up and grabs my arm. Now it so happens that I have a plastic lemon in my purse, you know how it always says you should carry a plastic lemon in your purse? I don't really do it, I tried it once but the darn thing leaked all over my chequebook, but in this fan-

---

* "Indian Summer" from *The Portable Dorothy Parker*, Revised and Enlarged Edition, edited by Brendan Gill. Copyright 1926 by Dorothy Parker. Copyright renewed in 1954 by Dorothy Parker. Reprinted by permission of Viking Penguin Inc.

tasy I have one, and I say to him, 'You're intending to rape me, right?' and he nods, so I open my purse to get the plastic lemon, and I can't find it! My purse is full of all this junk, Kleenex and cigarettes and my change purse and my lipstick and my driver's licence, you know the kind of stuff; so I ask him to hold out his hands, like this, and I pile all this junk into them and down at the bottom there's the plastic lemon, and I can't get the top off. So I hand it to him and he's very obliging, he twists the top off and hands it back to me, and I squirt him in the eye."

    I hope you don't think that's too vicious. Come to think of it, it is a bit mean, especially when he was so polite and all. [Atwood, 1977:105].

(Apparently, Atwood's last sentence accurately reflects women's attitudes. A female holder of a black belt in karate, who teaches women how to defend themselves against rapists, "complained that women often wait around to apologize after stunning their attackers." She teaches them to "get out of there and run like a bat" [*Calgary Herald*, 16 July 1982].)

We still await the "new masculine humor." Meanwhile, Jim Unger's (1979) Herman confronts the women's movement along with sadistic dentists, smart-ass children, unpleasant pets and thick-headed bosses. One cartoon shows Herman decked out in an apron, up to his elbows in dishwater. His wife, who sits reading the newspaper, informs him, "According to this quiz, you're a 'male chauvinist pig.'" Another shows a very large wife, occupied with a book and a box of chocolates. Herman, broom in hand, says, "There's a guy at the door wants to know what I think of 'women's lib.' What shall I tell him?"

Nonverbal Communication Patterns

Although language is our major mode of communication, human beings have many other ways of sending messages to one another. Staring, winking, frowning and shoulder shrugging are all well-recognized means of "speaking." Birdwhistell (1970:8), a pioneer in the study of nonverbal communication, says that the human face alone is capable of some 250,000 different expressions. Yet more subtle nonverbal cues are conveyed by the amount of space commanded by an individual, the arrangement of seating or the preferred conversational distance between speakers. Messages such as these may not even be consciously registered.

    Our culture's emphasis on verbal communication is indicated by the fact that language (grammar, structure, written composition) is taught in our schools. On the other hand, nonverbal communication is not taught; we never learn to analyze what certain postures, gestures and looks mean, or how to express ourselves better nonverbally. (Henley, 1975). Nevertheless, nonverbal communication is a matter of learning, not biology. Birdwhistell (1970:34) tells us that,

    . . . just as there are no universal words, no sound complexes, which carry the same meaning the world over, there are no body motions, facial expressions, or gestures which provoke *identical* responses the world over. A body can be bowed in grief, in humility, in laughter, or in readiness for aggression. A "smile" in one society portrays friendliness, in another embarrassment, and, in still another may contain a warning that, unless tension is reduced, hostility and attack will follow [emphasis in original].

Despite the fact that nonverbal communication is learned informally, some researchers argue that this mode constitutes the *core* of communication (Eakins and Eakins, 1978:147). Indeed, Argyle and his colleagues (1970) estimate that nonverbal communication carries four times the "conversational" weight of verbal communication. For instance, a study reported that subjects performed less well than they would by pure chance when asked to interpret spontaneous interaction from verbal transcripts. The experimental group who viewed videotapes of the same social interaction were significantly more accurate than the first group (Archer and Akert, 1977).

Do nonverbal communication patterns differ by sex? Considerable evidence supports the existence of *learned* (not instinctual) sex differences. For instance, Birdwhistell (1970:43) says that he has worked with both female and male informants from seven societies (Chinese, middle- and upper-class London British, Kutenai, Shuswap, Hopi, Parisian French and American) who had no trouble distinguishing typically male communication behavior from typically female communication behavior.

Our purpose in this section is to review some of the more central differences and to discuss interpretations of these differences. Our perspective is that nonverbal behavior reflects patterns of power and social control between the sexes. Researchers have consistently found that women engage in more *eye contact* than men (Exline, Ellyson and Long, 1974). Women look at one another more and hold eye contact longer with each other than men do with men (Eakins and Eakins, 1978:150). Women also gaze more at men than vice versa, and Lamb (1981) suggests a reason. In status-differentiated groups, the high-status person typically receives the most visual attention. Thus, the low-status person "looks to" the high-status person for direction, control or reward (Lamb, 1981:49). A related point is that people do more looking when they are listening to another speak. As mentioned earlier, in mixed-sex groups men do more talking than women (Eakins and Eakins, 1978:154). Also, women are more affected than men by visual cues (Eakins and Eakins, 1978:150). Therefore, women would be more likely to attend to this channel of information. In all these cases, we are *not* discussing the aggressive kind of staring that is used to sanction other people's behavior.

Women *smile* more than men (a finding you can check by looking at your high-school yearbooks to see which sex sports a smile and which a no-nonsense, stern pose) (Deaux, 1976:63). Apparently, women smile and laugh, whether or not they are happy or amused. The hypothesis advanced here is that since the traditional feminine role calls for affiliative, sociable behavior, women may smile more to meet social obligations than to express genuine warmth or friendliness (Frances, 1979:529). Children five to eight years old have caught on to the fact that fathers' smiles signal positive feelings, while mothers' smiles are indiscriminate. Mothers smile while making negative remarks. Therefore, the children are more likely to believe men's smiles and to ignore women's (Bugental, Love and Gianetto, 1971). In the early, angry days of the feminist movement, Shulamith Firestone (1971) described the smile as "the child/woman equivalent of the shuffle; it indicates acquiescence of the victim to his own oppression." She says she had to train herself out of that "phony smile, which is like a nervous tic on every teenage girl" (p. 90).

Females show more circumspection in their *demeanor*, a less casual *posture* and *bearing* than do males (Eakins and Eakins, 1978:159 ff.). Men tend to keep their legs apart at a ten- to fifteen-degree angle; women keep their knees together. The torso lean of the male in conversation is farther back (and more relaxed) than the female's. In general, women's bodily demeanor is more restrained and restricted than men's. Once again, a status explanation seems in order: "among nonequals in status, superordinates can indulge in a casualness and relative unconcern with body comportment that subordinates are not permitted" (Eakins and Eakins, 1978:159).

Women are *touched* by men more than men are touched by women. Henley (1975), among others, feels that touching has status connotations and quotes Goffman's (1956:74) description of the "touch system" in a hospital as an analogy: "The doctors touched other ranks as a means of conveying friendly support and comfort, but other ranks tended to feel that it would be presumptuous for them to reciprocate a doctor's touch, let alone initiate such a contact with a doctor." A sexual, as opposed to a status explanation, would not explain why higher-status women are less likely to be touched; secretaries and waitresses are felt or pinched more often than female executives. Touching may be seen as a nonverbal equivalent to first-naming. When both are used reciprocally, they indicate solidarity and intimacy. When used nonreciprocally, they indicate status (Henley, 1975:194). Studies show that women respond more positively to being touched than do men (Deaux, 1976:65), perhaps out of familiarity. Mothers report touching their girl babies more than their boy babies (Goldberg and Lewis, 1969). Also, females experience more same-sex touching than males. Apart from formal handshaking and locker-room swatting, male touching of other males carries homosexual connotations (Deaux, 1976:65).

A related observation is that men command more *personal space* than do women. Men prefer greater standing and sitting distances between themselves, than do women. Opposite-sex pairs require less interpersonal distance than female-female pairs, which require less than male-

male pairs (Wittig and Skolnick, 1978). Males find crowded situations more unpleasant than do women (Freedman et al., 1972). Males expansively dominate the space around them—they sprawl, they sit with legs spread out, they pace a room, they gesture extravagantly. By contrast, women condense or compress. They keep their legs crossed, elbows at their sides, move around the room or stage less when speaking in public, maintain a more erect posture and seem to be trying to take up as little space as possible.

Sex differences in the use of space are interpreted by most authorities as dominance-submission behaviors. Higher-status people command more space. They have larger houses, cars, offices, desks. Inferiors own less space and their personal space is more readily breached by others (Eakins and Eakins, 1978:169-71). However, a sociability hypothesis has also been advanced, which assumes that women engage in more behaviors that are interpreted as expressing warmth toward others (e.g., permitting/encouraging advances into their personal space bubbles; maintaining more eye contact). These behaviors, in turn, encourage others to put less personal distance between themselves and women.

In everyday situations, both sociability and low status may be found. However, an empirical study (Wittig and Skolnick, 1978) designed to untangle the effects of these two variables discovered status to be the important one. The authors suggested that women, as low-status individuals, may engage in more "suppliant" behaviors indicating warmth and liking. Perhaps the woman may wish to deflect displays of dominance by the high-status person by establishing a friendly atmosphere.

Nancy Henley's *Body Politics* (1977) was the first systematic treatment of the impact of gender upon nonverbal communication. All of the differences in nonverbal signals that Henley isolated—gaze, smiling, demeanor, touching, space use—were characteristic of status inequalities. Children, in learning the subtle lessons of body language, have their notions about male superiority-female inferiority reinforced. But children draw other inferences, as well. In the words of Tavris and Offir (1977:186):

> They may decide that females are more nurturant because their mothers usually comfort them when they're hurt, encourage lap-sitting, and rock them to sleep when they're sick. They may conclude that males are the more aggressive sex, because their fathers most often roughhouse with them, toss them into the air, and accept their invitations to play touch-football. Children probably generalize from personal experience to reach conclusions about the "natural" traits and duties of men and women.

We suspect that gender socialization lessons derived from the "silent language" are especially profound, for the simple reason that many of them remain below the level of conscious awareness.

Changing Sexist Language

Three general perspectives currently exist concerning prospects for changing sexist language.

One position resists change, and misunderstands and trivializes the issue. Martyna (1980) describes some mass-media expressions of this position. *Time* magazine called the language issue "ms.-guided." *TV Guide* wondered about the "women's lib redhots" with the "nutty pronouns." A syndicated columnist offered a critique of the "libspeak tantrum." Another columnist wrote, "Women are irrational, all women; when some women threaten to disembowel me unless I say 'personhole-cover,' I am surer even than I was that all women are irrational" (p. 484). (A Calgary, Alberta radio announcer jokingly talked about "bovine-persons" riding in the Calgary Stampede.) In general, people adopting this position see the sexist language issue as funny.

Proponents of the second perspective are quite sympathetic with feminists' desire for social change in order to equalize the positions of women and men. However, they believe that changing language is difficult, if not impossible. Moreover, they doubt whether tinkering with sexist language will improve women's situation. For them, linguistic change *follows* social change (Kramer, Thorne and Henley, 1978). Robin Lakoff (1975:43), who supports this perspective, claims that linguistic imbalances "are clues that some external situation needs changing, rather than items that one *should* seek to change directly [emphasis in original]." Furthermore, she warns that publicizing fanciful plans to reform the inequities of the English language, such as changing "his-tory" to "her-tory," create well-deserved ridicule. This ridicule then carries over "into other areas which are not ludicrous at all, but suffer guilt by association" (p. 45).

The third perspective advocates change in sexist usage and structure of language (Blaubergs, 1978; Martyna, 1980). Recognizing the importance of language both as a socializing influence and a reflection of society, some writers on the subject claim, "that changing the usage and structures of language constitutes at least a first step toward changing societal practices, if only by increasing the awareness of the existence of sexism in conventional language and/or by indicating a nonacceptance of such sexist usage" (Blaubergs, 1978:245). Many publishers and professional associations have put forth guidelines for conversion to nonsexist language.

In answer to the charge that language change is slow and cannot be forced, proponents of this position point to recent changes that have occurred in response to social movement pressure (Kramer, Thorne and Henley, 1978). The switch has been made from "Eskimo" to "Inuit" and from "Negro" to "Black." Because of the women's movement, various terms have been coined or have taken on new significance, e.g., "male chauvinist pig," "Ms.," "sisterhood." Job descriptions have been neutralized. Attempts are being made to eliminate generic masculine pronouns, through the invention of new pronouns or circumlocutions. However, deliberately altering language is not an easy task. Influencing sexism in nonverbal communication and in general interaction (e.g., interruptions and inattention to women) presents even more difficult challenges. The last chapter of this book will consider the prospects of changing the world to enhance the opportunities of both sexes to realize their human potential.

CONCLUSIONS

Chapter Six has examined the part played by these secondary and symbolic agents of gender socialization: the school, the church, the mass media and language. Two major conclusions emerge from our discussion. First of all, the secondary agents augment and elaborate upon family and peer group definitions of gender. Although further documentation is required of the linkages between primary and secondary agencies (and the connection of both to the pervasive influence of language), the emphasis placed on the family by gender socialization theorists seems to be appropriate. Second, the influence of all these gender socialization agencies upon the child appears to be consistent and cumulative in impact.

Women's (and men's) liberation groups, academicians and, to a certain extent, Canadians in general are coming to appreciate the fact that traditional sex stereotypes are arbitrary and damaging. Although the difficulties inherent in altering cultural values and familial behavior cannot be underestimated, thought is being given to healthier definitions of femininity and masculinity, and to the possibility that adult gender identities are not immutable. The general assumption made is that if sex differences are socially induced, they can be socially altered. Nevertheless, the ambiguity surrounding proper feminine and masculine behavior is bound to produce confusion in gender socialization patterns well into the future.

Up to this point, gender has been considered from a biological perspective and from a social-psychological perspective. The next chapter provides a social-structural analysis of the problem.

7 Social-Structural Explanations of Gender

THE COMPLEXITY of human social behavior is indicated by the existence of a variety of intellectual disciplines—psychology, sociology, economics, history, linguistics, anthropology, political science. All of them seek to understand why people do what they do. All of them offer distinctive, but perfectly legitimate, perspectives on the same problems, hence the expression, *explanation by discipline*. The criterion for evaluating one discipline's explanation against another is pragmatic: which one predicts best? Given the present state of knowledge in the social sciences, it is rare that alternative disciplinary explanations are mutually exclusive. Generally speaking, every explanation has something to contribute, and we need them all.

Because of disciplinary specialization, there are varying *levels of explanation*.[1] That is, there is a logical ordering of perspectives on human behavior, from the *biological* level, to the *psychological* level, to the *social-psychological* level, to the *social-structural* level. Behavior bearing a single label (e.g. aggression) may sometimes involve one level, sometimes another. (Often two or more levels are implicated, because social behavior usually has more than one cause.)

Take the unhappy example of suicide. Since the Golden Gate Bridge in San Francisco opened in 1937, there have been at least 708 suicides (more than one per month). A few years ago, local interest focused on who would be the five-hundredth jumper. After the bridge guards had stopped thirty people (including one with a big "500" daubed on a card fastened to his back), the dubious honor went to a young man who left a note saying that this was "just something [I] wanted to do." The civic government considered erecting antisuicide barriers on the bridge; however, after spending $27,000 on designing a model, the idea was rejected on the dual grounds of expense and aesthetics (*Calgary Herald*, 6 October 1975 and 28 July 1981). The next sequence of events may well be apocryphal. Apparently someone convinced the San Francisco city fathers that the installation of vending machines containing chocolate bars would be just as effective as physical barriers. The reasoning: low blood sugar causes depression and suicide. A would-be suicide (presumably equipped with change for the machines) would gulp some chocolate, feel happier and decide to go home, instead of jumping. The low blood sugar hypothesis approaches suicide from the *biological level*. (What level of explanation would we adopt to explain why the Golden Gate Bridge is perhaps the most popular location for suicide in the Western world?)

In Crewe (England) a few years ago, a fourteen-year-old boy burned himself to death on the school's rugby field. As dozens of helpless friends and teachers watched, Andrew Potter poured alcohol over himself and set himself on fire. The youth left a suicide note saying that he was under pressure at school, hated homework and resented the examination system (*Calgary Herald*, 24 January 1979). At first, the death of this troubled boy seems best explained at the *psychological level*. However, the newspaper reports went on to say that Potter had told a friend that he had been fascinated by a horror film, in a series called Theatre of Blood, which had ended in a gruesome self-immolation. This additional information suggests that the *social-psychological level* would provide a more appropriate explanation.

An illustration of suicide that seems best explained at the *social-structural* level is provided by anthropologist Bronislaw Malinowski's (1926) account of his visit to the Trobriand Islands: "One day an outbreak of wailing and a great commotion told me that a death had occurred somewhere in the neighbourhood. I was informed that Kima'i, a young lad of my acquaintance, of sixteen or so, had fallen from a coconut palm and killed himself." Much later, Malinowski discovered that the boy had committed suicide. He had violated his tribe's rules of exogamy with his cousin. Although people knew about the matter, nothing was done until the girl's discarded lover took the initiative.

> This rival threatened first to use black magic against the guilty youth, but this had not much effect. Then one evening he insulted the culprit in public—accusing him in the hearing of the whole community of incest and hurling at him certain expressions intolerable to a native.
> For this there was only one remedy; only one means of escape remained to the unfortunate youth. Next morning he put on festive attire and ornamentation, climbed a coconut palm and addressed the community, speaking from among the palm leaves and bidding them farewell. He explained the reasons for his desperate deed and also launched forth a veiled accusation against the man who had driven him to his death, upon which it became the duty of his clansmen to avenge him. Then he wailed aloud, as is the custom, jumped from a palm some sixty feet high and was killed on the spot. [pp. 77-79]

Because violation of the incest taboo led to the death of this Trobriand Islander, this particular suicide had a *social-structural* cause. (However, nothing social is simple, and social-psychological causation was also *operative*, that is, until his rival made a public accusation, punishment for violation of the taboo was not enforced [Becker, 1963:12].) Before moving from the example of suicide to the matter at hand—gender—a definition of *social structure* may be helpful.

> A society is not just a chaotic collection of randomly interacting people who happen to occupy the same area. Despite the human capacity for flexible and creative action, there is an underlying regularity, or pattern, to social behavior in any society. To sociologists, therefore, *social structure* refers to the organized relationships among the basic components in a social system. These basic components provide the framework for all human societies, although the precise character of the components and the relationships among them vary from one society to another. The most important components of social structure are statuses, roles, groups, and institutions (emphasis in original). [Robertson, 1981:80]

The structural inequality inherent in gender suggests Mills's (1959) distinction between "private troubles" and "public issues," between individual and societal inadequacies (Connelly and Christiansen-Ruffman, 1977). Sociologist Dorothy Smith (1977:10) tells us what this distinction, as interpreted by feminism and Marxism, has meant in her personal life: "[This discovery of what oppression means] is the discovery that many aspects of my life which I had seen privately—perhaps better, experienced privately as guilt, or as pathology, or that I'd learned to view as aspects of my biological inferiority—that all these things could be seen as aspects of an objective organization of a society—as fixtures that were external to me, as they were external to other women."

This chapter adopts the social-structural perspective, as the last link in our cumulative explanation of gender. Our analysis will stress sex stratification, as we seek to understand the extent to which female-male differences stem from structural inequalities. More particularly, attention will be given to structural inequalities at work and in the family. Women who labor under more than one source of structural inequality—the old, newcomers to this country, native Indians—will be briefly discussed.

SOCIAL STRATIFICATION AND SEX STRATIFICATION

In *The Vertical Mosaic*, Porter (1965:3-4) argued that Canadians hold a classless image of their society. Many people believe that Canadians are relatively equal in money earned, possessions and opportunities to get ahead in the world. The historical source of this image is a romanticized story of equality among pioneers in a frontier society. Gradually the image of rural equality has been replaced with the image of middle-level classlessness in the urban industrial setting. The myth of a classless or middle-class society persists partly because the middle classes are insulated from the very rich and the very poor. Nevertheless, despite the prevalence of such mistaken ideas, it is a sociological truism that inequality is ubiquitous, if not inevitable (Forcese, 1980).

To begin with, all societies are *differentiated* according to ascribed criteria (e.g., age, sex, ethnicity) as well as achieved criteria (e.g., occupation, education, earned wealth). These differences are also *evaluated*. In our society, the young are valued more highly than the old, WASPs more than recent, nonwhite immigrants, men more than women, engineers more than janitors. People in valued categories command a disproportionate share of material wealth, power and prestige. These resources help them to maintain their position. A *stratification* structure consists of two or more social classes or groups of relative equals regarded as superior or inferior to one another.

Stratification systems vary in terms of the extent of disparity in wealth, power and prestige. In preindustrial societies, a marked polarization is found between the very rich minority and the impoverished peasantry. In industrialized societies, such as our own, the extremes of wealth and poverty are there, but the majority of the population constitutes a middle stratum. In industrial societies, social standing is determined mainly by occupational status (Nielsen, 1979). Stratification systems also vary in the degree to which stratification is rigid or open, that is, in the amount of social mobility possible (Forcese, 1980:10-11). Nonetheless, "Whatever the precise composition of the inequality, it is important to realize that it is a structured thing, very resistant to change. In sociological terms, it is *institutionalized*; that is, persisting through inherited organization and learning or socialization [emphasis in original]" (Forcese, 1980:11).

Until very recently, social stratification theory and research excluded women almost entirely (Acker, 1973). Sociologists showed little interest in sex as a criterion of social differentiation. The assumption was made that in this area the family was the appropriate unit of analysis. The social position of the family is determined by the status of the male head of the household. Women were seen to derive their status, first from their fathers, and then from their husbands. Therefore, their own occupational endeavors simply were irrelevant. Although the claim that the social status of women was determined by that of their husbands may have had some justification at a time when few women worked after marriage, it is hardly tenable now (Treiman and Terrell, 1975). Remedial steps are being taken. For instance, in 1978 a Canadian socioeconomic index for employed women finally became available (Blishen and Carroll, 1978). "Compensatory" research, designed to offset the previous neglect of women, is now under way. For example, studies have examined the intergenerational mobility of women (Featherman and Hauser, 1976; Haller, 1981; McClendon, 1976), and sex differences in the determinants of occupational status (Boyd, 1982; England, 1979; Treiman and Terrell, 1975). As we shall see later on, stratification theory as it applies to women has recently taken quite an innovative turn (Nielsen, 1979). But first we must deal with some preliminary theoretical matters.

One of the most creative steps toward a structural explanation of gender relations was the placement of male dominance, as a "fundamental and universal feature of social life," within the context of universal social stratification (Walum, 1977:141). "Evaluating social categories as better and worse, or more or less important, and rewarding them accordingly, is called *social stratification*. Defining sex-specific categories as better or worse and rewarding them accordingly is called *sex stratification* [emphasis in original]" (Nielsen, 1978:10). Both social stratification in general and its subtype, sex stratification, involve the notion of hierarchy of positions, with differential rewards and access to power (Lipman-Blumen and Tickamyer, 1975:314). As noted above, before the women's movement, stratification theory had made very little of sex as an ascribed basis of social differentiation. Emphasizing the parallel features of social stratification and sex stratification has brought numerous theoretical advantages. For one thing, existing sociological theory could be brought to bear on specific problems of gender relations. For another, the realization dawned that stratification theory should apply to both halves of humanity.

ALTERNATIVE STRATIFICATION LABELS FOR WOMEN

Over the years, several attempts have been made to capture the structural inequality of men and women by devising stratification labels for women. These various alternatives are described below.

Women as Minority Group

Helen Hacker (1951) was the first sociologist to consider the appropriateness of the designation "minority group" to women. If the minority-group concept proved to be applicable, then the theory and methodology relating to the more thoroughly studied ethnic groups might contribute to an understanding of women's position. In viewing women's situation as a sociological problem, Hacker was well ahead of her time. Twenty years later, Hacker (1975:103), tongue-in-cheek, remarked that her classic paper "aroused so much interest that it took almost three years to get it published." Rejected as "polemical and journalistic" in 1950, it was praised for its "professional, impersonal tone" two decades later.

For her analysis, Hacker adopted Louis Wirth's (1945:347) definition: "A minority group is any group of people who because of their physical or cultural characteristics, are singled out from the others in the society in which they live for differential and unequal treatment, and who therefore regard themselves as objects of collective discrimination." Hacker argued successfully that women were indeed subjected to "differential and unequal treatment." They face job and wage discrimination, legal discrimination, discrimination relating to social conduct, and discriminatory socialization practices within the family (Abu-Laban and Abu-Laban, 1977). Moreover, they manifest group self-hatred. (Women say they dislike other women, prefer to work under men and find exclusively female gatherings repugnant.) Like other minority groups, women tend to develop a separate subculture. Said Hacker: "Only the acculturated male can enter into the conversation of the beauty parlor, the exclusive shop, the bridge table, or the kitchen. In contrast to men's interest in physical health, safety, money, and sex, women attach greater importance to attractiveness, personality, home, family, and other people" (p. 62).

Despite the above arguments, Hacker concluded that "minority group" was really not an apt label for women. The difficulty was that women feel no minority-group consciousness, no sense of group identification (also part of Wirth's definition). Some women do not know that they are being discriminated against on a group basis. Others affirm the propriety of differential treatment. Therefore, Hacker concluded that women could usefully be studied according to their minority group *status*.

Other scholars have subsequently reconsidered the pertinence of the minority-group/minority-status concept. Their arguments are usefully summarized in Abu-Laban and Abu-Laban (1977). All of the "pro" arguments have already been mentioned by Hacker. Arguments *against* the propriety of the minority label for women include the fact that women constitute more than one-half the population and that women are encompassed within the families of the supposed majority. Disagreements exist as to whether women have a distinctive subculture. Abu-Laban and Abu-Laban (1977:114) feel that while "to parsimoniously lump all the disadvantaged [including, for example, the aged] under the minority-group label may be ideologically useful," it is "analytically premature." They warn that the concept of "minority group" suffers from definitional ambiguities. Do others understand what we mean when we label women or the aged a "minority group"?

Eichler (1977c) also examined the minority-group concept and arrived at similar conclusions. In general, she believes that male-female relationships are far more complicated than this concept assumes. More particularly, it does not tell us anything about the nature of men's power over women. Female self-hatred and discrimination against women

(Hacker, 1951) merely describe some of the *results* of male dominance. Finally, we are left with the riddle of why women lack group consciousness.

Nonetheless, despite the shortcomings of the minority-group concept per se, the ethnic relations literature does contain some promising leads to gender relations questions (Mackie, 1977b). Take, for example, the problem of changing attitudes. The ethnic relations literature informs us that discrimination is *situational*. Back in 1956, Kohn and Williams (p. 104) said, "There is now abundant research evidence of situational variability in intergroup behavior: an ever-accumulating body of research demonstrates that allegedly prejudiced persons act in a thoroughly egalitarian manner in situations where that is the socially prescribed mode of behavior. . . ." Ehrlich (1973:167) presents the following as "the principle of change which is as close to a law as any generalization in the social sciences: *Changes in ethnic attitudes follow changes in established ethnic group relations* [emphasis in original]." Though sexism and racism may be different phenomena, it seems parsimonious to first assume similarity, and then to test the applicability of the extensive ethnic relations literature. The special issue on "Ethnicity and Femininity" in *Canadian Ethnic Studies* (Volume 13, 1981) contains some interesting ideas along this line.

Women as Caste

Another theoretical approach to the super- and subordination of the sexes has been to apply the concept of *caste* to women (Eichler, 1977c). This approach dates from Myrdal's *An American Dilemma* (1944). In the Appendix to his famous diagnosis of the "Negro" problems in the U.S., he drew parallels between the disadvantages of American blacks and American women. Myrdal himself did not say that women constitute a caste, as some people mistakenly think. Rather, he called Negroes a caste, and compared their situation with that of women. Another writer, Andreas (1971), did apply the caste concept directly to women.

A caste system is a *closed stratification system*, with clearly defined boundaries. A person's position is determined at birth and cannot be altered in any way. Caste systems are endogamous; people may marry only within their own group (Robertson, 1981:236).

Eichler (1977c:52) neatly describes Myrdal's comparison between Negroes and women:

> [Both] women and slaves are (were) under the paternal order. From the paternalistic order of society stem the following consequences: both women and Negroes suffer from negative stereotypes. They themselves believe in their inferior endowment and therefore women as well as men

resent having female supervisors. Men and whites prefer a more humanistic and less professional relationship with women and Negroes. The political disabilities, inferior education and economic disabilities are [rationalized in the myth of the "contented woman," which parallels the myth of the "contented Negro." Just as there are pet "niggers," so there are pet women.

Many contemporary analysts (Eichler, 1977c) are convinced that the term *caste* cannot accurately be applied to women. While gender is ascribed at birth and the sexes are hierarchically related, women are most definitely not endogamous. Also, the stratification system between women and men is more complicated than the vertical ranking of castes. While "women as a group are economically, socially and politically underprivileged in comparison with men, there is likewise no doubt that *some* women are economically and socially more privileged than some men" (Eichler, 1977c:53). Finally, since women associate a great deal with men, the social avoidance criterion of caste fails to characterize the relationship between the sexes.

Women as Class

In a class society, as opposed to a caste society, the stratification is more subtle and upward mobility is possible, even encouraged. "Classes are aggregates of persons distinguished by inherited access to wealth or income, by power, and by prestige or life style (Forcese, 1980:14). One's occupation determines one's class position. The class analysis of gender relations is closely associated with Marxist ideas and the Marxist definition of class: "In its simplest form, class stratification involves two groups . . . who are distinguished by their differential access to *both* the means and fruits of production [emphasis in original]" (Blumberg, 1978:15). Smith (1977:30) expands on this definition:

Capitalism establishes a division of society into two major classes. Those two classes have been described . . . as those who appropriate and control the means of production, and those who must sell their labour power to those who appropriate and control the means of production. [Although] two classes don't provide a comprehensive description of the class structure of the society, . . . these two classes provide the basis on which the struggle to change the society goes on actively.

Benston (1969) was one of the first to provide a class analysis of women's position (Eichler, 1977c).

Benston begins by observing that the "woman question" is usually ignored in analyses of the class structure of society. The reason: classes are defined by their relation to the means of production, and women are not supposed to have any unique relation to the means of production. The category of *women* seems to cut across all classes; there are working-class women, middle-class women, etc. Nevertheless, Benston argues that women's status is inferior to that of men and "that women as a group do indeed have a definite relation to the means of production and that this is different from that of men" (p. 13). The difference flows from the distinction in capitalist societies between commodity production (products created for exchange on the market) and the production of use-values (all things produced in the home). In a society based on commodity production, household labor, including child care, is "not usually considered 'real work' since it is outside of trade and the market place" (p. 15). Men have primary responsibility for commodity production, women for the production of use-values. Herein lies women's inferior status: "In a society in which money determines value, women are a group who work outside the money economy. Their work is not worth money, is therefore valueless, is therefore not even real work" (Benston, 1969:16).

According to Benston, women's situation will not improve until women are freed from private production in the home. Unfortunately, their unpaid work in the home serves the capitalist system. To pay women for their work would mean a massive redistribution of wealth. The status quo supports the present consuming functions of the family. And in the present situation, women constitute an elastic part of the industrial "reserve army." They are called into the labor force when they are needed (e.g., during wartime) and sent home when that need disappears. Benston argues that structural changes in production would be required to end women's "exploitation," and that such changes would require a revolution.

The major flaw in Benston's analysis is her emphasis on household labor and consequent neglect of employed women (Eichler, 1977c). Armstrong and Armstrong (1978) feel that Morton (1972) provides the necessary linkage between women's exploited position in the home and in the marketplace. Women's work outside the home *does* have structural importance: "The sense in which women's role in the labour force is peripheral is that women's position in the family is used to facilitate the use of women as a reserve army of labour, to pay women half of what men are paid, but women's work in the labour force is peripheral neither to the women's lives nor to the capitalist class" (Morton, 1972:52).

The system employs women in low-wage sectors of the economy. Because they are usually part of a family unit, women "can often survive with less pay and disappear back into the home when they are fired or laid off" (Armstrong and Armstrong, 1978:137). The dominant class, then, benefits from women's work both inside and outside the home.

The Marxian perspective continues to inform some social scientists' study of gender relations (see Connelly, 1978; Jaggar and Struhl, 1978;

Jamieson, 1981). For example, Connelly and Christiansen-Ruffman (1977) argue the inequality of Canadian women in these structural terms: "A glance at the Canadian social structure indicates that it is men who own and control the essential resources. . . . Ownership of the most important resource, the means of production, is mainly in the hands of a few men who have power over almost all women as well as other men. . . . Men also have control of the next most important resources, access to the occupational structure and control of policy making in the major areas of social life" (p. 168).

However, in line with our treatment of women-as-minority-group and women-as-caste, it is appropriate to consider some criticisms and extensions of the women-as-social-class concept.

The argument that women constitute a special class has been attacked from within Marxist sociology. Evelyn Reed (1978), for example, argues that women, like men, are a multiclass sex. A few are part of the plutocratic class at the top; more belong to the middle class; even more belong to the proletarian layers of society. An enormous spread divides the few wealthy "society" women from the millions of poor women. She argues further that "the notion that all women as a sex have more in common than do members of the same class with one another is false. Upperclass women are not simply bedmates of their wealthy husbands. As a rule they have more compelling ties which bind them together. They are economic, social and political bedmates, united in defense of private property, profiteering, militarism, racism—and the exploitation of other women" (p. 127). If all women compose a class, the oppressed class, then all men form a counterclass, the oppressor class. However, it is not men as such who represent women's main "enemy." Such a mistaken view, according to Reed, "crosses out the multitudes of downtrodden, exploited men who are themselves oppressed by the main enemy of women, which is the capitalist system" (p. 127). Women, in her view, are an oppressed sex whose situation can be usefully diagnosed according to Marxism.

Eichler (1977c) argues that the class model also fails to capture the complexity of female-male relations. In particular, previous attempts overlooked the fundamental difference between the relationship of employed women with men and that of full-time housewives with men. So far as employed women are concerned, sex constitutes another stratifying variable in addition to occupation, income, education, etc. "Women are present in all strata, but differ on two dimensions from men: first, in comparison with men they are under-represented in the upper strata; second, within each stratum, women as a group occupy a lower level than men" (p. 58). Nonemployed housewives are ranked solely in terms of the men to whom they are attached, usually their husbands. Their derived status is lower than their husbands', but usually higher than that of men their husbands outrank, irrespective of their own personal qualifications.

In terms of derived status, full-time housewives are found in every stratum. Eichler applies the concept "personal dependents" to housewives. Their dependency on husbands (or fathers) for economic, social and legal status gives the males authority over them. In her view, the two statuses are not unrelated. Married women in the labor force occupy both a derived and an independent status. Also, a woman may pass in and out of either status "by resuming or renouncing employment and/or marriage to a particular man" (p. 59). Lastly, a woman's derived status is always supposed to be above or at least equal to her independent status. That is, it is considered improper for a female lawyer to marry the milkman.

NEW DIRECTIONS IN STRATIFICATION RESEARCH

When stratification researchers first noticed women, they began asking the same questions about women that they had already asked about men (Nielsen, 1979). Because men's social status in industrialized societies is primarily determined by their occupation, research on women's status made very much the same assumption. Recently the wisdom of this approach has been questioned (Nielsen, 1979). First, the emphasis on occupational achievement has limited use for comparative analysis. Ideally, a general theory of sex stratification should explain cross-cultural and historical variation. Second, limiting definitions of status to occupation and giving women their husbands' social status is really a "cop-out." Third, even employed women are not in the labor force in the same way men are. Women's work efforts are affected by their family responsibilities much more than men's. A final limitation of the tendency to measure social status in terms of occupation is the ensuing neglect of other aspects of stratification, especially power.

An alternative perspective on sex stratification has been suggested by anthropological studies (Nielsen, 1979). Since these studies deal with entire societies, rather than aspects of very large ones, they have a more comprehensive view of women's social status. Two distinctions stressed by anthropological research are important for our purposes. One, the form of power exercised within a hierarchy of roles and considered legitimate by others, namely, authority, is distinguished from influence: "[Influence] is the ability to impose one's will in the absence of perceived legitimacy on the part of the person being influenced. In its most sophisticated and well-developed form, of course, this kind of power is exerted without the awareness of the one being influenced. Furthermore, its use requires a good deal of interpersonal skill and sensitivity to others" (Nielsen, 1979:331). (This conceptual distinction originates with Max Weber [1947].)

The second relevant distinction is the one made by Engels (1942) between private and public spheres of life. In industrial societies, workplace and home activities are sharply differentiated. Men engage in work that has exchange value in the public world, while (many) women are confined to the home. Their work has use-value, but not exchange value. Consequently, women do not have direct access to the status resources available in the larger society. Prior to industrialism, reproductive, subsistence and leisure activities took place in a single context.

The major hypothesis of anthropologists such as Rosaldo (1974), whose work was mentioned in Chapter Three, is that women's structural position (their lack of authority in the public world) facilitates their development of informal power strategies, i.e., influence, to achieve their goals.[2] "Because of its less than legitimate nature, . . . many societies have no concepts with which to define female power; [women's] influence is often labelled as deviant or disruptive and powerful women in modern societies are described as 'bitches' and 'castrating females' while those in more traditional ones are thought of as witches and sources of evil" (Nielsen, 1979:332). In societies where private and public spheres are more integrated, women's status and expression of power more closely resemble men's.

Sociologists such as Nielsen (1979) are not advocating that informal power measures of status be substituted for the traditional occupational measure. Rather, they argue that status differences in both the public and private worlds need to be appreciated, as well as the relationship between the two. We turn now to a discussion of the work that women do in their public and domestic worlds. Adopting Hall's (1969) definition permits us to treat women's activities in both spheres as work. (He uses "work" and "occupation" interchangeably.) "An occupation is the social role performed by adult members of society that directly and/or indirectly yields social and financial consequences and that constitutes a major focus in the life of an adult [emphasis deleted]" (pp. 5-6). We will deal first with women in the labor force and then with housewives.

SEX DIFFERENCES IN LABOR FORCE EXPERIENCES

Social scientists have shown considerable interest in women's structurally disadvantaged position in the labor force. Their emphasis on women's paid work is easily explained. Work is a central dimension of individual lives and of the societal structure. ("During the adult years work is rivaled only by sleep as a routine activity" [Hall, 1969:3].) As we shall see, the labor force participation of women is increasing. Therefore, a description of gender relations that omitted work would be quite unthinkable. Also, economic factors are primary for social scientists with a Marxist perspective. Finally, many of the academics studying gender relations are themselves women, and have a personal stake in an enhanced understanding of women's occupational experiences. It seems that understanding the group itself is high on the agenda of a disadvantaged group equipped with research skills.

The interest of social scientists in women's disadvantaged status in the labor force is much easier to explain than are the mechanisms that produce this state of affairs. In Almquist's (1977) view, this lack of explanatory power is attributable to the way research has been conducted. She says, "Most current research is macrosociological rather than microsociological, based on large-scale, impersonal, aggregated, and static data rather than small-scale, personal, disaggregated, and dynamic findings. From this we get a very firm appraisal of women's overall position in the labor force, but we do not know the processes by which they attained it" (pp. 853-54).

Labor Force Participation

The examination of changing labor force participation rates over time leads to some compelling observations regarding sex differences. According to Statistics Canada (1974:113), the "most marked changes in Canada in this century have been the drop in male participation (over 14 percentage points since 1911) and the rise in female participation." Female participation has risen from 16.1% in 1901 (Statistics Canada, 1974:113), to 48.9% in 1979. (The male participation rate in the latter year was 78.4%.) To put the matter another way, women represented 39.3% of the total Canadian labor force in 1979 (Women's Bureau, Labour Canada, 1980:Table 16). Experts such as those consulted by the *Royal Commission on the Status of Women in Canada* (1970) failed to predict the size of the increase in the participation rate of women, particularly certain age categories of women (Lupri and Mills, 1979:2). Growth has been greatest for middle-aged women, although the youngest and oldest female age groups have also increased (Gunderson, 1976:96). According to Lupri's and Mills's (1982:2-3) overview of Canadian women at work,

> . . . the single most dramatic and pervasive trend in the status of Canadian women since World War II has been the increase in the proportion of married women who work for pay. The five-fold increase in the proportion of married women entering the labour force has been increasing almost twice as fast as that for all women. But most important, the largest increase in labour force activity has occurred for the group generally viewed as least likely to work—mothers of preschool-age children.

In 1979, the female labor force consisted of 30% single women, 60% married women and 10% "other" (widowed, separated, divorced) women (Women's Bureau, Labour Canada, 1980:Table 56).

How are these participation rates to be explained? So far as male-female differences are concerned, women in general are less likely to participate than men. Married women continue to bear major responsibility for the family and for the work at home, whether or not they also work outside the home (Gunderson, 1976:95). This factor can be demonstrated statistically. If we look at single people aged twenty to sixty-four, 80.0% of the females and 83.3% of the males were in the labor force in 1979. However, among the married in the same age category, 93.4% of the males versus 51.3% of the females were in the labor force in the same year (Women's Bureau, Labour Canada, 1980:Table 25). Sex differences in part-time work also suggest the priority of women's home responsibilities. In 1979, 23.2% of the women compared with 5.8% of the men were engaged in part-time work (Women's Bureau, Labour Canada, 1980:Table 15). Although marriage and children still reduce women's labor force participation, they are weaker deterrents now than in the past. Last, the drop in male labor force participation since the turn of the century can be attributed to earlier retirement and to the longer period spent in school (Statistics Canada, 1974:113).

What factors account for women's increased labor force participation? Four reasons are particularly important:

1. The service sector has become more important in the Canadian economy than manufacturing and primary industries. The service sector is more labor-intensive and traditionally draws female participation (Statistics Canada, 1980:85). (The matter of industrial sectors will be discussed further in the next section.)
2. The increasing education of women enhances their labor force activity. Highly educated women have a higher earning capacity, which motivates them to seek work outside the home (Gunderson, 1976:99).
3. Although the presence of children is a weaker barrier to women's labor force participation today than in the past (Bruce, 1978), the decline in family size is a factor in women's increased labor force participation (Statistics Canada, 1980:85).
4. More and more married women are being "economically compelled" to enter the labor force. Connelly (1977:25) argues that "as the standard of living in Canada rises, married women whose husbands earn low incomes must work outside the home to maintain their relative standard of living." Double-digit inflation over the past few years has forced many women into the labor force.

Although these reasons partially explain why women are entering paid work "at a prodigious rate," the forces that create increased participation in the labor force have probably not been fully uncovered

(Almquist, 1977). Nor does the greater number of employed women signal equality of status.

Sex Segregation of Work

The dramatic growth in women's labor force participation, as well as the publicity given to female pioneers in nontraditional occupations such as construction work (see Braid, 1979), conveys the impression that significant improvements are occurring in women's work situation. In actual fact, the pace of change for women is "glacial" (Almquist, 1977). An analysis of census data carried out by the Canadian sociologists, Armstrong and Armstrong (1975; 1978), showed that although the female participation rate in the Canadian labor force rose sharply between 1941 and 1971, corresponding changes did not occur in the nature of women's work. "[Women] are still overwhelmingly slotted into specific industries and occupations characterized by low pay, low skill requirements, low productivity, and low prospects for advancement. There is women's work and there is men's work. And women continue to be disproportionately segregated into many of the least attractive jobs" (Armstrong and Armstrong, 1978:16).

Industrial segregation refers to the fact that employed women are concentrated more in some industries than in others (Armstrong and Armstrong, 1978:23). Women are particularly likely to be found in the following divisions of industry: trade (36.7% female); finance, insurance and real estate (51.5% female); community, business and personal services (57.6% female); public administration and defense (25.5% female) (Armstrong and Armstrong, 1978:Table 3). (The figures given are for 1971.) In 1979, 77% of the female labor force was engaged in these four industrial sectors (Women's Bureau, Labour Canada, 1980:Table 27b). The important point to note here is that the industries where females are concentrated are in the low productivity, low-wage sectors (Armstrong and Armstrong, 1978:27).

Occupational segregation by sex also occurs. That is, women tend to work in a relatively few traditionally "female" jobs and to dominate (outnumber men) in these occupations (Armstrong and Armstrong, 1975:373).

Table 7.1 shows that while women are concentrated in some occupations (clerical, medicine and health, teaching, service, social sciences), they are almost entirely absent from others (construction, religion, fishing, hunting, trapping, forestry and logging, mining and quarrying). Two-thirds of the women working are employed in clerical, health, teaching and service occupations. According to Armstrong and Armstrong (1975), the segregation of women in these relatively few,

TABLE 7.1
Sex Segregation in Canadian Occupations in 1979

Occupation	Women/Total % Employed in Occupation	Percentage Women	Distribution Men
Clerical	77.1	34.0	6.4
Medicine and health	76.4	8.7	1.7
Teaching	56.3	6.1	3.0
Service	53.9	17.9	9.7
Social sciences	49.7	1.8	1.2
Sales	39.9	10.7	10.3
Artistic and recreational	34.7	1.2	1.5
Managerial and administrative	25.4	5.0	9.3
Product fabricating, assembling and repairing	23.5	5.6	11.6
Agriculture	22.4	2.9	6.3
Materials handling	18.9	1.2	3.3
Processing	18.1	1.8	5.1
Other crafts and equipment operating	16.9	0.6	1.8
Natural sciences, engineering and mathematics	12.1	1.1	5.1
Machining	5.7	0.4	4.2
Transport equipment operating	5.3	0.6	6.4
Construction trades	1.4	0.2	10.3
Religion	*	*	0.4
Fishing, hunting, trapping	*	*	0.4
Forestry and logging	*	*	0.9
Mining and quarrying	*	*	0.9
All occupational categories	38.8	100.0	100.0

SOURCE: Adapted from Women's Bureau, Labour Canada, 1980:Table 9b.

* Figures too small to be reliable.

mostly low-skilled, poorly paid jobs, has remained stable since 1941. Although considerable publicity is given to female physicians, lawyers, university professors and pharmacists, each of these professions involves a tenth of one percent (or less) of all female workers (Armstrong and Armstrong, 1978:37).

International comparisons suggest that occupational and industrial segregation are universal phenomena among developed countries (Gunderson, 1976). However, patterns do differ from country to country. In the U.S.S.R., for example, three-quarters of the physicians and one-third of the lawyers are women. However, in that country, the presence of women deflates the status of these occupations, which are highly prestigious in North America.

Income

The money that women derive from their work represents a key indicator of progress toward equality. The facts are unequivocal: employed women earn considerably less money than their male counterparts. From a national survey, Goyder (1981) found that Canadian women earn less than half the average income of Canadian men. The earnings gap is greatest for "those with weak attachment to the labour force"—married, middle-aged, poorly educated and part-time female workers. Younger, single, educated females fare better. Women's family responsibilities negatively affect their earnings. For example, child rearing results in shorter, more intermittent periods in the labor force than is the case for men. Indeed, marriage is associated with increased earnings for males but not for females (Gunderson, 1976:119, 128). In fact, if we analyze sex differences in income by marital status, we find that married women earn about 40% of married men, but that single women earn about 80% of single men, and women in other categories earn about 60% of men in these same categories (Block and Walker, 1982).

Explaining sex differences in income represents a complicated statistical problem. Goyder (1981) concluded that sex differences in educational and occupational status are of little importance in explaining income inequality. However, when differences between the sexes in part-time versus full-time work and in career interruptions are adjusted for, female income reaches 67% of the male average. Most of the remaining margin of inequality reflects discrimination. However, "equal pay for equal work" legislation may not be the answer to discrimination because it may reinforce segregation rather than equalize pay. "Rather than raise women's wages to match those of their male counterparts, employers may simply hire women only and pay them all the same low rate" (Armstrong and Armstrong, 1978:40).

Additional Characteristics of Women's Work

Several other generalizations may be made about women's employment. First, it tends to be *unstable*. Female unemployment is becoming an increasingly serious problem in Canada (Marsden, 1977). In 1979, the unemployed labor force was made up of 8.8% women and 6.6% men. The female rate of unemployment in that year was higher in every province in Canada (Women's Bureau, Labour Canada, 1980:29, 35). According to Gunderson (1976:127), women have higher unemployment rates than men "in almost every occupation and industry, but women tend not to be clustered in high-unemployment industries or occupations." Although job loss and layoffs usually affect women first, the main factor explaining women's higher unemployment is that women move *out* of the labor force more often than men (Tangri, 1978). Here, noneconomic reasons (e.g., marriage, child rearing) appear to be more important than economic reasons (e.g., uninteresting, dead-end jobs).

In many ways, women's work in the labor force *parallels their work in the home* (Armstrong and Armstrong, 1978:46). In both contexts, they nurture and support others, cook and serve food, take care of the sick, sew clothes, clean rooms, wash hair.

Women's work typically *offers few opportunities for advancement*. The Canadian woman "frequently ends her working life where it began —doing the more menial, repetitious, and least prestigious jobs for others" (Armstrong and Armstrong, 1975:50). Put somewhat differently, men tend to have careers while women do not (Rosenfeld, 1979).

It almost goes without saying that women are much less likely than men to occupy *authority positions* in work organizations. Table 7.1 shows that only 5% of employed women are in managerial and administrative positions. Even fewer of these women are in high-level management. In addition, men are overrepresented in the higher-level positions of even traditionally female professions, such as teaching, librarianship and social work. In other words, women are much less likely than men to be in positions of authority, even when they do have equivalent educational qualifications. Research suggests that although women's lack of qualifications is an explanatory factor, even more important are discriminatory employer policies based on the assumption that women are unfit to supervise others (Wolf and Fligstein, 1979). Finally, evidence exists that the few women in management are structurally disadvantaged. For instance, Kanter (1977) hypothesized that the work performance and social integration of token persons are negatively affected *because* they are a highly visible, self-conscious minority. (A study by Spangler, Gordon and Pipkin [1978] of women law students supported Kanter's hypothesis.)

Finally, an increasing number of women are becoming *unionized*. Today almost 30% of Canadian union members are women, compared with 16% in 1962 (Briskin and Yanz, 1981). However, only 27% of Canadian female workers are unionized, compared with 43% of Canadian male workers (Baker and Robeson, 1981). Although the union movement is becoming a central arena for feminist activities, it was slow to afford help to working women's concerns (Baker and Robeson, 1981; Marchak, 1973). The main reason was the nature of women's work. White-collar workers and part-time workers are difficult for unions to organize (Marchak, 1973). In addition, union leaders tend to be blue-collar men, and blue-collar men tend to accept the traditional ideology that women's place is in the home. It was seen as advantageous to keep cheap female labor out of the marketplace. As well, women's double burden of home and work responsibilities sometimes discourages extensive union participation.

A Structural Explanation of Women's Work

To begin with, a *structural* explanation of sex differences in work experiences focuses on labor market characteristics, not individual attitudes or motives. Such an explanation stresses the fact that women are segregated into particular sectors of the industrial structure and into low-skill, low-paying jobs within these sectors (Armstrong and Armstrong, 1978). The demand for women's labor exists not in the goods-producing, "primary" sectors, characterized by high wages, employment stability and chances for advancement, but in "secondary" sectors, characterized by low wages, high labor turnover and little chance for promotion. Primary sector employers may screen out workers with a reputation for intermittent employment, such as women and members of certain ethnic groups. In addition, secondary sector employees may behave just the way management expects them to behave. If job commitment and continuity of employment are not rewarded, their employment may be discontinuous (Rosenfeld, 1979), thus creating a self-fulfilling prophecy. The critical factor here is the opportunity structure of the work organization, not the sex of the worker: "If women sometimes have lower aspirations, lesser involvement with work, and greater concern with peer group relations—so do men in positions of limited or blocked mobility" (Kanter, 1976:416).

The Marxian concept of a "reserve army of labor" augments the above analysis (Connelly, 1978). This concept focuses on factors that influence women's entry into the labor market (and reasons for their higher unemployment rate). Capitalism needs women's work in the home—consumption, childbearing and child rearing. However, capitalism also requires a flexible labor supply, which can be drawn into the labor force when needed and sent home when the need is past. The large pool of women competing for low-skill jobs gives women little bargaining power. In Rosenfeld's (1979) view, women are manipulated by being treated as wives and mothers when they are employed. They are assumed to be supplementary breadwinners and are paid low wages, despite the fact that an increasing number of women are primary earners in their families.

How do sociologists account for the fact that many women are not committed to their jobs, that their employment is discontinuous, that their absenteeism is higher than men's and that they fail to advance occupationally? One answer emphasizes the family. Another answer emphasizes work. The truth probably involves both institutions.

The "familial constraint" position argues that "the woman has the cultural mandate to give priority to the family" so that "even when working she is expected to be committed to her family first, her work second" (Coser and Rokoff, 1971:538). In early adulthood, locating and marrying a suitable man takes precedence over investing time and money in extensive job training. Looking ahead, the young woman's decision is not between family and work, but between family and *demanding* work. After marriage, her husband and *his* work are what counts. If his job requires geographic mobility, she gives up her job and goes with him. Whether she works outside the home or not, children and housework remain her responsibility (Meissner et al., 1975). Her work is disrupted by pregnancy, child rearing and family emergencies. But these disruptions really don't matter because her low-status work doesn't matter. In our society, the family is "a 'greedy institution' which demands total allegiance of women" (Coser and Rokoff, 1971:542). According to the traditional rules, "men are to get occupational status and women are to get men who will get such status" (p. 551).

This account sounds plausible enough. However, the pattern looks somewhat different when consideration is given to the work actually available for most women to do. Let us return to the adolescent on the brink of courtship. Laws (1976) challenges what she calls "the teleological shibboleth," which "holds that young women do not plan for their occupational future but rather, like the devout Navaho weaver, leave the design of their identity unfinished until knitted together by their future life partner" (p. 38). She asks, "[If] your options are lackluster, and none of them has irresistible incentives associated with it, why would you be excited about your occupational future?" (p. 38). As we have seen, other analysts attribute women's work performance to the work available for women to do: ". . . absenteeism, lack of job continuity, and low commitment are characteristic of all workers, male or female, who perform low-skilled, low-paid jobs which involve little control or responsibility" (Armstrong and Armstrong, 1978:146).

In short, in order to appreciate properly the work behavior of women (and men), the work and family spheres of life must be studied in *interaction*. Epstein's (1974b:16-17) point is well taken: "There is probably far more compatibility and structure to the performance of women in the institutions of the family and work than appears on the surface. Each institution supports the other. The demands by the family on the woman keep her out of real competition in the occupations; reciprocally, the lack of positive reinforcement she faces in the occupations sends her back to the home to seek rewards there."

WOMEN'S WORK IN THE HOME

If life is to proceed smoothly, someone has to prowl supermarket aisles in search of fresh broccoli, someone has to cook dinner, someone has to scrub toilet bowls, someone has to wipe children's runny noses. That someone is usually the wife. Regardless of individual variation in talent and inclination, society consigns "a large segment of the population to the role of homemaker solely on the basis of sex" (Bem and Bem, 1971:88). As mentioned earlier, outside work does not let women "off the hook": they carry two jobs. According to the Vancouver study of Meissner et al. (1975), when a childless wife goes out to work, the husband contributes an extra six minutes of housework each week. In couples with young children, the husband of an employed wife contributes, on the average, an hour more of housework a week.

Women receive neither pay nor status for doing housework on behalf of their families. Perhaps the greatest difference between women's work and men's work is that "men are paid for most of the work they perform, whereas women are not paid at all for most of the work they do" (Eichler, 1978:53). Unremunerated activity is denigrated in our materialistic society. Glazer-Malbin (1976:906) isolates the "axioms" that explain the second-class status of women's work in the home: (a) women belong in the family, while men belong at work; (b) therefore men work, while women do not work; (c) therefore housework is not a form of work; (d) monetary and social rights belong to those who work—to those who are economically productive; (e) women do not work but are parasitic; (f) therefore women are not entitled to the same social and economic rights as men.

Despite the fact that more than half of married Canadian women are full-time housewives and the rest devote some portion of their time to housework, until recently sociologists did not conceptualize housework as *work*. It is likely that male sociologists simply failed to notice, never mind to take seriously, this female activity. Eichler (1978:53) says that "it is one of the great achievements of the feminist movement that unpaid labour has been at least partially recognized for what it is, namely labour." We now have Canadian (Kome, 1982; Proulx, 1978), American (Berk, 1980; Lopata, 1971) and British (Gavron, 1966; Oakley, 1974) books available on the subject.

Sex Segregation of Home Labor

Many scholars believe that the same structural factors that explain the sex segregation of the labor market explain the segregation of domestic labor. Responsibility is attributed to a capitalistic, patriarchal system. The main question is, why does the economic system encourage women to be full-time (or at least part-time) housewives? Structural answers often draw upon Engels's analysis of the inequality of the sexes, *The Origins of the Family, Private Property and the State* (1942). The underlying assumption is that "capitalism is an economic system organized for the maximization of profit by those who control capital" (Glazer, 1977a:112). Three major arguments may be distilled:

1. The economic system relies on the existence of women as a "reserve army of labor." The cultural prescription that women belong in the home assures that women will return to the home when the labor force does not need them.

2. Women's primary allegiance to the family is used as an excuse for deploying them in menial, underpaid jobs. A large pool of unqualified women in competition for jobs depresses wages. Women are untrained, unreliable workers *because* their families come first. They require less money than men because they are secondary workers anyway. Or so the argument goes.

3. Women's unpaid labor directly and indirectly subsidizes men's paid labor (Eichler, 1978). Women keep house, provide meals, look after children, entertain husbands' business acquaintances, type, help with husbands' small businesses and farms, all without compensation. All of these services cost money when someone outside the family performs them. This sort of work allows husbands to devote their efforts to full-time paid work. Rowbotham (1973:67) says, "If it were admitted that the family is maintained at the expense of women, capitalism would have to devise some other way of getting the work done."

Although the topic of *solutions* is reserved for the last chapter, a few words are appropriate here. A structural analysis implies that some extremely radical changes would be required in order to equalize women's status with men's. If capitalism is the "villain," albeit an impersonal villain, then capitalism must "disappear." The implications of that statement are mind-boggling. The beneficiaries of an economic system do not simply fade away. In addition, the distinction between domestic and public domains of activity and the conviction that the domestic orientation of woman is *the* "critical factor in understanding her social position" (Rosaldo, 1974:24) call for profound changes in how housework is either presently remunerated or done. Proposals that housewives receive wages (e.g., by legislation ensuring that members of the household in the labor force share with those who do the domestic work) constitute the less radical route. (See Cook and Eberts, 1976.) Engels (1942:158) originally put the more radical proposal this way: ". . . the emancipation of women and their equality with men are impossible and must remain so as long as women are excluded from socially productive work and restricted to housework, which is private." Giving women greater familiarity with the public domain and men with the domestic domain would require significant alterations in traditional family structure.

The Prestige of "Occupation Housewife"

So far, two generalizations have been made concerning the status of housewives. First, in a society based on commodity production, household work is not considered "real work." Thus, the "non-recognition of women's labour in the home leaves them with no sense of value as a group at all" (Rowbotham, 1973:69). Second, full-time housewives are "personal dependents," to use Eichler's (1977c) term, and derive their status from their husbands.

Eichler (1977b) set out to answer questions such as these. Is the prestige of "occupation housewife" measurable? If so, how is the prestige of housewives affected by their husbands' occupation? How is the status of the family affected by the presence of a full-time housewife? How does housewives' prestige compare with that of other occupations? What role does sex play in this prestige assignment?

Respondents from the Waterloo-Kitchener area were asked to rank 93 occupational titles, including housewife and housekeeper, according to their own personal evaluation of the standing of each occupation.[3] Each title was ranked from 1 to 9, with 1 indicating the lowest social standing. The sample was randomly divided into three groups. One group evaluated occupational titles, with sex unspecified. The other two groups responded to occupational titles, with either "male" or "female" specified. Each occupational title was represented an equal number of times with male and female incumbents. For example, Group 1 evaluated accountant, typist, etc. Group 2 evaluated male accountant, female typist, etc., while Group 3 evaluated female accountant, male typist, etc.

Eichler reports that on the neutral scale, housewife ranked 52 among 93 occupations, where physician was highest (93) and newspaper peddler lowest (1). When the housewife was specified as "female," it ranked 52 out of 88 occupations. (Five occupations without female incumbents had been omitted.) When the housewife was specified as "male," it dropped to the eighth lowest rank.

Interestingly enough, the prestige of housewife was equivalent to the prestige of secretary/stenographer, the occupation that accounts for the highest percentage of employed women. With the exception of graduate nurses and elementary-school teachers, the other nine occupations involving the greatest absolute numbers of women were either equivalent to housewife in prestige (bookkeepers) or below them (waitresses, tellers, sales clerks). Thus, "the majority of women who choose a paid occupation over being a housewife cannot expect an increase in their occupational prestige and may, indeed, experience a loss in prestige when they enter the labour market after having been a housewife" (Eichler, 1977b:158). Housewife outranks housekeeper (on the female scale, 52 versus 45), perhaps because wives have more autonomy than employees. Finally, women ranked housewives lower on the neutral and female scales than did men, while men ranked male housewife lower than did women.

If previous researchers had been right in their assumption that housewives' status is completely derived from their husbands', wives' and husbands' scores should be identical. Eichler asked respondents to assess the prestige of housewives whose husbands were identified as physicians, social workers, plumbers, commercial farmers or elevator operators. The resulting prestige scores ranged from 81.5 (husband physician) to 37.1 (husband elevator operator). Apparently "there is some truth to the adage that a woman need not become a doctor, she can marry one" (Eichler, 1977b:163). However, when the prestige of the housewife married to each of the five occupational incumbents was compared with the prestige of the male incumbent (e.g., housewife of physician [81.5] with physician [92.7], housewife of elevator operator [37.1] with elevator operator [25.4]), the results showed that the housewife occupation possessed some independent status that interacted with the derived status. A high-prestige husband pulls up the housewife's status, but a low-prestige husband lowers her status, though not to his level.

In general, we may conclude from Eichler's results that housewifery can be treated as an occupation, despite the fact that it is unpaid, has no fixed working hours or accepted work procedures and is performed in isolation. Housewives are not entirely devoid of prestige. Their independent status interacts with their status derived from their husbands' occupation.

ROLE STRAIN OF WOMEN'S WORK

A substantial but confusing literature deals with the social-psychological effects of the structural constraints produced by women's work inside and outside the home. There are two senses in which this literature is confusing. First, it is *theoretically* confusing in that various categories of "feminine" role strain are discussed in isolation from the more general role theory that has developed in social psychology. Theoretical power to explain is thereby reduced. So far, the constraints experienced by both sexes have not been integrated within one conceptual framework. There is a series of scattered, imprecisely defined types of role dilemmas, whose interconnections remain unspecified. Though some eleven types (and a number of subtypes) can be conceptually isolated (see Mackie, 1976), a definition of *role strain*, the most general term, will satisfy our purposes. *Role strain* refers to the "*felt* difficulty in fulfilling role obligations [emphasis added]" (Goode, 1960). "*Felt*" has been italicized because, in order for a situation to be diagnosed as role strain, the women involved must subjectively experience a problem, must feel some anxiety or unhappiness (which emanates from the social structure).

A second reason for labelling this area "confusing" is that studies reach opposite conclusions about the extent to which modern women experience role strain. Some scholars claim that it is ubiquitous, part of the very definition of being female. Others report minimal problems. These contradictory findings are partially explained by variation in samples and concept measurement, and by the theoretical difficulties mentioned above. Although we cannot claim to resolve all these problems in the short space available, our strategy is to summarize briefly some of the contradictory ideas and findings for working women and full-time housewives respectively, and to discuss some Western Canadian data bearing this question.

Married Working Women

Over the years, a number of scholars have argued that married women attempting to combine work and family are bound to experience role strain. Epstein (1971:88) remarked that the problem of the many roles of modern women "has become a cliché even in the popular press." Gagnon (1975:12) says, "The model of the perfect woman is now one who is able to reconcile an active life outside the home with her traditional role as 'queen of the house.' . . . This is a model which the great majority of female workers who are not superwomen find absolutely impossible to attain." Turner (1970) discusses the "hazards of the combination" and draws an analogy between the married woman worker and the "marginal man." (An example of the latter is an immigrant to Canada who is caught between old and new countries and feels at home in neither.) According to Turner, she is suspended between two worlds, "in neither of which [she] can participate unreservedly enough to gain a genuine sense of self-respect" (p. 307). More particularly, Wilensky (1968) speaks of the "conflict between working wives' desire to work and their feeling it is wrong or harmful." Boyd's (1975a) Canadian poll results support Wilensky's observation. According to her, 59% of a national sample believe that labor force participation of married women has a harmful effect on family life. Four-fifths feel that women with young children should not work. Therefore, working mothers may very well experience guilt over adverse effects on their children, despite the contrary social-scientific findings (Etaugh, 1974).

A related problem attributed to working women is *role overload*—the constraint of coping with inordinate demands on one's time and energy, which are brought about by occupying several statuses. Indeed, all the time-budget evidence points to the fact that married women in the labor force are overworked, compared with their husbands and with full-time housewives (Meissner et al., 1975). It has been suggested (Coser and Rokoff, 1971) that the conflict (potential or actual) between job demands and family responsibilities is a major reason why women turn to unchallenging work and part-time employment, and show interrupted career patterns and low commitment to professional jobs.

Recently a contrary position has been expressed. Laws (1976) dismisses the "shibboleth of role conflict," the notion that role conflict "is inevitable for the woman who departs from her true vocation by seeking employment," especially a career. She is equally impatient with the "fallacy of monism"—the idea that "it is inconceivable that women could handle two sets of involvements" (p. 35). On a more general theoretical level, Sieber (1974) argues that sociologists have stressed role *obligations* and ignored the *rights and privileges* associated with roles. Moreover, he attacks the assumption that multiple roles are a source of role strain. Rather, he argues that the benefits accruing from multiple roles exceed the burdens. For example, a wide repertoire of roles may enrich the personality, enhance the self-concept and provide a buffer against failure. (Folk wisdom recommends not placing all one's eggs in the same basket.) Finally, few working women may encounter strain because few disobey the "cultural mandate" by insisting on high-level commitment to work. For example, Poloma (1972) reported that her sample of female physicians, lawyers and academics were not plagued by unmanaged role strain because their domestic lives took precedence over their professional lives.

Full-Time Housewives

Ambivalence also characterizes discussions of housewives' psychological reactions to their status. Friedan (1963) pioneered the negative position by publicizing the "problem that has no name." Women socialized to "desire no greater destiny than to glory in their own femininity, afraid to ask themselves 'Is this all?' " (p. 13), were saying "I feel empty somehow . . . incomplete" or "I feel as if I don't exist" (p. 18). (At least, that's what Friedan said they were saying.) Bernard (1974b) describes the "housewife as victim" and the circumstances attending her work as "pathogenic." Oakley (1974) found 70% of her British sample to be dissatisfied with *housework* (its monotony and loneliness). However, they were not necessarily dissatisfied with the *role of housewife*. Lopata (1971) also reported that some women were quite content with the whole role complex, which includes wife and mother. A number of authorities disagree. Their reasons include societal devaluation of the role, the fact that it is unpaid and consequent damage to the incumbents' self-esteem. Rowbotham (1973) expresses the difficulty women have in separating the self from their work, when she claims that housework "sucks you into itself as a person rather than a 'worker'" (p. 71) and "its space is the whole space of a woman's life" (p. 70). Although social class appears to affect housewives' reactions to their work, the situation is far from clear. For example, some authorities expect working-class women to find housework creative and autonomous in comparison with the outside jobs available to them (Glazer-Malbin, 1976). However, Ferree (1976) reported that working-class women did *not* prefer housework to paid work. Berheide, Berk and Berk (1976) found an upper-middle-class American sample to be neutral toward all household tasks except child care. Ninety percent were quite content with their lot. But Oakley (1974) reported no difference in level of dissatisfaction between her working-class and middle-class English respondents.

Calgary Study of Role Constraints

A study by the author (1976) provides Canadian data on married women's attitudes toward their role as housewife and (in the case of women in the labor force) their attitudes toward the combined housewife/paid worker roles. (This questionnaire-interview study of Calgary women has been referred to at several other points in this book.)

A number of questions sought to discover whether working women were operating under role strain. Eighty-two percent agreed with the statement, "I am working and I'm glad," and 12% chose the alternative statement, "I am working but I wish I weren't." (The remaining 6% did not respond.) Only 9% agreed with the statement, "All in all, I would say that the *burdens* of being a working wife outweigh the *rewards*. For me, it is not a satisfying way of life."[4] Clearly, most of these women like working. But do they experience conflict between the demands of work and domestic roles? Seventy-nine percent disagreed with the statement, "My job and family make conflicting demands on me so that I feel pulled in two directions." Many concurred with Sieber (1974) that occupancy of multiple roles is rewarding. The perceived benefits included enhanced self-esteem, protection from social isolation and satisfaction in contributing financially to the family. What about possible strain over parental obligations? While 21% of the working wives said they worry that they are not good mothers, 25% of the full-time housewives responded to this item in the same fashion. Do they experience conflict between work and husband's preferences? Only 4% agreed with the statement, "It's hard being a working wife because my husband objects to my working." Eighty-six percent felt that their work made them more interesting companions. We know that working women put in an inordinate number of work hours. Do they realize how hard they work? Do they resent it? In short, do they suffer from work overload? The answer to all three questions is yes. Fifty-three percent of the working wives (versus 35% of the housewives) agreed with the item, "A lot of the time I feel so tired." A substantial proportion of these women do resent the overload—43%

agreed that "It makes me mad to see my husband relax while I do housework." Indeed, working wives' role overload was the only serious type of role constraint isolated by the Calgary study.

This conclusion is corroborated by three other pieces of research. Lashuk's and Kurian's (1977) study of Calgary women reported that working wives and mothers did *not* exhibit more evidence of role conflict and stress than did full-time housewives. The examination of British Columbia suicide rates in 1961 and 1971 by Cumming, Lazer and Chisholm (1975) failed to support the role conflict hypothesis. According to these statistics, work protects women from suicide more than marriage does. Finally, a national American study (Campbell, Converse and Rodgers, 1976) measured people's happiness or general satisfaction with life. Although one would expect employed wives, laboring under the burden of two roles, to express more dissatisfaction with life than housewives, this did not prove to be the case. The author (1978b) reports identical findings on statements of own happiness by Western Canadian working wives versus housewives.

The full-time housewives also seemed relatively satisfied with their role. Seventy-five percent agreed with the statement, "I am not working and I'm glad I'm not." Seventy-three percent agreed that all in all, "running a household is more rewarding than an outside job." Eighty-one percent enjoy most of the work involved, while only 9% felt that "housework isn't a proper activity for an intelligent person." Ninety-two percent agree that it is important that the work they do is for people who care about them. Only 10% showed an interest in receiving monetary pay for being a housewife. On the negative side, 45% believed that housewives do not receive the respect that women who work outside the home do. Although 20% to 25% are lonely and bored most of the time, the majority enjoy the advantages of their unstructured time. Social class was not correlated with attitudes toward housewifery.

If we describe women who are engaged in major roles against their own inclinations as "conflicted," then 20% of the Calgary sample housewives are "conflicted housewives" and 12% of the women in the labor force are "conflicted workers." This is an unhappy situation to be caught in: "If women who wish to work, whether it is socially customary or because of their own career commitment, are held back from it, the evidence is that the results are likely to be damaging to their families as well as themselves. The reverse also holds; damage is likely to result if mothers who see (and may objectively have) good reasons for not working are nevertheless forced into work" (Fogarty, Rapoport and Rapoport, 1971:142).

However, the important conclusion is that most of these Western Canadian women are *not* suffering from role strain. Although some Marxists might see these women as deluded and label their contentment "false consciousness," it seems more respectful to take their sentiments at face value.

SEX DIFFERENCES IN FAMILIAL EXPERIENCES

Since 86% of the Canadian population are involved in families and since families are pivotal to the operation of gender relations, it is not surprising that that institution has already come up for discussion several times. (Chapter Five considered the family as the major agent of gender socialization, and the family figured prominently in this chapter's analysis of sex differences in labor market experiences.) Our concern here is to trace how the family, as social structure, impinges differently upon women and men.

Liberationists of both sexes complain about the family. Marlene Dixon (1971:170) claimed that the "institution of marriage is the chief vehicle for the perpetuation of the oppression of women; it is through the role of wife that the subjugation of women is maintained." The Royal Commission on the Status of Women in Canada (1970) offered twenty-eight recommendations in the area of the family. Men are also criticizing the family for the constraints it places upon them to be "iron men," to live up to the "success ethic," to take total financial responsibility for the family, to make all the decisions. Says Farrell (1974:130),

> Male polygamy—a man married to his job and wife (but barely to the latter)—causes many men who believe their devotion to the job will bring them love to find it has instead alienated them from those they love. This situation embitters many men, since they have invested their lives and status in something they expected would bring appreciation. Instead, they are ridiculed and resented by their children; and they find their marriage unsatisfying now that they have the money to make it work.

Roald Dahl's short story, "Mrs. Bixby and the Colonel's Coat" (1962), expresses a cynical view of marriage and the "success ethic":

> America is the land of opportunities for women. Already they own about eighty-five per cent of the wealth of the nation: Soon they will have it all. Divorce has become a lucrative process, simple to arrange and easy to forget; and ambitious females can repeat it as often as they please and parlay their winnings to astronomical figures. The husband's death also brings satisfactory rewards and some ladies prefer to rely upon this method. They know that the waiting period will not be unduly protracted, for overwork and hypertension are bound to get the poor devil before long, and he will die at his desk with a bottle of benzedrines in one hand and a packet of tranquillizers in the other.

Historical Changes in the Family

Urbanization and industrialization have deeply affected the family. A century ago, a woman participated in her family's production of goods. Her adult life was spent bearing six or seven children and working to maintain her large household (Royal Commission on the Status of Women, 1970:226-27). The doctrine of *legal unity* expressed women's subjugation under the law (McCaughan, 1977:2-3). In 1803 Blackstone described this doctrine: "By marriage, the husband and wife are one person in law; that is, the very being or legal existence of the woman is suspended during the marriage, or at least is incorporated and consolidated into that of the husband; under whose wing, protection, and cover, she performs everything [emphasis deleted]" (McCaughan, 1977:2). Indeed, anthropologists (Gough, 1971) tell us that throughout time, men have generally had higher status and authority over the women in their family. Contrary to popular belief, no truly matriarchal society has ever existed.

Nowadays marriage remains popular. Women are as likely to marry as they were in earlier times (Boyd, Eichler and Hofley, 1976:18). (Ninety percent of family heads in Canada are married and living together [Statistics Canada, 1980:Table 2.10].) However, the modern family is different. Industrialization has moved the father-provider from an agricultural to an industrial-business setting. For women, however, although the new technology has expanded job opportunities, their increased labor force participation does not provide them with an economically and socially rewarding, viable alternative to marriage (Gee, 1980). Rather, the occupational role supplements the familial role. "Indeed, one of the social changes occurring in the twentieth century has been the normative and legal acceptance of joint roles for women. In the past, the two roles were sharply segmented, i.e., a woman was either a wife-mother or a working woman" (Gee, 1980:462). Medical advances have brought contraceptive knowledge. (The average family now has 1.5 children [Statistics Canada, 1980:Table 2.1].) Although technology has changed the nature of housework, housewives spend as much time as ever doing it (Boyd, Eichler and Hofley, 1976:14). Now the mother tends to carry the sole responsibility for the children, rather than sharing it with the extended family (The Royal Commission on the Status of Women, 1970:237). With the advent of compulsory education and child labor laws, children have become more dependent on the family (Boyd, Eichler and Hofley, 1976:13). The legal status of women has improved since the time when they and their children were under the husbands' legal control. Whether traditional attitudes have changed to the same degree is quite another matter. "Society still expects a wife much more than a husband to adapt to the married status" (The Royal Commission on the Status of Women, 1970:228).

Although most Canadians still live in a nuclear family, variations in family structure are increasing. There is a growing number of one-parent families (10% of Canadian families fall into this category), and "living together" and common-law relationships are becoming more common. Family sociologist, Nett (1976:74-75), predicts how the changing family structure will affect the lifetime patterns of domesticity:

> Increased numbers of Canadians will be born into a nuclear family, live in a one-parent family after the divorce or death of a parent, re-enter a stepparental nuclear family, reside in a non-family household alone or with a nonrelative, marry into a first family of procreation, become a head of a one-parent family or live singly after divorce, remarry into a second family of procreation, head a one-person household after the death of the spouse, and end their lives in a "home" for the elderly.

Women's Family and Men's Family

Feminists have argued that marriage and the family have a differential impact on men and women and, further, that the family as presently constituted is the basic source of women's troubles. What evidence supports the allegation that, to paraphrase Bernard (1971), each family unit actually contains two families—his and hers?

His and Her Priorities

Females are expected to give priority to the family over alternative endeavors. To begin with, it is assumed that females will marry. In our society marriage is the sign of success for a woman, while occupational achievement is the sign of success for a man. The fact that women marry earlier than men indicates this sex difference in priorities. In 1975, the average age of Canadian brides and grooms at first marriages was 22.5 and 24.9 years respectively (Kalbach and McVey, 1979:314). Although changes are slowly occurring, the "failure to marry or failure in marriage is total failure for many women, while for men it is only a partial failure" (Glazer, 1977b:228). Witness the different connotations of "bachelor" and "spinster." "Bachelor" has a jolly, carefree air, while "spinster" "conjures up the vision . . . of a stringy old hen with a puckered mouth" (Dahl, 1962:138).

Two Australian researchers, Stolk and Brotherton (1981), measured attitudes toward single women to determine whether they are stereotyped as sexually frustrated old maids who have been rejected by men but are in constant search for a husband. More than half of their sample referred to single women in pejorative terms. However, a clear sex difference emerged. The men expressed mainly negative evaluations, while the women had predominantly positive attitudes.

The expectation that women will marry is apparently one source of discriminatory attitudes among credit officers. Kryzanowski and Bertin-Boussu (1981:229) report that in Montreal, "discrimination against single women appears to be based on greater uncertainties about a single woman's ability to repay due to possible future marriage and/or child-bearing. This unproven belief, in turn, depends upon two further unproven beliefs: (1) The average work expectancy of a single woman is less than that of a single man, and (2) Young women are just 'marking time' as wage earners until they marry or have children."

The fact that men are expected to give priority to their work, and women, both employed and full-time housewives, to their family is "old news" by now. However, studies of the male life cycle (Levinson, 1978) report priority shifts over time. Men in their 20s and 30s, during the early years of marriage and family formation, remain "largely passive spectators in the home setting." In mid-life there is a shift from this "high centrality of work to greater investment in family" (Rossi, 1980:11). The reason for this life-cycle change seems to be some combination of age, stress and failure in work. Although less attention has been paid to female life-cycle changes, the full-time housewife-mother eventually becomes interested in achievement outside the home. In *Passages* (1976), Sheehy provides an interesting example of the plight of women who have deferred achievement:

> Betty Friedan demonstrates this pattern in spades. She had an exquisite education at one of the top institutions, distinguished herself by graduating *summa cum laude*, then got married and moved to the suburbs to have babies. Although she had genuine feeling for her four children, she found that a large part of herself was frozen out of existence, but she couldn't imagine even at 35 how to put it into effect.
>
> If anyone doubts the difficulty of bringing a suppressed aspect of the self back into play, Friedan makes an astounding confession:
> "It was easier for me to start the women's movement than to change my own personal life."[p. 217]

Division of Labor

Familial priorities are closely connected with familial division of labor. In the traditional marriage, husbands and wives have distinctive responsibilities. The man is the head of the household and his major responsibility is to support the family financially, make the crucial decisions and possibly discipline the children. The woman has major responsibility for raising the children, caring for the home, keeping the marriage intact and maintaining ties with relatives (Baker and Bakker, 1980).

In his early theoretical discussion of gender roles, Parsons (1955b) argued that the major axis of family structure was along "instrumental-expressive" lines. According to him, this differentiation within the family is only a specific case of the generic tendency of small groups to develop both "instrumental" and "expressive" leaders. In experimental groups studied in the 1950s, an instrumental leader invariably emerged who pushed the group toward its goal, e.g., a group recommendation on a hypothetical human-relations problem. An expressive leader also emerged from within these groups, a person who encouraged group morale and reinforced individual efforts. Parsons saw these same two functions in the family. The mother became the expressive specialist, mainly because pregnancy and lactation are female experiences. The father became the instrumental specialist and supported the family. In addition to the biological basis for the division of labor, Parsons based his reasoning on the fact that in the experimental groups, the same person could not assume both instrumental and expressive leadership. Group members did not like the instrumental leader because he talked a great deal and ordered them about. Although Parsons's ideas have been influential, newer research shows that the role segregation he hypothesized is not a universal feature of family life. Aronoff and Crano (1975) examined how work was distributed among women and men in 862 societies and concluded that both sexes commonly share the instrumental function. In other words, women are providers as well as nurturers. They have been "gatherers, gardeners, fishers, poultry raisers, milk processors, and farm workers" (Bernard, 1975:224). The moral to the story: what may be true in our society does not necessarily have to be true.

Parenthood

Although child care constitutes one aspect of marital division of labor, parenthood's distinctive implications for women and men merit separate treatment. So far as the decision to procreate is concerned, husband and wife are fairly equal in power (Eichler, 1975b). Birth control means are freely available to both partners. (Until 1969, it was illegal in Canada to disseminate any information about birth control.) Once conception has occurred, the wife can obtain a therapeutic abortion without her husband's consent or go ahead with a pregnancy against his will.

Most societies assign child support to the father and child rearing to the mother. The law requires the husband to support his children (and wife), but the wife is not similarly obliged (Eichler, 1975b). Bernard (1974a:101) offers this observation on parenthood through law and custom:

Although there is a considerable corpus of law and legislation dealing with the family, including parent-child relationships, there is relatively little in it about mother-child relationships. Fatherhood has a large legal component; the legal rights, duties and obligations of fathers vis-à-vis children, and vice versa, constitutes a respectable part of the role script for fathers. Much of it deals with property, support, discipline, legitimacy. . . . [However] by and large, mothers are conspicuous for their absence in this body of family law. Motherhood rests on custom, tradition, convention, and the mores far more than on law or legislation. And these, in turn, presumably rest on mother-love rather than on law.

The "motherhood mystique" may serve as a functional alternative to the law in persuading women to nurture their children. The motherhood mystique teaches that a woman must experience maternity in order to find true happiness and feminine self-actualization. It holds that pregnancy and child rearing are "normal and natural and that motherhood is a necessary prerequisite for emotional maturity, psychological stability, and the demonstration of femininity" (Veevers, 1977:90). Recently, feminists have challenged both the wisdom of the universal applicability of the motherhood mystique and the manner in which our society interprets motherhood. With regard to the latter, Bernard (1979:124) argues: "The way we institutionalize motherhood in our society—assigning sole responsibility for child care to the mother, cutting her off from the easy help of others in an isolated household, requiring round-the-clock tender, loving care, and making such care her unique activity—is not only new and unique, but not even a good way for either women or . . . for children. It may, in fact, be the worst."

According to Bernard (1979), most societies throughout history have regarded the productive capacity of ablebodied adult women as too valuable to be spared for the exclusive care of children. Moreover, children in this situation are deprived of the care of fathers and other adults, while mothers are deprived of the opportunity for participation in other activities. Bernard goes on to argue that cross-culturally, the greater the burden of child care assigned to mothers, the less warmth they feel for their children.

Women are beginning to express aloud their reservations about motherhood. The irrevocable nature of parenthood is one consideration: "If marriages do not work out, there is now widespread acceptance of divorce and remarriage as a solution. The same point applies to the work world: we are free to leave an unsatisfactory job and seek another. . . . [However] there is little possibility of undoing the commitment to parenthood implicit in conception except in the rare instance of placing children for adoption. We can have ex-spouses and ex-jobs but not ex-children" (Rossi, 1977b:357). The Canadian poet, Mary Melfi (quoted in Griffiths, 1976:195), articulates the fear that society reduces women to "interchangeable baby-making machines":

a big hole,
  sits in my body,
   soon ready,
    to become me, entirely.*

Feminists object to the burden of responsibility of child rearing, a job for which most women are not trained and for which reliable advice is unavailable. They object to postponing their own career development until the children are grown (Maracek, 1978:266). Above all, they object to husbands' lack of involvement in parenting.

While a few men attend the birth of their child and participate in its feeding, diapering and amusement, most continue to delegate parenting to their wives. This fact has been variously interpreted. On the one hand, Polatnick (1975) argues that men do not rear children because they do not *want* to rear children. Men, as the more powerful marriage partners, are in a position to enforce their preferences. And men prefer being the principal family breadwinner to being a full-time parent. Breadwinners earn money, social status and power. Moreover, the conditions of the job of child rearing, as presently constituted—"no salary, low status, long hours, domestic isolation—mark it as a job for women only" (Polatnick, 1975:230). Therefore, men strongly support the motherhood mystique, even the maternal instinct, to ensure that the "weight of child-rearing responsibility falls on women's shoulders" (p. 218). Women's function as child-rearers reinforces their subordinate position, then. According to Polatnick (1975:230), this is "one of the vicious circles which keeps male power intact."

A somewhat different viewpoint on fatherhood is offered by Brenton (1975), who agrees though that men do little significant parenting. He laments the confusion surrounding the father role: his responsibility is emphasized, he feels guilty, it "seems that there's little he does or can do right" (p. 180). Advice and criticism are contradictory, since the experts have widely divergent opinions on the proper role of the father. The mother is glorified and idealized. Alas, no fatherhood cult exists! The " 'Thesaurus of Quotations' lists thirty-one 'apt thoughts' and 'felicitous expressions' for motherhood and a scant ten for fatherhood" (p. 183). Because it is difficult for fathers to relate emotionally to their children, they often view their offspring as economic liabilities to be resented.

Though it may be repetitive and boring to say so, times are slowly changing. Both skepticism regarding the motherhood mystique[5] and economic pressures are encouraging many women to delegate some child rearing to day-care centers and babysitters while they go out to work. Couples are producing one or two children, instead of three or four.

* Reprinted by the kind permission of the publisher of *Mother Was Not a Person*, comp. by Margret Andersen, Black Rose Books, Montreal, 1972.

There is increased tolerance for voluntary childlessness (Veevers, 1980). Since "raising a family seems to be one of those tasks, like losing weight or waxing the car, that is less fun to be doing than to have done" (Angus Campbell, 1975:39), couples may eventually regret their decision to keep the nest empty. But maybe they won't. Childless couples report happier marriages than do couples with children (Lupri and Frideres, 1981).

Marital Power

One consequence of the familial division of labor is asymmetry in conjugal power. Because our society values and rewards occupational achievement, husbands' status in the outside world typically spills over into the family in the form of enhanced power. In contrast, the bargaining position of the dependent wife, especially one encumbered with young children, is minimized. Although the topic of power differential came up in Chapter Five, we want to consider it here from another angle, namely, the "principle of less interest." This idea was put forth by Waller (Waller and Hill, 1951) and elaborated by Turner (1970). The "principle of less interest" holds that in a dyadic relationship, the person who cares less about the quality of the relationship or whether the relationship continues at all is in an advantageous position to dominate the other party to the relationship. The husband in a traditional marriage (or perhaps, any marriage) is the party of less interest. For one thing, he has alternative sources of gratification outside the family. For another, marriage is at the core of his wife's life and on the periphery of his own. Therefore, in all likelihood the wife is the marital partner to make concessions, to bend her will to that of her husband.

Marriage Dissolution

The rising numbers of Canadians who separate and divorce each year make it important to consider the differential effects of marriage dissolution on women and men. The 1978 divorce rate was 243.4 per 100,000 population, compared with 124.2 in 1969 (the year after Canadian divorce law was liberalized), and 37.6 in 1951 (Ambert, 1980:21). The figures for separation are even higher than those for divorce (McVey and Robinson, 1981). Abstract rates are difficult to grasp. In 1976, some 683,000 Canadians (nearly three out of every hundred persons), were separated or divorced (Ambert, 1980:23). Dependent children were involved in 56% of these divorces (Statistics Canada, 1980:Table 2.19). The median duration of marriage upon dissolution was 11.4 years in 1975 (Ambert, 1980:33) and the median ages of divorcing women and men in that year were 32.9 years and 35.9 years, respectively (Ambert, 1980:34).

Who initiates divorce? The "principle of less interest" would predict that the wife would have a greater stake than her husband in maintaining the marriage. "Since husbands have more money than wives, better jobs, more alternatives to meet persons of the other sex, and are less likely to bear total responsibility for the children if the marriage fails, we might expect that when a marriage is not satisfactory they will be more likely to be the first to suggest the possibility of divorce and then to seek it actively" (Ambert, 1980:43). Unfortunately, no Canadian study has focused on this question. However, American studies suggest that although the wife most often files for divorce, the husband engages in behavior that forces the wife to ask for divorce first (Ambert, 1980:44).

Custody of the children is another area where custom (but not the law) favors women. The mother is the custodial parent of over 85% of the children involved in divorce (Ambert, 1980:177). The father is often ordered to pay maintenance. "There is no explicit preference for this state of affairs in the current statutory laws of most provinces (except Saskatchewan where the mother is preferred until the child is 14)" (Prentice, 1979:1). The Divorce Act holds both parents "responsible for maintaining the 'children of the marriage'," and both parents are obliged to provide financial support, "subject to their relative financial abilities" (McCaughan, 1977:133). Strangely enough, feminists have taken little interest in encouraging fathers to share physical and legal custody after divorce (Kent, 1981b). However, a movement in support of joint custody is slowly growing, on the grounds that continuing mutual responsibility maintains the child's ties with both parents and does not overburden the mother (Roman and Haddad, 1978). A small, but growing, literature considers the role of the single father (Katz, 1979; Todres and Schlesinger, 1976).

The economic implications of divorce and separation are quite different for husband and wife. The end of the marriage often spells downward economic mobility, even poverty, for the women involved (Boyd, 1976). There are a number of reasons for this state of affairs. As we have seen, women generally earn less than men. Moreover, divorced and separated women suffer from the widespread assumption that men are the chief breadwinners and women merely secondary earners. Also, women returning to the labor market after years of full-time housewifery are unlikely to be well trained. The situation may "be further exacerbated both by the cost of child care support while the woman works and by a reduced or nonexistent credit rating" (Boyd, 1977:48).

A further reason for women's economic disadvantage was the failure of the law to recognize the contribution to the marriage of the wife who chose to be a full-time housewife or to work in a family business. The Murdoch case in the 1970s forced realization of this flaw in Canadian law. Irene Murdoch spent eight years fighting for a half interest in the

Turner Valley (Alberta) ranch she and her husband had built up during their marriage. In 1976, the Supreme Court of Canada awarded her 12% of her ex-husband's property and assets. However, in a 1978 landmark decision, the Supreme Court gave a Saskatchewan woman divorcing from a farmer one-half of the farm property. Many of the provinces are now introducing marital property laws that recognize the contribution of women's work in the home.

Finally (as noted in Chapter Five), divorced women are less likely to remarry than divorced men. Four-fifths of divorced men, but only two-thirds of divorced women, remarry (Ambert, 1980:189). The "double standard of aging" is the major factor involved here, with age being a greater barrier to remarriage than dependent children. Older women have less chance of remarriage because custom says they must marry someone at least their own age. In comparison, much younger women are considered suitable marriage partners for divorced men.

Women's age disadvantage is the fulcrum of the plot in the latest novel by Erich Segal, of "love-is-never-having-to-say-you're-sorry" fame (*Man, Woman and Child*, 1980). The wife has just learned that the husband had an affair ten years earlier, on a trip to France, which produced a child. The French woman has recently died. The wife agrees to take her husband's child into their home. " 'You're incredible,' he said. She shook her head. 'No, Robert, I'm just thirty-nine years old' " (Segal, 1980:24).

Gender and the Social-Psychological Consequences of Familial Participation

Labels such as "his and her marriages" and "his and her families" imply that the sexes' differing institutional experiences should result in differing social-psychological consequences. Indeed, an early proponent of this view, Jessie Bernard (1971), claimed that marriage benefited men and damaged women. However, a survey of general well-being done in the United States by Campbell, Converse and Rodgers (1976) does not support Bernard's position. They found no difference between married men's and married women's assessment of general well-being. Neither sex "feels itself generally disadvantaged throughout the marriage period" (p. 434). For both sexes, but for men especially, the psychological costs of remaining single are higher than those of marriage. (Cumming and Lazer [1981] report that marriage reduces the risk of suicide more for men than women.) Moreover, divorced people scored considerably lower than married people on the measure of general well-being. According to these data (as well as our own comments above), divorce is more difficult for women than for men. However, the phenomenon of family violence in general (Eekelaar and Katz, 1978) and husband-wife homicide in particular puts marriage and the family in a less rosy light. Chimbos (1976) tells us that about 20% of all Canadians murdered are murdered by their spouses and that in Canada, as elsewhere, wife slayers outnumber husband slayers by far. The murders he studied were very often the result of quarrels over extramarital affairs or sexual refusals.

SALIENT STATUS DUALITIES

Sociologists use the term *status* to refer to positions in the social structure. Often status is not clearly distinguished from the related term, *role*. However, status defines *who* a person is (e.g., man, elderly, pharmacist), while role defines *what* such a person is supposed to do (e.g., support a family, be dignified, understand drugs) (Zelditch, 1968), as well as related rights. There are two main types of statuses, *ascribed* and *achieved*. Individuals are placed in ascribed statuses, as a result of birth (e.g., gender). Achieved statuses are acquired through the individual's own achievements (e.g., occupation).

The *status set* refers to the combination of statuses held by any one individual at any one time (Merton, 1957). Mary Jones's status set includes woman, wife, mother, physician, Rotary Ann, middle-aged, YWCA member. Some of these statuses matter more than others to society at large. The fact that Dr. Jones is a female physician is more important, or more *salient*, than her affiliation with the Rotary Club. These salient statuses (Epstein, 1971) are pivotal in determining other people's responses and indeed the individual's life course. Examples are occupation, gender, race or ethnicity, and age. Salient statuses can be achieved or ascribed, socially valued or socially proscribed. With regard to the latter point, suppose a neighbor had a record for burglary, had nice table manners, was kind to his mother and voted Liberal. Chances are that his previous criminality would override all his other statuses and qualities.

Our concern is to explore the impact of gender on status combinations. Two major points are involved. The first we will discuss briefly, the second at some length.

One aspect of salient statuses is that "they may limit or facilitate the acquisition of other statuses" (Epstein, 1971:92). Some status-set combinations become more likely than others. They seem more natural and more acceptable to other people (Hughes, 1958). In addition to her sex status as female, a woman may be a wife, mother and nurse. The statuses of lumberjack or physician or Roman Catholic priest are unlikely additions to her status set. Similarly, a man may be a husband, father, brother and architect. Ballet dancer or stenographer are less probable. The woman or man who insists on nonconformity will encounter trouble. Eichler (1977b) documents one type of trouble: persons practising an occupation dominated by the other sex suffer loss of occupational prestige. Males in this situation lose more prestige than females. Years ago, Hughes

(1958:109) observed that, "this remains a white, Anglo-Saxon, male, Protestant culture in many respects. These are the expected characteristics for many favored statuses and positions." So far as gender is concerned, the fact of male privilege has until recently led analysts to concentrate on female disadvantage. Now people realize that gender can constitute a structural barrier for females and males alike.

The status-set problem that we wish to emphasize concerns the combination of gender with a second, devalued status. Because our society values masculinity more than femininity, the combination of gender with a denigrated salient status, such as elderly or immigrant, will be more costly for women than for men. Women's situation here has been described as the "double whammy" (Posner, 1975). Three of these "double whammied" groups will be discussed in turn: the elderly, immigrants and native Indians.

The Aged

Aging is as much a social as a biological phenomenon so far as timing and social reactions are concerned. No consensus exists as to when people in our society pass from middle-aged to elderly. The retirement dinner, the first pension check, the first grandchild all mark changes in status. But these events do not necessarily change personal or social identity from middle-aged to old (Matthews, 1979:58). Although the timing is sufficiently variable to keep people scrambling to hide liver spots and wrinkles, the fact that the old are considered less worthy than the young is abundantly clear. The reasons for "ageism" may be the closeness to death of the elderly, the repulsiveness of the biological aging process—the gray hair, wrinkled skin and weight loss that suggest the corpse (Posner, 1980:83-84), the obsolescence of their knowledge in fast-moving industrial societies. Novelist Mary Gordon (1978:137) expresses her view about why the old are second-class citizens:

> "The old are the invisible minority," she said. "They have no power; they're worse than blacks or women."
> "But they do have the power to menace us with our own inevitable futures. White people aren't afraid of becoming black or men of becoming women. Many people act as they do to old people because they're afraid of being like them. . . ."

Gender affects the aging process, so that women and men experience it somewhat differently. In our society, physical aging is much more traumatic for women than for men (Posner, 1980). Women find themselves doubly stigmatized in the last stage of their life cycle, but all along they have lived under the "double standard of aging." Women's magazines are full of ad copy such as, " 'Would He Like a Younger-

Looking Wife?' 'Would He Love You Looking Younger?' and 'Do People Guess Your Age Too Easily?' . . . The message is loud and clear and women are bombarded with it from all directions: Youth = Beauty, Beauty = Love, Aging = Evil. The rest of the message, barely more subtle, is that these truths apply almost solely to women" (Dulude, 1978:3).

However, the most serious problem faced by elderly women is lack of money. Older widows are especially likely to be poor (Matthews, 1980). The Canadian Advisory Council on the Status of Women (Dulude, 1978:95) reports that there are more than one million widowed and unmarried women over the age of fifty-five in Canada. At least two-thirds of them are attempting to survive on incomes below the poverty line. Shortage of money affects nearly every aspect of life, including shelter, nutrition and health.

"Bag ladies," women who live on the street and carry all their possessions in a shopping bag, are an extreme manifestation of this poverty. Skid row is no longer the exclusive domain of men. A Montreal woman tells of meeting an eighty-year-old bag lady while walking her dog in the park:

> It started to rain and I ran for cover under some concrete steps. I looked down and there was a dugout hole, a depression in the earth where there were some rags. The rags started to move. I just freaked! I thought, "Oh, my God, what's that?" I saw it was an old woman. She was just wearing a couple of coats and looked like a part of the earth. She sat up, and I said hello, and she said hello, and I felt embarrassed because I was in her home. She told me she would sleep there and then she'd leave and go down to Ogilvy's department store and use their washroom and sit the rest of the day on the benches of Ste-Catherine and Crescent streets. She was a really nice person. [Schull, 1981:16]

There are three major reasons why elderly women end up alone and destitute. Because of the double standard of aging, men choose women younger than themselves at both first and subsequent marriages. Second, women outlive men by seven years on the average (Dulude, 1978:23). As a result, in Canada there are ten unmarried women for every four unmarried men over the age of sixty-five (Dulude, 1978:75). Some women never marry. Some are divorcées who did not remarry, partly because divorced men remarry younger women. (Forty-five percent of divorced women were thirty-five years or older at the time of their divorce [Dulude, 1978:10].) Even more are widows. (There are more than one million widowed people in Canada, and 82% of them are women [Matthews, 1980].) Third, most elderly women are poor because they devoted their lives to their families without pay and believed they would always be taken care of. "When they become widows, as they almost inevitably must under our present marriage customs, the vast majority find that the promised security does not exist" (Dulude, 1978:95). Women of that generation were socialized to believe that they needed little education or job training. Many "end up working for low pay at subservient jobs that do not give access to pensions" (Dulude, 1978:95). In the end, women's lifelong preoccupation with the family fails to pay off.[6]

Old age is not a "bowl of cherries" for old men either, partly because old age serves to magnify the socioemotional disadvantages of the adult male role (Abu-Laban, 1980). Old men are more likely than old women to be friendless. Since adult children tend to be closer to their mothers than their fathers, even the parental role is weaker for elderly men. Although older men are statistically less likely to be widowed, the average widower is more vulnerable than the average widow. He has lost his closest confidant, he is less likely to seek emotional support from his own sex, he lacks homemaking skills and he is at high risk in terms of suicide potential, morbidity and mortality rates. The opportunity for remarriage is a well-recognized male advantage. However, the *rapidity* of male remarriage may indicate an "acute and devastating need for interpersonal support" (Abu-Laban, 1980:204).

If poverty and widowhood are the major problems of elderly women, retirement is a major problem for their male counterparts. The situation of both sexes can be viewed as "role loss." Males derive personal identity and social worth mainly from their work. Therefore, their greatest loss comes through retirement (Blau, 1973; Payne and Whittington, 1976). In contrast, women gain esteem and identity from their marital role. "Being a wife and being a wife of a particular man whose involvements reflexively give importance to his woman is still the focus of life for most women" (Payne and Whittington, 1976:493). Therefore, widowhood affects women more than retirement. Indeed, many women never retire, since homemaking *is* their work. Men in our society are trained to associate their masculinity with their work. When the work ends, life often becomes boring and self-esteem sags. The family income may decline sharply (Dulude, 1978:29). Simone de Beauvoir (1970:295) describes Ernest Hemingway's attitude toward retirement: "Hemingway said that the worst death for anyone was the loss of what formed the centre of his life and made him what he really was. Retirement was the most loathsome word in the language. Whether we chose it or whether we were compelled by fate, retiring, giving up one's calling—the calling that made us what we were—was the same as going down to the grave."

One of the most interesting gender comparisons in aging is the frequent reversal of power differential. Men lose power and women gain it. The retired husband, who has lost his occupationally derived advantages, may now be a twenty-four-hour-a-day nuisance in his wife's domestic domain. Meanwhile, the wife, as authority in the home, maintains and extends the informal feminine power that we spoke of earlier in this chapter. And the husband is likely to die seven years before the wife. To quote de Beauvoir (1970:543) again, "It is for women in particular that the last age is a liberation: all their lives they were subjected to their husbands and given over to the care of their children; now at last they can look after themselves." (Unfortunately, widows must do so on precious little money.)

Another example of what Bart (1969) describes as "turns of the social ferris wheel" has its source in the supposed asexuality of postmenopausal women. The idea of older women being sexually active is abhorrent to many people (Posner, 1975). Although this misperception has some unfortunate consequences, it also carries advantages, since men apparently fear women's sexuality (Safilios-Rothschild, 1979). Women's sexuality also interferes with their authority claims (the "soft body, soft mind" phenomenon [Ellmann, 1968:74].) Older women sometimes trade their *perceived* asexuality for power in the family, authority in professional work contexts and physical freedom. The voice of the matriarch carries weight. The gray-haired female professor knows what she is talking about. In some countries of the world where younger women are forbidden to leave home unescorted, "older women are free to walk alone at any time of the day or night, to go to bars, to swear, and to interact freely with men" (Safilios-Rothschild, 1979:214).

We conclude our discussion of the first "double whammy" category on an optimistic note. Some gerontologists (Neugarten, as interviewed by Hall [1980]) believe that ageism and the cult of youth are fading, as we move toward "age-irrelevancy." The social clock that previously dictated the proper time to marry, or to enter the labor market, or to go to university, or to have children is no longer so compelling. Growing old is not quite the *faux pas* it used to be. The reason? The average age of the population in Western societies, as well as the percentage of people in the older age categories, is increasing. The number of old people in our communities forces us to realize that the fate of everyone who is lucky enough is to grow old.

Immigrants to Canada

Recent immigrants (the first-generation foreign-born) constitute 15% of Canada's population (Kalbach and McVey, 1979:39). Almost half of the three million immigrants admitted since World War II are female (Royal Commission on the Status of Women, 1970:357). Many of these people are disadvantaged simply because they are newcomers to this country. Prior to the 1960s, Canadian immigration policy encouraged immigration from countries similar to Canada, particularly European countries. In the 1960s, discriminatory aspects of the Immigration Act were changed, and as a result there were massive increases in immigration from Third World countries (Statistics Canada, 1980:5). The visible distinctiveness of people from Asia, Africa, the West Indies and Latin America renders them especially disadvantaged. Although social-scientific studies have neglected immigrant women, recent work (Boyd, 1975b:406) indicates that they bear a "double burden with respect to their status in Canadian society."

The *Report of the Royal Commission on the Status of Women in Canada* (1970:357-64) recognized the dual disadvantage of immigrant women. Three of its recommendations (which were subsequently adopted by the federal government) illustrate how gender could influence immigrants' experiences in Canada. The first recommendation sought to ensure respect for the right of the wife to be an independent applicant for admission to Canada. Apparently the Immigration Service routinely assumed the husband to be the wage earner and the wife his dependent. A related recommendation of the Commission objected to the term "head of the family" in immigration regulations. These practices endangered the woman's admission to Canada and her right to remain. Often the wife is better qualified than her husband for entrance. Indeed, immigrant women work in proportionately greater numbers than Canadian-born women. The assumption that the wife is dependent on her husband also meant that when a deportation order was made against the head of the family, all dependent members of the family were deported under that order. Third, the Royal Commission noted that nonworking married women have particular difficulty in adjusting to their new society. Often these women are much more isolated than their husbands and children from the mainstream of Canadian life: "Often, they speak neither English nor French and, being unable to relate to their environment, they become prey to a psychological solitude which not only crushes their spirit but is also harmful for husband and children" (Royal Commission, 1970:361). The Commission's recommendation concerning programs for the special educational needs of immigrant women has been partially implemented.

Nine years later, the Canadian Advisory Council on the Status of Women issued a report, "Problems of Immigrant Women in the Canadian Labour Force" (Arnopoulos, 1979). The report, which describes them as the "most disadvantaged group" in the labor structure, shows that immigrant women continue to be caught in a "double whammy" situation. Although some are highly trained professional and technical workers, they tend to be overrepresented (in comparison with native-born women and foreign-born men) in low-wage service and manufacturing jobs. They are overworked, underpaid, segregated according to linguistic group, and unable to learn English or French at night school because of family responsibilities. Minimum labor standards legislation puts the onus on the workers to complain. However, immigrant workers are least able to complain effectively, because of communication difficulties, ignorance or fear. The new Immigration Act speaks vaguely of deportation for sub-versive activities. Immigrant workers refuse to insist on their labor rights because they are afraid that complaints will endanger their status in Canada. A final problem, unique to females, is the exploitation of domes-tic workers who have come here on work permits. At the time of the report, Prince Edward Island was the only province that covered these do-mestics under provincial minimum labor standards legislation.

Native Indians

It is ironic that indigenous Indians, like the newcomers discussed above, are marginal people in their own society. Stymeist (1975:62) says, "In-dians are regarded as outsiders, as people who have no real place in the community." Berry, Kalin and Taylor (1977) concluded from their na-tional survey that the native peoples occupy a "marginal" position in Canadian attitudes. While Canadians recognize their unique, aboriginal status, this appreciation is not enough to create positive attitudes, Berry (1981:219) provides an overview of the situation of the native peoples:

> Native people in general are economically poor, occupy housing of minimal standards, and have had little success in moving through the educational systems of the larger society. . . . They have experienced governmental policies which have kept them segregated on reservations, but more recently are facing assimilation policies. At the same time, economic, educational, religious, and telecommunications policies and programs of various institutions have placed enormous assimilation pressures on native peoples, but attitudes in the general population of the larger society have often been negative and discriminatory.

If Indians are badly off in comparison with whites, the plight of In-dian women is even more severe than that of Indian men. In an article describing native women's "multiple jeopardy," Kathleen Jamieson (1979:164-65) quotes an Indian woman: "Of all the people in this vast country, no one has been more downtrodden, has been more overlooked and bypassed, has been more maligned, than [the] Indian woman who is continuously classed as an object of scorn by modern society, who is con-temptuously referred to as 'squaw' and who is considered 'easy to get' by white men."

Indian women's situation as a "minority within a minority," (Jamieson, 1979) is encapsulated by Section 12(1)(b) of the Indian Act. This section states that an Indian woman who marries a non-Indian man ceases to be an Indian under Canadian law. Such a woman must leave her reserve upon marriage and must dispose of any reserve property she holds. Her children are not recognized as Indian. She may be prevented from returning to the reserve, even if she becomes poverty-stricken, sick, widowed, separated or divorced. Finally, her body may not be buried on the reserve with those of her ancestors. On the other hand, Indian men may marry whom they please. Indeed, through marriage, Indian men may confer full Indian rights and status upon non-Indian wives and children (Jamieson, 1978:1).

Jeannette Lavell, the Indian woman who contested this matter before the Supreme Court of Canada in 1973 on the grounds that this section of the Indian Act contravened the Canadian Bill of Rights, lost her case. One difficulty was that the male Indian leaders wanted the Indian Act retained in order to secure their aboriginal rights with regard to land claims. Although native women are organizing their own movements (Jamieson, 1979), Indian women's status under Section 12(1)(b) remains a "moral dilemma," which pits "the rights of all Indians against the rights of a minority of Indians, i.e. Indian women" (Jamieson, 1978:2). Male Indian opposition also stems from concern over the potential costs to the reserve if these women manage to regain their Indian status.

CONCLUSIONS

This chapter completes the trilogy of perspectives on gender: the biological, the social-psychological and the structural. Focusing on social institutions as causal agents of gender has increased our understanding of the phenomenon beyond that possible through the first two levels of explanation alone. "Sexual stratification" is a particularly useful concept, since it ties the matter of gender securely into existing sociological theory. Although we dealt extensively with society's two key institutional areas—work and the family—our inventory of structural constraints is by no means exhaustive. Space limitations precluded discussion of, for example, the legal system (Dranoff, 1977; McCaughan, 1977; McKie and Reed, 1981; Hagan and O'Donnell, 1978) and the political system (Cochrane, 1977; Vickers, 1978).

Who is affected most by the social-definition-of-gender situation, males or females? Can we go beyond the conclusion that the social structure places restrictions on the development and behavior of *both* sexes to make comparisons? On the one hand, women lack the power and prestige that men enjoy. They experience work segregation both at home and in the workplace (Armstrong and Armstrong, 1978). The socially embroidered demands associated with the family seem to be the major source of women's difficulties. However, men are also constrained by gender definitions, and their troubles seem to be increasing. Although men have more resources than women, they have less freedom. While women may now enter the labor market, "social expectations as well as legal requirements of marriage channel men almost exclusively into work activities" (Baker and Bakker, 1980:550). Moreover, the women's movement has placed many men in a "double bind" situation. They are expected to be successful according to the traditional norms, but they are also expected to explore the new, emerging gender norms (Baker and Bakker, 1980). New standards of achievement may stress the cultivation of interpersonal skills, rather than physical prowess or concrete production (Moreland, 1980). Put another way, male and female statuses are changing and ambiguity and confusion confront both sexes. However, females have more to gain and less to lose.

Alternative sources of data fail to shed much light on the perennial question, "Is it harder to be female than male?" Both Canadian (Mackie, 1978b) and American (Campbell, Converse and Rodgers, 1976) sources report no difference in male versus female "satisfaction with life" or "happiness" scores. So far as mental illness is concerned, "rates of mental illness reveal that there are more females than males with the diagnosis of depression, phobia, anxiety, hysteria, and chronic schizophrenia, and more males than females with the diagnosis of personality disorders (psychopathy, alcoholism, and addiction) and psychophysiological disorders (ulcers, heart, and respiratory disorders)" (Al-Issa, 1980:331). (Chessler [1972] and Gove and Tudor [1973] also report that the diagnosis and treatment of mental illness is related to gender.) Finally, males of all ages have the higher suicide rate (Cumming and Lazer, 1981).

At this point, we leave the question of how gender is to be explained. As research becomes more directive, the answer will doubtless become less inchoate. However, future explanations of gender, elegant though they may be, will almost certainly continue to incorporate all three levels of explanation—the biological, the social-psychological and the structural. We turn in our last chapter to the matter of changing definitions of gender.

8 Prospects and Avenues of Change

W HEN people feel neglected or frustrated or mistreated by the existing social order, they sometimes band together to seek a collective solution to their problems in a social movement. A social movement is "a large-scale, informal effort designed to correct, supplement, overthrow, or in some fashion influence the social order" (Toch, 1965:5). The 1960s saw women in many parts of the world beginning to organize in order to improve their lot. The emergence of the women's liberation movement caught most people by surprise. What on earth had women to complain about? (Freeman, 1973) During the past fifteen years or so, the sources of female discontent have been clearly articulated. Although gender as traditionally defined constrains *both* sexes, the more privileged males did not understand gender's negative implications until after the women had organized. This chapter, as an epilogue to our discussion of the development and operation of gender, will concentrate upon the women's movement in Canada, its history and its goals. Men's liberation will be discussed as one of several reactions to the women's movement.

HISTORICAL BACKGROUND

The history of feminism began in 1792 (three years after the start of the French Revolution), with the publication of Mary Wollstonecraft's *A Vindication of the Rights of Woman*. Like other heirs of the Enlightenment, Wollstonecraft believed that "reason, if properly cultivated through education, could set men and women free" (Rossi, 1973:3). Influenced by Rousseau, she wrote of her conviction that "the neglected education of my fellow-creatures is the grand source of the misery I deplore." Her analysis of women's situation aroused quite a storm. In her own time, she was described as a "hyena in petticoats" and one of the "philosophizing serpents we have in our bosom" (Rossi, 1973:32). She fared even less well

289

in this (excuse the expression) *argumentum ad hominem* written 150 years later: "Mary Wollstonecraft hated men. . . . [Her] life reads like a psychiatric case history. So, for that matter, do the lives of many later feminists. . . . [She] was afflicted with a severe case of penis-envy . . . that she was an extreme neurotic of a compulsive type there can be no doubt. Out of her illness arose the ideology of feminism, which was to express the feelings of so many women in years to come" (Lundberg and Farnham, 1947, quoted by Rossi, 1973:37).

John Stuart Mill's *The Subjection of Women*, published in 1869, lent the American suffrage movement prestige because, after all, it was written by a man (Rossi, 1973:183). The beginning paragraph of his essay reads in part as follows: "The principle which regulates the existing social relations between the two sexes—the legal subordination of one sex to the other—is wrong in itself, and now one of the chief hindrances to human improvement; . . . it ought to be replaced by a principle of perfect equality, admitting no power or privilege on the one side, nor disability on the other" (from Rossi, 1973:196).

Several other historical figures contributed analyses of women's condition, the most notable being Friedrich Engels's *The Origin of the Family, Private Property and the State* (1884). Ambert's (1976:170) observations here are interesting: "When one reads the new feminists side by side with the ones from previous generations, and even centuries, one is struck by the fact that, of what is being currently said and written, very little is new: it is an ever-repeating script. . . . [This] repetition attests to the overall lack of change that has taken place in the condition of women."

WOMAN'S SUFFRAGE IN CANADA

The campaign by Canadian women to win the vote parallels the efforts of women in Great Britain and the United States. In a way, the suffrage movement in this country grew out of the problems of Emily Stowe. In the 1860s Mrs. Stowe was having difficulty supporting her invalid husband and three children. By scrimping and saving part of her teaching salary, she managed to save enough to study medicine. Rejected by Canadian medical schools because of her sex, she graduated from an American school. Then she returned to Toronto as Canada's first woman physician and began to work for societal reform. Because of her efforts, the University of Toronto admitted women in 1886. The vote for women was regarded by Stowe and other like-minded women as a lever to open the way to other reforms. In 1876, Dr. Stowe launched the Toronto Women's Literary Club. The word "suffrage" was considered too bold (Cleverdon, 1974:19-20).

The Canadian women's struggle for the vote was peaceful in comparison with the militancy of Emmeline Pankhurst's group in England,

which made its point through hunger strikes and public suicide. The suffragettes here argued that it was unjust to pay taxes and obey laws
without having a share in making laws. They contended that the state
needed a woman's point of view. Failure of the male-run legislatures to
pass protective laws for women who were flooding into industry became a
powerful argument for extending the franchise to women. The final argument for political equality was women's contribution to the war effort in
1914-18 (Cleverdon, 1974:10-11).

The fact that it took half a century to win the vote (Cleverdon,
1974:3) indicates that the males were not easily persuaded by these
arguments. They countered that women were too weak to participate in
the excitement of elections, that since they took no share in the defense of
the country they were not entitled to the vote, that women did not have
the mental capacity to comprehend political problems, and besides, most
women did not want the vote anyway (Cleverdon, 1974:5). In the United
States, "scientists argued that if women used their brains excessively, they
would impair their fertility by draining off blood cells needed to support
the menstrual cycle. Many genuinely believed that the dawning feminist
movements threatened the survival of the race" (*Newsweek*, 18 May
1981:81).

The attention that has been given to people such as Dr. Emily
Stowe, Judge Emily Murphy, Joséphine Dandurand and Nellie McClung[1]
invites a "great woman" approach to the Canadian suffrage movement,
which is not altogether accurate. The time was one of reform and the
issue of woman's vote was associated with a wide range of social reforms,
relating to factory working conditions, alcoholism, poor health and diet
among working people in Canada (Marsden and Harvey, 1979:190).
These multiple issues explain why middle-class women's organizations,
such as the Women's Christian Temperance Union (WCTU) and the National Council of Women among urban women, and the Women's In-
stitutes among rural women, played a leadership role in the suffragist
movement. The WCTU, for example, was concerned with the problem of
alcoholism among working people. Its leadership was convinced that if
the women obtained the vote, they would then be in a stronger position to
influence liquor laws (Marsden and Harvey, 1979:191).

Women won the federal vote in 1918, under the impetus of the First
World War, and the provincial vote between 1916 and 1922 in every
province except Quebec, where it was not won until 1940. Another battle
was won in 1929 when the British Privy Council amended the British
North America Act to include women as legal "persons." Until that time,
"women under British Common Law were only considered to be persons
in 'the matter of pains and penalties, but not in the matter of rights and
privileges' " (Marchildon, 1981:101).

In a sense, though, the suffragettes had won the battle but lost the war. "Women got the vote and achieved a measure of legal emancipation, but the real social and cultural barriers to full equality for women remained untouched" (Dixon, 1971:166). Women's organizations continued to support various concerns, but no unifying issue emerged to ignite the imagination. The Depression fell upon the nation and the feminist movement became dormant for some forty years.

THE NEW FEMINIST MOVEMENT

The contemporary feminist movement in Canada officially began with the federal government's 1967 decision to establish a Royal Commission on the Status of Women in Canada (Morris, 1980). Prior to this political action, women's situation was not regarded as a social problem. However, the currents of intellectual thought in Canada, the United States and Western Europe, concerning equality of opportunity and human rights issues, were ripe for a reconsideration of women's rights. The economically prosperous 1960s were a decade of protest in the U.S. against the Vietnamese War, nuclear weaponry and the disadvantaged position of blacks, the poor and university students. The publication of Betty Friedan's *The Feminine Mystique* in 1963 led to the formation of the American National Organization of Women. The ideology spilling northward across the border through media and personal contacts mingled with the ideas of parallel, indigenous movements in this country (Morris, 1980). Women involved in these activist movements became aware of the subordinate position of their sex in organizations advocating freedom and equality for others. They were "only asked to do the cooking and cleaning, the licking of stamps, and the stuffing of envelopes . . . but never to advance their own ideas or become leaders themselves" (Marsden and Harvey, 1979:195). The Voice of Women (a "ban-the-bomb" organization) played a crucial role as a link between the New Left activist groups in Canada and elsewhere, and the mainstream, upper-middle-class women's organizations (Morris, 1980). It also served as a political training ground.

The enterprise of one individual, Laura Sabia, was crucial to the new feminist movement. As national president of the Canadian Federation of University Women, she invited all established women's organizations to send delegates to a meeting on women's status. On May 3, 1966, women representing thirty-two organizations met in Toronto and created a steering committee, headed by Sabia, to approach the government for the purpose of instituting a Royal Commission on the Status of Women. *Chatelaine* magazine editorials were timed to support this demand (Morris, 1980). The Cabinet agreed to establish the Commission, thus legitimizing "the social problem definition of the status of women" and publicly signifying the movement's beginning (Morris, 1980). In 1970 the Commission made 167 recommendations for change.

The Commission intensified communication on women's issues across the country. Formal briefs were prepared. Problems were now seen as social issues, not individual troubles. Two main types of people have been involved in this discussion: middle-class women in established groups, and university and college students or dropouts with affiliations in radical organizations (Marsden and Harvey, 1979:196). Since its emergence, the women's movement has been diffuse and decentralized (Morris, 1979). Frequently women share common sentiments and concerns, but not formal membership in specific organizations. There are two main branches of the movement. The more formal branch concentrates on women's legal and economic problems. The other branch, made up of younger women, is less formally organized and more radical in its philosophy (Freeman, 1973). A basic debate continues to oppose feminists who embrace a liberal-reform model for goal achievement and feminists who advocate a socialist-revolutionary model. The radical position is less popular, probably because "North American society is not at all revolutionary in its main political and philosophical currents," and because women's gender socialization has discouraged aggressive thinking and behavior (Morris, 1979:197). However, a recent development has been the intertwining of feminism with the trade union movement (Kates, 1981).

The women's movement in this country faces a number of peculiarly Canadian problems. It must cope with the division of powers between federal and provincial governments. (For example, at the time of writing, divorce is a federal matter, while the division of matrimonial property following divorce is a provincial matter.) Strong regional differences exist, for instance, between the women of Quebec and women in the rest of Canada, who live under different regimes of civil law. These regional interests are reinforced by the high costs of travel and communication. Further, working-class women (when they are involved at all) and middle-class women have somewhat different concerns (Marsden and Harvey, 1979:198). Our next task is to examine these contemporary feminist concerns in some detail.

FEMINIST CONCERNS

In contrast with the earlier suffrage movement, which emphasized one issue (votes for women), the ideology of the contemporary movement addresses an array of issues. Like all movements, the feminist movement promotes both specific changes and a conception of reality (or ideology) that justifies these changes. Ideologies represent political thought and combine factual propositions with value judgments (Turner and Killian, 1972:269). By examining these ideologies and goals in terms of biological, social-psychological and social-structural levels, we attempt to introduce some order into this diversity. (This classification is the author's, not the movement's.)

Biological Level

Feminists argue that in the past, anatomical, hormonal and genetic differences between males and females have been (1) grossly exaggerated and (2) used to justify women's inferior social status. The anatomical differences that distinguish women from men should be cherished. (Black is beautiful and female is, too.) If inferior social value is to attach to anyone's anatomy, it should be male, not female, anatomy (Safilios-Rothschild, 1974:8). However, their main point is that "biologically derived differences between the sexes are relatively minor and that a vast inequitable system has been built upon the assumption that such differences are basic and major" (Carden, 1974:11). Instead, the root of the matter is "oppressive socialization."

Feminist action ranges from scholarly refutation of "biology is destiny" interpretations (e.g., Osler, 1980) to "trashing" sisters for "wrong-headed" thinking. The latter point is illustrated by *Newsweek* (18 May 1981:72): " 'I found myself being screamed at—this time by the very people whose cause I had supported,' wrote sociologist Alice Rossi, after she landed in hot water for talking about the 'innate predisposition' of women for child-rearing. 'People are being really hounded,' agrees anthropologist Sarah Blaffer Hrdy, who found she could not even hypothesize about men's math abilities without provoking feminist wrath."

Sociopsychological Level

A basic tenet of feminist ideology is that traditional "masculine" and "feminine" behaviors have been induced through socialization and can therefore be altered by means of nontraditional socialization experiences (Safilios-Rothschild, 1974:8). Sociopsychological goals include resocializing other people and resocializing the feminists themselves, according to a revised image of the sexes.

Resocializing other people means changing the ideas that employers, teachers, librarians, etc., have about the potentialities and "proper" behavior of females and males. As Armstrong and Armstrong (1978:118) point out, the Royal Commission on the Status of Women assumed that women's situation results, in part, from false ideas planted in children's heads: "The stereotype of the ideal woman has its effect upon Canadian women. It appears that many women have accepted as truths the social constraints and mental images that society has prescribed, and have made these constraints and images part of themselves as guides for living" (Royal Commission on the Status of Women, 1970:14). The implication is that change will result through the correction of false stereotypes and promulgation of liberalized gender attitudes. Elimination of sexism in children's storybooks ("Little Miss Muffet Fights Back!") and in mass media programming and advertisements is part of this strategy.

In the early days, feminists' resocialization (and radicalization) of themselves took place through "consciousness-raising" groups. Each woman, through sharing of personal experiences with other women, "questions, rethinks, and revises her old conceptions of womanhood" in all facets of her life (Carden, 1974:33). *Chatelaine* magazine's *Guide to the Women's Movement in Canada* (Kreps, n.d.:12) said that consciousness-raising concentrates on "debunking male fantasies" and "getting correct data from the only valid place: women's own experience." Instructions were given on how to begin: "Just get together with eight to ten of your [female] friends, . . . agree to interrupt each other as little as possible, try to give everyone a chance to talk, and be honest—with yourself and with your sisters" (Kreps, n.d.:14). Suggested topics included problems of growing up as a girl, relationships with men and with women inside and outside the family, feelings about pregnancy, marriage and getting old, experiences as a "sex object" and life goals (Kreps, n.d.:15-16).

Assertiveness training for women in the 1970s has succeeded consciousness-raising as a tool for individual change (Smye and Wine, 1980). The popularity of such courses is indicated by their availability through YWCAs, universities and women's centers. Assertive behavior is behavior "which expresses that person's feelings, attitudes, wishes, opinions or rights directly, firmly, and honestly, while respecting the feelings, attitudes, wishes, opinions, and rights of other persons" (Alberti, 1977:367). Assertiveness training programs are based on the largely untested assumption that females are less skilled than males in interpersonal assertiveness (Smye et al., 1980). (However, sex stereotypes certainly picture women this way.) Goals here include enhancing self-respect and self-confidence, developing more emotionally satisfying relationships with others and increasing the possibility of getting one's own needs satisfied. Unlike consciousness-raising, which depends on insight to bring about change, assertiveness counselling teaches specific skills. However, the primary aim of both is to realize women's potential through altered states of consciousness.

Academic feminists in particular have been intrigued with the possibility of *androgyny*, as opposed to sex-typing, as the goal of socialization. *Androgyny*, which is derived from the Greek words for male and female, refers to "a state in which feminine and masculine elements are present, accepted and accessible within the individual [emphasis deleted]" (Laws, 1979:306). The idea is an ancient one (Singer, 1976). For example, in Greek mythology, Tiresias lived for seven years as a woman and seven years as a man in order to experience both sexes (Laws, 1979:308). In *A Room of One's Own*, Virginia Woolf (1929:102) wrote: "In each of us two powers preside, one male, one female, and in the man's brain, the man predominates over the woman, and in the woman's brain, the woman predominates over the man. The normal and comfortable state of being is that when the two live in harmony together, spiritually cooperating." Carl Jung (1926) introduced the idea of androgyny into psychology in his discussion of the animus (the male principle within the female) and the anima (the female principle within the male). Sandra Bem's (1974) research made the topic current in contemporary psychology.

A controversy is presently raging over the desirability of androgyny. For several years, feminists approved of the androgynous ideal because the assumption that an individual can be both feminine and masculine helped to free the human personality from the restricting prison of sex-role stereotyping (Bem, 1976:49). Some research does support the proposition that individuals who have both instrumental and expressive capabilities within their repertoires (about one-third of university student populations) are better off than sex-typed individuals (Bem, 1976). The implication is that androgyny is not completely extinguished by gender socialization. The practical question is then: how can androgyny be expanded? (Laws, 1979:356). However, not everyone is enthusiastic over the prospects of androgyny. More recent research suggests that androgyny benefits women more than men, since it is masculine behavior that our society rewards (Pyke, 1980). The most serious criticism of the androgyny notion is that it does not eliminate sex-role stereotypes, it just combines them in a new way (Pyke, 1980). Accordingly, the suggestion is made that "there are no such syndromes as feminine, masculine, or androgynous; there are only people, each equipped with a unique complex of psychological qualities" (Pyke, 1980:27). The ultimate goal of socialization according to this perspective is no gender at all; that is, societal expectations for individuals would have nothing at all to do with biological sex. A tall order, indeed.

The Social-Structural Level

Social movements are "organizations of the impatient" (Wilson, 1973:231). To many of the people attracted to the women's movement, the social-psychological strategies outlined above seem impossibly slow. These people raise questions such as the following about attitude change:[2] what point is there in propaganda campaigns extolling women's potential addressed to corporation executives if job segregation benefits capitalism?

What difference does it make if public schools operate with texts from which sexism has been expunged, and universities speak of their department chair*persons* (not chairmen) and *women* students (not girls), if the power and authority in these (and other institutions) are held by males?

Consciousness-raising and assertiveness training, critics argue, may indeed change movement members. However, changing a few people at a time is a mighty slow way to renovate a society. Besides, this therapeutic interest in individual women is a type of victim blaming (Ryan, 1971). The victim's defects are stressed, while the victimizing social forces are ignored. Translate "personal troubles into public issues" (Mills, 1959:187), they say. The personal *is* political. Change the social structure first, and attitude change and socialization practices will follow.

Movement people who emphasize structural rather than internal barriers to female equality and self-determination may be categorized as either "talkers" or "doers." The former tend to be university women, while the latter are organization women. These women have tackled a multiplicity of issues: equal job opportunities and pay; pensions; day care; abortion; education; divorce and marital property law reform; protection from rape. The "talkers" are engaged in theoretical analysis and education, while the "doers" lobby for specific societal changes. Oddly enough, the "talkers" are the "radical" feminists, while the "doers" are the "reformists" (Freeman, 1979:560).

The feminists engaged in intellectual work are of two main types (Jaggar and Struhl, 1978:82-85).

Socialist feminists (e.g., Mitchell, 1971) emphasize class analysis and augment Marx's and Engels's discussion of society by focusing on institutions such as the family, which are particularly responsible for women's oppression. Capitalism and sexism are seen to reinforce one another. Liberation for women will require a society that is both classless and genderless. "Genderless" means "a society in which the biological fact of sex received no social recognition (except, presumably, for reproductive purposes)" (Jaggar and Struhl, 1978:85).

Radical feminists view women's oppression as fundamental. Firestone (1970), for example, claims that oppression on the basis of sex provides the model for understanding racial and class oppression. Since women's childbearing function and subsequent dependence on men is the root of female oppression, only a biological revolution will free women. Possibilities are extrauterine reproduction or lesbianism. (These biological strategies adopted for political reasons simultaneously involve two levels of our classification scheme—the biological and the structural.)

Most of the feminist "doers" adopt a liberal ideology. The roots of women's oppression are assumed to lie in their lack of civil rights and educational opportunities (Jaggar and Struhl, 1978:82). "The majority choice, and therefore the central tendency within the North American women's movements is the liberal-reform model of achieving feminist goals. Even though this model has been informed [by the two frameworks mentioned above], it is still inherently reformist in that it does not link female oppression directly to the institution of private property and/or the nature and functioning of advanced capitalism" (Morris, 1979:197).

We turn now from the matter of feminist philosophies to one of the main consequences of the women's movement, namely, the men's movement.

MEN'S LIBERATION MOVEMENT

It is not difficult to devise a list of logical reasons to explain why a men's liberation movement ought to be alive and well in North America. (Equally cogent reasons explain why this should *not* be the case, but these can be ignored for the time being.) Because gender roles are interlocking and complementary, the dissatisfaction of women cannot help but affect men. Women's critical scrutiny of the traditional ways in which the sexes relate has forced men to become conscious of flaws in the status quo. With movement rhetoric and consciousness-raising, the women have become angry with the "system," with "male oppressors." For example, the Manifesto of SCUM (Society for Cutting Up Men) (Morgan, 1970:514) begins like this: "Life in this society being, at best, an utter bore and no aspect of society being at all relevant to women, there remains to civic-minded, responsible, thrill-seeking females only to overthrow the government, eliminate the money system, institute complete automation, and destroy the male sex." Although SCUM may be apocryphal, women's rage is both real and hard to ignore. Male-female role reciprocity means that both sexes must react to the small moves toward egalitarianism that have already occurred. Who reaches for the restaurant check? (Laner, Axelrod and Laner, 1979). Who lights cigarettes for whom? Who dances which part in the "door-opening ballet"? (Walum, 1974). These prickly situations are only symptoms of the underlying social ferment produced by the women's movement.

Moreover, various social policies that aim to liberate women would also liberate men (Safilios-Rothschild, 1974:72 ff.). If women insisted on being treated as equal human beings, not as inferiors and sex objects, both sexes would benefit (in theory at least) from new, mature relationships. Men would no longer need to take all the responsibility for initiating contact with women (or all of the risk of rejections). True female-male friendships would become possible. Egalitarian marriage would mean the sharing of decision making and economic burdens. "The economic independence of women would free men from the moral, social, and legal obligation to support all the 'dependent' women and children in their lives. This is a particularly important type of liberation for men who, up to now, have not had the option not to work, to work part-time, or occasionally to underachieve, or to fail occupationally and/or economically" (Safilios-Rothschild, 1974:73).

Men, too, could ignore occupational sex-typing and, if they wished, enter the nurturing, supportive occupations such as nursing and primary-school teaching (low-paying as they are), or the artistic, expressive occupations such as ballet dancing and acting. If women became liberated from twenty-four-hour-a-day motherhood, men would learn more about fatherhood. Finally, female criticism of sex stereotypes and touting of the androgynous ideal has taught males that there is no place in traditional masculinity for the tender, expressive, sensitive qualities, and further, that the rough, tough male is seriously disadvantaged in establishing relationships with women, children or other males.

Men have indeed reacted to the women's movement. Women's anger has provoked fear and ridicule and the publication of books on masculinity. A few men, mostly white, middle-class and university-educated (Snodgrass, 1975) became involved in male liberation groups. Initially, men confronted with radical feminists sought one another out to discuss sexist accusations and to learn what manners and attitudes such women might find inoffensive. Other men were simultaneously attracted because they too considered themselves to be injured by sexism. The "emotional deprivation" issue mentioned earlier was the basis of masculine protest. Movement men acknowledge the relatively greater oppression of women than men (Snodgrass, 1975).

To tell the truth, hen's teeth are probably more plentiful than men's groups in Canada. In the mid-1970s they apparently thrived in England (Tolson, 1977) and the United States (Farrell, 1974; Katz, 1976), and even in Montreal (Powers, 1978). Recently, though, things have been quiet. And for good cause. Fundamental to a social movement is the existence of a sizable number of discontented people convinced that their situation is intolerable. Such is not the case here.

"Male oppression" is a pretentious slogan. Men have not been discriminated against because they are *men* (Walum, 1977:210). Since they are the powerful, prestigious sex, most do not perceive themselves as victimized by the system. Although male liberation would widen the available choices, improve relationships with others and promote better health and longer lives, the costs in terms of power, status and money, all valued highly in our society, would be high (Baker and Bakker, 1980). Not many men are willing to pay the price.

FUTURE PROSPECTS

In order to provide a logical conclusion for my book, I must look to the future of gender relations in Canadian society. This is as much a personal as a professional task, so the impersonal modes of expression, "we" and "the writer," are abandoned. Thoughts about the prospects of gender provoke mixed feelings (over and above the trepidation experienced by any sociologist faced with the challenges of prediction). "Measured optimism" best describes my state of mind.

The feminist goal is equality of the sexes. Ideally, females and males should be valued equally and should have equal opportunity to realize their potentialities and to channel the course of their lives. More specifically, such equality entails ending work segregation in the labor market and in the home. Progress has certainly been made over the past fifteen years or so. Hence, my optimism. However, the agenda of unfinished business is formidable. Hence, my *qualified* optimism, even pessimism.

On the positive side, movement women have articulated the problems involved in gender relations and brought them to public attention. Innocence can never be regained. University and college courses are established and research is well under way (some of it under the auspices of the Canadian Research Institute for the Advancement of Women). Women's centers, rape crisis centers and shelters for battered women exist across the country. Progress has been made in attaining women's rights, some of it by the Canadian Advisory Council on the Status of Women. Canadian attitudes are becoming more egalitarian.

Notwithstanding the above, the fundamental axes of male-female relations remain unaltered. Most women continue to carry traditional family responsibilities. For many, housework and child care are heaped upon low-paying, menial, outside jobs. Egalitarianism will come about only if radical changes occur in the structure of the family and the structure of the economy.

Both institutions, but especially the family, which is charged with sentiment, are highly resistant to change. For instance, research (Komarovsky, 1976) shows that men who approve equality of access to occupational, economic and political rewards still demand traditional role differentiation within the family. Further, the 1976 census for the first time gave Canadians the option of listing either the husband or wife as head of their households, instead of automatically designating the husband as head. Only 1.5% chose the wife, 98.5% retaining that honor for the husband (Davids, 1980). *The Total Woman* (Morgan, 1975) and *Fascinating Womanhood* (Andelin, 1974) represent a backlash against feminism's threat to the traditional wife in the traditional family. Changing the economic system is not exactly child's play, either. Women have not flocked to outside jobs *because* the women's movement stimulated their ambition. Rather, women work as a consequence of inflation and the availability of service jobs that male workers do not want—"mainly part-time, in-and-out, temporary or dead end, and almost always poorly paid" (Harris, 1981:36). These economic changes were instrumental in producing the women's movement. Unfortunately, the conservatism associated with the economic stress and confusion of the 1980s does not bode well for gender equality.

Dreaming up utopian economic and family arrangements is a delightful pastime. However, real-life institutions do not voluntarily fade away, and revolutions take some doing. Revolutions are also extremely unpleasant affairs, which I, as a humanist, cannot countenance. I see a future with a great deal of work to be done and no guarantees of success.

Dedicated activists have little choice but to carry on, to address the many issues that still remain and to consolidate what has already been won. Social scientists with a professional interest in gender relations, too, must pursue their own incomplete work and find answers to the many questions spawned by their exploratory research.[3] I firmly believe that part of the social scientist's responsibility is to tell lay audiences when she is wearing her "scientist hat" and when she is wearing her "activist hat." The devil of it is that this postscript required both!

Notes

CHAPTER 1. INTRODUCTION AND OVERVIEW

1. Although space limitations make it impossible to pursue all the nuances of this complex issue, readers may find helpful the following definitions of *theory* and *theoretical orientation*. According to Shaw and Costanzo (1970:4), a theory is "a set of interrelated hypotheses or propositions concerning a phenomenon or set of phenomena," while an orientation is "a general approach to the analysis and interpretation of behavior" (p. 8). The feminist critique is aimed at both theories and orientations.

2. The meaning of *paradigm* in the context of sociology is somewhat confusing (Eckberg and Hill, 1979). Kuhn (1970), the major authority in these discussions, apparently used the term in twenty-one different ways. However, the feminists appear to be referring to Kuhn's "metaphysical paradigm," a total world view, gestalt or *Weltanschauung* within a given science (Ritzer, 1975:4).

Paradigm 1 → Normal science → Anomalies → Crisis → Revolution → Paradigm 2

According to Kuhn, major changes take place in any science through revolution rather than through slow, orderly transition. At any one point in time, the science is dominated by a specific paradigm. Normal science is a period of accumulation of knowledge, as researchers work under the aegis of the reigning paradigm. Eventually, such work produces anomalies, or things that the existing paradigm cannot explain. If these anomalies are significant, a crisis stage occurs, which may end in revolution. The reigning paradigm is discarded and a new one takes its place (Ritzer, 1975:3-4).

Proponents of this viewpoint evidently believe that the effect of the discovery of gender in sociology is sufficient to cause a crisis and a paradigmatic revolution.

3. Mills (1959:9) uses marriage as one illustration of his distinction between "personal troubles" and "the public issues of social structure." Inside a marriage, the wife and husband may well experience personal troubles. However, the fact that one marriage out of four ends in divorce is an indication of the structural issues involved in this particular marriage and in related institutions.

4. Carole Beere's (1979) five-hundred-page compilation of attitude scales and other measuring instruments used in research regarding women is a useful aid.

CHAPTER 2. FEMALE/MALE SIMILARITIES AND DIFFERENCES

1. *Webster's Third New International Dictionary* defines *myth* in several ways. These two definitions seem closest to the sociological usage:

(a) *a story that is usu. of unknown origin and at least partially traditional, that ostensibly relates historical events usu. of such character as to serve to explain some practice, belief, institution, or natural phenomenon, and that is esp. associated with religious rites and beliefs . . .*

(b) *a belief given uncritical acceptance by the members of a group, esp. in support of existing or traditional practices and institutions.*

2. Atwood (1972:200) offers as an example of the "nature-as-woman" metaphor E. J. Pratt's personification of the Canadian Shield in *Towards the Last Spike*:

> This folded reptile was asleep or dead:
> So motionless, she seemed stone dead—just seemed:
> She was too old for death, too old for life,
> For as if jealous of all living forms
> She had lain there before bivalves began
> To catacomb their shells on western mountains.
> Somewhere within this life-death zone she sprawled,
> Torpid upon a rock-and-mineral mattress. . . .

3. Said Napoleon Bonaparte: "Nature intended women to be our slaves. . . . They are our property; we are not theirs. They belong to us, just as a tree that bears fruit belongs to a gardener. What a mad idea to demand equality for women! . . . Women are nothing but machines for producing children" (McPhee, 1978).

4. The larger study examined the interrelationships between the institutions of work and family, with special emphasis on the changing roles of women in both spheres. The principal investigators in this research are Merlin B. Brinkerhoff, James S. Frideres, Eugen Lupri, Marlene Mackie and Donald L. Mills, all of the University of Calgary. Funds for the research were provided by the University of Calgary Research Policy and Grants Committee.

5. The content analysis of the Twenty Statement Test responses ignored the extreme modifiers attached to the Broverman et al. traits, such as "always," "very," "not at all."

CHAPTER 3. BIOLOGICAL EXPLANATIONS OF SEX DIFFERENCES

1. Probably because of its male orientation, sociology in general has yet to consider seriously the implications of the mother-infant bond for societal organization. However, a few female social scientists, such as Chodorow (1971; 1978) and Rossi (1977a), have been exploring the question of parent-child ties.

2. It should be noted that several anthropologists (Matthiasson, 1975; Schlegel, 1974) adopt what Lamphere (1977:616) labels a "complementary but equal" perspective on women's position. For example, Matthiasson (1975:xviii), in the editorial introduction to her book, *Many Sisters*, accepts Briggs's (1975) view of the Eskimo. The latter classifies them as a "complementary society" in which "women are valued for themselves and the contributions they make to society. In these societies, women are neither inferior nor superior to men, merely different."

3. This section is based on the discussion by Sayers (1980:242-43).

4. The evolutionary argument for the existence of two sexes instead of one or three sexes is amusing. Moreover, it makes sense. According to Tavris and Offir (1977:266), "There are two sexes, actually, because two is the most efficient minimum number for the exchange of genetic information. An organism that reproduces itself gains no new material. Two sexes are sufficient for assuring the genetic recombinations necessary for variation and adaptation. A third sex would add no new genes but lots of social aggravation and sexual inefficiency."

5. The *couvade* is a practice among some preliterate tribes, in which the father subjects himself to various taboos associated with pregnancy, experiences labor pains and a long recovery period. He may minimize contact with others, avoid eating certain foods during pregnancy, refrain from performing normal tasks during the postpartum period, etc. Quite likely, the *couvade* is motivated by the father's practical need to assert his claim on the child in situations where paternity

is quite uncertain, rather than by some mystic "womb envy" (Tavris and Offir, 1977:248-51). It may be recalled that the *couvade* was practised among the Arapesh (Mead, 1935).

6. Sex and gender taken together involve eight variables (Hyde, 1979, based in part upon Money and Ehrhardt, 1972). Earlier, we discussed four biological variables, *genetic sex, hormonal sex, gonadal sex* and *genital sex.* Genital sex may be further differentiated into *internal accessory organs* (uterus and vagina in the female; prostate and seminal vesicles in the male) and *external genital appearance* (vulva in the female; penis and scrotum in the male). Being female or male involves three additional social-psychological variables. *Assigned gender*, based on the appearance of the child's external genitals, is the gender the parents and the rest of society believe the child to be. It is the gender in which the child is raised. *Gender identity* is the person's own conviction of being male or female, which is expressed in personality and behavior. Finally, *choice of sexual partner* refers to the person's sexual attraction to members of the same sex or the opposite sex or both.

In most cases, an individual is consistently male or female across the above eight variables. That is, an individual with XX chromosomes has an endocrine system that produces estrogen, as well as internal and external female organs. This person has been designated a female from birth, and believes herself to be female. Finally, she is sexually attracted to males.

Occasionally, however, contradictions exist among these variables. A person whose gender identity contradicts the first six dimensions is called a *transsexual*. A person whose choice of sexual partner is at variance with the other components is called a *homosexual*. A person with contradictions among the biological variables (hormones, chromosome structure, anatomy) is called a *hermaphrodite*.

CHAPTER 4. GENDER SOCIALIZATION: THE SOCIAL-PSYCHOLOGICAL PERSPECTIVE ON SEX DIFFERENCES

1. This chapter draws upon two chapters previously written by the author on the topic of socialization: Mackie (1979) and Mackie (1980a).

2. Boyd (1975a) analyzed Gallup Polls taken from 1964 to 1973 with random probability cluster samples using quotas. The questions cited in Table 4.1 involved from 708 to 725 respondents. The Gibbins, Ponting and Symons (1978) study involved 1,832 randomly selected interviewees aged eighteen and over.

3. A second type of learning, *classical conditioning*, explains some of children's learning that is unintended by their parents. For example, a child may munch cookies while watching "Sesame Street." Before long, television becomes a signal to eat. Phobias provide another good illustration. Classical conditioning does not have much relevance for gender socialization.

CHAPTER 5. FAMILY AND PEER GROUP: PRIMARY SOURCES OF GENDER SOCIALIZATION

1. Goffman (1977:315) goes on to say that, "Brothers will have a way of defining themselves in terms of their differences from persons like their sisters, and sisters will have a way of defining themselves in terms of their differences from persons like their brothers. . . ." A prediction that the presence of opposite-sex siblings reinforces gender identity is inherent in these observations. As we shall see, the empirical evidence on this point is both limited and confusing.

2. In order to retain some balance in our discussion, we must register "Portnoy's

Mother's Complaint" that being a mother is not easy. Chodorow (1978:84) observes that the "mother is caught between engaging in 'maternal overprotection' (maintaining primary identification and total dependence too long) and engaging in 'maternal deprivation. . . .'" She cites a sentimental chapter epigraph: "They must go free/Like fishes in the sea/Or starlings in the skies/Whilst you remain/The shore where casually they come again" (p. 85).

>   Or perhaps this cynical version of another watery fable appeals more:
>   There is a story about an eagle who had to bring her [child] to safety when a flood covered the earth and it was too young to fly the great distance. She picked up the . . . child in her talons and began to fly. "I will always be grateful to you, mother," said the baby eagle. "Liar," said the mother, and dropped him into the flood (Friday, 1977:445).

3. Incidentally, there is no evidence that either lesbianism (Chodorow, 1978:175) or male homosexuality (Yussen and Santrock, 1978:376) correlate with growing up in homes where the father is absent.

4. The October 1979 issue of *The Family Coordinator* is devoted to the topic, "Men's Roles in the Family."

5. Meissner et al. (1975:438) share these case study comments with us regarding the attitudes of helping husbands:

>   A sales representative in his mid-forties said he is happy about his wife's full-time bank job and does the "outside chores" at home. About the "inside" housework, he feels: "I wouldn't want it. It doesn't interest me and women are more capable of doing it. It's her responsibility because it's just accepted that she looks after that area. It's just the same as finances. I don't want to be bothered with it and I think it's good for her to do it."

>   A machine operator in his mid-thirties, whose wife works nearly full time as a keypunch operator (three children aged three to eleven), on the subject of the "heavy work" which he takes as his share of the housework: "I think—why the hell do I have to scrub these bloody walls and she couldn't get up on a step ladder and do the same bloody thing. My dad never did it. Why the hell do I have to do them?"

6. As we mentioned earlier, Brinkerhoff (1977) did *not* find the fact of mothers working to be related to daughters' role-innovativeness (choice of male-dominated occupations).

7. The Irene Murdoch affair produced wide publicity for divorced women who were refused a fair share of the ranch or farm assets that had accrued partly from their labor. See Chapter Seven.

8. The English-Canadian/French-Canadian parental difference was reversed in Lambert, Yackley and Hein's (1971) analysis of working-class parents' reactions to a taped version of a child's demands for attention, help and comfort, and displays of anger and insolence. Here, although both French-Canadian and English-Canadian parents demanded more of boys than of girls, the French-Canadian parents perceived fewer gender differences than did the English-Canadians.

9. Theorists such as Jean Piaget (1928, 1932), working from a cognitive-developmental perspective, and George Herbert Mead (1934), from a symbolic interactionist perspective emphasize the importance of play and games for the child's social development. In many respects, childhood games are small-scale analogies of society. When children learn about game rules they are learning, at their level, about societal norms. Similarly, when they learn to play game roles, they are also learning something about playing societal roles. According to these theorists, both the self-concept and an awareness of morality emerge from children's play.

10. *Sociometry* is a research technique for measuring the attraction and repulsion patterns in small groups. Subjects are asked to designate a small number of people

they would prefer to associate with, usually for specific work and play activities. Sometimes they are also asked to name people they would prefer not to associate with.

11. Fay Weldon's *Female Friends* (1974) is a delightful fictional treatment of this topic.

12. Gender is only one of several demographic characteristics that correlate with leisure activities. The higher the income level, occupational class and educational status, the greater the number of leisure activities engaged in, and the greater the importance of "active" versus "passive" activities (Statistics Canada, 1977:133).

13. Food faddism is hardly new. In the nineteenth century, the Reverend Sylvester Graham invented the graham cracker "as a substitute for the meats and fats he believed inflamed his parishioners to sexual excess." The current enthusiasm for a high-fibre diet recalls the great constipation panic. In 1924 the Brinkler School of Eating in New York insisted that, "two or three evacuations a day are logical," and suggested that "the man with educated bowels will outstrip the man with educated brains in the race for life" (*Quest*, July 1980:25).

14. Brenton (1974:148-64) and Chafetz (1974:161-71) were major sources for this section.

15. Related to this matter of women being more easily dominated by older men is an observation made by anthropologist Robert Edgerton (1967) in an ethnographic study of the lives of forty-eight adult mental retardates. One reason these people managed to maintain themselves outside institutions was the development of a relationship with "benefactors" (normal persons who helped them with their problems). The relevant point is that eleven benefactors were husbands and only one, a wife. Further, Edgerton says, "Most of these husbands appeared to enjoy their extremely dominant relationship with their retarded wives" (p. 203).

16. Bess Kaplan's *Malke, Malke* (1977) is a delightful fictional account of a Jewish woman who advertises for her third husband in the personal column. The answer of one of her suitors provides a neat illustration of exchange theory:

> Dear Widow,
>
> My name is H. Schenkle. If you want we should meet, send me your picture. My wife died last year, and I'm a lousy cook. I am 69 years old. P.S. I have plenty money. I'm a rich man.
>
> Yours truly,
> H. Schenkle (Kaplan, 1977:24).

CHAPTER 6. SECONDARY AND SYMBOLIC AGENTS OF GENDER SOCIALIZATION

1. Since space limitations make it impossible to discuss *all* sources of gender socialization in the body of the book, the reader may find this more complete enumeration helpful. It is based on Lippitt (1968:335).

    a. The formal education system, public and private.

    b. The churches with their programs for children and youth.

    c. The leisure-time agencies with their recreational, cultural and character education programs.

    d. The social control and protection agencies such as the police, courts, traffic-safety agents, etc.

    e. The therapeutic, special correction and resocialization services such as counsellors, remedial clinics and programs for the handicapped.

    f. Employment offices and work supervisors who hire the young and supervise them on their paid jobs.

g. Political leaders who have an interest in involving the young in political activities.

The seven sources listed above offer more or less articulated programs and have professional socialization agents. They are the *secondary* socialization agents. The next two sources, the *primary* ones, are considerably more informal in their efforts, but they still involve direct agents:

h. The family.

i. The peer group.

The remaining two sources of socialization, the *symbolic* sources, lack direct agents:

j. The mass media.

k. Verbal and nonverbal forms of communication.

2. This section does not imply that occupational choice or career commitment are events that occur in adolescence and never again (Laws, 1976).

3. John Porter's *The Vertical Mosaic* (1965) tells us a great deal about Canadian elites, but very little about women. The reason is obvious: Women are the "missing sex" from the structures of power.

4. The term *church* is used to refer to "beliefs and rituals about the sacred, which bind people together in a moral community" (Walum, 1977:125).

5. According to Poelzer (1980), "feminist theology" is not theology done for and by women. Rather it is "theologizing done by any male or female person who as feminist recognizes that women have equal access to life opportunities, and to the development of their gifts, and to full equality as persons in relationship to men" (p. 36).

6. Although Chapter Seven treats social structural explanations of gender in depth, a brief discussion of the social structure of religion is included here for continuity's sake.

7. Margaret Atwood (1979:32) recalls the movie, *The Red Shoes*,

starring Moira Shearer, with beautiful red hair. A whole generation of little girls were taken to see it as a special treat for their birthday parties. Moira Shearer was a famous dancer but alas, she fell in love with the orchestra conductor, who, for some reason totally obscure to me at the time, forbade her to dance after they got married. This prohibition made her very unhappy. She wanted the man, but she wanted to dance as well, and the conflict drove her to fling herself in front of a train. The message was clear. You could not have both your artistic career and the love of a good man as well, and if you tried, you would end up committing suicide.

8. O'Kelly (1980:110) concludes that fine art has been a masculine domain. She says, "the artists, the patrons, the gallery owners, the art critics, and the museum curators have been predominately and often exclusively men. The human experiences reflected in art, therefore, are male experiences or what men conceive of as female experiences."

9. Miners (1976) analyzed the following novels: Ethel Wilson, *Swamp Angel*; Robertson Davies, *Leaven of Malice*; Adele Wiseman, *The Sacrifice*; John Marlyn, *Under the Ribs of Death*; Mazo de la Roche, *Morning at Jalna*; Mordecai Richler, *The Apprenticeship of Duddy Kravitz*; Mavis Gallant, *Its Image on the Mirror*; Leonard Cohen, *The Favourite Game*; Margaret Laurence, *A Jest of God*; Hugh MacLennan, *Return of the Sphinx*; Marian Engel, *No Clouds of Glory*; Robert Kroetsch, *The Studhorse Man*; Alice Munro, *Lives of Girls and Women*; Richard B. Wright, *The Weekend Man*; Margaret Atwood, *Surfacing*; Herbert Harker, *Goldenrod*.

10. For simplicity's sake, Albrecht's (1954) third function, "social control," has been omitted from the discussion.

11. The material in this subsection has been organized according to categories developed by Eakins and Eakins (1978). Additional major sources were Martyna (1980) and Miller and Swift (1977).

12. Major references for the subsection "Sex Differences in Language Use" are Thorne and Henley (1975) and Kramer, Thorne and Henley (1978).

CHAPTER 7. SOCIAL-STRUCTURAL EXPLANATIONS OF GENDER

1. Nettler (1970) tells us that "explanations are manipulations of symbols performed in an attempt to satisfy curiosity [emphasis deleted]" (p. 1). Further, a distinguishing characteristic of the scientific explanation is its "self-conscious use of facts as the building blocks, the elements, of its story." Empathetic and ideological explanations, by contrast, "talk to the heart" (p. 87).

2. Mackenzie's (1978) ethnographic study reported that Hutterite women did *not* manage to exercise informal power.

3. Eichler's (1977b) procedure varied only slightly from that used in Pineo's and Porter's (1967) study of occupational prestige.

4. Both these questions were taken from Nye and Hoffman (1963).

5. The skepticism of women in social science toward biological explanations of motherhood has a long history. Leta Hollingworth (quoted in Polatnick, 1975:202) argued as follows in a 1916 issue of *The American Journal of Sociology*:

> There is, to be sure, a strong and fervid insistence on the "maternal instinct," which is popularly supposed to characterize all women equally, and to furnish them with an all-consuming desire for parenthood, regardless of the personal pain, sacrifice, and disadvantage involved. In the absence of all verifiable data, however, it is only common-sense to guard against accepting as a fact of human nature a doctrine which we might well expect to find in use as a means of social control.

Contemporary social scientists such as Chodorow (1978) continue to be wary of bioevolutionary analyses of motherhood, such as that of Rossi (1977). An important reason for preferring structural explanations of parenthood is, of course, the plausibility of the evidence for such explanations and the deficiencies in the evidence for biological explanations.

6. See Lopata (1979) for discussion of the *social* implications of widowhood.

CHAPTER 8. PROSPECTS AND AVENUES OF CHANGE

1. Nellie McClung's *In Times Like These*, originally published in 1915, and reissued by the University of Toronto Press, provides an interesting personal account of the early twentieth-century feminist issues.

2. Armstrong and Armstrong (1978:115) report that during International Women's Year (1975), the Canadian government undertook an extensive advertising campaign to convince Canadians that men and women have equal potential. Decision Marketing Research Limited, who did an evaluation study for the government, found that there had been "no significant change, on average, in any of the attitudes." On the American scene, Mason et al. (1976) found little evidence that the influence of the women's movement alone had changed women's gender attitudes. On the contrary, the sizable changes in attitudes since 1964 may help explain the rise of the movement.

3. See Eichler (1980) for an insightful discussion of feminist research and proposals for social change.

Glossary

Achieved Status. Societal position acquired through the individual's own accomplishments, e.g., occupation.

Adult socialization. Socialization that occurs beyond the childhood years.

Agentic orientation. A masculine orientation that stresses achievement and occupational commitment (as opposed to relationships) and is accompanied by attitudes of aggressiveness, power, control and competitiveness. Also referred to as "instrumental orientation."

Aggression. Behavior intended to hurt another.

Anal stage. Freud's second stage of personality development (eighteen months to three years of age) in which the child becomes preoccupied with elimination of the bowels. The superego emerges from this conflict.

Androcentric. Dominated by males or masculine interests.

Androgyny. "A state in which feminine and masculine elements are present, accepted and accessible within the individual" (Laws, 1979).

Anima. A concept originated by Jung that refers to the female principle within the male.

Animus. A concept originated by Jung that refers to the male principle within the female.

Anorexia nervosa. A syndrome in which adolescents (90% female) starve themselves and sometimes die of malnutrition.

Argument-by-analogy research. Inferring human behavior from that of selected animals.

Ascribed status. A position in a social group, decided at birth (e.g., gender, race).

Asexuality. Being sexless or having no apparent sexuality.

Assertive behavior. Behavior "which expresses that person's feelings, attitudes, wishes, opinions or rights directly, firmly, and honestly, while respecting the feelings, attitudes, wishes, opinions and rights of other person(s)" (Alberti, 1977).

Assimilation. Process by which a group loses its distinctiveness and becomes similar to the dominant group.

Associationism. The assumption that behavior can be explained by studying the associations or linkages between stimuli and the accompanying changes in an organism's behavior, called responses.

Assumption of dichotomy. Males and females are considered to be complete opposites with entirely separate, nonoverlapping sets of characteristics. Also known as the "bipolarity assumption."

Authoritarianism. An undemocratic form of leadership where an aloof leader makes the group decisions.

Authority. Legitimized power to which people consent.

Avoidance learning. A type of conditioning in which the organism learns to prevent an aversive stimulus by making the appropriate response.

Axioms. Propositions or principles that have received general acceptance or which seem self-evident.

Behaviorism. A methodological position that psychology should deal only with the observable behavior, and not with what goes on inside the organism.

Biogenic. Resulting from biological, structural or biochemical factors.

Biological. Pertaining to the structure, functioning, growth or other life processes of living organisms that are not social or psychological in nature.

Biological determinism. The viewpoint that individual and social behaviors are determined by inborn biological propensities, such as genes or instincts.

Biosocial behavior. Social behavior considered to be the outcome of organic evolution.

Bipolarity assumption. See **Assumption of dichotomy**.

Bipolar trait. Any trait that can be categorized in terms of extremes or opposites (e.g., not at all aggressive—very aggressive).

Brain controversy. A controversy raging in the early twentieth century, when certain scientists were attempting to link brain size and intelligence, and were inferring the inferiority of certain racial groups and the entire female sex.

Bureaucracy. The administrative segment of a formal organization that operates according to explicit rules and procedures.

Canalization process. The channelling of behavior into familiar pathways, e.g., parents providing sex-typed playthings, which the children come to prefer.

Capitalist system. A class-based economic and political system based upon free enterprise and privately owned wealth.

Caste system. A closed stratification system with clearly defined boundaries that determine a person's position for life, at birth.

Castration complex. In Freudian theory, males' unconscious fear of losing their genital organs, as punishment for desiring their mothers.

Chauvinism. Zealous devotion to belief in the superiority of one's own sex.

Church. An established religious group bound together by similar beliefs and practices concerning the sacred.

Class. An aggregate of persons distinguished by inherited access to wealth or income, by power, and by prestige or life-style (Forcese, 1980).

Cognitive-developmental theory. A general psychological theory initiated by the Swiss psychologist, Jean Piaget, which attempts to identify the systematic changes that occur over time in children's thought processes.

Cohabitation. The practice of living together without being formally married. (Applies to partners of opposite sex.)

Cohort. A set of people in a population, grouped according to a common demographic event, e.g., year of birth.

Commodity production. The creation of products for exchange on the market.

Communal orientation. A feminine orientation that stresses relationships (as opposed to the male agentic orientation) and is accompanied by attitudes of nurturance and dependence. Also referred to as "expressive orientation."

Communal orientation to research. A general research style preferred by some feminists, which uses qualitative data and methods, and attempts to gain understanding by seeing the world through the eyes of the people being studied.

Concept. *An idea that includes all that is characteristically associated with . . . a term* (Webster's).

Conjugal. Refers to the wife-husband relationship.

Content analysis. A research procedure that systematically examines the content of recorded data such as mass media or government documents.

Control group. The group in an experiment that is observed but that does not receive any experimental manipulation.

Correlational studies. Studies that confirm the existence of a statistical association between or among variables, but which cannot establish a causal linkage.

Courtship. A recognized way for single persons to relate to each other with the goal of permanent mate selection (Laws and Schwartz, 1977).

Couvade. A practice among some preliterate societies, in which the father subjects himself to various taboos associated with pregnancy, experiences labor pains and a recovery period.

Criminology. A branch of sociology that studies the characteristics of crime, criminals and criminal behavior.

Cultural universal. A certain type of behavior found in many cultures, despite other variations in cultural patterns. This behavior is believed to be determined primarily by human genetic makeup.

Demeanor. Manner in which one conducts or presents oneself.

Demography. The scientific study of the characteristics of human populations.

Derived status. Status that is not dependent upon one's own personal achievement or ability but which is dependent upon the status of another, e.g. a wife's status is dependent in part upon that of her husband.

Deviation. Any variation (from a norm) that is considered socially significant.

Didactic. Intended or designed to teach or instruct.

Discrimination. Differential (usually harmful) treatment of others, which stems from their category membership rather than their individual characteristics.

Domestic orientation. Women's traditional sphere of activity, which is built around reproductive, affective and familial bonds.

Double sexual standard. According to this standard, the same behavior (e.g. premarital intercourse) brings different consequences for females and males.

Dyad. A two-person group.

Ecological. Refers to the relationship between living organisms and their environment.

Egalitarian family. One in which husband and wife have equal rights, duties and decision-making powers, and in which the children are provided with a nontraditional gender socialization environment.

Egalitarian sex roles. Women's and men's roles are not mutually exclusive. Both sexes participate equally in the domestic and economic sectors.

Empirical. (Knowledge) gained through the senses.

Environmental determinism. The position that individual and social behavior are the products of environmental influences in general and learning in particular. Extreme proponents deny the role of biology.

Erogenous zones. Areas of the body that respond sexually to stimulation and are associated by psychoanalysts with stages of development (e.g., oral zone, genital zone).

Ethnic group. A group with a shared sense of identity based on similar characteristics and sociocultural experiences.

Ethnographic study. Observational study of a group's way of life. The technique originated with anthropologists' studies of preliterate societies. Now applied to modern groups as well.

Etiology. The study of origins, causes or reasons.

Exchange theory of courtship. Females offer characteristics desired by males in exchange for the characteristics and the status they desire from males (Taylor and Glenn, 1976).

Exogamy. The custom of marrying outside of one's family group, community or other social unit.

Explanation by discipline. The way in which a discipline, such as biology, psychology or sociology, seeks to understand phenomena, and to offer its own distinctive, but legitimate, perspective.

Expressive leader. A person who encourages group morale and reinforces individual efforts rather than pushing the group toward its instrumental goal.

Expressive orientation. See **Communal orientation**.

Expressive skills. Skills traditionally considered feminine, and which focus on concern for the relation between self and others.

Extended family. Nuclear family (wife, husband, children) plus other relatives such as grandparents, aunts, uncles.

False consciousness. Marxian concept that emphasizes the failure of members of a class to share an awareness of their common situation and interests, an awareness that might lead to political action.

Feminist. A person, female or male, who advocates for women the same rights granted men. (See also **Radical feminist** and **Socialist feminist**.)

Franchise. The statutory right to vote.

Functionalists. Sociologists who view society as a system of interrelated parts that each contribute to its overall stability.

Gender. Sociocultural elaborations upon physiological sex.

Gender identity. An individual's personal conviction of being female or male. May conflict with physiological sex.

Gender ideology. Beliefs concerning the kinds of behavior appropriate for females versus males.

Gender imagery. Mental pictures, images or descriptions that people hold of females or males (as socially defined).

Gender norms. Informal rules, beliefs and standards that govern the behavior of females and males.

Gender socialization. The processes through which individuals learn to become masculine and feminine according to the expectations current in their society.

Genderless society. "A society in which the biological fact of sex receives no social recognition (except, presumably, for reproductive purposes)" (Jaggar and Struhl, 1978).

Generic. Relates to or describes an entire group or class.

Genetic sex. Male/female difference as determined by XX or XY chromosomes.

Genital sex. Male/female difference as determined by the presence of a penis or a clitoris and vagina.

Genital stage. Freud's fifth stage of personality development (adolescence) marked by a resurgence of sexual urges resulting from physiological maturation.

Gonadal sex. Male/female sex as determined by the presence of either ovaries or testes.

Group cohesion. The degree to which individual members are attracted to or committed to the group.

Group consciousness. The totality of ideas and beliefs held by a group and internalized by its members.

Hedonism. Assumption that the basic motivation for behavior lies in the individual's attempts to maximize rewards and minimize punishments.

Hegemony. Leadership or dominance of one group over another.

Hermaphrodites. Organisms that possess both male and female tissue.

Hormonal sex. Male/female difference as determined by relative levels of estrogen and testosterone.

Hypodermic needle model. Posits a direct relationship between mass media messages and subsequent actions of audience members.

Hypothesis. An assertion of a relationship between two or more variables that is subject to empirical verification.

Ideational creativity. The aspect of creativity that involves the production of unusual ideas.

Identification theory. Assumption that gender socialization occurs through children's modelling of adult behavior.

Ideological institutions. Institutions that both reflect and convey the ideas, beliefs, values and social needs of people (e.g., broadcasting and publishing organizations, schools, universities).

Ideology. A set of ideas, beliefs and values reflecting the needs of the people embracing the ideology to explain the social order.

Incest. Forbidden sexual relationship between persons of the same family.

Independent status. A status that in no way depends upon another person's status, but instead is based solely upon one's personal qualifications.

Industrial segregation by sex. Refers to the fact that employed women are concentrated more in some industries than in others.

Innate. Inborn or inherent, that is, not learned.

Institutionalized. Well-established social patterns.

Instrumental leader. One who pushes the group toward its goal, rather than placing emphasis on group morale or individual efforts.

Instrumental orientation. See **Agentic orientation**.

Instrumental skills. Skills traditionally considered masculine, and which focus on competence and accomplishment rather than interpersonal relations.

Internalization. To make external beliefs and values a part of one's own system of beliefs and values.

IQ (Intelligence quotient). A person's presumed abilities and skills as measured according to specific techniques.

Kinder, Küche, Kirche. The traditional notion that women's lives should revolve around children, kitchen and church.

Latency stage. Freud's fourth stage of personality development (six to twelve years), which consolidates the achievements of the preceding stages.

Lateralization. Specialization in the functioning of each hemisphere of the brain.

Learning Theory. See **Social learning theory**.

Lesbianism. Female homosexuality.

Linguistic. Relating to the nature and structure of human language.

Machismo research. The general research style allegedly preferred by male sociologists, which stresses the similarities between sociology and the natural sciences. Quantitative research is employed and data are statistically controlled and manipulated.

Macrosociological research. Research based on large-scale, impersonal, aggregated and static data.

Male bonding. Lionel Tiger's hypothesis that a particular relationship exists between males such that they react differently to members of their bonding unit, as compared to individuals outside it.

Marxism. The perspective originated by Karl Marx, which views class conflict as the major societal principle.

Masochism. Pleasure derived from being mistreated.

Mass media. Impersonal communication sources that reach large audiences and exist to entertain, inform and sell products (i.e., television, newspapers).

Matching hypothesis. People tend to relate to others of approximately equal beauty.

Matriarchate. A hypothetical form of society ruled by women.

Matrifocal. Social organization in, for example, ape societies, that develops from the mother-infant bond (Lancaster, 1976).

Mean. The sum of the scores divided by the total number of cases involved (Blalock, 1960).

Means of production. A term used by Marx to classify the equipment, resources and technology used in the production of goods and services.

Median. The category or value in a statistical distribution, above and below which lie an equal number of values.

Metaphysical. Based on very abstract or speculative reasoning.

Methodology. The logic and techniques of carrying out research.

Microsociological research. Research based on small-scale, personal, disaggregated and dynamic findings.

Minority group. Any group of people (regardless of size) with similar characteristics who receive differential and discriminatory treatment because of these characteristics (e.g., women, Indians).

Misogyny. The hatred of women.

Mode. The most frequently occurring score in a distribution.

Modelling. A type of learning whereby a new response is acquired through observation of another's behavior.

Momism. A situation in which maternal power is too strong and paternal power is in decline, allegedly existing in the U.S.A. in the 1950s.

Motherhood mystique. The belief that a woman must experience maternity in order to find true happiness and feminine self-actualization.

Mythology. Shared belief systems divorced from science, which provide people with means of control, as well as explanation (see Chapter Two Notes).

Narcissism. In psychoanalysis, a regression to the infantile state of development in which one is erotically interested in one's own body.

Nature-nurture controversy. A long debate over the relative importance of inheritance (nature) versus environment (nurture) in shaping a person's development.

Neologism. A newly invented word, phrase or expression (e.g., Ms.).

Normal curve. A smooth, symmetrical, bell-shaped frequency distribution based on an indefinitely large number of cases. Its mean, median and mode all coincide. This mathematical ideal can only be approximated by actual data (Blalock, 1960).

Norms. Standards of behavior and beliefs that are established either formally or informally within a culture, and which are both accepted and expected by the group members.

Nuclear family. The family consisting of the mating couple and their children.

Occupational segregation of females. The concentration of employed women in a few traditionally "female" jobs.

Oedipus conflict. Freudian assertion that the child craves sexual possession of the opposite-sex parent, while viewing the same-sex parent as the rival.

Operant conditioning. A type of learning whereby the organism makes a number of trial-and-error responses. The responses that are followed by reward (positive reinforcement) tend to be repeated on future occasions. Those responses followed by negative reinforcement, or by no reinforcement, tend to be extinguished.

Operational definition. The clear specification of the observable procedures used to identify a term or concept in question, e.g., defining aggression according to specific attitude tests designed to measure it.

Operationalize. See **Operational definition.**

Oral stage. Freud's first stage of personality development (birth to eighteen months) in which the infant is preoccupied with pleasures associated with the mouth.

Ordinal family position. The position a person holds in the age-ranking of the siblings of a family.

Orientation. A general theoretical approach to the analysis and interpretation of behavior.

Paradigm. A major theoretical framework of a scientific discipline.

Paralinguistic. Refers to optional vocal effects that accompany human speech. Examples include tone, pitch, depth of voice.

Paraphilia. Preference for unusual sexual practices.

Parsimony. Use of economy or simplicity of assumptions in stating an argument.

Parthenogenic approach to gender identity. The assumption that a child's identity will correctly emerge if there is at least one parent with whom the child experiences close interaction.

Particularistic expectations. The expectation one has of another, based upon that person's individual qualities and needs.

Paternalistic society. See **Patriarchial society.**

Pathology. Individual or group activity or behavior that is destructive to other individuals, groups or society.

Patriarchal society. A society oriented toward and dominated by males.

Patrilineal system. A system in which a person's descent is traced through the male line.

Pedestal-gutter syndrome. The apparently contradictory myths that males hold concerning women (e.g., goddess and devil, virgin and whore). All represent the attitude that woman is different from man.

Peer group. "An informal group of self-selected equals who coalesce around common interests, tastes, preferences, and beliefs" (Bensman and Rosenberg, 1979).

Penis envy. The envy of males experienced by females (according to Freud) from early childhood on because of the more visible male sex organs.

Personal space. The area around a person that he/she feels belongs uniquely to him/her. Invasion of this space brings negative reactions.

Phallic stage. Freud's third stage of personality development (at about four years old), which establishes gender identity through resolution of the Oedipal conflict.

Phylogenetic scale. A system of classification based upon the evolution of a genetically related group of organisms.

Physiological. Pertaining to the body, its life processes, activities and functions.

Platonic relationship. A relationship between a male and female that does not involve romance or sexual relations.

Plutocratic class. A term for upper social class, which owns the means of production.

Polygyny. A marriage arrangement in which the man has more than one wife at a time.

Pop sociology. Widely circulating notions about the operations of society, produced by sources other than professional sociologists.

Postmeasurement. Measurement made after the administration of the experimental variable.

Prejudice. A negative attitude toward an individual, based on the individual's category membership, not on his/her personal characteristics.

Premeasurement. Measurement made prior to administration of the experimental variable.

Primary relationships. Relationships based on the particular identities, qualities and needs of the individuals involved. The strength of the emotions in these relationships (e.g., family, friendship groups) makes them the most influential in the individual's socialization.

Primary sectors. Those segments of the economy characterized by high productivity, heavy capitalization and unionization, such as oil and gas, mining and some manufacturing and construction (extrapolated from Armstrong and Armstrong, 1978).

Primary socialization. The basic socialization that occurs in childhood and which involves development of language and individual identity, the learning of cognitive skills and self-control, the internalization of moral standards, attitudes and motivations, and some understanding of societal roles.

Primatology. The study of primates, including *homo sapiens*, apes, monkeys, lemurs, marmosets.

Primordial gender. The original, elementary forms of femininity and masculinity.

Principle of less interest. In a two-person relationship, the person who cares the least about the quality or continuation of the relationship is in an advantageous position to dominate the other person in the relationship (Waller and Hill, 1951).

Private sphere of life. Centers around home activities and their use-value. (See **Production of use-values.**) In industrial society, there is a sharp differentiation between workplace and home activities and the status, resources and value derived from each.

Production of use-values. Production of things in the home, which are outside the money economy.

Proletarian class. A term originated by Marx to mean the working class, or the social class that does not own the means of production.

Psychoanalytic perspective. A theory of personality and a system of therapy formulated by Freud and his disciples.

Psychodynamics. The view that behavior is the product of active (dynamic) mental (psychological) forces.

Psychological. Pertaining to the individual, particularly his/her mind and emotions.

Psychosexual. The mental, emotional and/or behavioral aspects of a person's biologically specified sex.

Public orientation. The traditional orientation of men's sphere of activity (e.g., politics, the military, religion, hunting). (It contrasts with the traditional *domestic* orientation of women.)

Qualitative research. Research that examines and interprets observations nonnumerically, for the purpose of discovering underlying meanings and relationships, e.g., participant observation.

Quantitative research. Research that numerically represents and manipulates observations for the purpose of explaining the phenomena in question, e.g., analyzing questionnaires by computer.

Queen Bee syndrome. Refers to women who have become successful in the male professional world and who treat women who have not as inferior (Staines et al., 1974).

Racism. Discrimination based on the alleged inferiority of a person's ethnicity.

Radical feminist. A Marxian-influenced thinker who views women's oppression as fundamental to all oppression, and who advocates revolution as the only solution.

Reference group. A group with which one identifies (but to which one does not necessarily belong), used as a standard for personal definition and evaluation.

Reflection hypothesis. States that the media are sexist because they mirror, rather than originate, cultural notions of gender.

Regionalism. Refers to the consciousness of the population of a distinct area, characterized by common interests, background or culture.

Repression. A defense mechanism used to prevent anxiety-producing experiences from entering the consciousness.

Reserve army of labor. According to Marx, women constitute a flexible labor supply, drawn into the labor market when needed and sent home when the need is past.

Resocialization. Occurs when a new role or situation requires that a person replace established patterns of behavior and thought with new patterns.

Resource theory of conjugal power. Assumes that the balance of power in a marriage rests on the resources that the partners contribute to the marriage (e.g., social status, distinguished lineage, money).

Reversal of success phenomenon. Refers to the observation that while females compete equivalently with males during school years, they have relatively low aspirations beyond high school.

Role. Defines what a person in a given status is supposed to do (e.g., support a family, look after children, perform surgical operations).

Role script. Those behaviors, activities and attitudes that are considered appropriate for the incumbent of a given status.

Role strain. Difficulty that is felt in fulfilling role obligations.

Salient statuses. Those of an individual's statuses that matter more than others to society at large. They can be achieved or ascribed, socially valued or socially proscribed.

Secondary agents of socialization. Formal agents, such as the school or the church, which purposely set out to equip individuals with knowledge required to fit into society.

Sex roles. Refers to behavior associated with sexual intercourse.

Sex stratification. Defining sex-specific categories as better or worse and rewarding them accordingly (Nielsen, 1978).

Sex-typing. The differential shaping of behavior for males and females.

Sexism. Discrimination based on the assumption that one sex (usually male) is superior.

Sexual dimorphism. The belief that males and females display quite different types of behavior, because of their sex.

Social desirability. The tendency for research subjects to respond in culturally preferred ways, at the expense of truthfulness.

Social identity. Broad social categories (e.g., gender, age, race) to which an individual can belong and be seen as belonging (Goffman, 1971).

Social institutions. Sets of beliefs, norms and values that resolve issues of societal importance (e.g., raising children, producing goods, making political decisions).

Social learning theory. A general psychological theory that has attempted to identify a comprehensive set of learning principles that apply equally well to humans and lower animals.

Social movement. "A large-scale, informal effort designed to correct, supplement, overthrow, or in some fashion influence the social order." (Toch, 1965).

Social psychology. The discipline that explores how the social environment impinges upon the individual.

Social stratification. The arrangement of social categories into hierarchial positions that are ranked unequally and rewarded (psychologically, socially, materially) accordingly.

Social structure. The organization of interrelated components that make up a social system (e.g., statuses, roles, groups).

Social system. A network of interacting units.

Socialist feminist. Emphasizes class analysis and augments Marx's and Engels's discussion of society by focusing on institutions, such as the family, which are particularly responsible for women's oppression.

Socialization. The lifelong, complex learning process through which individuals develop selfhood and acquire the knowledge, skills and motivations required for participation in social life.

Society. A relatively self-sufficient group of people distinguished from others by mutual interests, shared territory, shared institutions and a common culture, e.g., Canada (as a nation).

Sociobiology. "The analysis of social behavior as the outcome of organic evolution" (Boorman and Levitt, 1980).

Socioeconomic status. Refers to one's position in a stratification system based on power, prestige and material possessions. Occupation, income and education are important determinants in one's ranking.

Sociolinguistics. An interdisciplinary field of interest, which studies language as a social phenomenon.

Sociology. The study of human social behavior, social structures and social interaction.

Sociology of knowledge. The branch of sociology concerned with the relation between a person's thought and his/her location in the social structure.

Sociometry. A research technique for measuring the attraction and repulsion patterns in small groups.

Spatial skills. The ability to visually manipulate, locate or make judgements about the spatial relationships of items located in two- or three-dimensional space.

Status. Position in a social group, e.g., mother, old man, computer technician.

Status set. Combination of statuses held by any one individual at any one time (e.g., woman, wife, mother, daughter, student).

Stereotype. A folk belief about the attributes characterizing a social category (e.g. women), on which there is substantial agreement.

Stratification. See **Social stratification.**

Structural-functionalists. See **Functionalists.**

Subculture. A cultural subgroup with more or less distinctive beliefs, norms, symbols, values or other shared factors.

Substantive. That which has a solid, empirical basis.

Suffrage movement. The early-twentieth-century women's movement that fought for the right to vote.

Superego. The Freudian conscience.

Symbolic agents of socialization. Language and the mass media.

Symbolic interactionism. Microsociological theoretical perspective inspired by G. H. Mead, C. H. Cooley and W. I. Thomas, which emphasizes interaction, language and the self.

Theory. "A set of interrelated hypotheses or propositions concerning a phenomenon or set of phenomena" (Shaw and Costanzo, 1970).

Trait. A relatively enduring personality characteristic that is the product of an interplay between biological predispositions and social learning.

Transsexualism. A biologically normal person's overwhelming desire to be, or conviction of being, a member of the other sex.

Transvestism. The desire to dress in clothing of the opposite sex.

Universalistic expectations. The expectations one has of another based upon the objective standards one has for all people in that category (i.e., teacher/student).

Urbanization. The increase in the proportion of a population that lives in urban areas.

Values. Socially shared principles, standards or ideas about what is considered right, worthwhile or desirable.

Variable. A measurable dimension of a concept that has more than one magnitude (e.g., income that varies in dollars).

WASP. Refers to a person of white, Anglo-Saxon, Protestant descent.

Women's studies. The analysis of women conducted in a variety of fields within the humanities and social sciences.

Bibliography

Abbott, Susan. "Full-time farmers and week-end wives: an analysis of altering conjugal roles." *Journal of Marriage and the Family* 38 (1976):165-74.

Abell, Helen C. "Adaptation of the rural family to change." In *Marriage, Family and Society: Canadian Perspectives*, edited by S. Parvez Wakil, pp. 367-78. Toronto: Butterworths, 1975.

Aberle, D., and K. Naegele. "Middle-class fathers' occupational role and attitudes toward children." *American Journal of Orthopsychiatry* 22 (1952):366-78.

Abu-Laban, Sharon McIrvin. "Social supports in older age: the need for new research directions." *Essence* 4 (1980):195-210.

Abu-Laban, Sharon McIrvin, and Baha Abu-Laban. "Women and the aged as minority groups: a critique." *Canadian Review of Sociology and Anthropology* 14 (1977):103-16.

Acker, Joan. "Women and social stratification: a case of intellectual sexism." *American Journal of Sociology* 78 (1973):936-45.

Adler, F. *Sisters in Crime: The Rise of the New Female Criminal.* New York: McGraw-Hill, 1975.

Akers, F. C. "Negro and white automobile-buying behavior: new evidence." *Journal of Marketing Research*, August 1968: 283-89.

Alberti, R. E. "Principles for ethical practice of assertive behavior training." In *Assertiveness: Innovations, Applications, Issues*, edited by R. E. Alberti, pp. 365-74. San Luis Obispo, Calif.: Impact Publishers, 1974.

Albrecht, Milton C. "The relationship of literature and society." *American Journal of Sociology* 59 (1954):425-36.

Al-Issa, Ihsan. *The Psychopathology of Women.* Englewood Cliffs, N.J.: Prentice-Hall, 1980.

Allport, Gordon. *The Nature of Prejudice.* Reading, Mass.: Addison-Wesley, 1954.

Almquist, Elizabeth M. "Women in the labor force." *Signs* 2 (1977):843-55.

Ambert, Anne-Marie. *Sex Structure.* 2nd ed. Don Mills, Ontario: Longman Canada, 1976.

_____. *Divorce in Canada.* Don Mills, Ontario: Academic Press Canada, 1980.

Andelin, H. B. *Fascinating Womanhood.* New York: Bantam Books, 1974.

Andersen, Margret, ed. *Mother Was Not a Person.* Montreal: Black Rose Books, 1972.

Anderson, Alan B., and James S. Frideres. *Ethnicity in Canada: Theoretical Perspectives.* Toronto: Butterworths, 1981.

Andreas, Carol. *Sex and Caste in America.* Englewood Cliffs, N.J.: Prentice-Hall, 1971.

Archer, D., and R. M. Akert. "Words and everything else: verbal and nonverbal cues in social interpretation." *Journal of Personality and Social Psychology* 35 (1977):443-49.

Archer, John. "Biological explanations of psychological sex differences." In *Exploring Sex Differences*, edited by Barbara Lloyd and John Archer, pp. 241-66. New York: Academic Press, 1976.

Archibald, Linda; Leona Christian; Karen Deterding; and Dianne Hendrick. "Sex biases in newspaper reporting: press treatment of municipal candidates." *Atlantis* 5 (1980):177-84.

Argyle, M.; V. Salter; H. Nicholson; M. Williams; and P. Burgess. "The communication of inferior and superior attitudes by verbal and nonverbal signals." *British Journal of Social and Clinical Psychology* 9 (1970):222-31.

Armstrong, Hugh, and Pat Armstrong. "The segregated participation of women in the Canadian labour force, 1941-71." *Canadian Review of Sociology and Anthropology* 12 (1975), Part 1:370-84.

_____. *The Double Ghetto: Canadian Women and Their Segregated Work.* Toronto: McClelland and Stewart, 1978.

Arnopoulos, Sheila McLeod. *Problems of Immigrant Women in the Canadian Labour Force.* Ottawa: Canadian Advisory Council on the Status of Women, 1979.

Aronoff, Joel, and William D. Crano. "A re-examination of the cross-cultural principles of task segregation and sex role differentiation in the family." *American Sociological Review* 40 (1975):12-20.

Ashmore, Richard D., and Frances K. Del Boca. "Sex stereotypes and implicit personality theory: toward a cognitive-social psychological conceptualization." *Sex Roles* 5 (1979):219-48.

Atkin, C., and M. Miller. "The effects of TV advertising on children: experimental evidence." Paper presented to Annual Convention of the International Communication Association, Chicago, 1975.

Atwood, Margaret. *The Edible Woman.* Toronto: McClelland and Stewart, 1969.

_____. *Survival: A Thematic Guide to Canadian Literature.* Toronto: Anansi Press, 1972.

_____. *Surfacing.* Don Mills, Ontario: PaperJacks, 1973.

_____. "A reply." *Signs* 2 (1976):340-41.

_____. *Dancing Girls.* Toronto: McClelland and Stewart, 1977.

_____. "The curse of Eve—or, what I learned in school." *Canadian Women's Studies* 1 (1979):30-33.

Babchuk, Nicholas. "Primary friends and kin: a study of the association of middle-class couples." *Social Forces* 43 (1965):483-93.

Babchuk, Nicholas, and Alan P. Bates. "The primary relations of middle-class couples: a study in male dominance." *American Sociological Review* 28 (1963):377-91.

Bakan, David. *The Duality of Human Existence.* Chicago: Rand McNally, 1966.

Baker, Maureen, and J. I. Hans Bakker. "The double-bind of the middle-class male: men's liberation and the male sex role." *Journal of Comparative Family Studies* 11 (1980):547-61.

Baker, Maureen, and Mary-Anne Robeson. "Trade union reactions to women workers and their concerns." *Canadian Journal of Sociology* 6 (1981):19-31.

Bandura, Albert. "Social-learning theory of identificatory processes." In *Handbook of Socialization Theory and Research*, edited by David A. Goslin, pp. 213-62. Chicago: Rand McNally, 1969.

Barash, D. P. "Reflections on a premature burial." *The American Sociologist* 12 (1977a):66-68.

_____. *Sociobiology and Behavior.* New York: Elsevier, 1977b.

_____. *The Whisperings Within.* Markham, Ontario: Penguin, 1979.

Barclay, A., and D. R. Cusumano. "Father absence, cross-sex identity and field-dependent behavior in male adolescents." *Child Development* 38 (1961):243-50.

Bardwick, Judith M. "The development of sex differences." In *Readings on the Psy-*

chology of Women, edited by Judith M. Bardwick, pp. 1-3. New York: Harper and Row, 1972.

Bardwick, Judith M., and Elizabeth Douvan. "Ambivalence: the socialization of women." In *Woman in Sexist Society*, edited by Vivian Gornick and Barbara K. Moran, pp. 225-41. New York: Signet Books, 1971.

Barfield, Ashton. "Biological influences on sex differences in behavior." In *Sex Differences: Social and Biological Perspectives*, edited by Michael S. Teitelbaum, pp. 62-121. Garden City, N.Y.: Doubleday Anchor, 1976.

Barfoot, Joan. *Abra*. Toronto: McGraw-Hill Ryerson, 1978.

Baron, Robert A. and Donn Byrne. *Social Psychology*. 2nd ed. Boston: Allyn and Bacon, 1977.

Barry, Herbert; Margaret K. Bacon; and Irwin L. Child. "A cross-cultural survey of some sex differences in socialization." *Journal of Abnormal and Social Psychology* 55 (1957):327-38.

Bart, Pauline B. "Why women's status changes in middle age: the turns of the social ferris wheel." *Sociological Symposium* 3 (1969):1-18.

_____. "Depression in middle-aged women." In *Woman in Sexist Society*, edited by Vivian Gornick and Barbara K. Moran, pp. 163-86. New York: Signet Books, 1971a.

_____. "Sexism and social science: from the gilded cage to the iron cage, or, the perils of Pauline." *Journal of Marriage and the Family* 33 (1971b):734-45.

Barty, M. "Fear of success." Unpublished manuscript, 1971.

Baruch, G. K. "Maternal influences upon college women's attitudes toward a man and work." *Developmental Psychology* 6 (1972):32-37.

Bassett, Isabel. *The Parlour Rebellion: Profiles in the Struggle for Women's Rights*. Toronto: McClelland and Stewart, 1975.

Batt, Sharon. "Editorial." *Branching Out* 5, no. 4 (1978):2.

Bearison, David J. "Sex-linked patterns of socialization." *Sex Roles* 5 (1979):11-18.

de Beauvoir, Simone. *The Second Sex*. New York: Bantam Books, 1952.

_____. *Old Age*. Harmondsworth, England: Penguin Books, 1970.

Becker, Howard S. *Outsiders*. New York: Free Press, 1963.

_____. "A school is a lousy place to learn anything." In *Learning to Work*, edited by Blanche Geer, pp. 89-109. Beverly Hills: Sage Publications, 1972.

Beere, Carole A. *Women and Women's Issues: A Handbook of Tests and Measures*. San Francisco:Jossey Bass, 1979.

Bell, Inge Powell. "The double standard." *Trans-action* 8 (November-December 1970):75-80.

Bem, Sandra L. "The measurement of psychological androgyny." *Journal of Consulting and Clinical Psychology* 42 (1974):155-62.

_____. "Sex-role adaptability: one consequence of psychological androgyny." *Journal of Personality and Social Psychology* 31 (1975):634-43.

_____. "Probing the promise of androgyny." In *Beyond Sex-role Stereotypes: Readings toward a Psychology of Androgyny*, edited by Alexandra G. Kaplan and Joan P. Bean, pp. 48-62. Boston: Little, Brown, 1976.

Bem, Sandra, and Daryl J. Bem. "Training the woman to know her place: the power of a nonconscious ideology." In *Roles Women Play: Readings toward Women's Liberation*, edited by Michele Hoffnung Garskof, pp. 84-96. Belmont, Calif.:Brooks/Cole Publishing, 1971.

_____. "Does sex-biased job advertising 'aid and abet' sex discrimination?" *Journal of Applied Social Psychology* 3 (1973):6-18.

Benbow, Camilla Persson, and Julian C. Stanley. "Sex differences in mathematical ability: fact or artifact?" *Science* 210 (12 December 1980):1262-64.

Bensman, Joseph, and Robert Lilienfeld. "Friendship and alienation." *Psychology Today* (October 1979): 56, 57, 59, 60, 63, 66, 114.

Bensman, Joseph, and Bernard Rosenberg. "The peer group." In *Socialization and the Life Cycle*, edited by Peter I. Rose, pp. 79-96. New York: St. Martin's Press, 1979.

Benston, Margaret. "The political economy of women's liberation." *Monthly Review* 21 (1969):13-27.

Berger, Charlene, and Dolores Gold. "The relation between sex-role identification and problem-solving performance in young boys and girls." Paper presented at Research for Women: Current Projects and Future Directions, an Interdisciplinary Conference, Mount Saint Vincent University, Halifax, N.S., 1976.

Berger, Peter L. *The Noise of Solemn Assemblies*. New York: Doubleday, 1961.

Berger, Peter L., and Thomas Luckmann. *The Social Construction of Reality*. Garden City, N.Y.: Doubleday Anchor, 1966.

Berheide, Catherine White; Sarah Fenstermaker Berk; and Richard A. Berk. "Household work in the suburbs: the job and its participants." *Pacific Sociological Review* 19 (1976):491-518.

Berk, Sarah Fenstermaker, ed. *Women and Household Labor*. Beverly Hills: Sage Publications, 1980.

Berlyne, D. E. "Laughter, humor, and play." In *The Handbook of Social Psychology*, 2nd ed., vol. 3, edited by Gardner Lindzey and Elliot Aronson, pp. 795-852. Reading, Mass.: Addison-Wesley, 1969.

Bernard, Jessie. "The paradox of the happy marriage." In *Woman in Sexist Society*, edited by Vivian Gornick and Barbara K. Moran, pp. 145-62. New York: Mentor Books, 1971.

_____. "My four revolutions: an autobiographical history of the ASA." *American Journal of Sociology* 78 (1973):773-91.

_____. *The Future of Motherhood*. New York: Dial Press, 1974a.

_____. "The housewife: between two worlds." In *Varieties of Work Experience*, edited by Phyllis L. Stewart and Muriel G. Cantor, pp. 49-66. Cambridge, Mass.: Schenkman, 1974b.

_____. *Women, Wives, Mothers: Values and Options*. Chicago: Aldine, 1975.

_____. "Sex differences: an overview." In *Beyond Sex-role Stereotypes: Readings toward a Psychology of Androgyny*, edited by Alexandra G. Kaplan and Joan P. Bean, pp. 10-26. Boston: Little, Brown, 1976.

_____. "The mother role." In *Women: A Feminist Perspective*, 2nd ed., edited by Jo Freeman, pp. 122-33. Palo Alto, Calif.: Mayfield, 1979.

_____. *The Female World*. New York: Free Press, 1981.

Berry, John W. "Native peoples and the larger society." In *A Canadian Social Psychology of Ethnic Relations*, edited by Robert C. Gardner and Rudolf Kalin, pp. 214-30. Toronto: Methuen, 1981.

Berry, John W.; Rudolf Kalin; and Donald M. Taylor. *Multiculturalism and Ethnic Attitudes in Canada*. Ottawa: Supply and Services Canada, 1977.

Berscheid, E; K. Dion; E. Walster; and G. Walster. "Physical attractiveness and dating choice: a test of the matching hypothesis." *Journal of Experimental Social Psychology* 7 (1971):173-89.

Berscheid, Ellen, and Elaine Hatfield Walster. "Physical attractiveness." In *Advances in Experimental Social Psychology*, vol. 7, edited by L. Berkowitz. New York: Academic Press, 1974.

_____. *Interpersonal Attraction*, 2nd ed. Reading, Mass.: Addison-Wesley, 1978.

Bestsellers Staff. "Magazines that grow and change with the women who read them." In *American Mass Media*, edited by Robert Atwan, Barry Orton and William Vesterman, pp. 226-29. New York: Random House, 1978.

Beuf, Ann. "Doctor, lawyer, household drudge." *Journal of Communication* 24 (1974):142-45.

Bibby, Reginald W. "Religion." In *Sociology*, edited by Robert Hagedorn, pp. 387-427. Toronto: Holt, Rinehart and Winston, 1980.

Biller, Henry B. *Father, Child and Sex Role*. Lexington, Mass.: D. C. Heath, 1971.

Birdwhistell, Ray L. *Kinesics and Context*. Philadelphia: University of Pennsylvania Press, 1970.

Birrell, Susan. "Achievement-related motives and the woman athlete." In *Women and Sport: From Myth to Reality*, edited by Carole A. Oglesby, pp. 143-71. Philadelphia: Lea and Febiger, 1978.

Blalock, Herbert M. *Social Statistics*. New York: McGraw-Hill, 1960.

Blau, Peter M., and Otis Dudley Duncan. *The American Occupational Structure*. New York: Wiley, 1967.

Blau, Zena Smith. *Old Age in a Changing Society*. New York: New Viewpoints, 1973.

Blaubergs, Maija S. "Changing the sexist language: the theory behind the practice." *Psychology of Women Quarterly* 2 (1978):244-61.

Blishen, Bernard R. "A socio-economic index for occupations in Canada." *Canadian Review of Sociology and Anthropology* 4 (1967):41-53.

————. "Social class and opportunity in Canada." In *Social Stratification: Canada*, edited by James E. Curtis and William G. Scott, pp. 162-73. Scarborough, Ontario: Prentice-Hall, 1973.

Blishen, Bernard R., and William K. Carroll. "Sex differences in a socio-economic index for occupations in Canada." *Canadian Review of Sociology and Anthropology* 15 (1978):352-71.

Blishen, Bernard R., and Hugh A. McRoberts. "A revised socioeconomic index for occupations in Canada." *Canadian Review of Sociology and Anthropology* 13 (1976):71-79.

Block, W. E., and M. A. Walker, eds. *Discrimination, Affirmative Action, and Equal Opportunity*. Vancouver: The Fraser Institute, 1982.

Blood, Robert, and Donald Wolfe. *Husbands and Wives: The Dynamics of Married Living*. New York: Free Press, 1960.

Blumberg, Rae Lesser. *Stratification: Socioeconomic and Sexual Inequality*. Dubuque, Iowa: Wm. C. Brown, 1978.

Bock, E. Wilbur. "The female clergy: A case of professional marginality." *American Journal of Sociology* 72 (1967):531-39.

Boorman, Scott A., and Paul R. Levitt. "The comparative evolutionary biology of social behavior." *Annual Review of Sociology* 6 (1980):213-34.

Booth, Alan. "Sex and social participation." *American Sociological Review* 37 (1972):183-93.

Boskind-Lodahl, Marlene. "Cinderella's stepsisters: a feminist perspective on Anorexia Nervosa and Bulimia." *Signs* 2 (1976):342-56.

Boulding, Elise. *The Underside of History: A View of Women Through Time*. Boulder, Colo.: Westview Press, 1976.

Bowlby, John. *Maternal Care and Maternal Health*. Geneva: World Health Organization, 1952.

Boyd, Monica. "English-Canadian and French-Canadian attitudes toward women: results of the Canadian Gallup Polls." *Journal of Comparative Family Studies* 6 (1975a):153-69.

_____. "The status of immigrant women in Canada." *Canadian Review of Sociology and Anthropology* 12 (1975b), Part 1:406-16.

_____. "The forgotten minority: the socioeconomic status of divorced and separated women." In *The Working Sexes*, edited by Patricia Marchak, pp. 47-71. Vancouver: University of British Columbia, 1977.

_____. "Sex differences in the Canadian occupational attainment process." *Canadian Review of Sociology and Anthropology* 19 (1982):1-28.

Boyd, Monica; Margrit Eichler; and John R. Hofley. "Family: functions, formation, and fertility." In *Opportunity for Choice: A Goal for Women in Canada*, edited by Gail C. A. Cook, pp. 13-52. Ottawa: Information Canada, Statistics Canada, in association with the C. D. Howe Research Institute, 1976.

Braid, Kate. "Women in non-traditional occupations in British Columbia." Paper presented to the Annual Meeting of Canadian Sociology and Anthropology Association, Saskatoon, Sask., 1979.

Brenton, Myron. *Friendship*. New York: Stein and Day, 1974.

_____. "The paradox of the contempory American father: every day is Mother's Day." In *Sex: Male—Gender: Masculine*, edited by John W. Petras, pp. 179-85. Port Washington, N.Y.: Alfred Publishing, 1975.

Briggs, Jean. "Eskimo women: makers of men." In *Many Sisters*, edited by Carolyn J. Matthiasson, pp. 261-304. New York: Free Press, 1975.

Brill, A. A., ed. *The Basic Writings of Sigmund Freud*. New York: Random House, 1938.

Brim, Orville. "Family structure and sex role learning by children: a further analysis of Helen Koch's data." *Sociometry* 21 (1958):1-16.

Brinkerhoff, Merlin B. "Women who want to work in a man's world: a study of the influence of structural factors on role innovativeness." *Canadian Journal of Sociology* 2 (1977):283-303.

Brinkerhoff, Merlin, and Eugen Lupri. "Theoretical and methodological issues in the use of decision-making as an indicator of conjugal power: some Canadian observations." *Canadian Journal of Sociology* 3 (1978):1-20.

Briskin, Linda, and Lynda Yanz. "Women and trade unions." *Resources for Feminist Research* 10 (1981):1.

Brodzinsky, David M.; Karen Barnet; and John R. Aiello. "Sex of subject and gender identity as factors in humor appreciation." *Sex Roles* 7 (1981):561-73.

Bronfenbrenner, Urie. "Some familial antecedents of responsibility and leadership in adolescents." In *Leadership and Interpersonal Behavior*, edited by Luigi Petrullo and Bernard M. Bass. New York: Holt, Rinehart and Winston, 1961.

Brophy, Jere E. *Child Development and Socialization*. Chicago: Science Research Associates, 1977.

Broverman, I. K.; D. M. Broverman; F. E. Clarkson; P. Rosenkrantz; and S. R. Vogel. "Sex-role stereotypes and clinical judgments of mental health." *Journal of Consulting and Clinical Psychology* 34 (1970):1-7.

Broverman, I. K.; D. M. Broverman; F. E. Clarkson; P. S. Rosenkrantz; and S. R. Vogel. "Sex-role stereotypes: a current appraisal." *Journal of Social Issues* 28 (1972):59-78.

Brown, Bruce W. "Wife-employment and the emergence of egalitarian marital role prescriptions: 1900-1974." *Journal of Comparative Family Studies* 9 (1978):5-17.

Bruce, Christopher J. "The effect of young children on female labor force participation rates: an exploratory study." *Canadian Journal of Sociology* 3 (1978):431-39.

Bryden, M. P. "Evidence for sex-related differences in cerebral organization." In *Sex-Related Differences in Cognitive Functioning: Developmental Issues*, edited by M. A. Wittig and A. C. Petersen, pp. 121-43. New York: Academic Press, 1979.

Bugental, Daphne E.; Leonore R. Love; and Robert M. Gianetto. "Perfidious feminine faces." *Journal of Personality and Social Psychology* 17 (1971):314-18.

Butler, Matilda, and William Paisley. *Women and the Mass Media*. New York: Human Sciences Press, 1980.

Campbell, Angus. "The American way of mating: marriage si, children only maybe." *Psychology Today* (May 1975) 8:37-43.

Campbell, Angus; Philip E. Converse; and Willard L. Rodgers. *The Quality of American Life*. New York: Russell Sage Foundation, 1976.

Campbell, Ernest Q. *Socialization: Culture and Personality*. Dubuque, Iowa: Wm. C. Brown, 1975.

Canadian Advisory Council on the Status of Women. *The Status of Women and the CBC: A Brief by the Canadian Advisory Council on the Status of Women to the Canadian Radio-Television and Telecommunications Commission*. Ottawa, 1978.

———. *Ten Years Later: An Assessment of the Federal Government's Implementation of the Recommendations Made by the Royal Commission on the Status of Women*. Ottawa, 1979.

Cantor, Joanne R. "What is funny to whom? the role of gender." *Journal of Communication* 26 (1976):164-72.

Caplow, Theodore. *The Sociology of Work*. Minneapolis: University of Minnesota Press, 1954.

Carden, Maren Lockwood. *The New Feminist Movement*. New York: Russell Sage Foundation, 1974.

Carey, Patricia. "Farm wives: the forgotten women." *Canadian Women's Studies* 1 (1978-79):4-5.

Carter, C. S., and W. T. Greenough. "Sending the right sex messages." *Psychology Today* 13 (September 1979):112-14.

Carter, Novia. *Volunteers: The Untapped Potential*. Ottawa: The Canadian Council on Social Development, 1975.

Cash, T. F., and V. J. Derlega. "The matching hypothesis: physical attractiveness among same-sexed friends." *Personality and Social Psychology Bulletin* 4 (1978):240-43.

Centers, Richard; Bertram H. Raven; and Aroldo Rodrigues. "Conjugal power structure: a re-examination." *American Sociological Review* 36 (1971):263-78.

Chafetz, Janet Saltzman. *Masculine/Feminine or Human?* Itasca, Ill.: Peacock, 1974.

Chapman, Anthony J., and Nicholas J. Gadfield. "Is sexual humor sexist?" *Journal of Communication* 26 (1976):141-53.

Cheal, David. "Religion and the social order." *Canadian Journal of Sociology* 3 (1978):61-69.

Cherlin, Andrew, and Pamela Barnhouse Walters. "Trends in United States men's and women's sex-role attitudes: 1972 to 1978." *American Sociological Review* 46 (1981):453-60.

Chesler, Phyllis. *Women and Madness*. New York: Avon Books, 1972.

Chimbos, Peter D. "Marital violence: a study of husband-wife homicide." In *The Canadian Family*, rev. ed., edited by K. Ishwaran, pp. 580-99. Toronto: Holt, Rinehart and Winston, 1976.

Chodorow, Nancy. "Being and doing: a cross-cultural examination of the socialization of males and females." In *Woman in Sexist Society*, edited by Vivian Gornick and Barbara K. Moran, pp. 259-91. New York: New American Library, 1971.

_____. *The Reproduction of Mothering: Psychoanalysis and the Sociology of Gender*. Berkeley: University of California Press, 1978.

Cicourel, Aaron W. "The acquisition of social structure: toward a developmental sociology of language and meaning." In *Understanding Everyday Life*, edited by Jack D. Douglas, pp. 136-68. Chicago: Aldine, 1970.

Clark, John P., and Edward W. Haurek. "Age and sex roles of adolescents and their involvement in misconduct: a reappraisal." *Sociology and Social Research* 50 (1966):495-508.

Clarke, Juanne. "Sex differentiation and its future." *Journal of Comparative Family Studies* 9 (1978):223-29.

Clausen, John A. "Perspectives on childhood socialization." In *Socialization and Society*, edited by John A. Clausen, pp. 130-81. Boston: Little, Brown, 1968.

Clemens, Samuel L. *The Adventures of Tom Sawyer*. New York: The World's Popular Classics Books, 1876.

Clement, Wallace. *The Canadian Corporate Elite: An Analysis of Economic Power*. Toronto: McClelland and Stewart, 1975.

Cleverdon, Catherine L. *The Woman Suffrage Movement in Canada*. Toronto: University of Toronto Press, 1974.

Clifton, A. Kay; Diane McGrath; and Bonnie Wick. "Stereotypes of woman: a single category?" *Sex Roles* 2 (1976):135-48.

Cochrane, Jean. *Women in Canadian Life: Politics*. Toronto: Fitzhenry and Whiteside, 1977.

Cochrane, Jean; Abby Hoffman; and Pat Kincaid. *Women in Canadian Life: Sports*. Toronto: Fitzhenry and Whiteside, 1977.

Colley, T. "The nature and origins of psychological sexual identity." *Psychological Review* 66 (1959):165-77.

Collison, Robert. "The age of the wounded male." *Saturday Night* (Jan.-Feb. 1979):28-31.

Condry, J. C.; M. L. Siman; and V. Bronfenbrenner. "Characteristics of peer- and adult-oriented children." Unpublished manuscript, Cornell University, Ithaca, N.Y., 1968.

Connelly, Patricia. "The economic context of women's labour force participation in Canada." In *The Working Sexes*, edited by Patricia Marchak, pp. 11-27. Vancouver: University of British Columbia, 1977.

_____. *Last Hired, First Fired: Women and the Canadian Work Force*. Toronto: The Women's Press, 1978.

Connelly, M. Patricia, and Linda Christiansen-Ruffman. "Women's problems: private troubles or public issues?" *Canadian Journal of Sociology* 2 (1977):167-78.

Cook, Gail C. A., and Mary Eberts. "Policies affecting work." In *Opportunity for Choice*, edited by Gail C. A. Cook, pp. 143-202. Ottawa: Information Canada, 1976.

Cosby, Bill. "The regular way." In *Sex: Male—Gender: Masculine*, edited by John W. Petras, pp. 58-62. Port Washington, N.Y.: Alfred Publishing, 1975. (Originally printed in *Playboy*, 1968).

Coser, Rose L. "Some social functions of laughter." *Human Relations* 12 (1959):171-82.

_____. "Laughter among colleagues." *Psychiatry* 23 (1960):81-89.

Coser, Rose Laub, and Gerald Rokoff. "Women in the occupational world: social disruption and conflict." *Social Problems* 18 (1971): 535-54.

Courtney, A., and S. Lockeretz. "A woman's place: an analysis of the roles portrayed by women in magazine advertisements." *Journal of Marketing Research* 8 (1971):92-95.

Courtney, Alice E., and Thomas W. Whipple. *Canadian Perspectives on Sex Stereotyping in Advertising*. Ottawa: Advisory Council on the Status of Women, 1978.

Coyne, James C.; Richard C. Sherman; and Karen O'Brien. "Expletives and woman's place." *Sex Roles* 4 (1978):827-35.

Cumming, Elaine; Charles Lazer; and Lynne Chisholm. "Suicide as an index of role strain among employed and not employed married women in British Columbia." *Canadian Review of Sociology and Anthropology* 12 (1975), Part 1:462-70.

Cumming, Elaine, and Charles Lazer. "Kinship structure and suicide: a theoretical link." *Canadian Review of Sociology and Anthropology* 18 (1981):271-82.

Currie, Raymond F. "Belonging, commitment, and early socialization in a western city." In *Religion in Canadian Society*, edited by Stewart Crysdale and Les Wheatcroft, pp. 462-78. Toronto: Macmillan, 1976.

Curtis, James, and Ronald D. Lambert. "Culture and social organization." In *Sociology*, edited by Robert Hagedorn, pp. 79-121. Toronto: Holt, Rinehart and Winston, 1980.

Dahl, Roald. *Kiss Kiss*. Harmondsworth, England: Penguin Books, 1962.

Daly, Mary. "God is a verb." In *Women in a Changing World*, edited by Uta West, pp. 153-70. New York: McGraw-Hill, 1975.

_____. *Gyn/Ecology*. Boston: Beacon Press, 1978.

Daniels, Arlene Kaplan. "Feminist perspectives in sociological research." In *Another Voice: Feminist Perspectives on Social Life and Social Science*, edited by Marcia Millman and Rosabeth Moss Kanter, pp. 340-80. Garden City, N.Y.: Doubleday Anchor, 1975.

Danziger, Kurt. "The acculturation of Italian immigrant girls." In *The Canadian Family*, rev. ed., edited by K. Ishwaran, pp. 200-212. Toronto: Holt, Rinehart and Winston, 1976.

Davids, Leo. "Family change in Canada, 1971-1976." *Journal of Marriage and the Family* 42 (1980):177-83.

Davis, Kingsley. "Extreme social isolation of a child." *American Journal of Sociology* 45 (1940):554-64.

_____. "Final note on a case of extreme isolation." *American Journal of Sociology* 52 (1947):432-37.

Davy, Shirley. "Miss to Mrs: going, going, gone!" *Canadian Women's Studies* 1 (1978): 47-48.

Dawkins, Richard. *The Selfish Gene*. London: Oxford University Press, 1976.

Dean, Dwight G.; Rita Braito; Edward A. Powers; and Brent Bruton. "Cultural contradictions and sex roles revisited: a replication and a reassessment." *The Sociological Quarterly* 16 (1975):207-15.

Deaux, Kay. *The Behavior of Women and Men*. Monterey, Calif.: Brooks/ Cole, 1976.

Deaux, Kay, and Tim Emswiller. "Explanations of successful performance on sex-linked tasks: what is skill for the male is luck for the female." *Journal of Personality and Social Psychology* 29 (1974):80-85.

Deutsch, Helene. *Psychology of Women*. Vol. 1. New York: Grune and Stratton, 1944.

Deutsch, Morton, and Robert M. Krauss. *Theories in Social Psychology*. New York: Basic Books, 1965.

Deutscher, Irwin. "Words and Deeds: Social Science and Social Policy." *Social Problems* 13 (1966):235-54.

_____. *What We Say/What We Do: Sentiments and Acts*. Glenview, Ill.: Scott, Foresman, 1973.

Dion, K. K. "The incentive value of physical attractiveness for young children." *Personality and Social Psychology Bulletin* 3 (1977):67-70.

Dion, K., and E. Berscheid. "Physical attractiveness and social perception of peers in preschool children." Mimeographed. Minneapolis: University of Minnesota, 1972.

Dion, K.; E. Berscheid; and E. Walster. "What is beautiful is good." *Journal of Personality and Social Psychology* 24 (1972):285-90.

Dixon, Marlene. "Why women's liberation." In *Roles Women Play: Readings toward Women's Liberation*, edited by Michele Hoffnung Garskof, pp. 165-78. Belmont, Calif.: Brooks/Cole, 1971.

Dominick, Joseph R. "The portrayal of women in prime time, 1953-1977." *Sex Roles* 5 (1979):405-11.

Douvan, Elizabeth, and Joseph Adelson. The Adolescent Experience. New York: John Wiley and Sons, 1966.

Drabble, Margaret. *The Middle Ground*. Markham, Ontario: Penguin, 1980.

Dranoff, Linda Silver. *Women in Canadian Life: Law*. Toronto: Fitzhenry and Whiteside, 1977.

Driedger, Leo. "Introduction: ethnic identity in the Canadian mosaic." In *The Canadian Ethnic Mosaic: A Quest for Identity*, edited by Leo Driedger, pp. 9-22. Canadian Ethnic Studies Association. Toronto: McClelland and Stewart, 1978.

Driver, Anne Barstow. "Religion." *Signs* 2 (1976):434-42.

Drobot, Eve. "Half begun, half done." *Content* 85 (May 1978):3, 5-7, 26-31.

Dubbert, Joe L. *A Man's Place: Masculinity in Transition*. Englewood Cliffs, N.J.: Prentice-Hall, 1979.

Dulude, Louise. *Women and Aging: A Report on the Rest of Our Lives*. Ottawa: Canadian Advisory Council on the Status of Women, 1978.

Eakins, Barbara Westbrook, and R. Gene Eakins. *Sex Differences in Human Communication*. Boston: Houghton Mifflin, 1978.

Eckberg, Douglas Lee, and Lester Hill, Jr. "The paradigm concept and sociology: a critical review." *American Sociological Review* 44 (1979): 925-37.

Eder, Donna, and Maureen T. Hallinan. "Sex differences in children's friendships." *American Sociological Review* 43 (1978):237-50.

Edgerton, Robert B. *The Cloak of Competence: Stigma in the Lives of the Mentally Retarded*. Berkeley: University of California Press, 1967.

Eekelaar, John M., and Sanford N. Katz, eds. *Family Violence*. Toronto: Butterworths, 1978.

Ehrlich, Howard J. *The Social Psychology of Prejudice*. New York: Wiley, 1973.

Eichler, Margrit. "Sociological research on women in Canada." *Canadian Review of Sociology and Anthropology* 12 (1975a), Part 1:474-81.

_____. "The equalitarian family in Canada?" In *Marriage, Family and Society: Canadian Perspectives*, edited by S. Parvez Wakil, pp. 223-35. Toronto: Butterworths, 1975b.

_____. "Sociology of feminist research in Canada." *Signs* 3 (1977a):409-22.

_____. "The prestige of the occupation housewife." In *The Working Sexes*, edited by Patricia Marchak, pp. 151-75. Vancouver: University of British Columbia, 1977b.

———. "Women as personal dependents." In *Women in Canada*, rev. ed., edited by Marylee Stephenson, pp. 51-69. Don Mills, Ontario: General Publishing, 1977c.

———. "Women's unpaid labour." *Atlantis* 3 (1978), Part 2:52-62.

———. *The Double Standard: A Feminist Critique of Feminist Social Science*. New York: St. Martin's Press, 1980.

Ellmann, Mary. *Thinking about Women*. New York: Harcourt Brace Jovanovich, 1968.

Engel, Marian. *The Honeyman Festival*. Toronto: Anansi, 1970.

———. *Sarah Bastard's Notebook*. Don Mills, Ontario: PaperJacks, 1974.

———. *Bear*. Toronto: McClelland and Stewart, 1976.

Engels, Friedrich. *The Origin of the Family, Private Property, and the State*. 1884. Reprint. New York: International Publishers, 1942.

England, Paula. "Women and occupational prestige: a case of vacuous sex equality." *Signs* 5 (1979):252-65.

Ephron, Nora. *Crazy Salad: Some Things About Women*. New York: Knopf, 1975.

Epstein, Cynthia Fuchs. "Encountering the male establishment: sex-status limits on women's careers in the professions." *American Journal of Sociology* 75 (1970):965-82.

———. *Woman's Place*. Berkeley: University of California Press, 1971.

———. "A different angle of vision: notes on the selective eye of sociology." *Social Science Quarterly* 55 (1974a):645-56.

———. "Bringing women in: rewards, punishments, and the structure of achievement." In *Women and Success: The Anatomy of Achievement*, edited by Ruth B. Kundsin, pp. 13-21. New York: William Morrow, 1974b.

———. "The women's movement and the women's pages." In *Hearth and Home: Images of Women in the Mass Media*, edited by Gaye Tuchman, Arlene Kaplan Daniels, and James Benét, pp. 216-221. New York: Oxford University Press, 1978.

Erikson, Erik H. "Inner and outer space: reflections on womanhood." *Daedalus* 93 (1964):582-606.

Etaugh, Claire. "The effects of maternal employment on children: a review of recent research." *Merrill-Palmer Quarterly* 20 (1974):71-98.

Exline, R. V.; S. Ellyson; and B. Long. "Visual behavior as an aspect of power role relationships." In *Nonverbal Communication in Aggression*, edited by P. Pliner, L. Kramer, and T. Alloway, pp. 21-52. New York: Plenum, 1974.

Eysenck, H. J. "The effects of psychotherapy: an evaluation." *Journal of Consulting and Clinical Psychology* 16 (1952):319-24.

———. *The Effects of Psychotherapy*. New York: International Science Press, 1966.

Fagot, Beverley I. "The socialization of sex differences in early childhood." Paper presented to the Meeting of the Oregon Psychological Association, May 1978.

———. "Male and female teachers: do they treat boys and girls differently?" *Sex Roles* 7 (1981):263-71.

Fagot, B. I., and G. R. Patterson. "An *in vivo* analysis of reinforcing contingencies for sex-role behaviors in the preschool child." *Developmental Psychology* 1 (1969):563-68.

Farley, John. "Activities and pastimes of children and youth: age, sex and parental effects." *Journal of Comparative Family Studies* 10 (1979):385-410.

Farrell, Warren. *The Liberated Man*. New York: Random House, 1974.

Favreau, Olga Eizner. "Sex bias in psychological research." *Canadian Psychological Review* 18 (1977):56-65.

Featherman, David, and Robert M. Hauser. "Sexual inequalities and socioeconomic achievement in the United States." *American Sociological Review* 41 (1976):462-83.

Ferguson, Marjorie. "Imagery and ideology: the cover photographs of traditional women's magazines." In *Hearth and Home: Images of Women in the Mass Media*, edited by Gaye Tuchman, Arlene Kaplan Daniels, and James Benét, pp. 97-115. New York: Oxford University Press, 1978.

Fernberger, S. W. "Persistence of stereotypes concerning sex differences." *Journal of Abnormal and Social Psychology* 43 (1948):97-101.

Ferree, Myra Marx. "Working-class jobs: housework and paid work as sources of satisfaction." *Social Problems* 23 (1976):431-41.

Fink, Arlene, and Jacqueline Kosecoff. "Girls' and boys' changing attitudes toward school." *Psychology of Women Quarterly* 2 (1977):44-49.

Firestone, Shulamith. *The Dialectic of Sex*. New York: Bantam, 1971.

Fishman, Pamela M. "Interaction: the work women do." *Social Problems* 25 (1978):397-406.

Flora, Cornelia. "The passive female: her comparative image by class and culture in women's magazine fiction." *Journal of Marriage and the Family* 33 (1971):435-44.

Fogarty, Michael P.; Rhona Rapoport; and Robert N. Rapoport. *Sex, Career and Family*. London: George Allen and Unwin, 1971.

Forcese, Dennis. *The Canadian Class Structure*. 2nd ed. Toronto: McGraw-Hill Ryerson, 1980.

Forfeit, Karen G.; Terna Agor; Johnny Byers; John Larue; Helen Lokey; Michael Palazzini; Michele Patterson; and Lillian Smith. "Sex bias in the newspaper treatment of male-centered and female-centered news stories." *Sex Roles* 6 (1980):475-80.

Forgas, Joseph P., and Barbara Dobosz. "Dimensions of romantic involvement: toward a taxonomy of heterosexual relationships." *Social Psychology Quarterly* 43 (1980):290-300.

Fox, Greer Litton " 'Nice girl': social control of women through a value construct." *Signs* 2 (1977):805-17.

Frances, Susan J. "Sex differences in nonverbal behavior." *Sex Roles* 5 (1979):519-35.

Franzwa, Helen H. "Female roles in women's magazine fiction, 1940-1970." In *Woman: Dependent or Independent Variable?* edited by Rhoda Kesler Unger and Florence L. Denmark, pp. 42-53. New York: Psychological Dimensions, 1975.

Freedman, J. L.; A. S. Levy; R. W. Buchanan; and J. Price. "Crowding and human aggressiveness." *Journal of Experimental Social Psychology* 8 (1972):528-48.

Freeman, Jo. "The social construction of the second sex." In *Roles Women Play: Readings toward Women's Liberation*, edited by Michele Hoffnung Garskof, pp. 123-41. Belmont, Calif.: Brooks/Cole, 1971.

———. "The origins of the women's liberation movement." *American Journal of Sociology* 78 (1973):792-811.

———. "The women's liberation movement: its origins, organizations, activities, and ideas." In *Women: A Feminist Perspective*, 2nd ed., edited by Jo Freeman, pp. 557-74. Palo Alto, Calif.: Mayfield, 1979.

Freud, Sigmund. "Some psychological consequences of the anatomical distinction between the sexes." 1927. Reprinted in *Woman: Dependent or Independent Variable?* edited by Rhoda Kesler Unger and Florence L. Denmark, pp. 128-36. New York: Psychological Dimensions, 1975.

Freuh, T., and P. E. McGhee. "Traditional sex role development and amount of time spent watching television." *Developmental Psychology* 11 (1975):109.

Friday, Nancy. *My Mother, My Self.* New York: Dell, 1977.

Friedan, Betty. *The Feminine Mystique.* Harmondsworth, England: Penguin Books, 1963.

Frieze, Irene H.; Jacquelynne E. Parsons; Paula B. Johnson; Diane N. Ruble; and Gail L. Zellman. *Women and Sex Roles: A Social Psychological Perspective.* New York: W. W. Norton, 1978.

Fritz, Kathlyn Ann, and Natalie Kaufman Hevener. "An unsuitable job for a woman: female protagonists in the detective novel." *International Journal of Women's Studies* 2 (1975):105-28.

Fuller, Mary. "Sex-role stereotyping and social science." In *The Sex Role System: Psychological and Sociological Perspectives*, edited by Jane Chetwynd and Oonagh Hartnett, pp. 143-57. London: Routledge and Kegan Paul, 1978.

Gagnon, M. J. "Women and paid work—a difficult equation." In *Canada's Mental Health* 23 (International Women's Year Supplement) (1975):12.

Garfinkel, Harold. *Studies in Ethnomethodology.* Englewood Cliffs, N.J.: Prentice-Hall, 1967.

Garai, J. E., and A. Scheinfeld. "Sex differences in mental and behavioral traits." *Genetic Psychology Monographs* 77 (1968):169-299.

Garrison, Howard H. "Gender differences in the career aspirations of recent cohorts of high school seniors." *Social Problems* 27 (1979):170-85.

Gaskell, Jane S. "The sex-role ideology of working class girls." *Canadian Review of Sociology and Anthropology* 12 (1975), Part 1:453-61.

Gavron, Hannah. *The Captive Wife.* Harmondsworth, England: Penguin Books, 1966.

Gecas, Viktor. "The socialization and child care roles." In *Role Structure and Analysis of the Family*, edited by F. Ivan Nye, pp. 33-59. Beverly Hills: Sage Publications, 1976.

Gee, Ellen M. Thomas. "Female marriage patterns in Canada: changes and differentials." *Journal of Comparative Family Studies* 11 (1980):457-73.

Geise, L. Ann. "The female role in middle class women's magazines from 1955 to 1976: a content analysis of nonfiction selections." *Sex Roles* 5 (1979):51-62.

Gendell, Murray. *Swedish Working Wives.* Totowa: Bedminster Press, 1963.

Ghitan, George. "Female delinquency." Ph.D. candidacy examination, Department of Educational Psychology, University of Calgary, 1979.

Gibbins, Roger; J. Rick Ponting; and Gladys L. Symons. "Attitudes and ideology: correlates of liberal attitudes towards the role of women." *Journal of Comparative Family Studies* 9 (1978):19-40.

Gibbs, Margaret; Doris Auerbach; and Margery Fox. "A comparison of male and female same-sex friendships." *International Journal of Women's Studies* 3 (1980):261-272.

Glazer, Nona. "Introduction to part two." In *Woman in a Man-Made World*, 2nd ed., edited by Nona Glazer and Helen Youngelson Waehrer, pp. 101-13. Chicago: Rand McNally, 1977a.

———. "Introduction to part three." In *Woman in a Man-Made World*, 2nd ed., edited by Nona Glazer and Helen Youngelson Waehrer, pp. 227-30. Chicago: Rand McNally, 1977b.

Glazer-Malbin, Nona. "Housework: review essay." *Signs* 1 (1976):905-22.

Glock, Charles Y. "The role of deprivation in the origin and evolution of religious groups." In *Religion and Social Conflict*, edited by Robert Lee and Martin E. Marty, pp. 24-36. New York: Oxford University Press, 1964.

Goffman, Erving. "On cooling the mark out: some aspects of adaptation to failure." *Psychiatry* 15 (1952):451-63.

_____. "The nature of deference and demeanor." *American Anthropologist* 58 (1956):473-502.

_____. *Relations in Public*. New York: Basic Books, 1971.

_____. *Gender Advertisements*. New York: Harper and Row, 1976.

_____. "The arrangement between the sexes." *Theory and Society* 4 (1977): 301-31.

Gold, Dolores. "Full-time employment of mothers in relation to their ten-year-old children." Paper presented at Research for Women: Current Projects and Future Directions, an Interdisciplinary Conference, at Mount Saint Vincent University, Halifax, N.S., 1976.

Goldberg, Herb. *The Hazards of Being Male: Surviving the Myth of Masculine Privilege*. New York: Signet Books, 1976.

Goldberg, Philip A. "Are women prejudiced against women?" *Transaction* 5 (1968):28-30.

Goldberg, Steven. *The Inevitability of Patriarchy*. New York: William Morrow, 1973.

Goldberg, Susan, and Michael Lewis. "Play behavior in the year-old infant: early sex differences." *Child Development* 40 (1969):21-31.

Goldenberg, Naomi. "Women and the image of God: a psychological perspective on the feminist movement in religion." *International Journal of Women's Studies* 1 (1978):468-74.

Goleman, Daniel. "Special abilities of the sexes: do they begin in the brain?" *Psychology Today* (November 1978):48-49, 51, 54-56, 58-59, 120.

Goode, William J. "A theory of role strain." *American Sociological Review* 25 (1960):483-96.

_____. "Family and mobility." In *Class, Status, and Power*, 2nd ed., edited by Reinhard Bendix and Seymour M. Lipset, pp. 582-601. New York: Free Press, 1966.

Gordon, Chad. "Self-conceptions: configurations of content." In *The Self in Social Interactions*, vol. 1., edited by Chad Gordon and Kenneth J. Gergen, pp. 115-36. New York: John Wiley and Sons, 1968.

Gordon, Mary. *Final Payments*. New York: Ballantine Books, 1978.

Gornick, Vivian. "Introduction." In *Gender Advertisements*, edited by Erving Goffman, pp. vii-ix. New York: Harper and Row, 1976.

Gottlieb, Lois C., and Wendy Keitner. "Images of Canadian women in literature and society in the 1970s." *International Journal of Women's Studies* 2 (1979):513-27.

Gough, Kathleen. "The origin of the family." *Journal of Marriage and the Family* 33 (1971):760-71.

Gould, Lois. "X: a fabulous child's story." *Ms.* 1 (December 1972):74-76, 105-6.

Gould, Meredith, and Rochelle Kern-Daniels. "Toward a sociological theory of gender and sex." *The American Sociologist* 12 (1977):182-89.

Goulianos, Joan, ed. *By a Woman Writt*. Indianapolis: Bobbs-Merrill, 1973.

Gove, Walter R.; Michael Hughes; and Michael R. Geerken. "Playing dumb: a form of impression management with undesirable side effects." *Social Psychology Quarterly* 43 (1980):89-102.

Gove, Walter R., and Jeannette F. Tudor. "Adult sex roles and mental illness." *American Journal of Sociology* 78 (1973):812-35.

Goyder, John C. "Income differences between the sexes: findings from a national Canadian survey." *Canadian Review of Sociology and Anthropology* 18 (1981):321-42.

Gray, Vicky A. "The image of women in psychology textbooks." *Canadian Psychological Review* 18 (1977):46-55.

Greaves, Helen. "The view from the bench." *Branching Out* 5, no. 4 (1978):34-35.

Green, Maureen. *Fathering*. New York: McGraw-Hill, 1976.

Green, Richard. *Sexual Identity Conflict in Children and Adults*. Baltimore: Penguin, 1974.

Greenglass, Esther. "The psychology of women; or, the high cost of achievement." In *Women in Canada*, edited by Marylee Stephenson, pp. 108-18. Toronto: New Press, 1973.

Griffiths, Alison. "They who risked their delicate organs." *Branching Out* 5, no. 4 (1978):10-13.

Griffiths, N. E. S. *Penelope's Web: Some Perceptions of Women in Europe and Canadian society*. Toronto: Oxford University Press, 1976.

Groch, A. S. "Generality of response to humor and wit in cartoons, jokes, stories, and photographs. *Psychological Reports* 35 (1974):835-38.

Gunderson, Morley. "Work patterns." In *Opportunity for Choice: A Goal for Women in Canada*, edited by Gail C. A. Cook, pp. 93-142. Ottawa: Information Canada, 1976.

Hacker, Helen Mayer. "Women as a minority group." *Social Forces* 30 (1951):60-69.

_____. "Women as a minority group: twenty years later." In *Woman: Dependent or Independent Variable?* edited by Rhoda Kesler Unger and Florence L. Denmark, pp. 103-12. New York: Psychological Dimensions, 1975.

Hagan, John, and N. O'Donnell. "Sexual stereotyping and judicial sentencing." *Canadian Journal of Sociology* 3 (1978):309-19.

Hall, M. Ann. "Rarely have we asked why: reflections on Canadian women's experience in sport." *Atlantis* 6 (1980):51-60.

Hall, Elizabeth. "Acting one's age: new rules for old." (Interview of Bernice Neugarten.) *Psychology Today* 13 (April 1980):66-80.

Hall, Richard H. *Occupations and the Social Structure*. Englewood Cliffs, N.J.: Prentice-Hall, 1969.

Halleck, S. L. "Delinquency." In *Manual of Child Psychopathology*, edited by B. B. Wolman. New York: McGraw-Hill, 1972.

Haller, Max. "Marriage, women, and social stratification: a theoretical critique." *American Journal of Sociology* 86 (1981):766-95.

Hallinan, Maureen T. "Structural effects on children's friendships and cliques." *Social Psychology Quarterly* 42 (1979):43-54.

Harlow, Harry F. "Love in infant monkeys." *Scientific American* 200 (June 1959): 68-74.

_____. "The heterosexual affectional system in monkeys." *American Psychologist* 17 (1962):1-9.

_____. "Sexual behavior in the rhesus monkey." In *Sex and Behavior*, edited by Frank A. Beach, pp. 234-65. New York: Wiley, 1965.

Harris, Anthony R. "Sex and theories of deviance." *American Sociological Review* 42 (1977):3-16.

Harris, Marvin. "Why it's not the same old America." *Psychology Today* 15 (August 1981): 22-51.

Harrison, James B. "Men's roles and men's lives." *Signs* 4 (1978):324-36.

Hartley, Ruth E. "Sex-role pressures in the socialization of the male child." *Psychological Reports* 5 (1959):457-68.

Haskell, Molly. *From Reverence to Rape: The Treatment of Women in the Movies*. New York: Holt, Rinehart and Winston, 1974.

Heer, David M. "Dominance and the working wife." *Social Forces* 36 (1958):341-47.

Heirich, Max. "Change of heart: a test of some widely held theories about religious conversion." *American Journal of Sociology* 83 (1977):653-80.

Henley, Nancy M. "Power, sex, and nonverbal communication." In *Language and Sex: Difference and Dominance*, edited by Barrie Thorne and Nancy Henley, pp. 184-203. Rowley, Mass.: Newbury House, 1975.

_____. *Body Politics: Power, Sex and Nonverbal communication*. Englewood Cliffs: N.J.: Prentice-Hall, 1977.

Hennig, Margaret, and Anne Jardim. *The Managerial Woman*. New York: Pocket Books, 1976.

Hetherington, Mavis E. "Effects of parental absence on sex-typed behaviors in Negro and White preadolescent males." *Journal of Personality and Social Psychology* 4 (1966):87-91.

Hill, Charles T., Zick Rubin, and Letitia Anne Peplau. "Breakups before marriage: the end of 103 affairs." *Journal of Social Issues* 32 (1976):147-68.

Hiller, Harry H. "The Canadian sociology movement: analysis and assessment." *Canadian Journal of Sociology* 4 (1979):125-50.

Hitchman, Gladys S. "A report on the reports: the status of women in Canadian universities." *Canadian Sociology and Anthropology Association Bulletin* 35 (October 1974):11-13.

Hobart, Charles W. "Attitudes toward parenthood among Canadian young people." *Journal of Marriage and the Family* 35 (1973):93-101.

_____. "Church involvement and the comfort thesis in Alberta." *Journal for the Scientific Study of Religion* 13 (1974):463-70.

_____. "Sexual permissiveness in young English and French Canadians." In *The Canadian Family in Comparative Perspective*, edited by Lyle E. Larson, pp. 149-59. Scarborough, Ontario: Prentice-Hall, 1976a.

_____. "Youth and sex expression." In *The Canadian Family*, rev. ed., edited by K. Ishwaran, pp. 418-36. Toronto: Holt, Rinehart and Winston, 1976b.

_____. "Sources of egalitarianism in young unmarried Canadians." *The Canadian Journal of Sociology* 6 (1981):261-82.

Hochschild, Arlie Russell. "Making it: marginality and obstacles to minority consciousness." In *Women and Success: Anatomy of Achievement*, edited by Ruth B. Kundsin, pp. 194-99. New York: William Morrow, 1974.

_____. "The sociology of feeling and emotion: selected possibilities." In *Another Voice: Feminist Perspectives on Social Life and Social Science*, edited by Marcia Millman and Rosabeth Moss Kanter, pp. 280-307. Garden City, N.Y.: Doubleday Anchor, 1975.

Hoffman, Abby. *About Face. Toward a Positive Image of Women in Sport*. Toronto: The Ontario Status of Women Council, 1976.

Hoffman, Lois Wladis. "Effects of maternal employment on the child: a review of the research." *Developmental Psychology* 10 (1974):204-28.

Hoffman, M. L. "Sex differences in moral internalization and values." *Journal of Personality and Social Psychology* 32 (1975):720-29.

Hole, Judith, and Ellen Levine. *The Rebirth of Feminism*. New York: Quadrangle Books, 1971.

Hollander, E. P., and J. E. Marcia. "Parental determinants of peer orientation and self-orientation among preadolescents." *Developmental Psychology* 2 (1970):292-302.

Homans, George C. *The Human Group*. New York: Harcourt, Brace, 1950.

_____. *Social Behavior: Its Elementary Forms*. New York: Harcourt, Brace and World, 1961.

Horner, Matina. "Fail: bright women." *Psychology Today* 3 (November 1969):36, 38, 62.

Horney, Karen. "The dread of women." *International Journal of Psycho-Analysis* 13 (1932):348-60.

Howe, Florence. "Sexual stereotypes and the public schools." In *Women and Success: The Anatomy of Achievement*, edited by Ruth B. Kundsin, pp. 123-218. New York: William Morrow, 1974.

Hudson, Jackie. "Physical parameters used for female exclusion from law enforcement and athletics." In *Women and Sport: From Myth to Reality*, edited by Carole A. Oglesby, pp. 19-57. Philadelphia: Lea and Febiger, 1978.

Hughes, Everett C. *Men and Their Work*. Glencoe, Ill.: Free Press, 1958.

Hunter, Alfred A. *Class Tells: On Social Inequality in Canada*. Toronto: Butterworths, 1981.

Hyde, Janet. *Understanding Human Sexuality*. New York: McGraw-Hill, 1979.

Hyde, Janet S.; B. G. Rosenberg; and Jo Ann Behrman. "Tomboyism." *Psychology of Women Quarterly* 2 (1977):73-75.

Ishwaran, K., ed. *The Canadian Family*. Rev. ed. Toronto: Holt, Rinehart and Winston, 1976.

_____. "Childhood and adolescence in Canada: an overview of theory and research." In *Childhood and Adolescence in Canada*, edited by K. Ishwaran, pp. 3-36. Toronto: McGraw-Hill Ryerson, 1979.

_____. *Canadian Families: Ethnic Variations*. Toronto: McGraw-Hill Ryerson, 1980.

Jacobson, Helga E. "Women's perspectives in research." *Atlantis* 4 (1979):98-107.

Jaggar, Alison M., and Paula Rothenberg Struhl. *Feminist Frameworks: Alternative Theoretical Accounts of the Relations between Women and Men*. New York: McGraw-Hill, 1978.

Jamieson, Kathleen. *Indian Women and the Law in Canada: Citizens Minus*. Ottawa: Advisory Council on the Status of Women, 1978.

_____. "Multiple jeopardy: the evolution of a native women's movement." *Atlantis* 4 (1979), Part II:157-78.

_____. "Sisters under the skin: an exploration of the implications of feminist-materialist perspective research." *Canadian Ethnic Studies* 13 (1981):130-43.

Jourard, Sidney M. *The Transparent Self*. New York: Van Nostrand Reinhold, 1964.

Jung, C. G. *Psychological Types*. New York: Harcourt, Brace, 1926.

Kalbach, Warren E., and Wayne W. McVey. *The Demographic Bases of Canadian Society*. 2nd ed. Toronto: McGraw-Hill Ryerson, 1979.

Kalin, Rudolf; Janet M. Stoppard; and Barbara Burt. "Sex-role ideology and sex bias in judgments of occupational suitability." In *Sex Roles: Origins, Influences, and Implications for Women*, edited by Cannie Stark-Adamec, pp. 89-99. Montreal: Eden Press, 1980.

Kammeyer, K. "Sibling position and the feminine role." *Journal of Marriage and the Family* 29 (1967):494-99.

Kandel, Denise B., and Gerald S. Lesser. "Marital decision-making in American and Danish urban families: a research note." *Journal of Marriage and the Family* 34 (1972):134-38.

Kanter, Rosabeth Moss. "The impact of hierarchical structures on the work behavior of women and men." *Social Problems* 23 (1976):415-30.

_____. "Some effects of proportions on group life: skewed sex ratios and responses to token women." *American Journal of Sociology* 82 (1977):965-90.

Kaplan, Bess. *Malke, Malke*. Winnipeg: Queenston House, 1977.

Kappel, B. E., and R. D. Lambert. "Self-worth among the children of working mothers." Unpublished manuscript. Waterloo, Ontario: University of Waterloo, 1972.

Kates, Joanne. "Report from Canada: familiar issues—some new tactics." *Ms.* (August 1981):77-80.

Katz, Arnold J. "Lone fathers: perspectives and implications for family policy." *The Family Coordinator* (October 1979):521-28.

Katz, Barbara J. "Saying goodbye to Superman." In *The Forty-Nine Percent Majority*, edited by Deborah S. David and Robert Brannon, pp. 291-96. Reading, Mass.: Addison-Wesley, 1976.

Katzman, N. "Television soap operas: what's been going on anyway?" *Public Opinion Quarterly* 35 (1972):200-12.

Kaufman, Gloria, and Mary Kay Blakely, eds. *Pulling Our Own Strings: Feminist Humor and Satire*. Bloomington: Indiana University Press, 1980.

Kent, Jean F. "Portrayal of parenting roles in mass media." Unpublished manuscript. Calgary, Alberta: University of Calgary, 1981a.

_____. "Sexual equality in parenthood: after divorce." Unpublished manuscript. Calgary, Alberta: University of Calgary, 1981b.

Kessler, Suzanne J., and Wendy McKenna. *Gender: An Ethnomethodological Approach*. New York: John Wiley and Sons, 1978.

Kimball, Meredith M. "Women and success: a basic conflict?" In *Women in Canada*, edited by Marylee Stephenson, pp. 119-35. Toronto: New Press, 1973.

Klapper, Joseph T. *The Effects of Mass Communication*. New York: Free Press, 1960.

Kleinman, Sherryl. "Female premarital sexual careers." In *Shaping Identity in Canadian Society*, edited by Jack Haas and William Shaffir, pp. 101-17. Scarborough, Ontario: Prentice-Hall, 1978.

Klemmack, David L., and John W. Edwards. "Women's acquisition of stereotyped occupational aspirations." *Sociology and Social Research* 57 (1975):510-25.

Kohlberg, Lawrence. "A cognitive-developmental analysis of children's sex-role concepts and attitudes." In *The Development of Sex Differences*, edited by Eleanor Maccoby, pp. 82-172. Stanford, Calif.: Stanford University Press, 1966.

Kohlberg, Lawrence, and Edward Zigler. "The impact of cognitive maturity on the development of sex-role attitudes in the years 4 to 8." *Genetic Psychology Monographs* 75 (1967):89-165.

Kohn, Melvin L. *Class and Conformity*. 2nd ed. Chicago: University of Chicago Press, 1977.

Kohn, Melvin L., and Robin M. Williams, Jr. "Situational patterning in intergroup relations." *American Sociological Review* 21 (1956):164-74.

Komarovsky, Mirra. "Cultural contradictions and sex roles." *American Journal of Sociology* 52 (1946):184-89.

_____. *Blue-Collar Marriage*. New York: Random House, 1962.

_____. "Cultural contradictions and sex roles: the masculine case." *American Journal of Sociology* 78 (1973):873-84.

_____. *Dilemmas of Masculinity*. New York: W. W. Norton, 1976.

Kome, Penney. *Somebody Has to Do It: Whose Work is Housework?* Toronto: McClelland and Stewart, 1982.

Komisar, Lucy. "The image of women in advertising." In *Woman in Sexist Society*, edited by Vivian Gornick and Barbara K. Moran, pp. 304-17. New York: Basic Books, 1971.

Kramer, Cheris; Barrie Thorne; and Nancy Henley. "Perspectives on language and communication." *Signs* 3 (1978):638-51.

Kreps, Bonnie. *Guide to the Women's Movement in Canada*. Toronto: *Chatelaine*, n.d.

Kryzanowski, Lawrence, and Elizabeth Bertin-Boussu. "Equal access to credit: lenders' attitudes toward an applicant's sex and marital status." *International Journal of Women's Studies* 4 (1981):213-32.

Kuhn, Manford H., and Thomas S. McPartland. "An empirical investigation of self-attitudes." *American Sociological Review* 19 (1954):68-76.

Kuhn, Manford H. "Self-attitudes by age, sex, and professional training." *The Sociological Quarterly* 9 (1960):39-55.

Kuhn, Thomas. *The Structure of Scientific Revolutions*. 2nd ed. Chicago: University of Chicago Press, 1970.

Kunkel, John H. "Sociobiology vs. biosociology." *The American Sociologist* 12 (1977):69-73.

Labovitz, Sanford. "Some evidence of Canadian ethnic, racial, and sexual antagonism." *Canadian Review of Sociology and Anthropology* 11 (1974):247-54.

Lakoff, Robin. *Language and Woman's Place*. New York: Harper and Row, 1975.

Lamb, Theodore A. "Nonverbal and paraverbal control in dyads and triads: sex or power differences?" *Social Psychology Quarterly* 44 (1981):49-53.

Lambert, Helen H. "Biology and equality: a perspective on sex differences." *Signs* 4 (1978):97-117.

Lambert, Ronald D. *Sex Role Imagery in Children: Social Origins of Mind*. Royal Commission on the Status of Women in Canada, Study 6, Ottawa: Information Canada, 1971.

Lambert, Wallace E. "Social influences on the child's development of an identity." In *A Canadian Social Psychology of Ethnic Relations*, edited by Robert C. Gardner and Rudolf Kalin, pp. 57-75. Toronto: Methuen, 1981.

Lambert, W. E.; A. Yackley; and R. N. Hein. "Child training values of English Canadian and French Canadian parents." *Canadian Journal of Behavioural Science* 3 (1971):217-36.

Lamphere, Louise. "Anthropology: review essay." *Signs* 2 (1977):612-27.

Lancaster, Jane Beckman. "Sex roles in primate societies." In *Sex Differences: Social and Biological Perspectives*, edited by Michael S. Teitelbaum, pp. 22-61. Garden City, N.Y.: Doubleday Anchor, 1976.

Landau, Barbara. "The adolescent female offender: our dilemma." *Canadian Journal of Criminology and Corrections* 17 (1975):146-53.

Landers, Ann. "The new rules of the marriage game." *Family Circle* 2 (1981):14, 18, 19, 112.

Landis, M. H., and H. E. Burtt. "A study of conversations." *Journal of Comparative Psychology* 4 (1924):81-89.

Landy, D. *Tropical Childhood*. New York: Harper and Row, 1965.

Laner, Mary Riege; Morris Axelrod; and Roy H. Laner. "Sex and the single check." *Pacific Sociological Review* 22 (1979):382-400.

Langdon, M. Elizabeth. "Images and ideals of Victorian women, 1820-1850." Master's thesis, Department of History, University of Calgary, 1980.

Lashuk, Maureen Wilson, and George Kurian. "Employment status, feminism, and symptoms of stress: the case of a Canadian prairie city." *Canadian Journal of Sociology* 2 (1977):195-204.

Lauer, Robert H., and Warren H. Handel. *Social Psychology: The Theory and Application of Symbolic Interactionism*. Boston: Houghton Mifflin, 1977.

Laws, Judith Long. "Work aspirations of women: false leads and new starts." In *Women and the Workplace: The Implications of Occupational Segregation*, edited by Martha Blaxall and Barbara Reagan, pp. 33-49. Chicago: University of Chicago Press, 1976.

————. *The Second X: Sex Role and Social Role.* New York: Elsevier North-Holland, 1979.

Laws, Judith Long, and Pepper Schwartz. *Sexual Scripts: The Social Construction of Female Sexuality.* Hinsdale, Ill.: Dryden, 1977.

Lee, Betty. "Ms-taken identities: the birth-name game." *The Canadian* (27 March 1976):2.

Lee, Deborah, and Joan Hertzberg. "Theories of feminine personality." In *Women and Sex Roles: A Social Psychological Perspective*, edited by Irene H. Frieze, Jacquelynne E. Parsons, Paula B. Johnson, Diane N. Ruble, and Gail L. Zellman, pp. 28-44. New York: W. W. Norton, 1978.

Lefkowitz, Margaret B. "The women's magazine short-story heroine in 1957 and 1967." In *Toward a Sociology of Women*, edited by Constantina Safilios-Rothschild, pp. 37-40. Lexington, Mass.: Xerox, 1972.

Le Guin, Ursula K. *The Left Hand of Darkness.* New York: Walker, 1969.

Leibowitz, Lila. *Females, Males, Families: A Biosocial Approach.* North Scituate, Mass.: Duxbury Press, 1978.

Lenski, Gerhard. "Sociology and sociobiology: an alternative view." *The American Sociologist* 12 (1977):73-75.

Lester, Eva P.; Stephanie Dudek; and Roy C. Muir. "Sex differences in the performance of school children." *Canadian Psychiatric Association Journal* 17 (1972):273-78.

Lester, Julius, "Being a boy." Originally published in *Ms.* (July 1973) 2:112-13, Reprinted in *Sex: Male—Gender: Masculine*, edited by John W. Petras, pp. 54-57. Port Washington, N.Y.: Alfred Publishing, 1975.

Lever, Janet. "Sex differences in the complexity of children's play." *American Sociological Review* 43 (1978):471-83.

Levine, Joan B. "The feminine routine." *Journal of Communication* 26 (1976):173-75.

Levinson, D. J. *The Seasons of a Man's Life.* New York: Alfred A. Knopf, 1978.

Lewis, Michael. "Culture and gender roles: there's no unisex in the nursery." *Psychology Today* 5 (May 1972):54-57.

Lieberson, Stanley. "Bilingualism in Montreal: a demographic analysis." *American Journal of Sociology* 71 (1965):10-25.

Liebert, Robert M., and Rita W. Poulos. "TV for kiddies: truth, goodness, beauty —and a little bit of brainwash." *Psychology Today* 6 (November 1972):122-28.

Lightfoot, Sara Lawrence. "Family-school interactions: the cultural image of mothers and teachers." *Signs* 3 (1977):395-408.

Lindesmith, Alfred R., and Anselm L. Strauss. *Social Psychology.* Rev. ed. New York: Holt, Rinehart and Winston, 1956.

Lipman-Blumen, Jean, and Ann R. Tickamyer. "Sex roles in transition: a ten-year perspective." *Annual Review of Sociology* 1 (1975):297-337.

Lippitt, Ronald. "Improving the socialization process." In *Socialization and Society*, edited by John A. Clausen, pp. 321-74. Boston: Little, Brown, 1968.

Lofland, Lyn H. "The 'thereness' of women: a selective review of urban sociology." In *Another Voice*, edited by Marcia Millman and Rosabeth Moss Kanter, pp. 144-70. Garden City, N.Y.: Doubleday Anchor, 1975.

Lopata, Helena Z. *Occupation: Housewife.* New York: Oxford University Press, 1971.

————. "Sociology: review essay." *Signs* 2 (1976):165-76.

_____. *Women as Widows: Support Systems.* New York: Elsevier North-Holland, 1979.

Lowe, Marian. "Sociobiology and sex differences." *Signs* 4 (1978):118-25.

Lowenthal, Marjorie Fiske, and Clayton Haven. "Interaction and adaptation: intimacy as a critical variable." *American Sociological Review* 33 (1968):20-30.

Luce, S. "Motive to avoid success: a Canadian sample." Paper presented at the meeting of the Canadian Psychological Association, Vancouver, B.C., June 1973.

Lundberg, Ferdinand, and Marynia F. Farnham. *Modern Woman: The Lost Sex.* New York: Harper and Bros., 1947.

Lunneborg, P. W. "Stereotypic aspects in masculinity-femininity measurement." *Journal of Consulting and Clinical Psychology* 34 (1970):113-18.

Lupri, Eugen. "Contemporary authority patterns in the West German family: a study in cross-national validation." *Journal of Marriage and the Family* 31 (1969):134-44.

Lupri, Eugen, and Donald L. Mills. "The changing roles of Canadian women in family and work: an overview." In *The Changing Roles of Women in Family and Society: A Cross-Cultural Comparison*, edited by Eugen Lupri. Leiden: E. J. Brill, forthcoming (1982).

Lupri, Eugen, and James Frideres. "The quality of marriage and the passage of time: marital satisfaction over the family life cycle." *Canadian Journal of Sociology* 6 (1981):283-305.

Luxton, Meg. *More Than a Labour of Love: Three Generations of Women's Work in the Home.* Toronto: The Women's Press, 1980.

Lynn, David B. "A note on sex differences in the development of masculine and feminine identification." *Psychological Review* 66 (1959):126-35.

_____. *Parental and Sex Role Identification: A Theoretical Formulation.* Berkeley: McCutchan, 1969.

Maccoby, Eleanor Emmons, and Carol Nagy Jacklin. *The Psychology of Sex Differences.* Stanford, Calif.: Stanford University Press, 1974.

Mackenzie, Susan. "Hutterite women: work and assistance patterns." Master's thesis, Department of Anthropology, University of Calgary, 1978.

Mackie, Marlene. "The accuracy of folk knowledge concerning Alberta Indians, Hutterites, and Ukrainians." Ph.D. dissertation, University of Alberta (Edmonton), 1971.

_____. "Arriving at 'truth' by definition: the case of stereotype inaccuracy." *Social Problems* 20 (1973a):431-47.

_____. "Lay perception of heart disease in an Alberta community." *Canadian Journal of Public Health* 64 (1973b):445-54.

_____. "Role constraints and married women." Paper presented at Symposium on "The Working Sexes," University of British Columbia, Vancouver, October 1976.

_____. "On congenial truths: a perspective of women's studies." *Canadian Review of Sociology and Anthropology* 14 (1977a):117-28.

_____. "Professional women's collegial relations and productivity: female sociologists' journal publications, 1967 and 1973." *Sociology and Social Research* 61 (1977b):227-93.

_____. "The social psychology of names." Paper presented at the Pacific Sociological Association Meetings, Sacramento, Calif., 1977c.

_____. "Ethnicity and nationality: how much do they matter to western Canadians?" *Canadian Ethnic Studies* 10 (1978a):118-29.

_____. "The domestication of self." Paper presented at the International Socio-logical Association Meetings, Uppsala, Sweden, 1978b.

_____. "Gender socialization in childhood and adolescence." In *Childhood and Adolescence in Canada*, edited by K. Ishwaran, pp. 136-60. Toronto: McGraw-Hill Ryerson, 1979.

_____. "Socialization." In *Sociology*, edited by Robert Hagedorn, pp. 123-61. Toronto: Holt, Rinehart and Winston, 1980a.

_____. "The impact of sex stereotypes upon adult self-imagery." *Social Psychology Quarterly* 43 (1980b):121-25.

_____. "Ethnic relations in the prairies." In *A Canadian Social Psychology of Ethnic Relations*, edited by Robert C. Gardner and Rudolf Kalin, pp. 194-213. Toronto: Methuen, 1981a.

_____. "Lord of the carrot! Lord of the stick! What do fundamentalists get out of their religion?" Paper presented to the Annual Meeting of the Canadian Sociology and Anthropology Association, Halifax, N.S., May 1981b.

Mackie, Marlene, and Merlin B. Brinkerhoff. "Ethnicity's impact upon familial/gender attitudes: Social 'reality' or social 'fiction'?" *Canadian Ethnic Studies*, forthcoming (1982).

Madigan, F. C. "Are sex mortality differentials biologically caused?" *Millbank Memorial Fund Quarterly* 35 (1957):202-23.

Malinowski, Bronislaw. *Argonauts of the Western Pacific*. London: Dutton, 1922.

_____. *Crime and Custom in Savage Society*. New York: Humanities Press, 1926.

Marchak, Patricia M. "Women workers and white collar unions." *Canadian Review of Sociology and Anthropology* 10 (1973):134-47.

Marchildon, Rudy G. "The 'Persons' controversy: the legal aspects of the fight for women senators." *Atlantis* 6 (1981):99-113.

Marecek, Jeanne. "Psychological disorders in women: indices of role strain." In *Women and Sex Roles*, edited by Irene H. Frieze, Jacquelynne E. Parsons, Paula B. Johnson, Diane N. Ruble, Gail L. Zellman, pp. 255-76. New York: W. W. Norton, 1978.

Marini, Margaret Mooney, and Ellen Greenberger. "Sex differences in occupa-tional aspirations and expectations." *Sociology of Work and Occupations* 5 (1978):147-78.

Markle, Gerald E. "Sex ratio at birth: values, variance, and some determinants." *Demography* 11 (1974):131-42.

Marsden, Lorna R. "Unemployment among Canadian women: some sociological problems raised by its increase." In *The Working Sexes*, edited by Patricia Marchak, pp. 28-43. Vancouver: University of British Columbia, 1977.

Marsden, Lorna R., and Edward B. Harvey. *Fragile Federation: Social Change in Canada*. Toronto: McGraw-Hill Ryerson, 1979.

Martin, Wilfred B. W., and Allan J. Macdonell. *Canadian Education: A Sociological Analysis*. Scarborough, Ontario: Prentice-Hall, 1978.

Martyna, Wendy. "Beyond the 'he/man' approach: the case for nonsexist lan-guage." *Signs* 5 (1980):482-93.

Marx, Karl. *A Contribution to the Critique of Political Economy*. Translated from the 2nd German ed. by N. I. Stone. New York: International Library Publishing, 1904.

Marx, Karl, and Friedrich Engels. *On Religion*. New York: Schocken Books, 1964.

Mason, Karen Oppenheim; John L. Czajka; and Sara Arber. "Change in U.S. women's sex-role attitudes, 1964-1974." *American Sociological Review* 41 (1976):573-96.

Masters, W. H., and V. E. Johnson. *Human Sexual Response*. Boston: Little, Brown, 1966.

Mathes, E. W., and A. Kahn. "Physical attractiveness, happiness, neuroticism, and self-esteem." *Journal of Psychology* 90 (1975):27-30.

Matthews, Anne Martin. "Women and widowhood." In *Aging in Canada: Social Perspectives*, edited by Victor W. Marshall, pp. 145-53. Don Mills, Ontario: Fitzhenry and Whiteside, 1980.

Matthiasson, Carolyn J., ed. *Many Sisters*. New York: Free Press, 1975.

Maxwell, Mary Percival, and James Maxwell. "Women and the elite: the occupational choice of private school females 1966-1976." Paper presented to Annual Meeting of Canadian Sociology and Anthropology Association, Halifax, N.S., May 1981.

McArthur, L., and S. Eisen. "Achievements of male and female storybook characters as determinants of achievement behavior by boys and girls." *Journal of Personality and Social Psychology* 33 (1976):467-73.

McCall, Dorothy Kaufmann. "Simone de Beauvoir, *The Second Sex*, and Jean-Paul Sartre." *Signs* 5 (1979):209-23.

McCaughan, Margaret M. *The Legal Status of Married Women in Canada*. Toronto: Carswell, 1977.

McClelland, David C. "Wanted: a new self-image for women." In *The Woman in America*, edited by R. J. Lifton, pp. 173-92. New York: Houghton Mifflin, 1965.

McClendon, McKee J. "The occupational status attainment processes of males and females." *American Sociological Review* 41 (1976):52-64.

McClung, Nellie. *In Times Like These*. 1915. Reprint. Toronto: University of Toronto Press, 1972.

McGhee, Paul E. "Sex differences in children's humor." *Journal of Communication* 26 (1976):176-89.

McGhee, Paul E., and Terry Frueh. "Television viewing and the learning of sex-role stereotypes." *Sex Roles* 6 (1980):179-88.

McGrady, Mike. *The Kitchen Sink Papers*. Scarborough, Ontario: New American Library, 1975.

McKee, J. P., and A. C. Sherriffs. "Men's and women's beliefs, ideals, and self-concepts." *American Journal of Sociology* 64 (1959):356-63.

McKie, Craig, and Paul Reed. "Women in Canadian civil courts." *The Canadian Journal of Sociology* 6 (1981):485-504.

McMurry, Martha. "Religion and women's sex role traditionalism." *Sociological Focus* 11 (1978):81-95.

McNamara, Patrick H., and Arthur St. George. "Blessed are the downtrodden? an empirical test." *Sociological Analysis* 39 (1978):303-20.

McPhee, Nancy. *The Book of Insults Ancient & Modern*. Toronto: Van Nostrand Reinhold, 1978.

McVey, Wayne W., Jr., and Barrie W. Robinson. "Separation in Canada: new insights concerning marital dissolution." *The Canadian Journal of Sociology* 6 (1981):353-66.

Mead, George Herbert. *Mind, Self and Society*. Chicago: University of Chicago Press, 1934.

Mead, Margaret. *Sex and Temperament in Three Primitive Societies*. Reprint. New York: Mentor Books, 1935.

Meissner, Martin; Elizabeth W. Humphreys; Scott M. Meis; William J. Scheu. "No exit for wives: sexual division of labour and the cumulation of household demands." *Canadian Review of Sociology and Anthropology* 12 (1975), Part 1:424-39.

Mellen, Jean. *Women and Their Sexuality in the New Film*. New York: Horizon, 1973.

Merton, Robert K. *Social Theory and Social Structure*. 2nd ed. Glencoe, Ill.: Free Press, 1957.

Miall, Charlene Elizabeth. "Mass media and adolescent female fashion decisions." Master's thesis, University of Calgary, 1972.

Michel, Andrée. "Statut professionnel féminin et interaction dans le couple en France et aux Etats-Unis." In *La Sociologie de la famille: recueil de textes présentés et commentés*, edited by A. Michel, pp. 281-91. Paris: Mouton, 1970a.

———. "Working wives and family interaction in French and American Families." *International Journal of Comparative Sociology* 11 (1970b): 157-65.

Middlebrook, Patricia Niles. *Social Psychology and Modern Life*. New York: Alfred A. Knopf, 1974.

Mill, John Stuart. The Subjection of Women. Cambridge, Mass.: Massachusetts Institute of Technology Press, 1970.

Miller, Casey, and Kate Swift. *Words and Women*. Garden City, N.Y.: Doubleday Anchor, 1977.

Miller, George A., and David McNeill. "Psycholinguistics." In *The Handbook of Social Psychology*, 2nd ed., vol. 3, edited by Gardner Lindzey and Elliot Aronson, pp. 666-794. Reading, Mass.: Addison-Wesley, 1969.

Miller, Susan H. "The content of news photos: women's and men's roles." *Journalism Quarterly* 52 (1975):70-75.

Millman, Marcia. *Such a Pretty Face: Being Fat in America*. New York: Berkley Books, 1980.

Millman, Marcia, and Rosabeth Moss Kanter. "Editorial introduction." In *Another Voice: Perspectives on Social Life and Social Science*, edited by Marcia Millman and Rosabeth Moss Kanter, pp. vii-xvii. Garden City, N.Y.: Doubleday Anchor, 1975.

Mills, C. Wright. *The Sociological Imagination*. New York: Grove Press, 1959.

Milton, Brian Gerard. *Social Status and Leisure Time Activities: National Survey Analysis for Adult Canadians*. Canadian Sociology and Anthropology Association Monograph Series, no. 3, Montreal, Quebec: 1975.

Miners, Marion Frances. "Women in selected English-Canadian novels, 1954 to 1972." Master's thesis, University of Calgary, 1976.

Minton, C.; J. Kagan; and J. Levine. "Maternal control and obedience in the two-year-old child." *Child Development* 42 (1971):1873-94.

Mischel, W. "Sex-typing and socialization." In *Carmichael's Manual of Child Psychology*, edited by P. H. Mussen, pp. 3-72. New York: Wiley, 1970.

Mitchell, Juliet. *Woman's Estate*. New York: Pantheon Books, 1971.

———. *Psychoanalysis and Feminism*. New York: Pantheon Books, 1974.

Mitchinson, Wendy. "The Woman's Christian Temperance Union: a study in organization." *International Journal of Women's Studies* 4 (1981):143-56.

Modleski, Tania. "The disappearing act: a study of Harlequin Romances." *Signs* 5 (1980):435-48.

Mol, Hans. "Major correlates of churchgoing in Canada." In *Religion in Canadian Society*, edited by Stewart Crysdale and Les Wheatcroft, pp. 241-54. Toronto: Macmillan, 1976.

Molotch, Harvey L. "The news of women and the work of men." In *Hearth and Home: Images of Women in the Mass Media*, edited by Gaye Tuchman, Arlene Kaplan Daniels, and James Benét, pp. 176-85. New York: Oxford University Press, 1978.

Money, John, and A. A. Ehrhardt. *Man and Woman, Boy and Girl: The Differen-*

tiation and Dimorphism of Gender Identity from Conception to Maturity. Baltimore: Johns Hopkins University Press, 1972.

Money, John, and Patricia Tucker. *Sexual Signatures: On Being a Man or a Woman.* Boston: Little, Brown, 1975.

Montagu, Ashley. *The Natural Superiority of Women.* New York: P. F. Collier, 1952.

Moreland, John. "Age and change in the adult male sex role." *Sex Roles* 6 (1980): 807-18.

Morgan, M. *The Total Woman.* New York: Pocket Books, Simon and Schuster, 1975.

Morgan, Robin, ed. *Sisterhood is Powerful: An Anthology of Writings from the Women's Liberation Movement.* New York: Vintage Books, 1970.

Morris, Cerise. "Paradigms and politics: the ideas of the women's movement." *International Journal of Women's Studies* 2 (1979):189-201.

_____. " 'Determination and thoroughness': the movement for a Royal Commission on the Status of Women in Canada." *Atlantis* 5 (1980):1-21.

Morris, Jan. *Conundrum.* New York: Harcourt Brace Jovanovich, 1974.

Morris, Monica B. "Newspapers and the new feminists: blackout as social control?" *Journalism Quarterly* 50 (1973):37-42.

Morton, Peggy. "Women's work is never done." In *Women Unite! An Anthology of the Canadian Women's Movement*, pp. 46-68. Toronto: Canadian Women's Educational Press, 1972.

Munro, Alice. *Lives of Girls and Women.* New York: McGraw-Hill Ryerson, 1971.

Murstein, Bernard I. "Stimulus-value-role: a theory of marital choice." *Journal of Marriage and the Family* 32 (1970):465-82.

_____. "Physical attractiveness and marital choice." *Journal of Personality and Social Psychology* 22 (1972):8-12.

Mussen, Paul H. "Early sex-role development." In *Handbook of Socialization Theory and Research*, edited by David A. Goslin, pp. 707-31. Chicago: Rand McNally, 1969.

Myrdal, Gunnar. *An American Dilemma: The Negro Problem and Modern Democracy.* New York: Harper and Bros., 1944.

Neilsen, Joyce McCarl. *Sex in Society: Perspectives on Stratification.* Belmont, Calif.: Wadsworth, 1978.

_____. "From corrective to creative progress in sex stratification: sociological and anthropological contributions." *International Journal of Women's Studies* 2 (1979):324-39.

Nelson, Fiona. "Sex stereotyping in Canadian schools." In *Women in the Canadian Mosaic*, edited by Gwen Matheson, pp. 167-80. Toronto: Peter Martin Associates, 1976.

Nemiroff, Greta Hoffman. "Rationale for an interdisciplinary approach to women's studies." *Canadian Women's Studies* 1 (1978):60-68.

Nett, Emily. "The changing forms and functions of the Canadian family: a demographic view." In *The Canadian Family*, rev. ed., edited by K. Ishwaran. Toronto: Holt, Rinehart and Winston, 1976.

_____. "Definitions of femininity and masculinity in selected Canadian textbooks: some sources and consequences." Paper presented to Annual Meeting of Canadian Sociology and Anthropology Association, Saskatoon, Sask., June 1979.

Nettler, Gwynn. *Explanations.* New York: McGraw-Hill, 1970.

_____. "Sociologist as advocate." In *Sociology's Relations with the Community,* edited by Marlene Mackie. Calgary: Department of Sociology, University of Calgary, 1980.

Neufeld, E. D.; D. Langmeyer; and W. Seeman. "Some sex-role stereotypes and personal preferences: 1950 and 1970." *Journal of Personality Assessment* 3 (1974):247-54.

Nye, F. Ivan, and Lois W. Hoffman, eds. *The Employed Mother in America.* Chicago: Rand McNally, 1963.

Oakley, Ann. *Sex, Gender and Society.* New York: Harper and Row, 1972.

_____. *The Sociology of Housework.* Bath, England: The Pitman Press, 1974.

O'Dea, Thomas F. *The Sociology of Religion.* Englewood Cliffs, N.J.: Prentice-Hall, 1966.

O'Kelly, Charlotte. "Sex-role imagery in modern art: an empirical examination." *Sex Roles* 6 (1980):99-111.

O'Leary, Virginia E.; and Charlene E. Depner. "College males' ideal female: changes in sex-role stereotypes." *Journal of Social Psychology* 95 (1975):139-40.

Orbach, Susie. *Fat Is a Feminist Issue.* New York: Berkley, 1978.

Osler, Margaret J. "Sex, science and values: a critique of sociobiological accounts of sex differences." *Resources for Feminist Research,* Special Publication 8 (1980):119-24.

Packard, Vance. *The Sexual Wilderness.* New York: David McKay, 1968.

Parish, Thomas S., and Merton E. Powell. "A comparison of adult women's and men's ascription of negative traits to the same and opposite sex." *Sex Roles* 6 (1980):457-62.

Parker, Dorothy. *The Portable Dorothy Parker.* New York: Viking Penguin, 1976.

Parlee, Mary Brown. "The sexes under scrutiny: from old biases to new theories." *Psychology Today* (November 1978) 12:62-69.

Parlee, Mary Brown, and the Editors of Psychology Today. "The friendship bond." *Psychology Today* (October 1979):43-45, 49, 50, 53, 54, 113.

Parsons, Talcott. "The American family: its relation to personality and to the social structure." In *Family Socialization and Interaction Process,* edited by Talcott Parsons and Robert F. Bales. Glencoe, Ill.: Free Press, 1955a.

_____. "Sex roles and family structure." In *Family Socialization and Interaction Process,* edited by Talcott Parsons and Robert F. Bales. Glencoe, Ill.: Free Press, 1955b.

_____. "The school as a social system." *Harvard Educational Review* 29 (1959):297-318.

Payne, Barbara, and Frank Whittington. "Older women: an examination of popular stereotypes and research evidence." *Social Problems* 23 (1976):488-504.

Pederson, F., and K. Robson. "Father participation in infancy." *American Journal of Psychiatry* 39 (1969):466-72.

Percival, Elizabeth, and Terrance Percival. "Is a woman a person? Sex differences in stereotyping." *Atlantis* 4 (1979):71-77.

Peter, L. J. *Peter's Quotations: Ideas for Our Time.* New York: William Morrow, 1977.

Petryszak, Nicholas G. "Sociological theory and human nature." *Pacific Sociological Review* 23 (1980):131-50.

Pheterson, G. T.; S. B. Kiesler: and P. A. Goldberg. "Evaluation of the performance of women as a function of their sex, achievement, and personal history." *Journal of Personality and Social Psychology* 19 (1971):114-18.

Phillips, E. Barbara. "Magazines' heroines: Is *Ms.* just another member of the *Family Circle*?" In *Hearth and Home: Images of Women in the Mass Media,* edited by Gaye Tuchman, Arlene Kaplan Daniels, and James Benét, pp. 116-29. New York: Oxford University Press, 1978.

Piaget, Jean. *Judgment and Reasoning in the Child*. New York: Harcourt, 1928.

_____. *The Moral Judgment of the Child*. New York: Harcourt, 1932.

Pike, Robert M. *Who Doesn't Get to University and Why?* (Undertaken for the Association of Universities and Colleges of Canada.) Ottawa: The Runge Press, 1970.

Pineo, Peter, and John Porter. "Occupational prestige in Canada." *Canadian Review of Sociology and Anthropology* 4 (1967):24-40.

Pingree, Suzanne. "The effects of nonsexist television commercials and perceptions of reality on children's attitudes about women." *Psychology of Women Quarterly* 2 (1978):262-77.

Poelzer, Sr. Irene A. "Feminist theology: implications and significance for women as persons." *Resources for Feminist Research*, Special Publication 8 (1980):36-38.

Polatnick, Margaret. "Why men don't rear children: a power analysis." In *Sex: Male—Gender: Masculine*, edited by John W. Petras, pp. 199-235. Port Washington, N.Y.: Alfred Publishing, 1975.

Poloma, Margaret M. "Role conflict and the married professional woman." In *Toward a Sociology of Women*, edited by Constantina Safilios-Rothschild, pp. 187-98. Lexington, Mass.: Xerox, 1972.

Porter, John. *The Vertical Mosaic*. Toronto: University of Toronto Press, 1965.

Posner, Judith. "Dirty old women." *Canadian Review of Sociology and Anthropology* 12 (1975), Part 1:471-73.

_____. "Old and female: the double whammy." In *Aging in Canada: Social Perspectives*, edited by Victor W. Marshall, pp. 80-87. Don Mills, Ontario: Fitzhenry and Whiteside, 1980.

Powers, Patrick. "Reflections on male consciousness." *Canadian Women's Studies* 1 (1978):35-37.

Pratt, David. "The social role of school textbooks in Canada." In *Socialization and Values in Canadian Society*, vol. 1, edited by Elia Zureik and Robert M. Pike, pp. 100-126. Toronto: McClelland and Stewart, 1975.

Prentice, Beverly. "Divorce, kids, and custody: a quantitative study of three legal factors." Paper presented to Annual Meeting of the Canadian Sociology and Anthropology Association, Saskatoon, Sask., 1979.

Propper, Alice Marcella. "The relationship of maternal employment to adolescent roles, activities, and parental relationships." *Journal of Marriage and the Family* 34 (1972):417-21.

Proulx, Monique. *Five Million Women: A Study of the Canadian Housewife*. Ottawa: Advisory Council on the Status of Women, 1978.

Pyke, S. W. "Children's literature: conceptions of sex roles." In *Socialization and Values in Canadian Society*, vol. 2, edited by Robert M. Pike and Elia Zureik, pp. 51-73. Toronto: McClelland and Stewart, 1975.

_____. "Androgyny: a dead end or a promise?" In *Sex Roles: Origins, Influences, and Implications for Women*, edited by Cannie Stark-Adamec, pp. 20-32. Montreal: Eden Press, 1980.

Pyke, S. W., and J. C. Stewart. "This column is about women: women and television." *The Ontario Psychologist* 6 (1974):66-69.

Queen, Ellery, ed. *The Female of the Species: The Great Women Detectives and Criminals*. Boston: Little, Brown, 1943.

Rapoport, Rhona, and Robert N. Rapoport. *Dual-Career Families Re-examined*. New York: Harper and Row, 1977.

Reed, Evelyn. "Women: caste, class or oppressed sex?" In *Feminist Frameworks:*

Alternative Theoretical Accounts of the Relations between Women and Men, edited by Alison M. Jaggar and Paula Rothenberg Struhl, pp. 119-29. New York: McGraw-Hill, 1978.

Rheingold, H., and K. Cook. "The content of boys' and girls' rooms as an index of parent behavior." *Child Development* 46 (1975):459-63.

Richardson, Laurel Walum. *The Dynamics of Sex and Gender*. 2nd ed. Boston: Houghton Mifflin, 1981.

Richer, Stephen. "Sex-role socialization and early schooling." *Canadian Review of Sociology and Anthropology* 16 (1979):195-205.

Richmond, Marie L. "Beyond resource theory: another look at factors enabling women to affect family interaction." *Journal of Marriage and the Family* 38 (1976):257-66.

Rickel, Annette U., and Linda M. Grant. "Sex role stereotypes in the mass media and schools: five consistent themes." *International Journal of Women's Studies* 2 (1979):164-79.

Ringwood, Gwen Pharis, et al. "Women and theatrical tradition." *Atlantis* 4 (1978):154-58.

Ritchie, Marguerite. "Alice through the statutes." *McGill Law Journal* 21 (1975):702.

Ritzer, George. *Man and His Work: Conflict and Change*. New York: Appleton-Century-Crofts, 1972.

_____. *Sociology: A Multiple Paradigm Science*. Boston: Allyn and Bacon, 1975.

Rivlin, Lilly. "Lilith: the first woman." *Ms.* 1 (December 1972):92-97, 114-115.

Robb, A. Leslie, and Byron G. Spencer. "Education: enrolment and attainment." In *Opportunity for Choice*, edited by Gail C. A. Cook, pp. 53-92. Ottawa: Information Canada, 1976.

Robbins, Thomas, and Dick Anthony. "The sociology of contemporary religious movements." *Annual Review of Sociology* 5 (1979):75-89.

Robertson, Ian. *Sociology*. 2nd ed. New York: Worth Publishers, 1981.

Robson, R. A. H., and M. Lapointe. *A Comparison of Men's and Women's Salaries and Employment Fringe Benefits in the Academic Profession*. Royal Commission on the Status of Women in Canada, Substudy 1. Ottawa: Queen's Printer, 1971.

Rohrbaugh, Joanna Bunker. "Femininity on the line." *Psychology Today* 13 (August 1979): 30-42.

Roman, Mel, and William Haddad. *The Disposable Parent: The Case for Joint Custody*. Harmondsworth, England: Penguin Books, 1978.

Romer, Nancy, and Debra Cherry. "Ethnic and social class differences in children's sex-role concepts." *Sex Roles* 6 (1980):245-63.

Rosaldo, Michelle Zimbalist. "Woman, culture, and society: a theoretical overview." In *Woman, Culture and Society*, edited by Michelle Zimbalist Rosaldo and Louise Lamphere, pp. 17-42. Stanford, Calif.: Stanford University Press, 1974.

_____. "The use and abuse of anthropology: reflections on feminism and cross-cultural understanding." *Signs* 5 (1980):389-417.

Rosenberg, B. G., and B. Sutton-Smith. "Family interaction effects on masculinity-femininity." *Journal of Personality and Social Psychology* 8 (1968): 117-20.

Rosenberg, Bernard, and Norris Fliegel. "Prejudice against female artists." In *The Professional Woman*, edited by Athena Theodore, pp. 660-65. Cambridge, Mass.: Schenkman, 1971.

Rosenberg, M. *Society and the Adolescent Self-image*. Princeton, N.J.: Princeton University Press, 1965.

Rosenberg, Marie Barovic, and Len V. Bergstrom. *Women and Society*. Beverly Hills: Sage Publications, 1975.

Rosenberg, Miriam. "The biologic basis for sex role stereotypes." In *Beyond Sex-role Stereotypes: Readings toward a Psychology of Androgyny*, edited by Alexandra G. Kaplan and Joan P. Bean, pp. 106-23. Boston: Little, Brown, 1976.

Rosenblatt, Paul C., and Michael R. Cunningham. "Sex differences in cross-cultural perspective." In *Exploring Sex Differences*, edited by Barbara Lloyd and John Archer, pp. 71-94. New York: Academic Press, 1976.

Rosenfeld, Rachel A. "Women's occupational careers: individual and structural explanations." *Sociology of Work and Occupations* 6 (1979):283-311.

Rosenthal, R., and K. Fode. "The effect of experimental bias on the performance of the albino rat." *Behavioral Science* 8 (1963):183-89.

Ross, Aileen. "Businesswomen and business cliques in three cities: Delhi, Sydney, and Montreal." *Canadian Review of Sociology and Anthropology* 16 (1979):425-35.

Rossi, Alice S. "Naming children in middle-class families." *American Sociological Review* 30 (1965):499-513.

Rossi, Alice S., ed. *The Feminist Papers*. New York: Bantam Books, 1973.

Rossi, Alice S. "A biosocial perspective on parenting." *Daedalus* 106 (1977a):1-31.

_____. "Transition to parenthood." In *Family in Transition*, edited by Arlene S. Skolnick and Jerome K. Skolnick, pp. 351-62. Toronto: Little, Brown, 1977b.

_____. "Life-span theories and women's lives." *Signs* 6 (1980):4-32.

Rowbotham, Sheila. *Woman's Consciousness, Man's World*. Harmondsworth, England: Penguin Books, 1973.

Rowe, Mary Potter. "Child care for the 1980s: traditional sex roles or androgyny?" In *Women Into Wives: The Legal and Economic Impact of Marriage*, edited by Jane Roberts Chapman and Margaret Gates, pp. 169-93. Beverly Hills, Calif.: Sage Publications, 1977.

Royal Commission on the Status of Women in Canada. *Report*. Ottawa: Information Canada, 1970.

Rubin, Lillian. "Editorial." *Social Problems* 23 (1976):369-70.

Rubin, Zick. *Liking and Loving*. New York: Holt, Rinehart and Winston, 1973.

_____. *Children's Friendships*. Cambridge, Mass.: Harvard University Press, 1980.

Rubin, J. Z.; F. J. Provenzano; and Z. Luria. "The eye of the beholder: parents' views on sex of newborns." *American Journal of Orthopsychiatry* 44 (1974):512-19.

Ruether, Rosemary R. *Religion and Sexism: Images of Woman in the Jewish and Christian Traditions*. New York: Simon and Schuster, 1974.

Russell, Susan. "Learning sex roles in the high school." Paper presented to Annual Meeting of Canadian Sociology and Anthropology Association, Saskatoon, Sask., June 1979.

Ryan, William. *Blaming the Victim*. New York: Vintage, 1971.

Saario, Teresa; C. N. Jacklin; and C. K. Tittle. "Sex-role stereotyping in public schools." *Harvard Educational Review* 43 (1973):386-416.

Saegert, S., and R. Hart. "The development of environmental competence in girls and boys." In *Women in Society*, edited by P. Burnet. Chicago: Maaroufa Press, 1976.

Safilios-Rothschild, Constantina. "A comparison of power structure and marital satisfaction in urban Greek and French families." *Journal of Marriage and the Family* 29 (1967):345-52.

_____. "Family sociology or wives' family sociology: a cross-cultural examination of decision-making." *Journal of Marriage and the Family* 31 (1969):290-301.

———. *Women and Social Policy*. Englewood Cliffs, N.J.: Prentice-Hall, 1974.

———. "Sexuality, power, and freedom among 'older' women." In *Dimensions of Aging*, edited by Jon Hendricks and C. Davis Hendricks, pp. 213-16. Cambridge, Mass.: Winthrop, 1979.

Sanford, N. "The dynamics of identification." *Psychological Review* 62 (1955): 106-18.

Sapir, E. "Language." In *Encyclopaedia of the Social Sciences*, vol. 9, pp. 155-69. New York: Macmillan, 1933.

Sargent, Pamela. "Introduction: women in science fiction." In *Women of Wonder: Science Fiction Stories by Women About Women*, edited by Pamela Sargent, pp. xiii-lxiv. New York: Vintage Books, 1974.

Sayers, Janet. "Biological determinism, psychology and the division of labour by sex." *International Journal of Women's Studies* 3 (1980):241-60.

Scaife, Michael. "Observing infant social development: theoretical perspectives, natural observation, and video recording." In *Emerging Strategies in Social Psychological Research*, edited by G. P. Ginsburg, pp. 93-116. Toronto: John Wiley and Sons, 1979.

Scanzoni, John. *Opportunity and the Family*. New York: Free Press, 1970.

Schellenberg, James A. *Masters of Social Psychology*. New York: Oxford University Press, 1978.

Schlegel, Alice. "Women anthropologists look at women." *Reviews in Anthropology* 1 (1974):553-60.

Schlesinger, Benjamin. *The One-Parent Family*. 3rd ed. Toronto: University of Toronto Press, 1975.

Schlossberg, N. K., and J. A. Goodman. "Woman's place: children's sex stereotyping of occupations." *Vocational Guidance Quarterly* 20 (1972):266-70.

Schneider, Joseph W., and Sally L. Hacker. "Sex role imagery and use of the generic 'man' in introductory texts: a case in the sociology of sociology." *The American Sociologist* 8 (1973):12-18.

Schreiber, E. M. "The social bases of opinions on women's role in Canada." *Canadian Journal of Sociology* 1 (1975):61-74.

Schull, Christiane "Bag ladies." *Today* (25 April 1981):15-16.

Schulz, Muriel R. "The semantic derogation of woman." In *Language and Sex: Difference and Dominance*, edited by Barrie Thorne and Nancy Henley, pp. 64-75. Rowley, Mass.: Newbury House, 1975.

Schutz, A. *The Phenomenology of the Social World*. Evanston, Ill.: Northwestern University Press, 1967.

Schwendinger, Julia, and Herman Schwendinger. "Sociology's founding fathers: sexists to a man." *Journal of Marriage and the Family* 33 (1971):783-99.

Sears, P. S., and D. A. Feldman. "Teacher interaction with boys and girls." In *And Jill Came Tumbling After: Sexism in American Eduction*, edited by J. Stacey. New York: Dell, 1974.

Segal, Erich. *Man, Woman and Child*. New York: Ballantine Books, 1980.

Selman, Robert L., and Anne P. Selman. "Children's ideas about friendship: a new theory." *Psychology Today* 13 (October 1979):71, 72, 74, 79, 80, 114.

Serbin, L. A., and K. D. O'Leary. "How nursery schools teach girls to shut up." *Psychology Today* 9 (1975):56-57, 102-103.

Serbin, L.; K. O'Leary; R. Kent; and I. Tonick. "A comparison of teacher response to the preacademic and problem behavior of boys and girls." *Child Development* 44 (1973):796-804.

Shaw, Marvin E., and Philip R. Costanzo. *Theories of Social Psychology*. New York: McGraw-Hill, 1970.

Sheehy, Gail. *Passages*. Toronto: Clarke, Irwin, 1976.

Shepard, Winifred. "Mothers and fathers, sons and daughters: perceptions of young adults." *Sex Roles* 6 (1980):421-33.

Sherriffs, A. C., and R. F. Jarrett. "Sex differences in attitudes about sex differences." *Journal of Psychology* 35 (1953):161-68.

Sherriffs, A. C., and J. P. McKee. "Qualitative aspects of beliefs about men and women." *Journal of Personality* 25 (1957):451-64.

Shields, Stephanie A. "Functionalism, Darwinism and the psychology of women." *American Psychologist* 30 (1975):739-54.

Sidorowicz, Laura S., and G. Sparks Lunney. "Baby X revisited." *Sex Roles* 6 (1980):67-73.

Sieber, Sam D. "Toward a theory of role accumulation." *American Sociological Review* 39 (1974):567-78.

Silverman, I. "Physical attractiveness and courtship." *Sexual Behavior* (September 1971):22-25.

Simon, R. J.; G. Crotts; and L. Mahan. "An empirical note about married women and their friends." *Social Forces* 48 (1970):520-25.

Singer, J. *Androgyny*. Garden City, N.Y.: Doubleday Anchor, 1976.

Skinner, B. F. *Science and Human Behavior*. New York: Macmillan, 1953.

Smith, Dorothy E. "Women's perspective as a radical critique of sociology." *Sociological Inquiry* 44 (1974):7-13.

_____. "An analysis of ideological structures and how women are excluded: considerations for academic women." *Canadian Review of Sociology and Anthropology* 12 (1975), Part 1:353-69.

_____. *Feminism and Marxism—A Place to Begin, A Way to Go*. Vancouver: New Star Books, 1977.

Smuts, Robert W. *Women and Work in America*. New York: Schocken Books, 1959.

Smye, Marti Diane, and Jeri Dawn Wine. "A comparison of female and male adolescents' social behaviors and cognitions: a challenge to the assertiveness literature." *Sex Roles* 6 (1980):213-30.

Smye, Marti Diane; Jeri Dawn Wine; and Barbara Moses. "Sex differences in assertiveness: implications for research and treatment. In *Sex Roles: Origins, Influences, and Implications for Women*, edited by Cannie Stark-Adamec, pp. 164-75. Montreal: Eden Press, 1980.

Snodgrass, Jon. "The women's liberation movement and the men." Paper presented to the Pacific Sociological Association Meetings, Victoria, B.C., 1975.

Sontag, Susan. "The double standard of aging." *Saturday Review* 55 (1972):29-38.

Span, Paula. "Marketers busily rewriting ads for new generations: 15-75." Reprinted from the *New York Times Magazine*. Calgary: *The Calgary Herald*, 27 June 1981.

Spangler, Eve; Marsha A. Gordon; and Ronald M. Pipkin. "Token women: an empirical test of Kanter's hypothesis." *American Journal of Sociology* 84 (1978): 160-70.

Spears, Betty. "Prologue: the myth." In *Women and Sport: From Myth to Reality*, edited by Carole A. Oglesby, pp. 3-15. Philadelphia: Lea and Febiger, 1978.

Spence, Janet T., and Robert L. Helmreich. *Masculinity and Femininity: Their Psychological Dimensions, Correlates, and Antecedents*. Austin: University of Texas Press, 1978.

Spencer, Byron G., and Dennis C. Featherstone. *Married Female Labour Force Participation: A Micro Study*. Ottawa: Statistics Canada, Queen's Printer, 1970.

Spillane, Frank Morrison (Mickey). *Kiss Me Deadly*. New York: E. P. Dutton, 1952.

Squire, Anne M. "Feminist theology: toward personhood for women." *Resources for Feminist Research*, Special Publication 8 (1980):34-36.

Staines, Graham; Carol Tavris; and Toby Epstein Jayaratne. "The queen bee syndrome." *Psychology Today* 7 (January 1974): 55-60.

Starer, Ruana, and Florence Denmark. "Discrimination against aspiring women." In *Who Discriminates against Women?* edited by Florence Denmark, pp. 67-72. Beverly Hills: Sage Publications, 1974.

Stark, Rodney, and William Sims Bainbridge. "Networks of faith: interpersonal bonds and recruitment to cults and sects." *American Journal of Sociology* 85 (1980):1376-95.

Statistics Canada. *Perspective Canada I.* Ottawa: Information Canada, 1974.

_____. *Perspective Canada II. A Compendium of Social Statistics 1977.* Ottawa: Ministry of Supply and Services, 1977.

_____. *Culture Statistics: Recreational Activities 1976.* Ottawa: Catalogue 87-501, 1978.

_____. *Perspective Canada III.* Ottawa: Ministry of Supply and Services, 1980.

Stephenson, Marylee, ed. *Women in Canada.* Toronto: New Press, 1973.

Sternglanz, Sarah H., and Lisa A. Serbin. "Sex-role stereotyping in children's television programs." *Developmental Psychology* 10 (1974):710-15.

Stockard, Jean, and Miriam M. Johnson. *Sex Roles: Sex Inequality and Sex Role Development.* Englewood Cliffs, N.J.: Prentice-Hall, 1980.

Stolk, Yvonne, and Patricia Brotherton. "Attitudes towards single women." *Sex Roles* 7 (1981):73-78.

Stroller, R. J. *Sex and Gender: On the Development of Masculinity and Femininity.* New York: Science House, 1968.

Stymeist, D. H. *Ethnics and Indians: Social Relations in a Northwestern Ontario Town.* Toronto: Peter Martin Associates, 1975.

Sutherland, Sharon L. "The unamibitious female: women's low professional aspirations." *Signs* 3 (1978):774-94.

Sutton-Smith, B., and B. G. Rosenberg. "Sixty years of historical change in game preferences of American children." In *Child's Play*, edited by R. E. Heron and B. Sutton-Smith, pp. 18-50. New York: Wiley, 1971.

Sydie, Rosalind. "Women painters in Britain: 1768-1848." *Atlantis* 5 (1980): 144-75.

Szalai, Alexander, ed. *The Uses of Time: Daily Activities of Urban and Suburban Populations in Twelve Countries.* The Hague: Mouton, 1972.

Tangri, Beverly. "Women and unemployment." *Atlantis* 3 (1978), Part 2:85-92.

Tauer, Carol A. "Freud and female inferiority." *International Journal of Women's Studies* 2 (1979):287-304.

Tavris, Carol. "Men and women report their views on masculinity." *Psychology Today* 10 (January 1977):34-38, 42, 82.

Tavris, Carol, and Carole Offir. *The Longest War: Sex Differences in Perspective.* New York: Harcourt Brace Jovanovich, 1977.

Taylor, Norma. " 'All this for three and a half a day': the farm wife." In *Women in the Canadian Mosaic*, edited by Gwen Matheson, pp. 151-64. Toronto: Peter Martin Associates, 1976.

Taylor, Patricia Ann, and Norval D. Glenn. "The utility of education and attractiveness for females' status attainment through marriage." *American Sociological Review* 41 (1976):484-98.

Tedesco, N. S. "Patterns of prime time." *Journal of Communication* 24 (1974): 119-24.

Temerlin, Maurice K. "My daughter Lucy." *Psychology Today* 9 (November 1975):59-62, 103.

Terry, R. L., and S. L. Ertel. "Exploration of individual differences in preferences for humor." *Psychological Reports* 34 (1974):1031-37.

Thatcher, T. C. "Report of the Royal Commission on Violence in the Communications Industry." In *Violence in Canada*, edited by Mary Alice Beyer Gammon, pp. 218-51. Toronto: Methuen, 1978.

Theodore, Athena. "The professional woman: trends and prospects." In *The Professional Woman*, edited by Athena Theodore, pp. 1-35. Cambridge, Mass.: Schenkman, 1971.

Thorndike, E. L. *Animal Intelligence*. New York: Macmillan, 1898.

_____. *The Psychology of Learning*. New York: Columbia University Press, 1913.

Thorne, Barrie, and Nancy Henley. "Difference and dominance: an overview of language, gender, and society." In *Language and Sex: Difference and Dominance*, edited by Barrie Thorne and Nancy Henley, pp. 5-42. Rowley, Mass.: Newbury House, 1975.

_____. *Language and Sex: Difference and Dominance*. Rowley, Mass.: Newbury House, 1975.

Thornton, Arland, and Deborah S. Freedman. "Changes in the sex role attitudes of women, 1962-1977: evidence from a panel study." *American Sociological Review* 44 (1979):832-42.

Tiger, Lionel. *Men in Groups*. New York: Random House, 1969.

Timson, Judith. "The magnificent Margaret Atwood." *Chatelaine* 54 (1981):42, 43, 56, 60, 64, 65, 68, 70.

Toch, Hans. *The Social Psychology of Social Movements*. Indianapolis: Bobbs-Merrill, 1965.

Todres, R., and B. Schlesinger. "Motherless families: an increasing societal pattern." *Child Welfare* 55 (1976):533-38.

Tolson, Andrew. *The Limits of Masculinity*. London: Tavistock, 1977.

Treiman, Donald J., and Kermit Terrell. "Sex and the process of status attainment: a comparison of working women and men." *American Sociological Review* 40 (1975):174-200.

Tresemer, David. "Fear of success: popular but unproven." *Psychology Today* 7 (1974):82-85.

_____. "Assumptions made about gender roles." In *Another Voice: Feminist Perspectives on Social Life and Social Sciences*, edited by Marcia Millman and Rosabeth Moss Kanter, pp. 308-39. Garden City, N.Y.: Doubleday Anchor, 1975.

Trofimenkoff, Susan Mann, and Alison Prentice, eds. *The Neglected Majority: Essays in Canadian Women's History*. Toronto: McClelland and Stewart, 1977.

Tuchman, Gaye. "Introduction: the symbolic annihilation of women by the mass media." In *Hearth and Home: Images of Women in the Mass Media*, edited by Gaye Tuchman, Arlene Kaplan Daniels, and James Benét, pp. 3-38. New York: Oxford University Press, 1978a.

_____. "The newspaper as a social movement's resource." In *Hearth and Home: Images of Women in the Mass Media*, edited by Gaye Tuchman, Arlene Kaplan Daniels, and James Benét, pp. 186-215. New York: Oxford University Press, 1978b.

_____. "Women's depiction by the mass media." *Signs* 4 (1979):528-42.

Tudiver, Judith G. "Parents and the sex-role development of the preschool child." In *Sex Roles: Origins, Influences and Implications for Women*, edited by Cannie Stark-Adamec, pp. 33-49. Montreal: Eden, 1980.

Tumin, M. *Social Stratification: The Form and Functions of Inequality*. Englewood Cliffs, N.J.: Prentice-Hall, 1967.

Turk, James L. "Who has the power?" In *Marriage, Family and Society: Canadian Perspectives*, edited by S. Parvez Wakil, pp. 237-55. Toronto: Butterworths, 1975.

Turk, James L., and Norman W. Bell. "Measuring power in families." *Journal of Marriage and the Family* 34 (1972):215-22.

Turner, Ralph H. *Family Interaction*. New York: John Wiley and Sons, 1970.

Turner, Ralph H., and Lewis M. Killian. *Collective Behavior*. 2nd ed. Englewood Cliffs, N.J.: Prentice-Hall, 1972.

Unger, Jim. *The First Treasury of Herman*. Kansas City, Mo.: Andrews and Mc-Meel, 1979.

U.S. Commission on Civil Rights. *Window Dressing on the Set: Women and Minorities in Television*. Washington, D.C.: 1977.

U.S. Department of Health, Education, and Welfare. *Television and Growing Up: The Impact of Televised Violence*. Report to the Surgeon General from the Scientific Advisory Committee on Television and Social Behavior, Washington, D.C., 1972.

van den Berghe, Pierre L. *Man in Society: A Biosocial View*. New York: Elsevier, 1975.

_____. "Response to Lee Ellis' 'The decline and fall of sociology.' " *The American Sociologist* 12 (1977):75-76.

Vanderbilt, Amy. *Everyday Etiquette*. Rev. ed. Garden City, N.Y.: Doubleday, 1967.

van Herk, Aritha. *Judith*. Toronto: McClelland and Stewart, 1978.

Vaughter, Reesa M. "Psychology review essay." *Signs* 2 (1976):120-46.

Veevers, J. E. "The child-free alternative: rejection of the motherhood mystique." In *Women in Canada*, rev. ed., edited by Marylee Stephenson, pp. 90-108. Don Mills, Ontario: General Publishing, 1977.

_____. *Childless by Choice*. Toronto: Butterworths, 1980.

Veevers, J. E., and D. F. Cousineau. "The heathen Canadians: demographic correlates of nonbelief." *Pacific Sociological Review* 23 (1980):199-216.

Venkatesan, M., and J. Losco. "Women in magazine ads: 1959-71." *Journal of Advertising Research* 15 (1975):49-54.

Vickers, Jill McCalla. "Where are the women in Canadian politics?" *Atlantis* 3 (1978):40-51.

Vickers, Jill McCalla, and June Adam. *But Can You Type?* Toronto: Clarke, Irwin and Company in association with the Canadian Association of University Teachers, 1977.

Viorst, Judith. *How Did I Get to be Forty and Other Atrocities*. New York: Simon and Schuster, 1976.

Vroegh, Karen. "The relationship of birth order and sex of siblings to gender role identity." *Developmental Psychology* 4 (1971):407-11.

Wagner, L., and J. Banos. "A woman's place: a follow-up analysis of the roles portrayed by women in magazine advertisements." *Journal of Marketing Research* 10 (1973):213-14.

Walker, Kathryn. "Time used by husbands for household work." *Family Economics Review* (June 1970):8-11.

Walker, Nancy. "Do feminists ever laugh? women's humor and women's rights." *International Journal of Women's Studies* 4 (1981):1-9.

Wallace, Cecelia. "Changes in the churches." In *Women in the Canadian Mosaic*, edited by Gwen Matheson, pp. 93-128. Toronto: Peter Martin Associates, 1976.

Waller, Willard. *The Family: A Dynamic Interpretation*. New York: Dryden, 1938.

Waller, Willard, and Reuben Hill. *The Family: A Dynamic Interpretation.* New York: Dryden, 1951.

Wallin, Paul. "Cultural considerations and sex roles: a repeat study." *American Sociological Review* 15 (1950):288-93.

Walum, Laurel Richardson. *The Dynamics of Sex and Gender: A Sociological Perspective.* Chicago: Rand McNally, 1977.

_____. "The changing door ceremony." *Urban Life and Culture* 2 (1974):506-15.

Ward, Dawn, and Jack Balswick. "Strong men and virtuous women: a content analysis of sex role stereotypes." *Pacific Sociological Review* 21 (1978):45-53.

Wargon, Sylvia T. "Family." In *Perspective Canada III*, pp. 21-31. Statistics Canada. Ottawa: Ministry of Supply and Services Canada, 1980.

Waters, H. F., and P. Malamud. "Drop that gun, Captain Video." *Newsweek* 85 (10 March 1975):81-82.

Wax, Rosalie H. "Gender and age in fieldwork and fieldwork eduction: no good thing is done by any man alone." *Social Problems* 26 (1979):509-22.

Weber, Max. *The Theory of Social and Economic Organization* (trans. and ed. by A. M. Henderson and Talcott Parsons). London: Oxford University Press, 1947.

Weiner, Nella Fermi. "Lilith: first woman, first feminist." *International Journal of Women's Studies* 2 (1979):551-59.

Weisstein, Naomi. "Psychology constructs the female, or the fantasy life of the male psychologist." In *Roles Women Play: Readings toward Women's Liberation*, edited by Michele Hoffnung Garskof, pp. 68-83. Belmont, Calif.: Brooks/Cole, 1971.

Weitz, Shirley. *Sex Roles: Biological, Psychological, and Social Foundations.* New York: Oxford University Press, 1977.

Weitzman, L. J.; D. Eifler; E. Hokada; and C. Ross. "Sex-role socialization in picture books for preschool children." *American Journal of Sociology* 77 (1972):1125-50.

Welch, Mary Scott. *Networking: The Great New Way for Women to Get Ahead.* New York: Harcourt Brace Jovanovich, 1980.

Weldon, Fay. *Female Friends.* London: Pan Books, 1974.

West, Candy. "Sexism and conversation: everything you always wanted to know about Sachs (but were afraid to ask)." Master's thesis, Department of Sociology, University of California (Santa Barbara), 1973.

Weyant, Robert G. "The relationship between psychology and women." *International Journal of Women's Studies* 2 (1979):358-85.

White, Carol. "The effects of marriage on women's friendships." B. A. Honors Essay, Department of Sociology, University of Calgary, 1974.

Whitehurst, Carol A. "An empirical investigation of women's self-evaluation." *International Journal of Women's Studies* 2 (1979):76-86.

_____. "Images of the sexes in science fiction." *International Journal of Women's Studies* 3 (1980):327-37.

Whorf, B. *Four Articles on Metalinguistics.* Washington, D.C.: Foreign Service Institute, Department of State, 1949.

Wilensky, L. "Women's work: economic growth, ideology, structure." *Industrial Relations* 7 (1968):235-58.

Williams, Juanita H. *Psychology of Women: Behavior in a Biosocial Context.* New York: Norton, 1977.

_____. "Woman: myth and stereotype." *International Journal of Women's Studies* 1 (1978):221-47.

Williams, Tannis M. "Canadian childrearing practices and the response of Canadian universities to women as childbearers and childrearers." *Canada's Men-*

tal Health (Special International Women's Year Supplement, September 1975) 23:6-9.

Wilson, Edward O. *Sociobiology: The New Synthesis.* Cambridge: Harvard University Press, 1975.

Wilson, John. *Introduction to Social Movements.* New York: Basic Books, 1973.

Wilson, Sam; Bryan Strong; Leah Miller Clarke; and Thomas Johns. *Human Sexuality.* St. Paul: West Publishing, 1977.

Winick, Charles. "The social contexts of humor." *Journal of Communication* 26 (1976):124-28.

Wirth, Louis. "The problem of minority groups." In *The Science of Man in the World Crisis,* edited by Ralph Linton, pp. 347-72. New York: Columbia University Press, 1945.

Wittig, Michele Andrisin, and Paul Skolnick. "Status versus warmth as determinants of sex differences in personal space." *Sex Roles* 4 (1978):493-503.

Wolf, Wendy C., and Neil D. Fligstein. "Sex and authority in the workplace: the causes of sexual inequality." *American Sociological Review* 44 (1979):235-52.

Wolfenstein, Martha. "Children's humor: sex, names, and double meanings." In *The World of the Child,* edited by Toby Talbot, pp. 266-84. Garden City, N.Y.: Doubleday Anchor, 1968.

Wollstonecraft, Mary. *A Vindication of the Rights of Woman.* New York: W. W. Norton, 1967.

Women's Bureau, Labour Canada. *Women in the Labour Force, 1978-1979, Part I: Participation.* Ottawa: Minister of Supply and Services Canada, 1980.

Woodcock, George. Preface to *Women in Canadian Life: Literature,* by M. G. McClung. Toronto: Fitzhenry and Whiteside, 1977.

Woolf, Virginia. *A Room of One's Own.* New York: Harcourt, Brace and World, 1929.

Wylie, Philip. *Generation of Vipers.* New York: Rinehart Pocket Books, 1955.

YWCA Women's Centre. "A study of sexism in grade one readers." Unpublished manuscript. Montreal, 1977.

Yorburg, Betty. *Sexual Identity: Sex Roles and Social Change.* New York: John Wiley and Sons, 1974.

Young, Michael, and Peter Willmott. *The Symmetrical Family: A Study of Work and Leisure in the London Region.* London: Routledge and Kegan Paul, 1973.

Yussen, Steven R., and John W. Santrock. *Child Development.* Dubuque, Iowa: Wm. C. Brown, 1978.

Zelditch, Morris, Jr. "Social status." *International Encyclopedia of the Social Sciences,* edited by David L. Sills, pp. 250-57. New York: Collier-Macmillan, 1968.

Zikmund, Barbara Brown. "The feminist thrust of sectarian Christianity." In *Women of Spirit: Female Leadership in the Jewish and Christian Traditions,* edited by Rosemary Ruether and Eleanor McLaughlin, pp. 205-24. New York: Simon and Schuster, 1979.

Zimbardo, Philip G., and Wendy Meadow. "Becoming a sexist—in one easy laugh: sexism in the Reader's Digest." Paper presented at the Annual Meetings of the Western Psychological Association, San Francisco, 1974.

Index